CONTENTS

W9-BNJ-503

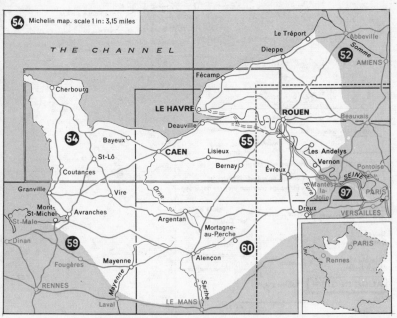

Michelin map. scale 1 in: 3,15 miles

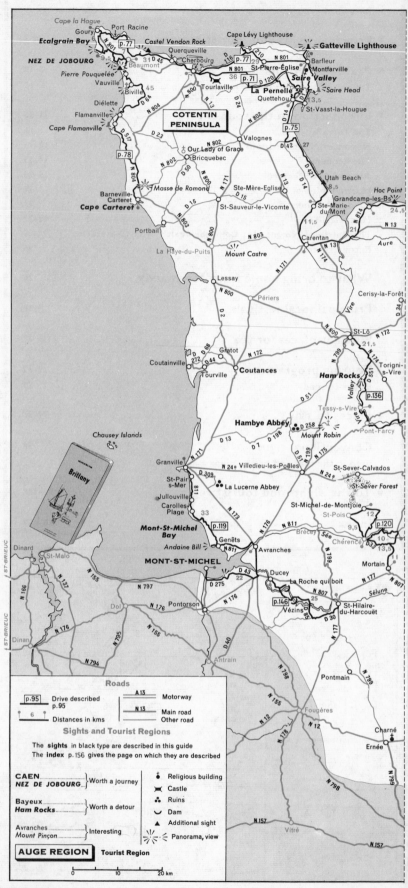

Cape la Hague
Goury
Port Racine
Cape Lévy Lighthouse
Ecalgrain Bay p.77 Castel Vendon Rock
Gatteville Lighthouse
Querqueville
NEZ DE JOBOURG Beaumont 31 D 45 Cherbourg 116 p.77 29 N 801 Barfleur
Montfarville
9,5 D 901 N 801 St-Pierre-Église **Saire Valley**
Pierre Pouquelée 36 p.71 120
Vauville **La Pernelle** 13,5 Saire Head
Biville 45 D 6A Tourlaville **D 24** Quettehou St-Vaast-la-Hougue
Diélette D 14 D 901
Flamanville N 804 **COTENTIN** N 802 p.75
Cape Flamanville D 23 **PENINSULA** D 42 27
D 57 D 804 N 802 Valognes
p.78 D 50 Our Lady of Grace Utah Beach
Bricquebec N 171 D 421 8,5 Hoc Point
Masse de Romont D 15 N 13 Grandcamp-les-Bs
Barneville- Ste-Mère-Église D 14 Ste-Marie- 24,5
Carteret D 15 du-Mont N 814 N 13
Cape Carteret St-Sauveur-le-Vicomte 11,5 21
Portbail N 803 Carentan Aure
La Haye-du-Puits N 803 N 13
Mount Castre N 171 N 174
Lessay N 174 21,5
N 800 Périers St-Lô N 172
Cerisy-la-Forêt
D 2 N 800 D 34
D 68 Gratot N 172 Torigni-
Coutainville D 172 N 799 s-Vire
D 44 **Coutances** D 551
Tourville D 51 **Ham Rocks** p.136
Vire Valley
Tessy-s-Vire
Chausey Islands **Hambye Abbey** D 258 Pont-Farcy
D 13 D 198 Mount Robin
Brittany D 7 D 551 N 175
N 171 D 199
Granville N 24e Villedieu-les-Poêles St-Sever-Calvados
D 309 N 24e St-Sever Forest
St-Pair- 811 **La Lucerne Abbey** St-Michel-de-Montjoie
s-Mer St-Pois 12 p.120
Jullouville N 173 9,5
Carolles 33 N 176 N 811 Brécey See 10
Plage p.119 D 13,5
Mont-St-Michel Genêts N 811 Chérencé
Bay Avranches N 199 Mortain
Andaine Bill Ducey N 177 N 807
MONT-ST-MICHEL D 43 La Roche qui boit N 807
St-Malo D 275 22 25 Sélune
Dinard N 137 N 797 D 30 St-Hilaire-
N 155 p.146 du-Harcouët
N 166 D 40 Vézins
Dol N 176 Pontorson N 176 N 177
Dinan N 176 N 795 N 155
N 794 Pontmain N 799
Antrain N 798
N 155 Fougères
N 12 Charné
N 157 N 12 Ernée
N 178
N 796
N 798
Vitré N 157

Roads

p.95	Drive described p.95	A 13	Motorway
6	Distances in kms	N 13	Main road
			Other road

Sights and Tourist Regions

The **sights** in black type are described in this guide
The **index** p.156 gives the page on which they are described

CAEN *NEZ DE JOBOURG*	} Worth a journey
Bayeux *Ham Rocks*	} Worth a detour
Avranches *Mount Pinçon*	} Interesting

● Religious building
⚔ Castle
⋮ Ruins
∪ Dam
▲ Additional sight
☼ Panorama, view

AUGE REGION Tourist Region

0   10   20 km

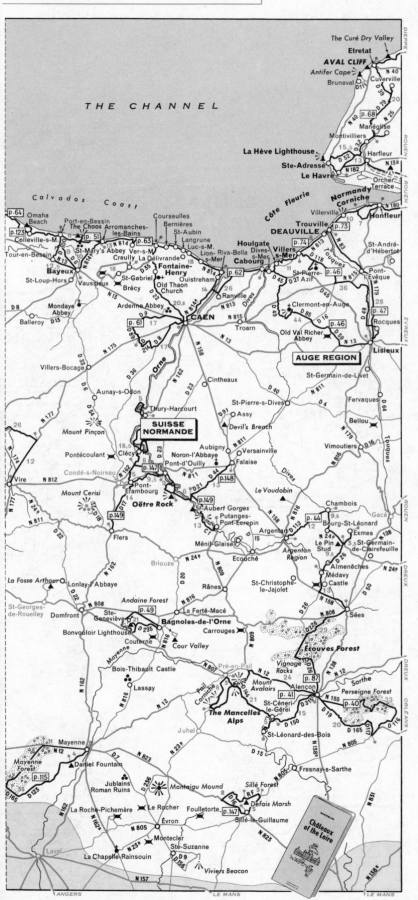

THE CHANNEL

DIEPPE

The Curé Dry Valley

Etretat
AVAL CLIFF
Antifer Cape
Bruneval
Cuverville
N 40
D 11
N 29
D 79
20

p. 68
Manéglise
Montivilliers
N 40
N 25

La Hève Lighthouse
Ste-Adresse
Le Havre
15,5
D 52
N 13
Harfleur
N 182
D 13B

Orcher
Terrace

ROUEN
ROUEN

Calvados Coast

Côte Fleurie
Normandy Corniche
N 180

Villerville
p. 10
Honfleur

p. 64
Omaha Beach
p. 123
Colleville-s-M.
Tour-en-Bessin
Port-en-Bessin
The Chaos
Arromanches-les-Bains
p. 51
N 814
D 13
St-Mary's Abbey
Creully
La Délivrande
Ver-s-M.
p. 63
Courseulles
Bernières
St-Aubin
Langrune
Luc-s-M.
Lion-s-Mer
Riva-Bella-s-Mer
Cabourg
Houlgate
Dives-s-Mer
Villers-s-Mer
Trouville
DEAUVILLE
p. 73
p. 74
St-André-d'Hébertot
N 83
St-Pierre-Azif
Pont-l'Évêque
p. 46
N 815
N 179

Bayeux
St-Loup-Hors
Vaussieux
D 6
St-Gabriel
Brécy
Fontaine-Henry
D 35
Old Thaon Church
Ouistreham
p. 62
N 814
Ranville
N 813
Dives
Clermont-en-Auge
D 85
D 16
p. 46
Old Val Richer Abbey
D 59
Rocques
p. 47
D 48
D 45
28
36

Mondaye Abbey
D 13
Balleroy
D 8
Ardenne Abbey
p. 61
CAEN
Troarn
N 815
D 45
D 49
44
D 85
AUGE REGION
Lisieux
EVREUX

Villers-Bocage
D 33
N 175
Orne
N 162
Cintheaux
St-Pierre-s-Dives
D 40
D 4
Fervaques
D 64
St-Germain-de-Livet

Aunay-s-Odon
D 54
Assy
D 91
Devil's Breach
Versainville
N 811
Vimoutiers
D 16
Bellou
N 179
Touques
ROUEN

26
N 177
Mount Pinçon
Thury-Harcourt
Aubigny
Noron-l'Abbaye
Falaise
SUISSE NORMANDE
Le Vaudobin
N 816
Chambois
Bourg-St-Léonard
p. 44
Gacé
D 274
12
Pontécoulant
18,5
Clécy
p. 147
Pont-d'Ouilly
D 811
p. 148
D 44
D 21
Argentan
D 113
Exmes
N 24B
D 138
St-Germain-de-Clairefeuille
D 26
Vire
N 812
Condé-s-Noireau
Pont-Érambourg
Oëtre Rock
p. 149
St-Aubert Gorges
Putanges-Pont-Écrepin
Le Pin Stud
N 24B
Almenêches
Médavy Castle
N 24B
D 22
Mount Cerisi
p. 149
D 18
Flers
Ménil-Glaise
Écouché
Argentan Region
N 158
D 26
Sées
DREUX

La Fosse Arthour
Lonlay-l'Abbaye
D 22
N 808
Andaine Forest
p. 49
La Ferté-Macé
Briouze
N 24B
Rânes
N 809
D 20
St-Christophe-le-Jajolet
Écouves Forest
D 226
N 808
D 50

St-Georges-de-Rouelley
Domfront
Ste-Geneviève
Bonvouloir Lighthouse
Couterne
D 235
Bagnoles-de-l'Orne
Carrouges
Cour Valley
N 816
Pré-en-Pail
N 807
Vignage Rocks
Sées
D 26
D 908
ORLEANS

Bois-Thibault Castle
N 162
Lassay
N 816
Poil Corniche
Mount Avaloirs
St-Céneri-le-Gérei
The Mancelles Alps
Alençon
p. 87
p. 41
N 155
Perseigne Forest
p. 40
D 311
D 19
Sarthe
D 165
DREUX

Mayenne
N 12
Daniel Fountain
D 7
N 923
N 23B
Juhel
St-Léonard-des-Bois
D 150
D 15
20

Mayenne Forest
p. 115
D 123
Jublains Roman Ruins
Montaigu Mound
Foulletorte
p. 147
Sillé Forest
Défais Marsh
Sillé-le-Guillaume
N 138B
D 16
Fresnay-s-Sarthe
N 805
N 831

La Roche-Pichemère
Le Rocher
Évron
Montecler
Ste-Suzanne
La Chapelle-Rainsouin
D 9
D 156
Viviers Beacon
N 823
N 159B

Laval
N 162B
N 805
N 157
ANGERS
LE MANS
LE MANS

Châteaux of the Loire

5

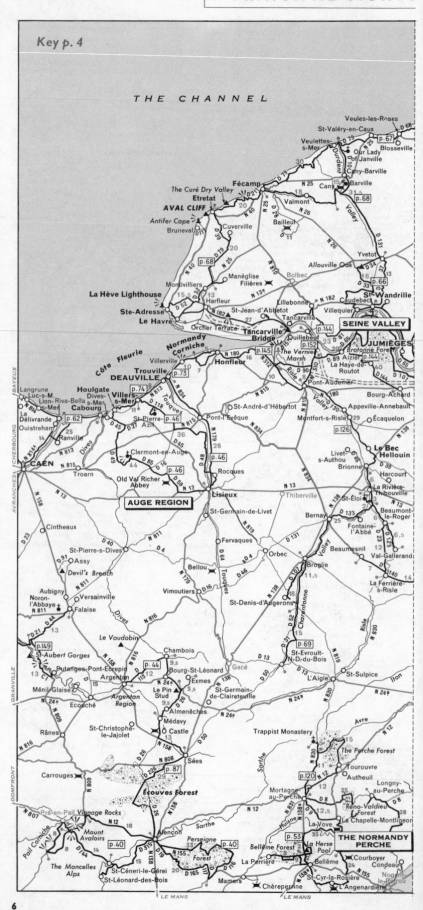

Key p. 4

THE CHANNEL

Veules-les-Roses
St-Valéry-en-Caux
Veulettes-s-Mer
Our Lady of Janville
Blosseville
p. 67
Cany-Barville
Barville
Cany
p. 68
Valmont
Bailleul
Fécamp
The Curé Dry Valley
p. 21
Etretat
AVAL CLIFF
Antifer Cape
Bruneval
Cuverville
Yvetot
Allouville Oak
p. 68
Montivilliers
Manéglise Filières
Bolbec
St-Wandrille
p. 66
Harfleur
Lillebonne
Caudebec
La Hève Lighthouse
Ste-Adresse
Le Havre
St-Jean-d'Abbetot
Villequier
Orcher Terrace
Tancarville
Tancarville Bridge
SEINE VALLEY
Quillebeuf
p. 144
Normandy Corniche
The Vernier Marsh
JUMIÈGES
Brotonne Forest
p. 152
Côte Fleurie
Villerville
Honfleur
La Haye-de-Routot
p. 144
Pont-Audemer
DEAUVILLE
p. 73
Trouville
p. 74
Bourg-Achard
Houlgate
Villers-s-Mer
St-André-d'Hébertot
Appeville-Annebault
Écaquelon
Cabourg
Langrune
Luc-s-M.
Lion-Riva-Bella
s-Mer
La Délivrande
p. 62
St-Pierre-Azif
p. 46
Pont-l'Évêque
Montfort-s-Risle
p. 126
Ouistreham
Ranville
Dives
Clermont-en-Auge
p. 46
Rocques
Le Bec Hellouin
Livet-s-Authou
Brionne
CAEN
Troarn
Old Val Richer Abbey
p. 46
Lisieux
Thiberville
Harcourt
La Rivière-Thibouville
St-Éloi
AUGE REGION
St-Germain-de-Livet
St-Eloi
Beaumont-le-Roger
Cintheaux
St-Pierre-s-Dives
Fervaques
Bernay
Fontaine-l'Abbé
Assy
Orbec
Beaumesnil
Val-Gallerand
Devil's Breach
Bellou
Broglie
La Ferrière-s-Risle
Aubigny
Noron-l'Abbaye
Versainville
Vimoutiers
St-Denis-d'Augerons
Falaise
St-Denis-d'Augerons
Le Vaudobin
Chambois
St-Evroult-N-D-du-Bois
p. 149
St-Aubert Gorges
p. 44
Bourg-St-Léonard
Gacé
L'Aigle
St-Sulpice
Putanges-Pont-Écrepin
Argentan
Exmes
St-Germain-de-Claireteuille
Ménil Glaise
Le Pin Stud
Écouché
Argentan Region
Almenêches
Trappist Monastery
Rânes
Médavy
Ô Castle
Avre
St-Christophe-le-Jajolet
The Perche Forest
Sées
Touvourve
Carrouges
p. 87
Écouves Forest
p. 120
Autheuil
Longny-au-Perche
Mortagne-au-Perche
Reno-Valdieu Forest
La Chapelle-Montligeon
Pré-en-Pail
Vignage Rocks
La Vove
THE NORMANDY PERCHE
Pail Corniche
Mount Avaloirs
p. 40
Alençon
Perseigne Forest
p. 40
Bellême Forest
p. 53
La Herse Pool
Courboyer
Condeau
The Mancelles Alps
St-Céneri-le-Gérei
St-Léonard-des-Bois
La Perrière
Mamers
Chèrepernne
St-Cyr-la-Rosière
L'Angenardière
Nogent-le-Rotrou

LE MANS
LE MANS

BAYEUX
AVRANCHES | CHERBOURG
GRANVILLE
DOMFRONT

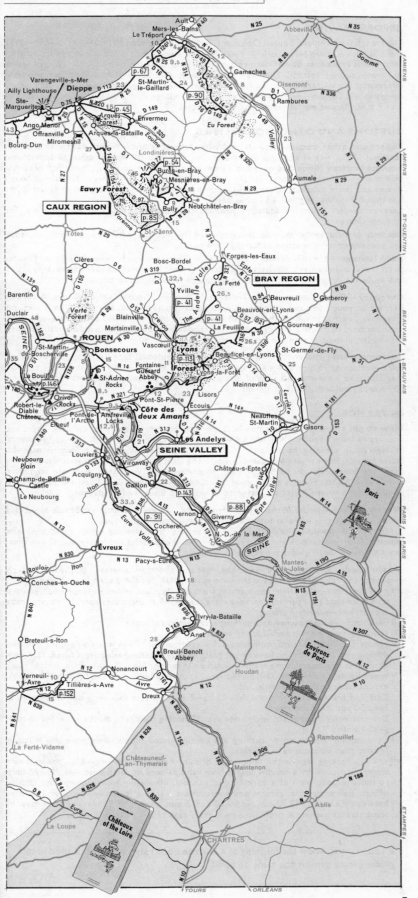

Ault
Mers-les-Bains
Le Tréport
N 25
Abbeville
N 35
Somme
N 28
N 1
N 336
AMIENS
Eu
D 49
Gamaches
Oisemont
D 1
Ramburs
p. 67
St-Martin-le-Gaillard
24
p. 90
Breslé Valley
23
Varengeville-s-Mer
Ailly Lighthouse
Ste-Marguerite
Dieppe
D 113
N 25
p. 45
D 149
Eu Forest
6
N 1
AMIENS
Ango Manor
Offranville
Miromesnil
Bourg-Dun
Arques Forest
Arques-la-Bataille
Envermeu
Equine
D 149
N 320
N 27
Londinières
N 28
N 320
Aumale
N 29
ST-QUENTIN
Eawy Forest
Buren-en-Bray
p. 54
Mesnières-en-Bray
18
Neufchâtel-en-Bray
N 29
p. 85
Bully
CAUX REGION
p. 97
St-Säens
N 28
N 314
Tôtes
N 29
Forges-les-Eaux
Epte
Clères
D 155
Bosc-Bordel
N 319
D 7
La Ferté
N 327
15
BRAY REGION
N 13e
Barentin
N 27
D 6
32,5
Yville
p. 41
26,5
D 84
Beuvreuil
Gerberoy
N 30
N 1
BEAUVAIS
Verte Forest
D 12
Blainville
Crevon
Ry
The Andelle Valley
La Ferté
p. 41
Beauvoir-en-Lyons
D 57
D 2
Gournay-en-Bray
BEAUVAIS
Duclair
48
N 28
SEINE
N 182
ROUEN
Martainville
N 30
Vascœuil
Lyons
p. 113
Forest
La Feuille
N 316
26,5
N 30
St-Germer-de-Fly
N 31
St-Martin-de-Boscherville
D 51
Bonsecours
N 14
Fontaine-Guérard Abbey
Lyons-la-Forêt
D 14
Mainneville
25
N 15
N 181
La Bouille
p. 146
St-Adrien Rocks
N 158
8,5
Beauficel-en-Lyons
Lavière
D 17
Orival Rocks
N 321
Pont-St-Pierre
23
Lisors
Écouis
N 14e
Neaufles-St-Martin
Gisors
N 153
Robert-le-Diable Château
Amfreville Locks
Côte des deux Amants
N 14
Pont-de-l'Arche
Elbeuf
12,5
31,3
Les Andelys
D 10
N 840
N 313
Louviers
Vironvay
SEINE VALLEY
Château-s-Epte
D 146
N 15
Paris
Neubourg Plain
D 133
Acquigny
Gaillon
30
N 313
N 181
N 14
PARIS
Champ-de-Bataille Castle
Le Neubourg
N 836
22
p. 143
D 5
p. 88
Epte Valley
N 13
p. 91
Vernon
Giverny
N-D.-de la Mer
N 183
A 13
Mantes-la-Jolie
N 190
PARIS
Iton
Évreux
Cocherel
SEINE
N 830
Pacy-s-Eure
N 13
N 183
N 13
N 191
Rouloir
Iton
Conches-en-Ouche
18
Eure Valley
p. 91
N 307
Environs de Paris
N 840
Ivry-la-Bataille
N 836
Breteuil-s-Iton
D 143
Anet
N 833
28
N 12
N 10
PARIS
Breuil-Benoît Abbey
Houdan
N 12
Verneuil-s-Avre
N 12
Tillières-s-Avre
p. 152
Nonancourt
Avre
Dreux
N 12
N 829
Rambouillet
N 841
N 839
N 828
N 154
N 306
La Ferté-Vidame
Châteauneuf-en-Thymerais
N 183
Maintenon
N 188
D 8
N 828
N 839
Eure
N 841
Châteaux of the Loire
Ablis
ÉTAMPES
La Loupe
CHARTRES
TOURS
ORLÉANS

USEFUL INFORMATION

BEFORE LEAVING

The French Government Tourist Office at 178 Piccadilly, London WIV 0AL ☎ 01—493—3171 and 610 Fifth Avenue New York ☎ Plaza 7—1125 will provide information and literature. **Local Tourist Information Offices**—*Syndicats d'Initiative* or *S.I.*—are to be found in larger towns and many tourist resorts. They can supply large scale town plans, timetables and local information on entertainment, facilities, sport and sightseeing. Someone on the staff nearly always speaks English—opening hours variable but in large towns usually 9 a.m. to noon and 2 to 7 p.m. (closed out of season in smaller places).

CUSTOMS AND OTHER FORMALITIES

Papers and other documents.—A valid **British Passport** or **British Visitor's Passport** is all that is required in the way of personal documents. For the car a **UK driving licence**, an **International Insurance Certificate** (**Green Card** obtainable from your insurance company, motoring organisation or even, in an emergency from the police on the quay at your port of arrival—although slower and more expensive), car registration papers (log-book) and **GB plates** (measuring not less than 6·9 inches long and 4·5 inches deep).

Caravan owners must, in addition, produce the **caravan log-book** and an inventory, for customs clearance.

Assistance provided by the Motoring Organisations.—The AA and RAC run accident insurance and breakdown service schemes for their members.

Health Insurance.—There is a reciprocal Health Service agreement between Britain and France, but it is advisable to make inquiries before leaving. Most insurance companies, travel agencies and motoring organisations have health insurance schemes at low premiums.

Currency.—Carry your money in Travellers' Cheques, obtainable from Cooks, American Express or your bank and exchangeable at banks (hours: 9 a.m. to noon, 2 to 4 p.m. on weekdays), exchange offices (*bureaux de change*) and in some hotels and shops—you need your passport both when buying and cashing cheques. Take a small amount of local currency for incidental expenses on the first day.

Customs.—**Going into or returning from France:** your personal luggage, 1½ bottle of spirits, 300 cigarettes or 75 cigars or 400 grammes of tobacco for those over 15 can go in free. You may also take 2 cameras, 10 rolls of film per camera, a portable radio, record player (and 10 records) and a musical instrument.

IN FRANCE

How to get there.—You can go by boat, plane or hovercraft, and your car also. There are boat trains from London which link up with the cross-Channel ferries at Dover, Folkestone or Newhaven crossing to Boulogne, Calais, Dieppe or Dunkirk, also a Southampton–Le Havre service, from where you can drive or catch local trains or buses to your destination; there are hovercraft run by British Rail, Hoverlloyd and Thorensen; there are scheduled and charter flights. Enquire at any good travel agent and remember, if you are going in the holiday season or at Christmas, Easter or Whitsun, to book well in advance.

Where to stay.—In the *Michelin Guide France* you will find a selection of hotels at various prices in all areas. It will also list local restaurants—again with prices.

Alternatively consult the *Michelin Guide Camping & Caravaning* which gives sites and indicates facilities, outlook and charges, and by means of an atlas and local maps, shows their exact situation. Both guides are revised annually.

On the road.—In France you drive on the right and, therefore, overtake on the left. A large number of the rules of the road are the same as in the UK but there are a few differences:

I road junctions—the driver approaching from the right has priority except when you are on a main road (and turnings on your right are therefore secondary roads). Priority roads are marked—*priorite à droite*;

II flash your headlights when approaching intersections at night;

III sounding your horn is forbidden in towns;

IV yellow headlights are not compulsory for tourists but if you are doing a lot of night driving you are advised to have amber bulbs or yellow cellophane covers fitted. Dip your headlights before oncoming traffic; switch on in mist or fog;

V speed limits in towns are 37 mph (60 kmph); outside built up areas, 56 mph (90 kmph), except where otherwise indicated.
   Cars and trailer caravans more than 22 ft.—7 m—in length following one another must keep 50 yds. between them.
   Drivers, including tourists, within one year of passing their test, must not exceed 56 mph —90 kmph;

VI signposts for a junction or turning are usually placed immediately after the junction (rather than before it as in Britain);

VII the No Parking sign is the same as in Britain. Regulated parking—blue zones (*zones bleues*), indicated by a narrow bright blue band painted on lamp-posts—is allowed only to those in possession of a parking disc (*disque*), obtainable from customs and tourist offices, police stations, garages and tobacconists. Parking is limited to 1 or 1½ hours between 9 a.m. and 12.30 p.m. and 2.30 and 7 p.m. except on Sundays and holidays. In some streets parking is prohibited on certain days of the week or month.

If you want to know the meaning of a **conventional sign or symbol** used in this guide, please consult the table on p. 38.

A FRENCH MENU

A menu in France should provide you with anticipatory relish—so don't be afraid, embark and enjoy it! The waiter will be glad to answer your queries and advise on wine.

Restaurants display their menus with prices outside, so you can see what is being offered before entering. All restaurants have to provide a 'tourist menu' or set price meal. This sometimes includes the service charge—*service compris* or *tout compris*—or you should add on 12–15%. Very exceptionally wine will also be included—*vin* or *boisson compris*.

The *plat du jour* should always be considered seriously as it is the chef's special effort of the day and probably well worth while, also the restaurant's own specialities.

Set menus are usually good value and there is generally a fairly wide choice. The card offered, perhaps handwritten, may well be divided under the following headings.

   I (a) *hors-d'œuvre* or a preliminary dish or (b) soup
  II an *entrée* or fish or made up dish of poultry or white meat or an egg course
 III a red meat, poultry or game course
 IV vegetables or salad served with (iii) or separately
  V cheese
 VI a dessert course or *entremets*
VII fruit.

This enables you to have a copious repast or to select a meal in accordance with your immediate taste and appetite. An obvious principle is that you precede your main course by an appetiser and round off the meal with a contrast. For example take (i), (iii), (iv), (v) and (vii) for a substantial meal; substitute (ii) for (iii) and possibly (vi) for (v) and (vii) and you have a much lighter meal, etc.

Hors-d'œuvre often consist of a single item e.g. tomato salad, artichoke hearts, sardines, oysters etc. each served as the course dish. *Crudités* are mixed shredded vegetables.

Soups are thick (*crème*) or clear (*consommé*) and are nearly always consumed at the evening meal. *Bisques* are shellfish soups.

The fish, white meat (veal or chicken) or egg course will probably gain its savour and substantiality from the sauce in which the basic ingredient is served. A dish from this group could be substituted for (i) to serve as a prologue, or if you want a light meal, take a dish from this course as your main dish.

It is at the point (ii) and (iii) that you realise the difference in French and English cooking: chicken may have wine or cream added at some stage in their cooking (*coq au vin*, *poulet à la crème*), fish will be in a wine or cream sauce, even vegetables will be different.

On (iii) will depend the weight of your meal. Some regional meat dishes—stews: *ragouts*, *cassoulets*—can be heavy. They are delicious, but beware what you take beforehand!

Cheese (*fromage*) is served from a board. You select several varieties and pieces are cut for you or you cut them yourself. Ask which are cream, hard, goat's (*chèvre*) or ewe's (*brebis*).

Dessert dishes (*entremets*) are a sweet course between the cheese and fruit. They include *soufflés*, tarts, ices etc. Always ask if there is a *tarte maison*—it may well not be on the menu, will almost certainly be homemade and is generally delicious. It will take the form of a large— about 12–15 inches in diameter—open fruit tart served in slices.

To drink with all this? A medium dry white wine with *hors-d'œuvre*, fish, cold chicken, eggs; a light red with roast chicken, poultry; a more robust red with red meat and game; a white, even a champagne (it costs less in France!) with dessert and fruit.

Not to be despised by any means are the wines most restaurants serve *en carafe*.

Tea and coffee.—Coffee is never included in a set price menu. If you ask for tea—*thé*—you may get tea with lemon (*thé citron*); if you want tea with milk ask for *thé au lait*. You must be equally precise about your coffee: *café au lait* is breakfast coffee *i.e.* coffee with hot milk; *café crème* is black coffee with cream or cold milk; *un café* or *café noir* is black coffee.

Food in France is something to relish, simply and without fuss or mystique, whether it's your first apéritif—a *pernod*?—or coffee, picnic, shellfish or pancake tea, midday meal on the road or evening meal on arrival at your overnight stop. May you enjoy it and remember it from your study of the menu to your final coffee and calvados! *Bon appétit!*

WORKING HOURS, SHOPS AND SHOPPING

Foodshops are open from 8 or 9 a.m. to 12.30 p.m. and 2 to 6.30 or 7 p.m. on weekdays— small ones may close for several hours at midday. Some open on Sunday mornings and public holidays; many remain closed all day Monday. If you are going on a picnic shop early, don't wait until you arrive or the shop keepers may have gone to their own lunch!

Tobacconists (*bureaux de tabac*) in France sell **tobacco** and **cigarettes** (a state monopoly), also **stamps** (post boxes are usually nearby, coloured yellow and fixed to a wall), and discs or *jetons* when needed for **public telephones**. Tobacconists can be spotted by their barber's pole type of sign looking like a deep red carrot.

Poste Restante.—Mail can be sent to you *poste restante* at the main post offices in larger towns. There is a small collection charge; take your passport as identification.

It is probably possible to get round a supermarket without speaking a word, but obviously shopping is most fun in the small shops unlike those at home.

The baker's—*la boulangerie*—where the bread (*pain*) may be made on the premises. The traditional long French loaf is a *baguette*, the thinner version, a *ficelle*. Rolls are *petits pains*. *Croissants* and *brioches* are not bread at all—try them for breakfast or a mid-morning coffee with or without butter and jam. **The cakeshop or pastrycook's**—*la patisserie*—is the place to find homemade pastries and cakes. They may be expensive but they are delicious.

Dairies and cheeseshops—*la laiterie*, *la crémerie*. In the first you buy milk—sold by the litre (see p. 10) and cream; in the second, all dairy products but especially cheese.

The grocer's—*l'épicerie*. As in England the grocer's range of items seem infinite. It will include wine and sometimes vegetables and fruit, though these will be more various at the greengrocers—the *marchand de légumes* or the market (see below). Take an empty bottle when going to buy wine, you can then buy your wine loose, which is cheaper!

The cold meats shop—*la charcuterie*. These shops, sometimes with mouthwatering window displays, exist all over France. They sell cold meats (*viandes froides*), *patés* or meat pastes, *terrines* or potted meats, made up salads—everything for a picnic. A great many items will be homemade (see p. 10 for weight equivalents).

The market—*le marché*. Markets abound all over France. Go early in the day.

SIGHTSEEING VOCABULARY

Abbatiale=abbey buildings
Abbaye=abbey
Amont=upstream
Anse=bay
Auberge=inn or small hotel
Aval=downstream
Bac=ferry
Bassin=dock, basin
Basse Ville=Lower Town
Beaux arts=fine arts
Beffroi=belfry
Bois=wood (trees) also timber
Borne=stone post (kilometre post)
Boucle=river loop
Carrefour=crossroads
Centrale Thermique=power station
Chapelle de La Vierge=Lady Chapel
Château=feudal castle; if 17C or later not translated in this guide (eg. Fontaine Henry Château)
Chêne=oak
Circuit=circular tour, car race track
Clocher=belfry, tower
Côte=hill, also coast
Croix=cross
Digue=breakwater, dyke
Donjon=castle keep
Ecluse=river lock
Embarcadère=landing stage
Evêché=bishopric
Falaise=cliff
Fleuve=river
Forêt=forest or large wood
Galet=shingle
Gare=railway station
  Gare maritime=harbour station
  Gare routière=bus station
Halles=covered market
Haras=stud farm
Haute Ville=Upper Town
Hêtre=beech
Horloge=clock
Hôtel=hotel, also a large town house or mansion

Hôtel de Ville=town hall
Impasse=blind alley
Jardin (public)=public garden
Jardin des Plantes=botanical garden
Lacet=hairpin bend in road
Magasin=shop
Mairie=town hall
Maison=house
Marais=marsh
Mare=marsh
Méandre=bend, curve
Notre-Dame=Our Lady
Palais de Justice=Law courts
Pays=a country, also a region
Parfumerie=perfume, cosmetic shop
Phare=lighthouse
Pharmacie=chemist's (medicine)
Plage=beach
Port=harbour, port
  Port de commerce=commercial port, quay
  Port de pêche=fishing port or harbour
  Port de plaisance=harbour for pleasure craft
  Port de voyageurs=passenger port, quay
Poteau=post
Quai=quay, embankment
Roche, rocher=rock
Ruisseau=stream
Sable=sand
Salle (des cartes)=(map) room
Sapin=fir tree
Saut=leap
Syndicat d'Initiative=tourist information office (abbreviated to SI)
Tour=tower, car trip
  Tour de l'horloge=clock tower
Vallée=valley
Valleuse=dry, hanging valley
Vallon=small valley
Ville=town
  Ville Close=walled town
Voie=way, traffic line

WEIGHTS AND MEASURES

Weight

1 kilogramme=1000 grammes=2 lb. 3 oz.
500 grammes=a bit over 1 lb.
250 grammes=9 oz.
100 grammes=$3\frac{1}{2}$ oz.
1 lb.=just over 450 grammes
$\frac{1}{2}$ lb.=just under 250 grammes
$\frac{1}{4}$ lb.=just over 100 grammes
1 oz.=just over 25 grammes

Length

1 cm=just over $\frac{3}{8}$ inch
1 m=39 inches
1 km=$\frac{5}{8}$ mile
1 inch=$2\frac{1}{2}$ cm
1 ft.=30 cm

1 yd.=90 cm
1 mile=1 km 600 m
(to convert miles to km divide by 5 and multiply by 8
to convert km to miles divide by 8 and multiply by 5
or very roughly divide km by 2 and add a bit on for the mileage)

Volume

1 litre—all liquids (milk, wine, oil, petrol)=$1\frac{3}{4}$ pints or 0·22 British Imperial Gallon
50 litres=11 gallons
1 pint=just over $\frac{1}{2}$ litre
1 gallon=$4\frac{1}{2}$ litres

PUBLIC HOLIDAYS IN FRANCE

Public Holidays, when museums, other buildings, public services and shops may be closed or vary their hours are:

New Year's Day
Easter Sunday and Monday
Labour Day, 1 May
Ascension Day
Whit Sunday and Monday

France's National Day, 14 July
The Assumption, 15 August
All Saints Day, 1 November
Armistice Day, 11 November
Christmas Day.

INTRODUCTION TO THE TOUR

THE TERRAIN

Normandy has two faces geographically: that of the northwest, the Paris Basin and that which, looking towards Brittany, consists of an eroded foundation of ancient rocks.

Armorican Normandy.—The Cotentin Peninsula and the Normandy Bocage or Woodlands today form the eastern end of the ancient Hercynian Chain of the eroded Primary Era Armorican Massif. Parallel strata of soft shale and hard sandstone, interspersed with great granite rocks make up the geological structure. Apart from enclosed valleys, the most obvious features of the confused topography are the long crests of uniform height such as those linking Mortain and the Ecouves Forest. These crests are broken by transverse cuts which provide interesting settings for towns like Mortain, Domfront and Bagnoles. The highest points of the crests are the tallest mountains in western France—Mount Avaloirs and the Ecouves Forest beacon each: 1,368 ft.—417 m—high.

Sedimentary Normandy.—The ancient foundation was overlaid in the Secondary Era, at the time of the great marine invasions of the land, by chalk several hundred feet thick. This was soon covered by a flint deposit made up of rocks decomposing in a climate both hotter and wetter than our own. In the Tertiary Era the chalk plateau was shaken by vast undulations which brought about a series of fractures running in the same direction, giving rise to the original relief of the Perche Region.

The plateau, with a mean height of 413 ft.—126 m—bears west, turning into a huge gully walled to the northeast by the Bray Region's volcanic cone and to the southwest by the hills of the Normandy Perche. Erosion attacked the heights and a "button-hole" opened up in the Bray Region (see p. 54). The valleys which cut their way down from these large watersheds through the chalk have a striking similarity in their convex shape and wide alluvial covered floors. The alluvial deposits of clay and silex were washed down when the valleys were being hollowed out in the great glaciary periods and have given rise to many different varieties of agricultural land.

The cretaceous deposits of the late Secondary Era, however, did not reach the Armorican Massif; when almost in sight of the low wooded hills of the Bocage they fell away, exposing older underlying Jurassic layers. The movements of the original rock foundation, so close and therefore violent, in this hybrid zone, produced many natural divisions—a mosaic of small "regions" (details p. 12).

Open countryside and woodland.—Two types of landscape are to be found in the province, existing without reference to the geological subsoil. In the strictest sense the countryside is open with dry and windswept plains where cereals predominate and the population is concentrated in large villages of houses of solid stone. Gradually local character is being lost as progress takes place in agriculture.

Woodlands are typical of the farmlands of the Armorican Massif; they outrun the original land mass considerably to the east, reaching the Maine, the Perche and the Auge Regions. A network of hedges, each topping an earth bank, encloses fields and meadows, so that from a distance the countryside appears almost wooded. The people in the innumerable hamlets scattered along the low lying roads continue their traditional self-sufficient lives and raise cattle—a relatively new occupation in the region, but one which suits the Bocain temperament.

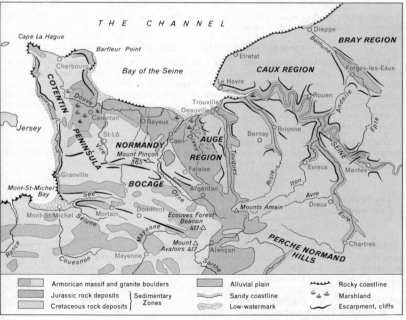

Armorican massif and granite boulders	Alluvial plain	Rocky coastline
Jurassic rock deposits } Sedimentary Zones	Sandy coastline	Marshland
Cretaceous rock deposits }	Low-watermark	Escarpment, cliffs

NORMANDY'S LOCAL REGIONS

Upper and Lower Normandy are major divisions within which lie Normandy's local regions. These can be grouped roughly by their vegetation into two totally different types, the *open countryside* and the *woodland* or *bocage region* (see p. 11), both of which have their counterparts in England.

UPPER NORMANDY

Upper Normandy is the sedimentary Normandy of chalk lands (see map p. 11) and the Lower Valley of the Seine. The countryside is predominantly open and the region is centred on Rouen.

THE OPEN COUNTRYSIDE REGIONS

The Neubourg Plain and the Evreux–St. André Countryside.—A flat and monotonous landscape is covered with arable crops, typical of large scale farming, with hardly a tree in sight.

The Caux Region.—This vast chalk plain is bordered, on the Channel side, by cliffs famous for their hanging valleys (see p. 66), and to the south by the Seine Valley. Alluvial mud makes it fertile, producing wheat and such industrial crops as flax (see p. 15) and sugar beet.

The landscape, however, is not without relief—silex clay deposits retain moisture, enabling trees to grow in occasional clumps on the plateau itself and on the hillsides of the surrounding valleys.

The Normandy Vexin.—This second chalk plain, a continuation southeast of the Caux Region, ends only where it is cut by the Epte and Andelle Valleys. The particularly thick coating of alluvial mud has made it an intensive arable area, primarily of wheat and sugar beet.

THE TRANSITIONAL REGIONS

Roumois and Lieuvin.—These plains, divided by the Risle Valley, appear as a transitional belt between the Caux and Auge Regions.

By tradition an area for rotation crop farming, it is transformed at its western end by the appearance of hedges and apple orchards into a woodland landscape.

The Ouche Region.—The scenery is more sombre than that of the Roumois and Lieuvin, for the land, lacking an alluvial deposit, supports only trees and sparse crops with here and there a hedge or meadow.

THE WOODLAND REGIONS

The Bray Region.—The Norman part of this region abuts, in the east, on the Caux and consists of a vast clay depression, known as the "button-hole" (see p. 54), bordered by two chalk hills. It is a woodland, cattle farming area—its dairy produce and apples destined for the Paris market.

The Auge.—This region, which spreads into both Upper and Lower Normandy, is different from the others. The chalk strata have been deeply cut by a network of valleys, resulting in the appearance of many non-porous, clay, areas on the valley floors.

Local humidity favours pastureland, hedges and cider orchards. Scattered farmsteads, some still with ancient half-timbering, appear part hidden beside the low lying roads. In some ways it is a lush woodland area, the Normandy of "meadowland, brilliant green and glistening dew" of the Norman poet Lucie Delarue-Mardrus (see p. 21).

LOWER NORMANDY

This is Armorican Normandy—with its halo of Jurassic terrain (see p. 11). Perhaps because it does not lie at the region's centre, Caen has never had the same influence on Lower Normandy as Rouen on Upper Normandy.

THE OPEN COUNTRYSIDE REGIONS

The Caen-Falaise Countryside.—This area of windswept fields is typical of the open countryside regions. Its fertility would seem to encourage large scale arable farming but aridity precludes pasturage and the landscape remains bare, treeless, monotonous.

Scattered amongst these cultivated flat lands are stone quarries—the stone has been used for hundreds of years, and is still, for building both in France and overseas: Westminster Abbey is built of Caen stone. Iron, also found in the area, has fostered local large scale industrial development.

The Argentan-Sées-Alençon Region.—These minute chalk regions lying north of the Sarthe Valley and the Mancelles Alps are gradually losing their exclusively cereal producing character: horses and cattle may now be seen grazing in the open orchards.

THE TRANSITIONAL REGION

The Normandy Perche.—This region of steep hills, the bridge between the Paris Basin and the Armorican Massif, is given over to that most plutocratic husbandry—horse breeding.

THE OPEN COUNTRYSIDE REGIONS

The Normandy Bocage.—A perfect example of *bocage* or open woodland country may be seen south of the Bessin where, in a landscape of meadows surrounded by tall hedges, small scattered villages and apple orchards, local farmers raise dairy cattle and Breton ponies.

Dense woods cover the south.

The people, for so long dependent on themselves alone, complemented their slender resources by cottage and light industries. These have survived and today at places such as Flers, Vire and St-Lô are expanding and specialising.

The Bessin.—Normandy cows graze the lush pastures which flourish on the clay soil and produce the milk, cream and butter which have made the name of Isigny famous not only in France but also abroad—note how many cheeses imported into England carry the name.

Bayeux is the capital of this open woodland region.

The Cotentin.—The Cotentin, thought by John Ruskin in 1848 to resemble Worcestershire except that it was more beautiful, has retained many of the qualities he appreciated, being so remote.

The peninsula, which is divided from the Normandy Bocage by a sedimentary depression which is flooded at certain times of the year, consists of three distinct areas within its own region—the Cotentin Pass, the Saire Valley and the Hague Point (see p. 74).

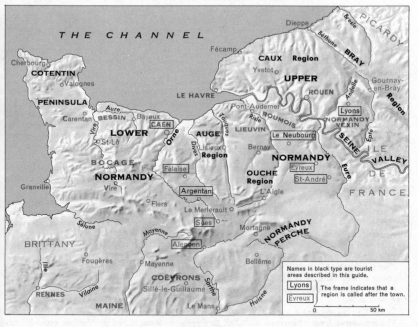

THE COAST

The coast of Normandy from the Valley of the Bresle in the north to that of the Sélune in the south is as varied as its hinterland. The Caux Region (see p. 12) matches the cliffs of Dover with high chalk cliffs of its own which have won for it the name of the Alabaster Coast. Shingle bottomed creeks break the line of the cliff wall. As rocks are undercut by the sea and fall, hanging valleys can be seen forming in the chalk (see p. 81).

The Calvados coast (see p. 62) is made up of the low Auge and Bessin cliffs and the sand dunes and salt marshes which intersperse them, particularly around Caen. Further east, the Côte Fleurie (see p. 73) offers miles of fine sand beaches where there may be a difference in depth on the strand of 1,000 yds. between high and low water. It is also an outstandingly sunny region. To the west are the sand or sand and shingle beaches of the bracing Côte de Nacre (see p. 62).

The Cotentin Peninsula (p. 74) reminds one of Cornwall and Brittany with its rocky inlets, although there are also long stretches of sand dunes and beaches along the coast where the continental rock base does not reach the shore.

Mont-St-Michel Bay is known for its vast sands from which the sea seems to withdraw completely at times.

The present coastline was drawn after the great upheavals of the Quaternary Era when the sea finally divided the Channel Islands from the Continent. No sooner had the continental shoreline been established than the sea began slowly but endlessly to wear away protruding sectors and to fill more sheltered spots with debris—the sea brought shingle to the Caux beaches; it brings the mud that silts up the Seine Estuary; it has killed more than one port (in Gallo-Roman times Lillebonne was a seaport), and it has raised the level of several of the Calvados beaches.

The Tides and Life on the Beach.—The first thing to do is to learn the rhythm of the tides—a rhythm almost as important as that of the sun. High or flood tide occurs twice every 25 hours. The waves remain at high water for only a few minutes before beginning to die away; eventually they reach the ebb tide or low water mark only to start again on the flood inland.

Tide time-tables are usually displayed in hotels, on quaysides and in the local press.

High tide, which attracts a horde of bathers to the beaches, is the time when beach and watersport enthusiasts display all their energy. High tide is also the best time for a drive along the coast or a visit to a port or harbour.

Fishermen and many others, on the other hand, wait impatiently for low tide to look for the crabs, shrimps, mussels, cockles, clams, etc., which lurk among seaweed covered rocks and in the wet sand.

> **Guarded beaches**
> Most beaches along the Normandy coast are entirely safe for bathing—many are guarded. If flags are hoisted—green for safe bathing, red for too dangerous to bathe—obey them: if the beach is unguarded take local advice in case there are currents, hidden rocks or shelving.

THE ECONOMY

STOCK BREEDING

Cattle.—With 6 million head of cattle, the Normandy breed predominates among the thirty or so to be found in France as a whole. The stock is all-purpose and fertile, and produces more than a quarter of the country's meat, milk and other dairy products.

The Manche with some 700,000 head has the most of any department and the proportion of these in milk makes it also the leading milk and dairy produce area.

The Cattle Breeders' Association with their *Normandy Herd Book* are engaged in improving the breed in cooperation with the Testing and Insemination Society.

Productivity is also being studied scientifically by the Milk Control Board which checks the weight and fat content of milk produced by each cow against its food ration. This procedure has been applied particularly in the Orne Department since 1965 where a good cow gives 4½ to 6½ gallons—20 to 30 litres—a day of milk rich in the cream which gives Normandy butter its flavour. Production is entirely absorbed by the local milk and butter cooperatives, cheese making, dried and condensed milk factories.

The Normandy breed is known by the three colour markings on its hide—white, cream and dark brown. The head is white with brown patches round the eyes—the lack of these "spectacles" bars a beast from entry in the *Herd Book*. Veal calves are sold for slaughter at 6 to 7 weeks when they weigh 12½ to 14 stone—80 to 90 kg. The fattening of bullocks and barren heifers is an industry in itself—pasturelands such as those of the Cotentin Peninsula allow a fattening rate of 900 lb. liveweight per acre—1,000 kg per ha—or 2¼ lb. liveweight on a 13 cwt. bullock eating just over 1 cwt. of grass per day—1 kg × 650 kg × 60 kg—and the meat has a splendid flavour!

Cattle markets and fairs such as the one held at Lessay (*see p. 110*) are a common sight and any interested tourist near Caen in the last two weeks in September should see the Cattle Show.

Horses.—The centre of Normandy horsebreeding is Ste-Mère-Eglise, although the Cotentin has remained the principal birthplace. Tradition has it that to grow strong bones a horse must graze grass upon limestone plains, which is why horsebreeding also centres on the pastures round Merlerault.

Thoroughbreds, cross-breeds, Bretons and Percherons are magnificently represented in the national studs at St-Lô (*see p. 135*) and Le Pin (*see p. 125*) and in local private studs.

The **thoroughbred**, descended from Asian stallions and English mares, has been bred in Normandy since the early 18C as a racehorse.

A yearling sale attended by buyers from the region and abroad is held each year in Deauville (*see p. 81*).

The **trotter** is now also a pure breed with its own stud book.

The **cross-breed**, from a Norman mare and an English thoroughbred or Norfolk cross-breed sire, is used for the increasingly popular pastime of hacking, the occasional star emerging as a racehorse. There is also the **cob**, a sturdy horse capable of pulling a ton at lively speed.

The **Percheron**, dappled grey or black with powerful fore and hind quarters, is a dray horse of great pulling power, good natured and known for its immense strength. Some say the breed goes back to the Crusades; what is certain is that it now contains Arab stock. All Percherons today are descended from the "great ancestor", the early 19C stallion Jean Le Blanc. Since his day the Percheron Horse Society has kept a stud book jealously marking out the areas where future generations may be bred in Perche, Mayenne and the Auge.

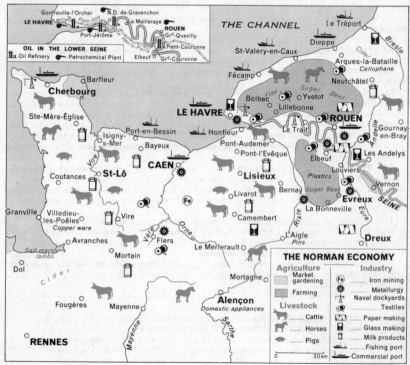

TWO NORMAN CROPS

Grassland cultivation is highly developed in Normandy but the fertile soil also lends itself to many other crops, two of the most typical being apples and flax.

Apples.—Apple blossom time, always enchanting, lasts for the four weeks of the *floréal* (20 April to 19 May—the former eighth month of the First Republic).

Normandy's cider orchards each year produce thousands of bushels of apples—some red, some pale as old ivory.

Early varieties of eating apples from the Bocage Region, tender and sweet, are ripe by September and October; mid-season apples (15 October to the end of November) are crisper, while the late varieties, which are the speciality of the Auge Region, are hard. These are picked as late as possible when they are almost ready to fall, but before the first frost. They are then stored in vast barns until they appear for sale between early December and late February.

Flax.—Some 20 miles—30 km—of the Caux coastline and a total area of 25,000 acres—10,000 ha—are devoted to flax which requires a silica-clay soil and a warm damp climate. One quarter of the crop is exported, the remainder is worked locally. This consists, in the early stages, of cutting it by machine—practically none is now hand cut—and leaving it to dry out and stiffen. Then it is either left longer to ret on the spot or tied in bundles for export to Belgium or dispatched to a factory for water retting.

INDUSTRY

Norman industry derives, in part, from its crafts of former times: Pont-Audemer is still a tanning town; bell casters and copper beaters are still found in the town which takes its name from metal craft work, Villedieu-les-Poêles—*poêles* are frying pans; Ezy, in the Eure Valley, is still known for its combs and La Couture-Boussey, on the neighbouring plateau, for reed instruments.

Other industries, equally typical of the region, but more highly developed and requiring more capital equipment are to be found at such places as Elbeuf, long associated with cloth weaving, Flers with furnishing materials and ticking. The workshops of the Ouche Region have been succeeded by metallurgical works treating non-ferrous metals at La Bonneville and in the Aigle area, drawing steel for the production of pins, needles, staples, etc.

The glassworks of the Bresle Valley specialise in bottles and flagons.

New industries such as records have come to places like Louviers, motor assembly works to the areas around Elbeuf and Le Havre, while a factory making a prosaic domestic utensil—a vegetable grinder and food mill—has transformed the local economy of the small market town of Alençon.

Heavy industry, dependent on weighty raw materials most economically transported by sea and river, has developed particularly around the ports of Rouen, Caen, Le Havre and along the Lower Seine Valley. The Rouen complex includes a wide variety of industries (*see map p. 133*) among the largest being newsprint which supplies nearly 50% of the national need. The Lower Seine is punctuated by four oil refineries, shipping yards and their attendant industries, including the ever extending petro-chemical establishments for detergents, plastics, synthetic rubber, etc.

Caen, linked by canal to the sea, has always been the natural outlet for the iron mines of Lower Normandy. The future economic goal of the area is, therefore, the creation of a planned industrial zone alongside the blast furnaces and steel works of Mondeville.

MARITIME INTERESTS

Life in the Ports.—The great **commercial ports** of Normandy handle approximately one third of France's seagoing commerce. Proof of their continuing vitality was the post-war establishment in Le Havre of the National Institute of Merchant Shipping.

Crowds always gather on the quays and jetties to watch the sailing of a transatlantic or other liner from Le Havre, Cherbourg or Dieppe. As the siren sounds, everyone dreams that he is under way!

Among **fishing ports**, Fécamp stands out as the largest cod-landing port in France. In all the many harbours, large and small, along the coast the throb of the diesel engine is heard everywhere, although it is still held that ability to sail a boat is the real test of seamanship. The passing land lubber will enjoy the early morning fish auction with its noisy bidding by fishmongers for sole, turbot, skate, mackerel, whiting, cod, and other fish.

Lighthouses.—The lighthouses along the Normandy coast make good vantage points for those who do not mind spiral staircases. The oldest houses are the tallest—modern electrical and optical equipment having been so improved that carrying power is no longer so dependent on height.

ART AND ARCHITECTURE IN NORMANDY

Richness in Stone.—The architecture of Normandy is as typical as its apple trees and its green fields: the wealth of historic buildings which gives the province an individual character is an expression of the people. The Norman, who has an inborn respect for property, loves stone, and he is never mean when it comes to building for God or himself. The riches of the country and affluence of the inhabitants have resulted, therefore, in many vast constructions —churches, abbeys, castles and manorhouses. The Norman builds a great deal and he builds well.

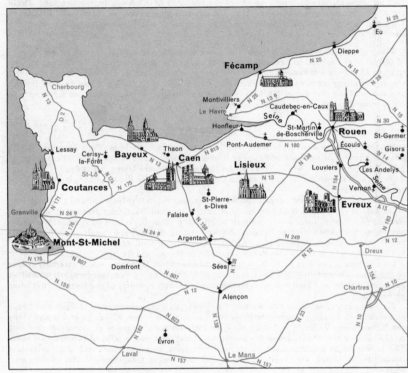

The Great Churches of Normandy

Norman material.—The stone in these buildings, which symbolise the industry and taste of the people, is local, often quarried from the very land which it later embellishes. Rouen and the towns of the Seine in Normandy are built of the soft stone found in the chalky cliffs bordering the river. The oolitic limestone of Caen, which is harder and with a fine grain, was used for buildings in the town and neighbouring countryside, and, after the Norman Conquest, for buildings in England, including Westminster Abbey.

A similar affinity exists between the natural local materials and the buildings in the Caux Region, where small stones are widely set in flowing mortar, and in the hamlets of the Suisse Normande, where the houses covered with shale have a mountain character. Norman clay, so abundant and economical, served for the cob walls and cobwork between the beams of thatched cottages long ago, and to make the bricks which are often laid ornamentally.

Sandstone and granite have a sobering effect on the architecture of the Bocage and the Cotentin, anticipating that of Brittany.

A CHURCH'S GROUND PLAN

The terminology of church architecture may not be familiar to all. The brief description and plan below explain and place the most usual features.

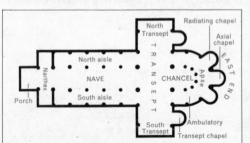

The Plan.—A church consists basically of a chancel where the clergy officiate and where the high altar and relics are placed, and a nave in which the faithful stand. Sometimes a porch precedes the west door. Early churches were all built simply to this plain rectangular or basilical plan.

Romanesque architects created the Catholic type of church with a ground plan based on the outline of a cross. A narthex at the entrance received those who had not been baptised, and provided a place for special pilgrim services. The nave was widened by the addition of side aisles. Pilgrimage churches were adapted by the extension of the aisles round the chancel, forming an ambulatory and thus allowing pilgrims to circulate. Chapels were sometimes built off the apse (absidal or radiating chapels) or the transept (transept chapels).

ROMANESQUE ARCHITECTURE (11C–early 12C)

The Benedictines and Romanesque Design.—In the 11C, after the period of the Invasions, the Benedictines returned to their building: they cleared land, they built monasteries, they constructed abbeys.

These monk-architects, inheritors of an ancient tradition, employed the barrel vault—the same that the Romans had used for their bridges and their triumphal arches or, sometimes, as an alternative, erected domes, using, however, not the original oriental but the more robust Carolingian methods of construction. Finally they created a new architectural style, named by the 19C Norman archaeologist, Arcisse de Caumont, who first (in 1840) outlined the theory of regional schools of architecture, "Romanesque". In England, however, the style has remained known as "Norman".

The Romanesque vault, a solid cover, weighed heavily upon its supporting walls so that solidarity took precedence over elegance and the Romanesque church emerged as a massive thick-set edifice with rare openings. A square belfry sometimes dominates the heavily buttressed and closed looking building. Nevertheless within its apparent simplicity Romanesque architecture is wonderfully diverse.

The Norman School and its Abbey Churches.—The Benedictines, supported by the Dukes of Normandy, played an immensely important part in the whole life of the province; only their work as architects and creators of the Norman school is described below.

The first religious buildings of importance in Normandy were the churches of the rich abbacies. Early monastic buildings may have disappeared or been modified, particularly after the Maurian reform (see p. 20), but there remain, as evidence of the "Benedictine flowering", such fine abbey ruins as Jumièges, and churches as St. Stephen and the Holy Trinity at Caen, St. George at St-Martin-de-Boscherville, Mont-St-Michel, Cérisy-la-Forêt and others.

The Norman school is characterised by pure lines, bold proportions, sober decoration and a beautiful sense of display. The style spread to England after the Norman Conquest (see p. 73) —it was in Durham Cathedral that rib vaulting officially first appeared, and certainly on such a scale, at the beginning of the 12C.(Other fine examples include Westminster Abbey as rebuilt by Edward the Confessor, the two façade towers and square crossing tower at Canterbury and Southwell, Winchester and Ely.)

Norman design also appeared in Sicily in the 11C in the wake of noble Norman adventurers (see p. 75) while, more widely in France, it opened the way for the Gothic style.

The abbeys are characterised by robust towers on either side of the façade, giving the west face an H-like appearance, and a square lantern tower above the transept crossing which also served to increase the light inside.

The towers, bare or decorated only with blind arcades below, get lighter with multiple pierced bays the higher they rise (many were crowned by spires quartered by pinnacles in the 13C).

(After Ed. Arthaud photo)

Caen.—The Abbaye aux Hommes (St. Stephen's Church (p. 57))

Romanesque belfries often surmount delightful country churches—their saddleback roofs rising like a circumflex accent or four sided wood or squat stone pyramid coverings, embryonic Gothic spires, marking them from afar.

The interior light and size of Norman abbeys is very striking. The naves are wide with two series of openings above great semicircular arches—an amazingly bold concept for a Romanesque construction. The explanation lies in the fact that the design was not intended to support a heavy barrel vault: the Norman monks deliberately rejected this style of covering in favour of a beamed roof over the nave and galleries, reserving groined stone vaulting (the crossing of two semicircular arches) for the aisles.

The vast galleries on the upper level opening on to the nave through wide bays repeat the design of the aisles. Finally, on a level with the upper windows, a gallery circles the church, passing through the thickness of the walls. A dome over the transept crossing supports a magnificent lantern tower which lets in the daylight through tall windows.

Norman Decoration.—The abbey churches, like all others of Romanesque design, were illuminated on a considerable scale with gilding and bright colours as were the manuscripts of the time. The main themes were those of Byzantine iconography.

Norman sculpture does not rival other Romanesque schools; the decoration is essentially geometric: different motifs stand out—mouldings, human heads, or animal masks emphasise a curve, an archivolt, a cornice. Occasionally the monks transposed a motif from a material, an ivory or a piece of oriental gold or silver work, carving it in low relief—such is the origin of the cornerstones of the main arches at Bayeux (see p. 50). Figured capitals are rare, most are gadroons or decorated with stylised leafwork.

GOTHIC ARCHITECTURE (12–15C)

The style, conceived in the Ile-de-France, apart from rib vaulting which was brought back from Norman England, was known as "French work" or "French style" until the 16C when the Italians of the Renaissance, unwilling to accept it as Parisian, gave it, to their minds, the disparaging appellation of Gothic art. The name, with no disparaging connotation, remains.

Development of the Gothic style.—Using crossed, pointed arches and their corollary, buttresses, the master masons of the Ile-de-France developed the style until it had both incomparable boldness and grace. The weight of the roof was balanced between the pointed arches meeting in a keystone above the centre of a bay and the ribs which took the weight of the supporting walls. Outside, these were supported by buttresses and flying buttresses, allowing the intervening wall space to be replaced by windows. Heavy masonry was superseded by glass; naves rose to a tremendous height. The French, elsewhere, for a time, copied the H-shaped façades and great galleries of the Norman abbeys (the façade of Notre-Dame in Paris is based on that of the Holy Trinity of Caen and its galleries on those of St. Stephen's) but after a transitional period, the Ile-de-France masons developed a style on their own which ultimately spread throughout the Christian world.

The Cathedrals.—Gothic is a style made for cathedrals, symbolising the sweeping religious fervour of the people, the growing prosperity of the towns. In an all-embracing enthusiasm, a whole city would participate in the construction of the house of God: some would bring offerings, others lend their strength and skill. Under the enlightened guidance of bishops and master builders, city corporations contributed to the cathedral's embellishment: stained glass makers, painters, wood and stone carvers went to work. The doors became the illustrated pages of history.

(After Yvon photo)

Coutances.—The Cathedral (p. 79)

Gothic Architecture in Normandy.—In turn the national Gothic style seeped gradually back to Normandy, preceding the seizure of the province by Philippe Auguste. The St. Romanus tower of Rouen Cathedral and particularly Lisieux Cathedral show the degree of French Gothic influence in Normandy by the end of the 12C.

In the 13C the Gothic and traditional Norman styles fused: Coutances Cathedral is the best example of the result. There Norman pure proportions and tall bare outlines combine marvellously with Gothic sophistication, particularly in the lantern tower.

This was also the period of the superb belfries of the Caen and Bessin plains, typified by their tall stone spires, often pierced to offer less resistance to the wind, and quartered with pinnacles.

The magnificent Merveille buildings of Mont-St-Michel give an idea of total Norman Gothic ornament. Sobriety provides the foundation over which foliated sculpture reigns supreme: plants of every variety decorate the round capitals, cover the cornerstones, garland the friezes. The three and four leafed clover in relief or hollowed out is a repeated motif but statuary is rare.

Flamboyant Gothic.—By the 14C, the period of great cathedral building had come to an end. The Hundred Years War killed architectural inspiration: bits were added, buildings were touched up, little created. When the war was over a taste for virtuosity alone remained—and Flamboyant Gothic was born. Rouen is the true capital of Flamboyant Gothic, which was particularly widespread in Upper Normandy.

In this new style, supplementary ribs—liernes and tiercerons—divide the vaults and main ribs fuse directly into columns which have no capitals. The triforium disappears and the space is taken over by tall windows; the tracery of bays and rose windows resembles wavering flames—the derivation of the term Flamboyant. Stone is cut like a jewel, worked until it is like lace; architecture is clouded by proliferating decoration.

Flamboyant Gothic produced such single masterpieces as the Church of St. Maclou at Rouen, the Butter Tower on Rouen Cathedral, the belfries of Our Lady at Caudebec and the Magdalene at Verneuil and beautifully decorated adjuncts in the form of cloisters, chapels, screens and traceries. A local school of statuary was established at Verneuil: an often repeated theme in Normandy became the Descent into the Tomb. Civil architecture developed in importance and passed from Flamboyant Gothic to Renaissance—a change symbolised in the gables, pinnacles, balustrades of the Law Courts at Rouen.

Gothic architecture in England developed through three distinct stages. From Early English in the 13C (of which Salisbury Cathedral is the most complete example), it progressed to Decorated during the 14C. Buildings became more ornate and tracery more naturalistic. Exeter Cathedral is an example of this period. In Perpendicular style Gothic architecture reached the height of its virtuosity and the last stage of its evolution in buildings such as King's College Chapel, Cambridge, built during the 15C.

FEUDAL ARCHITECTURE

In mediaeval Normandy permission to build a castle was granted to the barons by the ruling duke, who, prudent as well as powerful, reserved the right to billet his own garrison inside and forbade all private wars. Over the years the building of castles along the duchy's frontiers was encouraged—Richard Lionheart bolted the Seine with the most formidable fortress of the period, Castle Gaillard.

Castles were sited so as to command the horizon and be invincible to surprise attack. Originally only the austere keeps were inhabited, but from the 14C a courtyard and more hospitable and pleasing quarters were constructed within the fortifications. This evolution in military architecture can be seen in some of the Perche manors and particularly in the 15C Dieppe Castle.

A taste for comfort and adornment appeared in civil architecture: rich merchants and burgesses built tall houses where wide eaves protected half-timbered upper storeys which in turn overhung stone walled ground floors. The results were as capricious as they were picturesque: corner posts, corbels and beams were all vividly carved. In the 16C decoration became richer and less impulsive, but the wooden architectural style remained the same. Although many of these old houses disappeared, good examples may still be seen in, among other places, Honfleur, Bayeux and Rouen.

RENAISSANCE ARCHITECTURE (16C)

Georges d'Amboise, Archbishop and patron of Rouen, Cardinal Minister to Louis XII, introduced Italian methods and taste to Normandy. Skilful and sophisticated decoration replaced the more spontaneous Gothic art which had sprung from the people. Luxury and art became the prerogatives of the court and the rich. Mediaeval art had been anonymous and collective; the Renaissance was to mark the triumph of the individual.

The Italian Fashion.—A totally Italian style of decoration was applied by Italian artists to the feudal structure of Gaillon Castle by Georges d'Amboise. The new motives—arabesques, foliated scrollwork, medallions, shells, urns, etc.—were combined with Flamboyant Gothic art.

Gradually crossed pointed arches were replaced by coffered ceilings, keystones became elongated until they resembled stalactites; pilasters took the place of columns, the basket handle of the broken barrel arch; spires gave way to small domes flanked by lanterns. The outstanding works of this period are the main doorway of Rouen Cathedral, Gisors Church and the apse in St. Peter's at Caen, a masterpiece of exuberance.

The form of the statues of antiquity haunted the imagination of sculptors: allegorical and mythological personages combined with sacred themes—Olympus replaced the Gospel. The vaulting of Tillières Church (*damaged by fire in 1969*) is a good example of this invasion by the profane. Finally funerary statuary developed to major importance.

Fontaine-Henry.—The Château (*p. 64*)

Castles, Manors and Old Mansions.—The Renaissance style reached its fullest grace in domestic architecture. At first older buildings were ornamented in the current taste or a new and delicately decorated wing was added (Ô Castle and Fontaine-Henry Château); parks and gardens were laid out where fortifications once stood. The Classicism rediscovered by humanists took hold so that, among others, Philibert Dolorme, architect of Anet Château, sought above all correct proportion and the imposition of the three Classical Orders of Antiquity. Imperceptibly the search for symmetry and correctness mortified inspiration: pomposity drowned fantasy. In Normandy, the Gothic spirit survived, appearing most successfully in small manorhouses and innumerable country houses with pretense feudal moats, turrets and battlements incorporated in either half-timbering or stone and brick.

Norman towns contain many large stone Renaissance mansions. The outer façade is always plain and one has to enter the inner courtyard to see the architectural design and the rich decoration (Escoville Mansion, Caen).

CLASSICAL ART AND ARCHITECTURE (17–18C)

In this period, French architectural style, now a single concept and no longer an amalgam of individual techniques, imposed its rationalism on many countries beyond its borders.

Louis XIII and the so-called Jesuit Style.—The reign of Henri IV, following the civil wars, marked an artistic rebirth. An economical method of construction was adopted in which bricks played an important part: it was a time of beautiful châteaux with plain rose and white façades and steep grey-blue slate roofs.

The first decades of the 17C also coincided with a strong Catholic reaction. The Jesuits built many colleges and chapels—cold and formal edifices, their façades characterised by superimposed columns, a pediment and returned consoles or small wings joining the front of the main building to the sides.

Two Classical Normans.—Nicolas Poussin, initiator and master of Classical painting in France, was born at Les Andelys in 1594 (d. 1665); generations of schoolchildren are still imbued with the Classical spirit through the works of Corneille (1606–1684).

These two solemn Normans, passionate supporters of order and reason, were followers of Antiquity. A strong personality, allied to great sensibility, allowed each, however, to escape academic frigidity and create original work. From them emerged the ethic of the French Classical spirit which was to reach its climax in art with the advent of Le Brun and Le Nôtre and the construction of Versailles, a balanced whole and symbol of French grandeur.

The "Grand Siècle" in Normandy (18C).—The symmetrical façades of the Classical style demanded space for their appreciation as can be seen in the châteaux at Balleroy, Cany, Beaumesnil, Champ de Bataille and elsewhere.

The Benedictine abbeys, which had adopted the **Maurian Reform**, rediscovered their former inspiration. At the beginning of the 18C, the monastery buildings of the Abbaye aux Hommes in Caen and at Bec-Hellouin were remodelled by a brother architect and sculptor, **Guillaume de la Tremblaye** (see pp. 52 and 58). The original plan was conserved but the design and decoration were given an austere nobility. Finally, towns were transformed by the addition of magnificent episcopal palaces, town halls with wide façades and large private houses.

Ceramics and Pottery.—The glazed pavement in the chapterhouse of the 13C St-Pierre-sur-Dives demonstrates how far back ceramic art goes in Normandy. In the 16C Masséot Abaquesne was making decorated tiles in Rouen which were greatly prized and, simultaneously, potteries in Le Pré-d'Auge and Manerbe (near Lisieux) were also making "earthenware more beautiful than is made elsewhere". In 1644 **Rouen pottery** made its name with blue decoration on a white ground and vice versa. By the end of the century production had so increased that when the royal plate had to be sacrificed to replenish the treasury, "the Court", wrote Saint-Simon, "had changed to chinaware in a week". The radiant style, reminiscent of wrought ironwork and embroidery for which the town was well known, was succeeded by Chinoiserie and, in the middle of the 18C by the Rococo with its "quiver" decoration and the famous "Rouen cornucopia" in which flowers, birds and insects flow from a horn of plenty. A trade treaty in 1786, allowing the entry of English chinaware to France, ruined the industry.

MODERN ART

Painting took first place among the arts in 19C France. Landscape totally eclipsed historical and stylised painting in this century in Normandy which was to become the cradle of Impressionism.

The Open Air.—While the Romantics were discovering inland Normandy, Eugène Isabey, a lover of seascapes, began to work on the still deserted coast. **Richard Bonington**, 1801–1828, an English painter who went to France as a boy, trained there, and caught, in his watercolours, the wetness of sea beaches. A few years later a thoughtful young peasant, **J. F. Millet**, observed country life on the plains round The Hague. He became a painter and, retaining his realistic vision with deep feeling, drew or painted from memory, aided sometimes by a hasty sketch, scenes of work on the land.

In the second half of the 19C artistic activity was concentrated, with **Eugène Boudin** (1824–1898), around the Côte de Grâce. This painter from Honfleur, named "king of the skies" by Corot, encouraged a young 15-year-old from Le Havre, **Claude Monet**, to drop caricature for painting and urged his Parisian friends to come and stay in his St-Siméon farmstead.

Faced with luminous Norman skies and the delicate tints of the coast, the mid-19C school of painting known as the Barbizon school after the village of the same name in the Forest of Fontainebleau and comprising Millet, Théodore Rousseau and Diaz, cleaned their palettes of dull colours and began painting unprettified pictures of peasant life and scenery on the spot, this last characteristic making them the precursors of Impressionism.

Impressionism.—The younger painters, nevertheless, were to outstrip their elders in the search for pictorial light. They wanted to portray the vibration of light, hazes, the trembling of reflections and shadows, the depth and tenderness of the sky, the fading of colours in full sunlight. They—Monet, Sisley, Bazille and their Paris friends, Renoir, Pissarro, Cézanne and Guillaumin especially—were about to form the Impressionist School.

From 1862 to 1869 the Impressionists remained faithful to the Normandy coast and the Seine Estuary. After the Franco-German War they returned only occasionally—although it was in Normandy, at Giverny, that Claude Monet set up house in 1881 and remained until he died in 1926 in the full glory of his work.

Impressionism, in its turn, gave birth to a new school, **Pointillism**, which divided the tints with little touches of colour, applying the principle of the division of white into seven basic colours, to get ever closer to luminous effect. Seurat and Signac, the pioneers of this method, also came to Normandy to study its landscapes.

For half a century, therefore, the Côte de Grâce, the Caux Region, Deauville, Trouville and Rouen, were the sources of inspiration of a multitude of paintings.

20C Painters.—Painters still came to Normandy in the first half of the 20C, notably Valloton, Marquet, Gernez, Raoul Dufy, Othon Friesz who particularly enjoyed Honfleur and Van Dongen, painter of the worldly and the elegant and frequent guest at Deauville.

NORMAN MEN OF LETTERS

Letters, like architecture, began as a monastic art.

There is nothing surprising, therefore, in the fact that from the 13C onwards, Normandy, so rich in abbeys and one of the most prosperous civilised regions of France, should be the home of much French literature. Travellers and pilgrims brought news to the abbeys where there were monks and clerks learned in history and legend; poets went to the abbeys for inspiration and documentation for their epic verse chronicles, filled with the wonders of Christianity. It was, perhaps, from sources such as these that the *Song of Roland* was composed.

During the Hundred Years War, France's misery inspired Olivier Basselin, a clothworker from Les Vaux de Vire (see p. 154), to make up songs so full of spirit they passed from man to man.

In the 15C a university was founded at Caen, a Jesuit College at Rouen. In the same period, the name of Alain Chartier of Bayeux spread far as a poet.

Malherbe, imperious purist from Caen, not content with purifying the language also wished to put order into ideas and rationalise poetry! He opened the way, however, for the Classicists.

Corneille, who was born in Rouen, remains the great Classic writer. In the battles of conscience which he portrays in the theatre, this poet of free will usually makes reason triumph over emotion but without losing all heart. His taste for grandeur and human truth is always allied, in true Norman style, to restraint.

Fontanelle, with his positive character, incarnates the Norman temperament. His dry, but clever and lucid mind, made him prefer philosophy to letters. He was also from Rouen.

In the 19C literature and painting (see p. 20), both turned to the portrayal of provincial life. **Flaubert**, the Romantic who settled down and another Rouennais, conceived art as a means of discovery. He, who fulfilled the natural richness and duality of the Norman temperament, described himself as the lover of words and lyricism and yet the confirmed delver and seeker after truth. *Madame Bovary* remains one of the greatest modern novels.

Maupassant, subjected to harsh discipline in his style by Flaubert, was no less a minute observer of humanity. He retains considerable popularity abroad.

The founder of Norman regionalism is **Barbey d'Aurevilly**, a great nobleman of the Cotentin (see p. 137). In a style, both warm and bright, illuminated with brilliant imagery and original phrases, he sought, like the Impressionists, to convey the atmosphere, the quality, the uniqueness of his region.

Lucie Delarue-Mardrus, faithful until her death to Honfleur, sang well of her province.

Jean de la Varende, a man from the Ouche, also recalls in his works the eternal Normandy.

FOOD AND DRINK

See also p. 9

The variety and quality of Normandy's copious products has given rise to good cooking, characterised by the widespread use of cream.

Cream and Normandy Sauce.—Cream is the mainstay of the Normandy kitchen: ivory in colour, velvety in texture and mellow in taste, it goes as well with eggs and fish as with chicken, white meat, vegetables and even game. This delicious cream is at its best in the so-called Normandy Sauce—*Sauce Normande*—which elsewhere is nothing but a plain white sauce, but in Normandy both looks and tastes quite different.

Cheeses.—If cream is the queen of Normandy cooking, cheese is the king of all fares. *Pont-l'Evêque* has reigned since the 13C; *Livarot* is quoted in texts of the same period; the world renowned *Camembert* first appeared early in the 19C (details p. 45). To be really creamy and soft, a *Pont-l'Evêque* should be made on a farm in the Auge Region when the milk is still warm from the cow. *Livarot*, whose strong odour alarms the uninitiated, is made from milk which has stood. Although *Camembert* is now made in factories all over France, only Normandy *Camembert* is authentic.

Finally there are the fresh cheeses from the Bray Region—the *Suisses*, demi-sel and double creams—whose repute is more recent but none the less firmly established.

Cider and Calvados.—In Normandy the most fastidious gourmet will drink cider with shrimps, mussels, chicken from the Auge Valley, tripe or leg of lamb from the salt meadows. True cider, *bon bère*, is pure apple juice fermented. When the cork is drawn, *bon bère* should remain still in the bottle, only sparkling and then without a froth, when poured into the glass. For daily needs, the Norman dilutes his cider with water.

Auge Valley cider is famous (see pp. 28, 45) but other local ciders are also good.

Calvados is to the apple what cognac is to the grape. This cider spirit, or apple-jack, more than any other, needs to mature—twelve to fifteen years bring it to perfection. In the middle of his copious meal, the Norman breathes deeply for a moment and then swallows a small glass of *Calvados*: this is the famous "Norman hole" or *trou Normand*; at the end of the meal come cups of black coffee accompanied by further small glasses of *Calvados*.

Gastronomic Specialities.—Normandy tradition has it that one eats duck in Rouen, tripe in Caen and at La Ferté-Macé, an omelette at Mont-St-Michel and that at some point one should also taste Dieppe sole, Duclair duckling, Auge Valley chicken garnished with tiny onions, Vire chitterlings and Avranchin white pudding.

The only problem for the lover of sea food is the one of choice between the shrimps and cockles of Honfleur, the mussels of Villerville and Isigny, the oysters of Courseulles and St-Vaast and the lobsters of La Hague and Barfleur.

Finally for those with a sweet tooth there are Rouen sugar apples and Caen *chiques* or caramels.

	B.C.	The Celts inhabit parts of France The Seine becomes the "tin road" (see p. 140)	Gaul an independent area
ROMAN PERIOD	56 B.C. 1 C 2 C 3 C 260 284 4 C 364	Sabinius crushes the Unelli in the Mount Castre area The major towns develop (Rouen, Evreux, Coutances, etc.) Nordic (Saxon and Germanic) invasions of the Bessin region Conversion to Christianity St. Nicaise founds the Bishopric of Rouen Nordic invasion Nordic invasion	Roman conquest (58–51) Reign of Diocletian 284–305
FRANKISH DOMINATION	497 511 6 C 709	Clovis occupies Rouen and Evreux Clovis' son, Clothaire, inherits Neustria or the Western Kingdom The first monasteries founded (see p. 140: The Castles of God) Aubert, Bishop of Avranches, consecrates Mount Tombe to the cult of St. Michael (see p. 47)	The Merovingians
NORMAN INVASIONS	820 836 875 885 911	The Normans ravage the Seine Valley (see p. 141) Christians persecuted in the Cotentin Region Further persecution in the West The Normans besiege Paris Treaty of St-Clair-sur-Epte; Rollo, first Duke of Normandy (see p. 88)	The Carolingians
THE INDEPENDENT DUKEDOM	10–11 C 1035–1087 1066 1087–1135 1152 1154–1189 1195 1202 1204	Consolidation of ducal powers. Restoration of the abbeys. Creation of new monasteries William the Conqueror The invasion of Britain (details p. 73). The Duke of Normandy, now also King of England, becomes a threatening vassal to the King of France William I's heirs are divided. Henry I, Beauclerc, restores ducal authority (King of England 1100–1135) Henry II, Plantagenet, marries Eleanor of Aquitaine Henry II, King of England Richard I, Lionheart, builds Gaillard Castle John of England loses his Norman possessions Normandy reunited to the French throne	Hugues Capet (987–996) Louis VI (1108–1137) Louis VII (1137–1180) Philippe-Auguste (1180–1223)

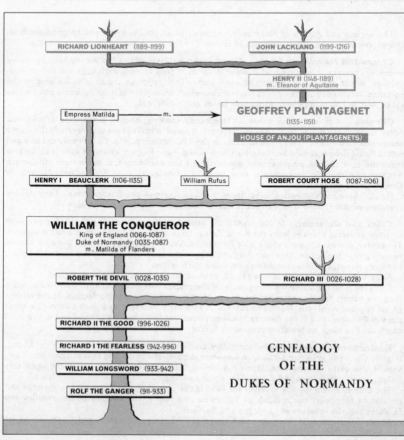

GENEALOGY
OF THE
DUKES OF NORMANDY

THE FRENCH DUKEDOM	1315	The Norman Charter, the symbol of provincial status, is granted and will remain in being until the Revolution	Philip the Fair (1285–1314)
	1339	Fresh invasion of Normans into England	
	1346	Edward III of England invades Normandy	Battle of Crécy (1346)
	1364–1384	The Battle of Cocherel marks the start of Du Guesclin's victorious campaigns	Battle of Poitiers (1356)
	1417	Siege of Rouen (see p. 127: The Goddons)	Battle of Agincourt (1415)
	1420	Henry V of England recognised as King of France under Treaty of Troyes.	
	1431	Trial and execution of Joan of Arc at Rouen (details p. 127)	Charles VII (1429–1461)
	1437	Founding of Caen University	
	1450	Normandy is recovered by French throne after victory at Formigny and recapture of Cherbourg	
	1469	The ducal seal is broken as Charles of France, last Duke of Normandy, is dispossessed of his dukedom	Louis XI (1461–1483)
THE PROVINCE OF NORMANDY	1514	The Rouen Exchequer becomes the Parliament of Normandy	
	1517	Foundation of Le Havre (details p. 102)	François I (1515–1549)
	1542	Caen and Rouen created self-governing cities	
	1562	Start of the Wars of Religion	
	1589	Henri of Navarre victor at Arques (details p. 44) and, the following year, at Ivry-la-Bataille (p. 91)	Henri IV (1589–1610)
	1625	Alençon created an autonomous city	Louis XIII (1610–1643)
	1639–1640	The introduction of the Gabelle—the salt tax—provokes the Revolt of the Barefoot Peasants (see p. 47)	
	1685	Revocation of the Edict of Nantes	Louis XIV (1643–1715)
	1771–1775	Suppression of the Parliament at Rouen	Louis XV (1715–1774)
CONTEMPORARY NORMANDY	1789	The Caen revolt	Louis XVI (1774–1793)
	1793	The Girondins' attempted uprising Siege of Granville	The Convention
	1795–1800	Insurrection of the Norman royalists, the Chouans	The Directory-Consulate
	1843	Inauguration of the Paris–Rouen railway	Louis-Philippe (1830–1848)
	1870–1871	Franco-Prussian War—occupation of Upper Normandy and Le Mans	Napoleon III (1851–1870)
	1883	Creation of the Norman Herd Book (see p. 14)	Third Republic
	1928	The Lower Seine becomes the River of Petrol (see p. 142)	
	June 1940	Piercing of the Bresle front; the cities and towns of Upper Normandy ravaged by fire	
	August 1942	Dieppe commando raid by the Canadian and British troops (p. 82)	
	6 June 1944	Allied Landing; massive bombardments. Battle of Normandy (pp. 24–25, 62)	

The Normans and History (9th to 17th centuries)

Several different kinds of expedition emphasise the "Norman epic": the first of these were war-like reconnaissances led by the Vikings along all the sea routes of the North Atlantic and the Mediterranean. Whenever these Northmen settled down, new states were created such as Normandy. But the map below gives special place to the achievements by Normans of Normandy: the founding of kingdoms in the 11 and 12C, then, after the Hundred Years War, discoveries (or re-discoveries) of lands accompanied by efforts at colonisation which were more or less successful.

The Norman Kingdoms

① 1066 Conquest of England by William of Normandy (see p. 73)

② 1042–1194 The descendants of Tancrède de Hauteville (details p. 75) found the Norman kingdom of Sicily.

③ 1099 During the First Crusade, Bohémond, son of Robert Guiscard (see p. 75), sets up a principality near Antioch. His descendants stay there until 1287.

Norman Discoveries

④ 1364 Men of Dieppe land on the coasts of Guinea (Sierra Leone of today) and found Little Dieppe (Petit Dieppe).

⑤ 1402 Jean de Béthencourt, of the Caux Region, goes in search of adventure and becomes King of the Canary Islands, but soon cedes the islands to the King of Castile.

⑥ 1503 Paulmier de Gonneville, gentleman of Honfleur, reaches Brazil in the Espoir.

⑦ 1506 Jean Denis, sailor from Honfleur, explores the mouth of the St. Lawrence, preparing the way for Jacques Cartier.

⑧ 1524 Leaving Dieppe (see p. 82: Jean Ango and Privateers' War), in the caravel La Dauphine, the French-Florentine Verrazano, navigator to François I, reconnoitres the New France and discovers the site of New York, which he names Land of Angoulême.

⑨ 1555 Admiral de Villegaignon sets up a colony of Huguenots from Le Havre on an island in the bay of Rio de Janeiro but they are driven away by the Portuguese.

⑩ 1563 Led by René de la Laudonnière, colonies of Protestants from Le Havre and Dieppe settle in Florida and found Fort Caroline but are massacred by the Spaniards.

⑪ 1608 Samuel Champlain, Dieppe ship builder, leaves Honfleur, to found Quebec (see p. 107: Canada, a Norman colony).

⑫ 1635 Pierre Belain of Esnambuc takes possession of Martinique in the name of the King of France. The colonisation of Guadeloupe follows soon after.

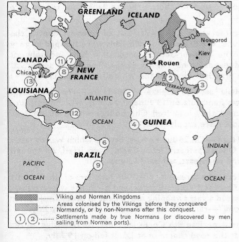

Viking and Norman Kingdoms
Areas colonised by the Vikings before they conquered Normandy, or by non-Normans after this conquest.
①, ② Settlements made by true Normans (or discovered by men sailing from Norman ports).

⑬ 1682 Cavelier de la Salle, of Rouen, after reconnoitring the site of Chicago, sails down the Mississippi and takes possession of Louisiana.

THE BATTLE OF NORMANDY

A landing on the continent of Europe was envisaged in England from the autumn of 1941, but it was only with the entry of the United States that offensive action on such scale could be seriously considered. The COSSAC plan, approved at the Churchill-Roosevelt meetings in Washington and Quebec in May and August of 1943, foresaw the landing of invasion troops along the Calvados coast, defended by the German 7th Army.

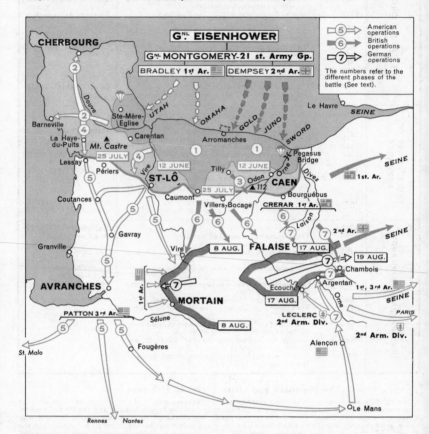

Preparation.—The building of artificial ports—a lesson learnt as a result of the costly Dieppe commando raid of 1942 (pp. 82, 45)—and the construction of landing craft was carried out with other training in the winter of 1943/44. On 24 December 1943 General Eisenhower was named Chief of the Allied Expeditionary Force and General Montgomery made responsible for tactical coordination of all land forces (21st Army Group) for Operation Overlord.

Marshal Rommel had covered the beaches and their approaches with obstacles. Aerial bombardment to paralyse the French railway system began on 6 March 1944.

①—**The First Week of the Landing.**—At dawn on D-Day, 6 June 1944, British and Commonwealth ground forces established beachheads at Sword, Juno and Gold and rapidly linked up with the airborne troops dropped to their east (p. 62). The Americans, landing on the beaches of Omaha and Utah, only joined up with their airborne flank after the capture of Carentan on 12 June (p. 123).

Layout of the Bridgehead.—Advances were substantial but of unequal depth: the Americans threatened Caumont on 13 June; the British and Canadians were stopped by very fierce fighting 4 miles north of Caen in the Tilly-sur-Seulles sector on 7 June and only got through on 20th—the village changed hands some twenty times. The Caen sector, as Montgomery had foreseen, became the principal hinge of the whole front (pp. 56, 61).

②—**The Cutting of the Cotentin Peninsula and the Capture of Cherbourg.**—The Americans launched their attack across the Cotentin Peninsula on 13 June and cut it, with the capture of Barneville, on the 18th. Turning north they assaulted Cherbourg, which fell on 26th (details p. 70)—a victory in the battle to ensure supply lines.

③—**The Battle of the Odon and Capture of Caen.**—On 26 June a hard battle, which was to last a month, began for a crossing over the Odon upstream from Caen. Caen itself, on the left bank, attacked in force from the west and northeast, fell on 9 July (p. 56).

Break-through Preparation.—"Keep the greatest possible number of the enemy divisions on our eastern flank, between Caen and Villers-Bocage, and pivot the western flank of the Army Group towards the southeast in a vast sweeping movement in order to threaten the line of retreat of the German divisions"—ran a Montgomery directive of early July.

④—**The Battle for St-Lô.**—On 3 July the American 8th Corps launched its offensive, in the face of fierce German resistance, towards the road centre of St-Lô. It fell on 19 July.

Progress at this time was slow in the Caen sector. For one, seemingly endless, week—19-25 July—bad weather suspended operations on all fronts.

⑤—**The Break-through (Operation Cobra).**—At midday on 25 July, following intense aerial bombardment (p. 135), the 7th Corps attacked west of St-Lô, the 8th between Périers and Lessay. By the 28th, Allied armour was driving down the main roads, carrying out vast encircling movements. Coutances fell on 28 July, Granville and Avranches on 31st. On 1 August, General Patton, taking command of the 3rd Army, hurled it into the lightning war. The 8th Corps burst west into Brittany, while the 15th Corps and the French 2nd Armoured Division under General Leclerc moved east towards Laval and Le Mans (9 August).

⑥—**The Thrust south of Caen.**—Under Montgomery, the 1st Canadian Army (General Crerar) was brought up to the Caen–Falaise road and the British divisions, pushing southeast from Caumont and Villers-Bocage (5 August), overwhelmed the last defences on the left bank of the Orne (pp. 43, 44).

⑦—**Battle of the Falaise–Mortain Pocket.**—Faced with the American 15th Corps to their rear and south and the British to the north, the German 7th Army began a westerly counterattack on 6/7 August in the Mortain region; the Allied air forces smashed the move at daybreak. After a week of bitter fighting the Germans retreated east (12 August).

The French 2nd Division took Alençon on 12 August and on 13th cut the Paris–Granville road at Écouché. On 19 August the Canadians and Americans met at Chambois, cornering the German 7th Army and forcing its surrender (see p. 44).

By the night of 21 August the Battle of Normandy was over—it had cost the Germans 640,000 men, killed, wounded or taken prisoner. *The battle is recalled in detail in the War and Liberation Museum in Cherbourg (see p. 70).*

RECONSTRUCTION

The Scale of Devastation.—Normandy, like Britain and unlike many other French and European territories, is not on any European invasion route and so had remained unscathed since the Wars of Religion; towns had scarcely altered since the 16C. The German invasion of 1940 and the air raids and army operations of 1944 caused widespread devastation: more than 200,000 buildings were destroyed or damaged and nearly all the great towns suffered— Rouen, Le Havre, Caen, Lisieux. Of the 3,400 towns and villages of Normandy, 586 have been totally reconstructed to new plans.

Town Planning and Reconstruction.—Modern town planning has altered what were narrow winding main streets into wide straight highways suitable for car and other traffic. Public gardens, parks and car parks have been provided.

Houses, flats and offices have been built and towns and villages have once more found an individual character; limestone is seen again in buildings on the Norman sedimentary plain and plateaux (see p. 11), sandstone, granite and brick in the woodland regions, combining with modern materials and slate or brown tiles on the roofs. For further details see p. 16.

Many historic monuments were damaged but most have been restored and look as before —often in improved settings—destruction having cleared away sordid or irrelevant surrounding buildings. Caen castle is a supreme example.

COMMONWEALTH WAR GRAVES

The cemeteries and churchyards listed contain more than one hundred graves. Commonwealth war graves also lie in many other burial grounds throughout the area. For reasons of space, these have had to be omitted from the list below.

ARQUES-LA-BATAILLE BRITISH CEMETERY
  3 miles southeast of Dieppe (D 1)
BANNEVILLE-LA-CAMPAGNE WAR CEMETERY
  6 miles east of Caen (N 815)
BAYEUX WAR CEMETERY
  On southwestern outskirts (D 5)
BENY-SUR-MER CANADIAN WAR CEMETERY, REVIERS
  9 miles northwest of Caen (D 35)
BOISGUILLAUME COMMUNAL CEMETERY AND EXTENSION
  4½ miles northeast of Rouen (N 28)
BRETTEVILLE-SUR-LAIZE CANADIAN WAR CEMETERY
  8 miles south southeast of Caen (N 158)
BROUAY WAR CEMETERY
  9 miles west northwest of Caen (D 217)
CAMBES-EN-PLAINE WAR CEMETERY
  4 miles north of Caen (D 79)
DIEPPE CANADIAN WAR CEMETERY, HAUTOT-SUR-MER
  1½ miles south of the town (west of N 27)
ETRETAT CHURCHYARD AND EXTENSION
  In northern part of town
FONTENAY-LE-PESNEL WAR CEMETERY, TESSEL
  9 miles west of Caen (D 173)
HERMANVILLE WAR CEMETERY
  8 miles north of Caen (D 60)
HOTTOT-LES-BAGUES WAR CEMETERY, TILLY-SUR-SEULLES
  12 miles west of Caen (D 9)
JANVAL CEMETERY, DIEPPE
  in the southern part of the town
  rue Montigny prolongee

LA DELIVRANDE WAR CEMETERY, DOUVRES
  8 miles north of Caen (D 7)
LE TREPORT MILITARY CEMETERY
  1 mile south of railway station (N 25)
MONT HUON MILITARY CEMETERY, LE TREPORT
  1½ miles south of railway station
RANVILLE WAR CEMETERY
  6 miles northeast of Caen (D 223)
RYES WAR CEMETERY, BAZENVILLE
  1½ miles southeast of Ryes (D 87)
ST-CHARLES DE PERCY WAR CEMETERY
  6¼ miles northeast of Vire (N 177)
ST-DESIR WAR CEMETERY
  2¾ miles west of Lisieux (N 13)
ST-DESIR WAR CEMETERY
ST-MANVIEU WAR CEMETERY, CHEUX
  7½ miles west of Caen (D 9)
STE-MARIE CEMETERY, LE HAVRE
  In northern part of the town
ST-SEVER CEMETERY AND EXTENSION, ROUEN
  2 miles south of the Cathedral
ST-VALERY-EN-CAUX FRANCO-BRITISH CEMETERY
  In southeastern outskirts of the town
SECQUEVILLE-EN-BESSIN WAR CEMETERY
  7½ miles northwest of Caen (D 126)
TILLY-SUR-SEULLES WAR CEMETERY
  12 miles west of Caen (D 13)
TOURGEVILLE MILITARY CEMETERY
  3 miles south of Deauville/Tourgeville (D 275)

WHAT TO BRING HOME FROM NORMANDY

An object which displays a local craftsman's skill is surely one of the best souvenirs of a pleasant holiday spent in a town, a village, a region. Passing rapidly by the mass-produced items on the stalls which line many a national highway, the tourist will find a wide variety of craftwork in the more lively towns or even sometimes in a secluded hamlet. Taste, originality and quality are the essentials to look for.

Lace.—Touring Normandy and approaching **Alençon**, **Argentan** or **Bayeux** one immediately recalls the wonderful love of the past. Certainly today no one thinks of lace as a key industry or a point of high fashion; the people of Argentan no longer spend time in inventing a new design to outdo those of Alençon, nevertheless one can still buy at the lace schools of Alençon and Bayeux, delightful small pieces of lace, handkerchiefs, table mats and cloths which have taken hours and hours to work. A visit to the Benedictine Abbey at Argentan (see p. 43) enables the stranger to see all the detailed skill required in the Argentan stitch. The quality of the lace—and its price—leave machine-made lace in the shade!

Pottery.—At **St-Aquilin-de-Pacy** is the Buisson de May pottery, in an enchanting setting in an old restored mill. The coffee cups and pots, mugs, bowls and other objects are attractive and not expensive.

Noron-la-Poterie (see also p. 51) is one of the most famous centres in France for salt glaze ware and all the traditional Norman utensils can be found there, including the dark brown or lustre coloured Saint-Gorgon cider pitcher, the *guichon* or small individual soup bowl, the *bobin* or small milk jug and the *machon* or pot in which eggs, meat, fish or vegetables were salted down.

The ware is fired at full heat continuously for three days and nights in a kiln which burns beechwood; the salt glazing is done at the end of the firing.

Tradition is most marked at the **St-Jacques-de-Néhou** pottery—the only Cotentin pottery where the baking is done over a wood fire. For centuries they have made *cohans* here, great vessels from which the workers in the fields used to drink.

Woodwork and cabinet-making.—**Domfront**, a woodworking centre on the edge of the Andaine Forest, manufactures a host of articles such as copper banded wooden pitchers, small barrels filled with *Calvados*, etc. Wood craftsmen may also be found at Randonnai and Trouville.

Wrought Ironwork.—Ironwork in Normandy goes back to the time when smiths beat out the red-hot metal into nails and horseshoes; this was followed by the period when wardrobe and other items of furniture were ornamented with elaborate iron locks and hinges. It is this adornment of furniture, both rustic and modern, that continues as a craft today and may be seen at **Gaillon** and **Conches** on the Eure and **Chanu**, **Bellême** and **Monceaux** in the Orne area.

CRAFTWORK
0   50 km

THE CHANNEL

Cherbourg
St-Jacques-de-Néhou
• *Pottery*
Bayeux   *Lace*
Noron-la-Poterie
Remilly-sur-Lozon   St-Lô   *Pottery*
Basketry   *Vire*
Villedieu-les-Poêles   • Vire
Copper   Chanu
Avranches
Domfront   *Wrought ironwork*
Cooperage
Fougères ○   Alençon   *Lace*
Mayenne
Wrought ironwork, Ceramics

Dieppe *Ivory*
Veules-les-Roses
Wrought ironwork
SEINE   *Jewellery*
LE HAVRE   ROUEN
Trouville   *Woodwork and*   *Ceramics*
cabinet making   Igoville
Périers-sur-le-Dan   *Weaving*   *Muids*
Weaving   *Pottery*   Gaillon
CAEN   Ouilly-du-Houley   *Wrought*   *Pottery*
Lisieux   *making*   St-Aquilin-de-Pacy
Wrought ironwork   Conches   Dreux ○
Argentan *Lace*   Randonnai
Woodwork and
cabinet making   *Monceaux*
Mortagne-au-Perche   *Wrought ironwork, Icons*
Bellême   Chartres
Ceramics

Weaving.—Fine furnishing materials are to be found at Périers-sur-le-Dan in Calvados and at **Muids** in the Eure.

The workshops also produce original scarves and ties.

Copper.—Copper has been hammered at **Villedieu-les-Poêles** since the end of the 17C. A most varied range of beaten items (some, by the way, of considerable value) are offered to the tourist: magnificent Normandy *cannes* or milk pitchers (see p. 154), ewers and old-fashioned vases.

The bell foundry in Pont-Chignon Street is interesting and picturesque (see p. 154).

Basketwork.—The people of **Remilly-sur-Lozon**, a small village in the Manche Department, have been weaving willow into baskets for bread, fruit and other things since time immemorial.

Ivory.—From the 16 to the 19C **Dieppe** was an important centre of ivory carving as may be seen from the remarkable ancient pieces displayed in the Castle Museum (see p. 84). One craftsman is still engaged locally in making ivory jewellery and small objects.

Miscellaneous.—The towns and villages marked on the map above will provide interesting and attractive examples of local craftwork which can also be found on many stalls in the old streets of Dreux.

Finally there are farms in Normandy where old cider presses and Calvados utensils, salt barrels and other items have been transformed into useful pieces of furniture with considerable decorative effect.

Customs.—Total purchases of a value of less than £10 do not have to be declared unless they are antiques—i.e. more than 100 years old. If your total purchases, however, amount to £10 or more in value they must be declared; they may be liable to customs duty. Antiques should be authenticated.

PRINCIPAL LOCAL FESTIVALS

DATE	PLACE	PAGE	EVENT
17 January	Pontmain	125	Pilgrimage to the Virgin
Whit Monday	Bernay	53	Pilgrimage to Our Lady of La-Couture—Procession of regional Brotherhoods of Charity (see below)
Whit Sunday and Monday	Honfleur	107	Seamen's Festival—Sunday: blessing of the sea—Monday morning: pilgrimage and Procession of small boats to the Côte de Grâce. Open air Mass in front of Our Lady of Grace
Sunday nearest 30 May	Rouen	127	Joan of Arc Festival
3rd Sunday after Whit-sun (every 4 years—1975, 1979, etc.)	Villedieu-les-Poëles	154	The Great Rite (Grand Sacre)—Procession particularly for dignitaries of Order of St. John of Malta
16 July	La Haye-de-Routot	144	The St. Clair Fireworks—Participants pull flaming brands from a bonfire as a protection against fire
25 July and following Sunday	St-Christophe-le-Jajolet	155	St. Christopher Pilgrimage—Procession and blessing of cars and lorries
Sunday preceding or following 26 July	La Heuze Chapel	86	St. Christopher Pilgrimage—Preceded, the evening before, by an outdoor festival, the St. Christopher Bonfire
Last Sunday in July	Granville	100	Pardon of the Corporations of the Sea—Procession of guilds with their banners. Open air Mass. Torchlight procession
15 August	Lisieux	110	Procession to the "Virgin with a Smile"—This statue was particularly revered by St. Theresa
15 August, following Thursday and 8 September	La Délivrande	63	Pilgrimage to the Virgin
9, 10, 11 and 12 September	Lessay	110	St. Cross Fair—The biggest and the most typical fair in Normandy
Last Sunday in September, 30 September and 3 October	Lisieux	110	St. Theresa's Festival—Processions with the shrine containing the relics of the saint
29 September	Mont-St-Michel	116	Feast of the Archangel Michael—Mass in the abbey church served by many prelates
Second Sunday in October	Le Pin Stud	125	Race Meeting—Cross-breed steeplechase, enthusiastically attended by the people of the area
18 October	Biville	67	St. Thomas Pilgrimage—Midnight Mass

The Brotherhoods of Charity.—In the country churches between the Seine and the Dives, tourists will frequently see, set along the churchwarden's pew, rows of often delicately worked small lamps. These are the special symbols of the "brotherhoods of charity" of Normandy. The brotherhoods, whose origin goes back at least to the 12C, have as their essential mission the assurance of a Christian burial for the dead. The "brothers" wear hoods, carry banners and the little lamps as they walk in procession, preceded by bell-ringers ringing their handbells (tintenelles) to an immutable rhythm. The procession always looks as though it has come straight from the Middle Ages.

PLEASANT PLACES FOR TEA

Normandy is a good region, with its country restaurants or *fermes*, in which to stop and try the local specialities or simply enjoy a cup of tea in such attractive surroundings as an apple orchard or *clos*. Listed below are a selection of establishments well away from main roads.

Cider, particularly that of the Auge Region, makes a good accompaniment to any Norman dish and the sea food to be found in every fishing port (*for further details see p. 21*). Perry is found only in the Domfront area.

One final injunction: do not insist on bottled cider! If your host recommends his draft cider, accept—there are some very good ones.

PLACE NAMES	Page of guide or Michelin map no. and fold	ESTABLISHMENTS Name and phone no.	Very comfortable / Comfortable / Plain	Setting and attractions ≪ Interesting or extensive view
L'Aigle	39	Aub. St-Michel (2 miles east) ℡ 2.29	●●	Rose garden
Les Andeleys	42	Salon de Thé la Rotonde ℡ 1.63	●●	≪ Seine
Bagnoles-de-l'Orne	48	Vallée de la Cour ℡ 0.85	●	≪ pool in the heart of the forest
		La Roseraie (at Tessé-la-Madeleine) Tessé ℡ 5.21	●●	Flower garden
Barneville	81	Aub. de la Source, Penne-depie ℡ 24	●	Terrace and garden
Le Bec-Hellouin	52	Aub. de l'Abbaye ℡ 2	●●	Terrace and garden
Bénouville	63	Manoir d'Hastings ℡ 39	●●●	Old priory and flower garden
Caudebec-en-Caux	65	Manoir de Rétival ℡ 0.67	●●	Park; ≪ Seine Valley
Clécy	147	Château de Surosne ℡ 19	●●	≪ countryside, woods, valleys
		Moulin de Vey (½ mile east) Clécy ℡ 8	●●	Shady setting beside the Orne; park
Commes	54 ⑭	Host. du Bosq ℡ 92.72.81	●●●	18C country house in its own park
Conteville	57 ⑫	Aub. du Vieux Logis ℡ 16	●●	Rural setting
Courseulles-sur-Mer	79	Domaine de l'Ile de Plaisance ℡ 83.45.48	●●	Norman thatched house
Deauville	81	Golf ℡ 88.19.01	●●●	≪ golf course, the sea and the valley
Duclair	85	Parc (½ mile west) ℡ 76.50.31	●	Flower garden; ⇒ Seine
Etretat	88	Dormy-House ℡ 30	●●●	≪ cliffs and the sea
Fourges	155 ⑱	Moulin de Fourges ℡ 12	●●	Old mill beside the Epte
Port de Goury	78	Aub. du Port, Auderville ℡ 1	●	≪ sea
Honfleur	107	Roche Vasouy ℡ 26	●●	≪ park, the sea and the Seine Estuary
		Ferme de la Grande Cour ℡ 1.62	●●	Farm set in the heart of an orchard
Houlgate	109	Ferme des Aulnettes, Cabourg ℡ 7.28	●●	Orchard; flowers
		Ferme Vimard ℡ 8.76	●●	Norman thatched house
		Ferme du Lieu Marot, Cabourg ℡ 8.44	●●	Farm set in the heart of an orchard
Ivry-la-Bataille	91	Moulin d'Ivry ℡ 36.40.51	●●	Garden and terrace beside the Epte
La Londe	55 ⑥	Relais Hippique ℡ 77.70.42	●●	Park, racing club
Lyons-la-Forêt	114	La Licorne ℡ 2	●●	Flower garden and miniature golf course
		Domaine St-Paul ℡ 0.57	●	Meadows on the edge of the forest
Martin-Eglise	45	Aub. Clos Normand ℡ 85.64.01	●●	Rustic interior; riverside terrace
Le Mesnil-Val	52 ⑤	Vieille Ferme, Criel-Plage ℡ 2.10	●●	Norman house, flower garden
Nez de Jobourg	78	Aub des Grottes, Jobourg ℡ 4	●	≪ sea
Roche d'Oëtre	148	Salon de Thé, Mesnil-Villement ℡ 19	●●	Pinewood ≪ Rouvre Gorges
Le Pin au Haras	60 ③	Host. Tourne-Bride ℡ 2	●●●	Hostelry on the edge of the forest; old furniture
Pont-Audemer	125	Aub. Vieux Puits ℡ 1.48	●●●	17C inn with old furniture and fittings
Port-Villez	55 ⑱	La Gueulardière ℡ 478.01.95	●●●	Rustic dining room and shaded terrace
La Roque	55 ⑦	Port La Roque ℡ 3	●●	≪ Seine and the cliffs
St-Adrien	55 ⑥	Manoir du Becquet ℡ 75.31.05	●●	Old priory in a garden; ≪ Seine
St-Denis-sur-Sarthon	60 ②	La Faïencerie ℡ 27.30.16	●●	Park
St-Germain-des-Vaux (Le Port Racine)	54 ①	Erguillière, Auderville ℡ 31	●●	≪ sea
St-Lô	135	Le Chant des Oiseaux ℡ 57.04.04	●●	Building on piles
St-Ouen-sous-Bailly	52 ⑤	Prieuré Bailly Bec ℡ 85.71.37	●●	Old priory and garden; ≪ Bec
St-Valery-en-Caux	137	Stade Valeriquais Tennis ℡ 61	●	Shaded valley
Thury-Harcourt	150	Roche à Busnel ℡ 2.56	●●	In the Orne Valley; rustic interior
Trelly	54 ⑫	Verte Campagne ℡ 15	●●	Old Norman farm
Varengeville	67	Les Sapins ℡ 85.11.45	●●	≪ flower garden
Villequier	154	Grand Sapin ℡ 8	●●	≪ Seine, flowered terrace
Villers-sur-Mer	74	Pommerose ℡ 87.01.85	●●	Orchard; flowers
Villerville	74	Manoir de Grand-Bec ℡ 88.09.88	●●●	Terrace; ≪ sea
Vironvay	143	Les Saisons, Louviers ℡ 2.56	●●	Park with trees and flowers
Yport	52 ⑫	Le Deun ℡ 33	●●	≪ sea and cliffs

TOURING PROGRAMMES

Two tours are suggested, one through Upper the other through Lower Normandy. Both start from the coast and they can be combined.

5 days (487 miles—784 km) in Upper Normandy.

Round trip starting from Dieppe . . . . see pp. 30–31

This trip can be combined with that of Lower Normandy (making a total of 12 days—1,079 miles—1,737 km) by going from Lisieux, on the 4th day, to St-Pierre-sur-Dives and Caen, thus joining the tour of Lower Normandy (on its 2nd day).

10 days (933 miles—1,502 km) in Lower Normandy.

Round trip starting from Cherbourg - . . . . see pp. 32–33

THE SEASONS

The real holiday season is from July to September although the mildness of the coastal climate makes it possible to visit Normandy at any time of the year.

Spring.—The blossoming of the apple trees in April and May transforms the Normandy countryside. Apples, the "kings" of the Normandy orchards, flower last, after the Gaillon cherries and the Domfront pears. Apple blossom time, praised so often, is really without equal, and this would, therefore, be the ideal time to explore the countryside by driving through the Auge Region and along the Valley of the Seine.

Summer.—Hot weather comes earlier inland than on the coast, and the beach season does not begin before June, when the last storms have died away. Then, from Le Tréport to Mont-St-Michel, the coast is taken over by people in search of sea air, relaxation and amusement. The sky remains hazy, delighting artists; the sunshine has a special quality. The changes in the weather—you must resign yourself to these with good humour—are felt most inland.

Those who enjoy bracing sea air will go to the beaches of the Caux Region, those who look for more even temperatures to the Bay of Mont-St-Michel, near the Brittany border. The Calvados coast is also well known for its bracing air.

Autumn.—"Rain, life's most usual companion", is an accurate description of Normandy from the beginning of October, the wettest month of the year. But as November approaches there are many magnificent days. The opportunity should be taken to go and see the wonderful tints of the forest trees. The light is incomparably soft, making some stone buildings appear all the more substantial. It is never very cold.

Winter.—Storms follow one another under uniformly dark skies but the damp is more of a mist than a real rain. Wild-fowlers, at this season, face the squalls of the Calvados coast and the Orne Estuary to enjoy their pleasure, while the art lover waits for a bright Sunday to visit a museum or building. Distances are short, the countryside you pass through is never sad and the falling of the leaves opens up unsuspected views.

BOOKS TO READ

Detailed accounts of the Allied Landings and the Battle of Normandy will be found in the official History of the War, memoirs and autobiographies:

Official History of the War (*H.M.S.O.*)

The Second World War by WINSTON CHURCHILL (*Cassel*)

Normandy to the Baltic by Field-Marshal Lord MONTGOMERY (*Hutchinson*)

Crusade in Europe by DWIGHT EISENHOWER (*Doubleday*)

The Seine by ANTHONY GLYN (*Weidenfeld & Nicolson*)

Madeleine Young Wife by Mrs. ROBERT HENREY (*Dent*)

Notes from an Odd Country by GEOFFREY GRIGSON (*Macmillan*)

St. Joan by BERNARD SHAW (*Constable*)

A Holiday History of France by RONALD HAMILTON (*Chatto & Windus*)

An Outline of European Architecture by N. PEVSNER (*Penguin*)

The Impressionists by WILLIAM GAUNT (*Thames & Hudson*)

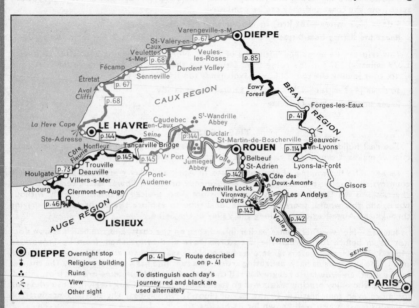

1st day

Dieppe—Le Havre

84 miles—135 km—plus 4¼ hours walking or sightseeing

The road affords views of the cliffs of the Côte d'Albâtre, but for the most part it runs across the great open spaces of the Caux plateau, where monotony is broken by patches of farmland around small hamlets.

At Varengeville* you can go to the little church and walk through the interesting small sailors' cemetery that surrounds it.

Veules-les-Roses, snug in a narrow valley, is a typical seaside resort on this coast.

At St-Valery (¼ hour) go up the Aval Cliff to see the monument to the 2nd Cavalry Division—the view from the cliffs is worth the short walk.

On leaving Veulettes and its beautiful beach, you go up the Durdent Valley* which is particularly pleasant around the delightful church at Barville.

Lunch at Fécamp or Etretat

On the run between Senneville and Fécamp there are immense views along the coast towards Etretat.

Fécamp** (1½ hours), first cod-fishing port of France, is also a town with fine buildings. Besides the impressive abbey church, dedicated to the Holy Trinity, there are the Benedictine museum and distillery.

Etretat** (1 hour), a fashionable resort, is famous for its cliffs, which are amazingly cut away, and are one of the natural wonders of France. You should not miss the fine walk to the Aval Cliff.

The Lézarde Valley brings you to Bléville and the Cape La Hève Lighthouse. A fine winding road down, with a view of the Le Havre roadstead, leads to Ste-Adresse.

Le Havre** (1½ hours), ravaged in September 1944, has been rebuilt on a huge scale. A quick tour through the modern quarter and the docks is suggested.

2nd day

Le Havre—Lisieux

83 miles—134 km—plus 1¼ hours walking or sightseeing

This stage will allow you to see the life and luxury of the Côte Fleurie resorts and above all the rustic charm of the Auge Region with its green countryside.

After crossing the Seine Estuary by the Tancarville Bridge**, the cliffs merge into the steep grassy slopes of the Normandy Corniche.

Honfleur** (¾ hour) has preserved its great charm with its old port, surrounded by picturesque tall houses, its curious wooden church and its museums, recorded by artists enchanted by its atmosphere. From the Côte de Grâce, near the little chapel sheltering in its lee, there is a good view of the Seine Estuary and Le Havre.

Lunch at Trouville or Deauville

Follow the beaches of fine sand of the Côte Fleurie, where everything invites one to laze. Trouville** is a great city holiday resort, full of life and gaiety. Deauville***, an international resort, maintains a reputation for luxury.

Villers-sur-Mer** is followed by Houlgate**. By way of Dives, ancient pilgrimage city, continue to Cabourg**.

About the middle of the hilly drive that follows, stop at Clermont-en-Auge* (¼ hour) to go on foot to the church, which stands apart, overlooking a vast panorama.

Lisieux**, capital of the Auge Region, was badly bombed in the war. The cathedral (¼ hour) is fortunately intact and the pilgrim can follow the steps in the brief life of "little sister Theresa" from her home at Les Buissonnets to Carmel and the basilica.

Refer to the index, pp. 156–158, to find the pages on which the towns mentioned above are described

NORMANDY
from Dieppe (487 miles—784 km)

3rd day

Lisieux—Rouen

91 miles—114 km—plus 5¾ hours sightseeing

This day of the trip is spent for the most part on a tour of Rouen, the museum city.

Crossing the grasslands of Lieuvin and then the little town of Pont Audemer*, you reach the majestic Valley of the Seine at Vieux Port. By first going along the left bank, you enter, briefly, the pleasant woodlands of the Brotonne Forest.

A ferry takes you across to Caudebec* (¼ hour), badly hit by the war but always proud of its church, crowned by a Flamboyant belfry.

At the Abbey of St-Wandrille** (½ hour) you may hear the traditional Benedictine prayers and rite.

The ruins of Jumièges*** (½ hour), seen against a background of greenery and sky, are amongst the most striking and moving in France.

After Duclair, where shady quays call for a halt, visit the Church of St-Martin-de-Boscherville* (¼ hour), an ancient minster of severe style.

On leaving Canteleu, a downhill run along the side of a valley affords the first view of Rouen, port and museum city.

A tour of Rouen*** (4 hours) is a marvellous experience: despite war damage, there are an enormous number of fine things to see. After a walk in the old town, drive along the Corniche de Rouen*** at nightfall (¼ hour), to see from the top of the Ste-Catherine Hill, a most impressive urban panorama.

Lunch at Rouen or Duclair

4th day

Rouen—Paris

114 miles—183 km—plus 1¾ hours walking or sightseeing

The art lover, unable to visit Rouen's two great museums the day before, can do so in the morning before leaving.

The Seine, at first still flanked by factories, becomes prettier above Belbeuf-St-Adrien.

The locks at Amfreville* (¼ hour), with the Poses dam, form a sight that is both attractive and impressive.

During the climb up the Deux Amants Hill** (¼ hour) there are views of the Seine Valley, and at the top an even larger panorama, including the confluence of the Seine and the Andelle.

The river is crossed by the fine new bridge of St-Pierre-du-Vauvray by which you reach Louviers* (½ hour): the church, with its exuberant Flamboyant charm and its statues, is worth the small detour.

Leaving the Eure Valley, you again enter, beyond Vironvay Church, the delightful Seine Valley countryside. There is a fine view between Villers-sur-le-Roule and Tosny.

Arrival at Les Andelys** (½ hour) brings you face to face with Gaillard Castle in all its fierce grandeur. A tour of the ruins of this formidable fortress affords another view over the valley.

At Vernonnet the road crosses the Seine once again to reach Vernon*, a small residential town in a pretty setting, and then, following the now "French" Seine, reaches the capital.

Lunch at Vironvay or Les Andelys

Paris

Suggestions for a short or long stay in Paris will be found in the English edition of the **Michelin Green Guide Paris**

5th day

Paris—Dieppe

135 miles—218 km—plus 1½ hours walking or sightseeing

You re-enter Normandy at Gisors* (1 hour), where the feudal castle, an ancient frontier fortress, recalls the struggles between the Dukes of Normandy and the Kings of France. The keep and its battlements are a fine example of Norman military architecture.

Lyons-la-Forêt* is a relaxing holiday place set in the heart of magnificent beech woods, interspersed by numerous clearings.

From the church at Beauvoir-en-Lyons (¼ hour), there is a good view of the vast Bray lowland region.

Forges-les-Eaux, where ferruginous springs have been known since the 17C, has a pleasant thermal spa in a park.

Climbing up to the Caux plateau you enter the splendid glades of the Forest of Eawy**. The straight stretches of the Limousins Alley afford attractive views.

Dieppe**, doyen of French seaside resorts, owes its attraction to its huge beach, the liveliness of its streets and port and to its many other entertainments. In St. James' Church (¼ hour) can be seen the chapels contributed by the rich ship-builders who made the city's fortune long ago.

Lunch at Lyons-la-Forét or Forges-les-Eaux

Walkers, campers, smokers . . . **take care!**
Fires are fatal to forestlands.

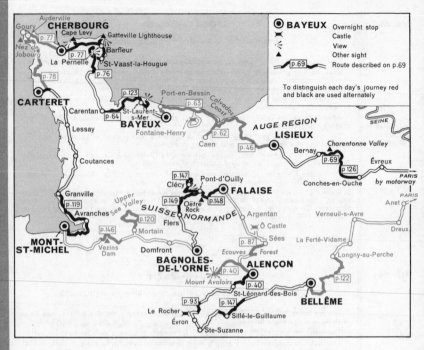

BAYEUX — Overnight stop
— Castle
— View
▲ — Other sight
p.69 — Route described on p.69

To distinguish each day's journey red and black are used alternately

---

1st day

Lunch at Auderville or take a picnic

Cherbourg—Carteret
60 miles—97 km—plus 1½ hours walking

The drive through the wild world's end of La Hague is most impressive. The sea dashes against great promontories or washes into graceful little coves.

By going to Goury* you will see the cliffs of the Channel Island of Alderney which stand out with astonishing clarity.

The Nez de Jobourg*** headland (½ hour) is a grand sight when seen from the Nez de Voidries. The scenery is less austere at the end of the drive as sand dunes appear.

Carteret* (¾ hour) is sheltered by a superb rocky cape.

2nd day

Lunch at Granville or Avranches

Carteret—Mont-St-Michel
84 miles—135 km—plus 4¼ hours sightseeing

The day is devoted to art, architecture and history.

Lessay possesses an Abbey** in the purest Romanesque style.

Coutances** (¼ hour) is grouped round its cathedral, a building with wonderful sweeping lines.

Granville* (1 hour) is a lively resort. The upper town, on the Pointe du Roc spur, has kept its mediaeval character.

Mont-St-Michel can be seen very well indeed from the botanical gardens at Avranches* (¾ hour). Documents on the abbey may be seen in the town hall.

The approach to Mont-St-Michel*** (2 hours) and the tour of the abbey are unforgettable.

3rd day

Lunch at Mortain

Mont-St-Michel—Bagnoles-de-l'Orne
96 miles—155 km—plus 1 hour walking or sightseeing

The road passes through the Bocage Region, cut by many hedgerows.

The reservoir behind the Vézins Dam* forms a beautiful lake.

At Mortain* (¼ hour) the great cascade should be seen and the climb made to the Little Chapel from which there is a fine panorama.

The Upper Valley of the Sée* is, at times, beautiful.

Domfront* (¼ hour) has a well situated public garden. At its foot, the Church of Our Lady by the Water is a charming Romanesque building.

Bagnoles-de-l'Orne**, a large spa, is well known for its picturesque setting and the pleasant forests which surround it.

4th day

Lunch at Pont-d'Ouilly or Clécy

Bagnoles-de-l'Orne—Falaise
66 miles—106 km—plus 1 hour walking or sightseeing

This day is devoted to a visit to the Suisse Normande where the rivers flow in deep beds between steep rock banks.

From Flers the narrow Valleys of the Vère and Noireau lead to Pont-d'Ouilly, from which a good mountain road leads to Clécy*, a centre for walks.

The view from the Faverie Cross* (¼ hour) is of almost classical beauty. The amazing site of the Oëtre Rock (¼ hour) will make the tourist forget the traditionally tranquil scenery of Normandy.

Falaise* (¼ hour) is dominated by the formidable mass of the castle where William the Conqueror was born.

TOUR

NORMANDY
from Cherbourg (933 miles—1,502 km)

5th day

Lunch at Sées or take a picnic

Falaise—Alençon

77 miles—124 km—plus 1¾ hours walking or sightseeing

Argentan (¼ hour) suffered badly in the war, but its Church of St-Germanus is worth a visit.
The outlines of Ô Castle* (¼ hour) stand reflected in its moat.
At Sées* (¼ hour) a visit to the cathedral is a "must".
There are good views during the drive through the tall trees of the Ecouves Forest** (¾ hour) and especially on the walk to the Vignage Rocks.
From the Avaloirs Mountain* belvedere the views are long and distant.
Alençon* (¼ hour), the lace town, has a remarkable Flamboyant style church.

6th day

Lunch at Ste-Suzanne or Sillé-le-Guillaume

Alençon—Bellême

101 miles—162 km—plus 2 hours sightseeing

The road leaves Alençon to cross the Mancelles Alps with their attractive enclosed valleys. St-Léonard-des-Bois* is a typical beauty spot.
The Maine spreads wide its beautiful wooded countryside.
Le Rocher Château* (½ hour), near Mézangers, is an elegant example of Renaissance architecture.
The Church of Our Lady at Evron* (½ hour) is one of the most lovely in the Mayenne; there is an outstanding treasure to be seen in the St. Crispin Chapel.
A walk round the ramparts at Ste-Suzanne (½ hour) leads to an appreciation of the site of this old stronghold.
By way of Sillé-le-Guillaume, laid out in a semicircle on the wooded Coëvrons slopes, Fresnay-sur-Sarthe and Mamers you eventually arrive at Bellême (½ hour), standing on a spur within sight of its magnificent forest*.

7th day

Lunch at Verneuil

Bellême—Paris

124 miles—200 km—plus 2½ hours sightseeing

This stage takes the visitor, between Bellême and Longny-au-Perche, through the Perche Region* with its low hills and wide valleys scattered with fine manorhouses.
The particularly pleasant setting of Longny-au-Perche in the green Jambée Valley can be well appreciated from the terrace near the delightful Renaissance Chapel of Our Lady of Pity.
After driving through the Longny and Ferté-Vidame Forests you come to Verneuil-sur-Avre* (1 hour), where the admirable Magdalen Tower reminds one of the Butter Tower at Rouen. There are some outstanding statues in the Church of Our Lady.
Go from Dreux* (1 hour) with its belfry and St-Louis Chapel, to Anet*, where the castle (½ hour) is an example of the successful mingling of many styles. Continue to Paris.

Paris

Suggestions for a short or long stay in Paris will be found in the English edition of the **Michelin Green Guide Paris**

8th day

Lunch at Conches or take a picnic lunch

Paris—Lisieux

125 miles—202 km—plus 2 hours sightseeing

On returning to Normandy, the visitor will find himself in the rich countryside of the Auge Region.
Evreux** (1 hour) is grouped round its cathedral, whose windows and wooden screens are famous. The reliquary of St. Taurinus, masterpiece of 13C goldsmith's work, can be seen in the church consecrated to this bishop.
At Conches* (½ hour), the Church of St. Foy possesses a rich collection of 16C windows.
Before leaving the pretty Charentonne Valley, a pleasant drive can be made to the hillside road of Les Monts from Bernay (¼ hour).
Lisieux**, holy town of Normandy, lost its famous wooden houses in 1944, but the cathedral (¼ hour) is intact and the visitor can follow, from Les Buissonnets to Carmel and the basilica, the events in the short life of "little sister Theresa".

9th day

Lunch at Caen

Lisieux—Bayeux

94 miles—151 km—plus 4¼ hours walking or sightseeing

After the valleys of the Auge Region come the flat stretches of the Caen countryside from which rise the belfries of magnificent churches, and the coast of Calvados where the men of the British 2nd Army landed in June 1944.
Caen*** (2 hours), capital of Lower Normandy, centre of culture and industry, is a Benedictine city. Its fine minsters (The Trinity and St. Stephen's), the Malherbe School and St. Peter's Church make a fascinating tour.
Leaving the coast for a moment, the tourist should see Fontaine-Henry** (½ hour) and its fine Renaissance château, then the charming church at Thaon* (½ hour), set at the bottom of the valley. From Arromanches, where the remains of a gigantic artificial port can still be seen, you reach the picturesque harbour of Port-en-Bessin*.
Bayeux** (1¼ hours), spared by the war, conserves the famous Bayeux Tapestry near the huge cathedral.

10th day

Lunch at St-Vaast

Bayeux—Cherbourg

106 miles—170 km—plus 2½ hours walking or sightseeing

This lap will leave you with impressive memories of the war; it is also marked by the crossing of the Saire Valley, "golden belt" of the Cotentin.
The American cemetery of St-Laurent, with its lines of graves facing the sea, is very moving. From a nearby belvedere one can see the desolate battlefield of Omaha Beach (¾ hour).
By way of Carentan and Ste-Mère-Eglise, another historic spot, one comes to the Cotentin coast at Quettebou. Only a short distance away is the Saire Valley** (¼ hour), which affords an extensive panorama.
By St-Vaast and Barfleur, little ports with a Breton appearance, you reach the Gatteville Lighthouse** (½ hour) then the Cape Lévy Lighthouse* (¼ hour). From the top of these there are fine views in all directions.
By the Corniche road you go on to Cherbourg* (¾ hour), naval base and transatlantic port, best seen from the Roule Fort, where a war memorial and museum of the liberation have been arranged.

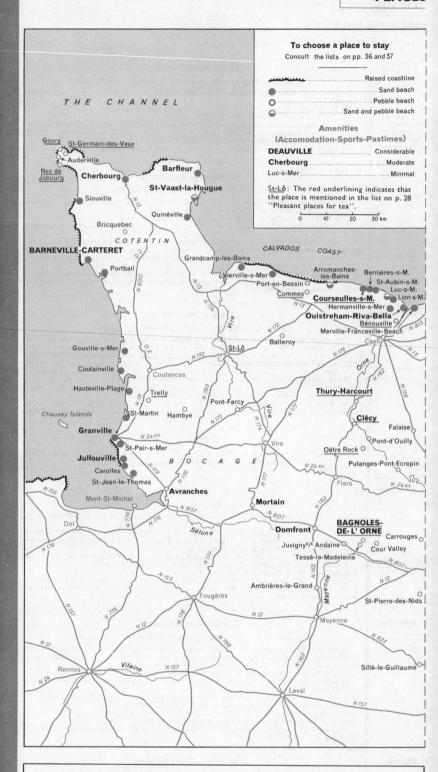

To choose a place to stay
Consult the lists on pp. 36 and 37

‒‒‒‒‒‒‒‒ Raised coastline
● ‒‒‒‒‒‒‒‒ Sand beach
○ ‒‒‒‒‒‒‒‒ Pebble beach
◎ ‒‒‒‒‒‒‒‒ Sand and pebble beach

Amenities
(Accomodation-Sports-Pastimes)
DEAUVILLE ‒‒‒‒‒‒‒‒ Considerable
Cherbourg ‒‒‒‒‒‒‒‒ Moderate
Luc-s-Mer ‒‒‒‒‒‒‒‒ Minimal

St-Lô : The red underlining indicates that
the place is mentioned in the list on p. 28
''Pleasant places for tea''.

0   10   20   30 km

THE CHANNEL

Goury
St-Germain-des-Vaux
Auderville
Nez de Jobourg
Cherbourg
Siouville
Barfleur
St-Vaast-la-Hougue
Quinéville
Bricquebec
COTENTIN
BARNEVILLE-CARTERET
Portbail

CALVADOS   COAST
Grandcamp-les-Bains
Vierville-s-Mer
Port-en-Bessin
Commes
Arromanches-les-Bains
Bernières-s-M.
St-Aubin-s-M.
Luc-s-M.
Lion-s-M.
Courseulles-s-M.
Hermanville-s-Mer
Ouistreham-Riva-Bella
Bénouville
Merville-Franceville-Beach
Caen
Balleroy

Gouville-s-Mer
Coutainville
Hauteville-Plage
St-Lô
Coutances
Trelly
St-Martin
Hambye
Pont-Farcy
Thury-Harcourt
Clécy
Falaise
Pont-d'Ouilly
Oëtre Rock
Putanges-Pont-Ecrepin

Chausey Islands
Granville
St-Pair-s-Mer
Jullouville
Carolles
St-Jean-le-Thomas
BOCAGE
Vire
Flers

Mont-St-Michel
Avranches
Mortain
Domfront
BAGNOLES-DE-L' ORNE
Carrouges
Cour Valley
Juvigny-s/s Andaine
Tessé-la-Madeleine

Dol
Sélune
Ambrières-le-Grand
St-Pierre-des-Nids

Fougères
Mayenne
Rennes
Vilaine
Laval
Sillé-le-Guillaume

CAMPING & CARAVANNING

The Michelin Guide **Camping-Caravaning en France**
(revised annually)

lists selected sites with full details
of their facilities, situation and
amenities.

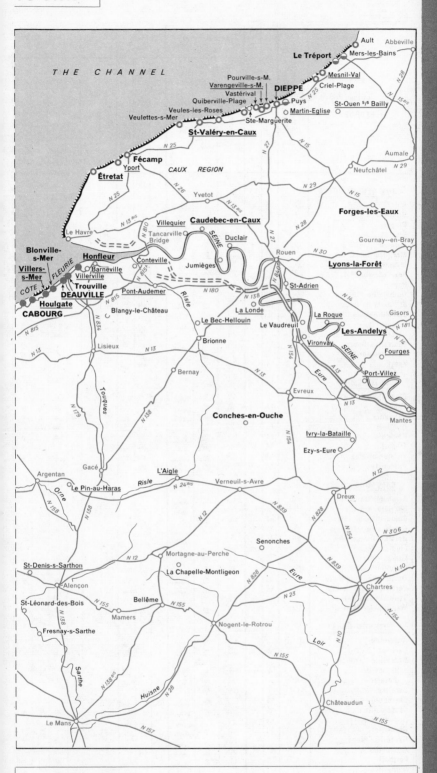

THE CHANNEL

Ault
Abbeville
Le Tréport
Mers-les-Bains
Pourville-s-M.
Mesnil-Val
Varengeville-s-M.
DIEPPE
Criel-Plage
Vastérival
Quiberville-Plage
Puys
St-Ouen s/s Bailly
Veules-les-Roses
Martin-Eglise
Veulettes-s-Mer
Ste-Marguerite
St-Valéry-en-Caux
Aumale
Fécamp
CAUX REGION
Neufchâtel
Yport
Étretat
Forges-les-Eaux
Yvetot
Le Havre
Villequier
Caudebec-en-Caux
Tancarville
Bridge
SEINE
Duclair
Gournay--en-Bray
Conteville
Rouen
Blonville-s-Mer
Honfleur
Jumièges
Lyons-la-Forêt
Barneville
Villers-s-Mer
Villerville
St-Adrien
CÔTE
FLEURIE
Trouville
Pont-Audemer
DEAUVILLE
Risle
La Londe
La Roque
Houlgate
Blangy-le-Château
Le Vaudreuil
Gisors
CABOURG
Le Bec-Hellouin
Les-Andelys
Brionne
Vironvay
Fourges
Lisieux
SEINE
Port-Villez
Touques
Bernay
Evreux
Mantes
Conches-en-Ouche
Eure
Gacé
Ivry-la-Bataille
Argentan
L'Aigle
Ezy-s-Eure
Le Pin-au-Haras
Risle
Verneuil-s-Avre
Dreux
St-Denis-s-Sarthon
Senonches
Mortagne-au-Perche
Alençon
La Chapelle-Montligeon
Eure
Chartres
St-Léonard-des-Bois
Bellême
Mamers
Fresnay-s-Sarthe
Nogent-le-Rotrou
Loir
Sarthe
Huisne
Châteaudun
Le Mans

NAME of the RESORT	Page in guide or no. of Michelin map and section 1 in. : 3.15 miles	M = Doctor	+ = Chemist	Number of rooms	Best hotel	Best camping site	Picturesque site	Woods nearby	Harbour	Tennis courts	Swimming pool	Sailing school (2)	Horse riding	Golf course	Casino
CAUX REGION COAST															
Ault	52-⑤	M	+	65	●	⛺				🎾					♠
Criel-Plage	52-⑤	M	+	..	●	⛺		🌲							♠
Dieppe	82	M	+	241	●	⛺	◁		⚓	🎾	🏊	V	🐎	18	♠
Étretat	88	M	+	134	●	⛺	◁			🎾		V	🐎	18	♠
Fécamp	95	M	+	114	●	⛺	◁		⚓	🎾			🐎		♠
Mers-les-Bains	67	M		43	●	⛺				See Le Tréport					
Mesnil-Val (Le)	52-⑤			36	●	⛺				🎾					
Pourville-sur-Mer	67	M		20	●	⛺		🌲		🎾					
Puys	52-④	M	+	10	●					🎾					
Quiberville-Plage	52-④			..		⛺									
St-Valery-en-Caux	137	M	+	19	●	⛺		🌲	⚓	🎾					♠
Ste-Marguerite	67			25	●	⛺							🐎		
Tréport (Le)	150	M		79	●	⛺			⚓	🎾	🏊		🐎		♠
Vastérival	52-④			28	●			🌲							
Veules-les-Roses	67	M	+	28	●	⛺	◁	🌲		🎾			🐎		♠
Veulettes-sur-Mer	67			9	●	⛺		🌲		🎾					
Yport	52-⑫	M	+	14	●	⛺	◁	🌲	⚓						♠
COTE FLEURIE															
Blonville-sur-Mer	74		+	47	●	⛺				🎾		V	🐎		♠
Cabourg	55	M	+	46	●	⛺			⚓	🎾		V	🐎	18	♠
Deauville	81	M	+	1067	●	⛺			⚓	🎾	🏊	V	🐎	18	♠
Honfleur	107	M	+	128	●	⛺	◁		⚓	🎾			🐎		
Houlgate	109	M	+	69	●	⛺	◁	🌲		🎾			🐎		♠
Trouville	151	M	+	343	●	⛺	◁	🌲	⚓	🎾	🏊		🐎		♠
Villers-sur-Mer	74	M	+	89	●	⛺		🌲		🎾		V	🐎		♠
Villerville	74	M	+	76	●	⛺		🌲		🎾			🐎		♠
CALVADOS COAST															
Arromanches-les-Bains	45			18	●		◁								
Bernières-sur-Mer	63	M		..		⛺									
Courseulles-sur-Mer	79	M	+	55	●				⚓	🎾		V	🐎		
Grandcamp-les-Bains	64	M	+	..					⚓	🎾		V	🐎		
Hermanville-sur-Mer	54A-⑯	M		..		⛺				🎾					
Lion-sur-Mer	63	M	+	14	●	⛺				🎾			🐎		
Luc-sur-Mer	63	M		55	●	⛺				🎾			🐎		
Merville-Franceville	54A-⑯	M		35	●	⛺				🎾			🐎		
Ouistreham-Riva-Bella	124	M	+	39	●	⛺			⚓	🎾		V	🐎		
Port-en-Bessin	64	M	+	20	●	⛺			⚓				🐎		
St-Aubin-sur-Mer	63	M	+	57	●	⛺				🎾			🐎		♠
Vierville-sur-Mer	124			13	●		◁						🐎		
COTENTIN COAST															
Auderville	54A-①			13	●		◁		⚓	🎾					
Barfleur	77	M	+	39	●	⛺	◁		⚓	🎾					
Barneville-Carteret															
Barneville	49	M	+	16	●				⚓	🎾					
Carteret	49	M	+	93	●		◁		⚓	🎾		V			
Carolles	64	M	+	36	●	⛺	◁			🎾					
Cherbourg	70	M	+	202	●	⛺			⚓	🎾	🏊	V			♠
Coutainville	80	M	+	32	●	⛺				🎾			🐎	9	♠
Gouville-sur-Mer	54A-⑫	M	+	..		⛺							🐎		
Granville	100	M	+	59	●	⛺	◁		⚓	🎾	🏊	V	🐎	18	♠
Hauteville-Plage	54A-⑫			16	●	⛺						V	🐎		
Jullouville	119	M	+	86	●	⛺		🌲		🎾		V	🐎		
Portbail	49	M		12	●	⛺				🎾		V	🐎		
Quinéville	76			..		⛺						V	🐎		
St-Germain-des-Vaux	54A-①			10	●		◁			🎾			🐎		
St-Jean-le-Thomas	59-⑦			45	●	⛺				🎾			🐎	9	
St-Martin	59-⑦	M				⛺				🎾			🐎		
St-Pair-sur-Mer	119	M	+	22	●	⛺				🎾	🏊	V	🐎		♠
St-Vaast-la-Hougue	76	M	+	18	●	⛺	◁		⚓	🎾		V	🐎		
Siouville	54A-①			50	●	⛺	◁			🎾			🐎		

(1) As in the Michelin Guides "France" and "Camping Caravanning en France", the red sign indicates a pleasant hotel or camping site.

(2) School recognised by the Ministry of education.

pp. 34 and 35.

NAME of the RESORT	Page in guide or no. of Michelin map and section 1 in.: 3.15 miles	M = Doctor	+ = Chemist	Accommodation (1) Number of rooms	Best hotel	Best camping site	Characteristics Picturesque site	Woods nearby	Sports and pastimes Tennis courts	Swimming pool	Fishing	Horse riding	Golf course	Casino
INLAND														
Ambrières-le-Grand	59-20	M	+	..										
Andelys (Les)	42	M	+	37										
Àvranches	47	M	+	144										
Bagnoles-de-l'Orne	48	M	+	511										
Balleroy	49	M	+	10										
Le Bec-Hellouin	52	..	..	10										
Bellême	53	M	+	10										
Blangy-le-Château	54-18	..	..	..										
Bricquebec	55	M	+	20										
Brionne	55	M	+	25										
Carrouges	64	M	+	11										
Caudebec-en-Caux	65	M	+	65										
Chapelle-Montligeon (La)	123	..	..	20										
Clécy	147	M	+	52										
Conches-en-Ouche	72	M	+	18										
Cour (Vallée de la)	49	..	..	12										
Domfront	84	M	+	89										
Ezy-sur-Eure	91	M	+	14										
Falaise	94	M	+	44										
Forges-les-Eaux	98	M	+	89										
Fourges	55-18	..	..	10										
Fresnay-sur-Sarthe	99	M	+	12										
Hambye	107	M	+	10										
Ivry-la-Bataille	91	M	+	30										
Jumièges	109	..	..	..										
Juvigny-sous-Andaine	60-1	..	..	22										
Lyons-la-Forêt	114	M	+	25										
Martin-Église	45	..	..	10										
Mortain	120	M	+	43										
Pont d'Ouilly	148	M	+	29										
Pont-Farcy	59-9	..	..	6										
Putanges-Pont-Écrepin	149	M	+	15										
St-Léonard-des-Bois	41	..	..	20										
St-Pierre-des-Nids	60-2	M	+	..										
Senonches	60-6	M	+	15										
Sillé-le-Guillaume	147	M	+	16										
Tessé-la-Madeleine	48	M	+	98						See Bagnoles-de-l'Orne				
Thury-Harcourt	150	M	+	35										
Le Vaudreuil	55-7-17	..	+	14										
Vironvay	143	..	..	16										

(1) *As in the Michelin Guides "France" and "Camping-Caravaning en France", the red sign indicates a pleasant hotel or camping site.*

ABBREVIATIONS
AND KEY TO SIGNS

✲✲✲ **ROUEN**	Worth a journey	N	Trunk road
✲✲ **Fécamp**	Worth a detour	D	Secondary road
✲ Ecouis } Touques }	Interesting	V 13	Local road
Yvetot	See if possible	R.F.	Forest road
Ourville	Reference point	Rtn	Return: Round trip

Pop: Total population

⑤⑤-④ Number and section of Michelin map
(scale 1 inch = 3,15 miles)

All the heights are indicated in metres on the local maps of this guide

Maps and Plans

②	Approach road number common to Michelin maps and guides		Railway
	Through route		Tram or trolleybus
	Sightseeing route		Cable railway
	Wide street		Road crossing rail
	Fairly wide street		Rail crossing road } Railway crossings
	Narrow street		Level crossing
→	One-way street	2T	Load limit on bridge
	Street of uncertain usability		Car ferry
	Street closed or impassable	Bac B	Pedestrian ferry
	Road planned here, under construction		Route described
	Tree-lined street		Alternative route or excursion
	Steps		Go on foot
	Footpath	A13	Motorway
	Street passing under arch tunnel or gateway		Other roads
		12	Distance in kilometres

	Interesting religious building		Public building	S.I.	Tourist Office
	Place of interest, main entrance		Castle or château Ruins		Main Post-Office (with poste restante)
⋊	Interesting castle or château		Fountain, Cross or Calvary		Establishment A pleasant place for Tea (see table p. 28)
♣	Interesting ruins	☆☆	Fort		
▲	Other things to see		Lighthouse		
⊤	Viewing-table	✿ ✿	Factory		Hospital
▪	Monument, statue		Covered market		Barracks
	Panorama, view	POL.	Police (in big cities, police headquarters)		Forest
	Race-course	C	Chamber of commerce		Fine woodland
	Tennis	G	Gendarmerie		Public garden
	Outdoor or indoor Swimming pool	H	Town Hall		Private garden
	Landing stage	J	Law courts		Cemetery
✈	Aerodrome	M	Museum		
	Ramparts	P	Prefecture, sub-prefecture	START	Start of sightseeing tour
	Golf and no. of holes	T	Theatre	P	Car Park
	Church, chapel	U	University		

The companion guides in English in this
series on France are:

Brittany   **Paris**   **French Riviera**

Châteaux of the Loire

TOWNS, SIGHTS
AND TOURIST REGIONS
in alphabetical order

L'AIGLE—Michelin map ⑥⓪ ⑤—pop. 9,288.

Aigle, between the Ouche (see p. 12) and Perche Regions (see p. 12) and one of the larger towns in the Upper Risle Valley, maintains its metalwork tradition with modern steel drawing mills producing needles, staples, etc.

St. Martin's.—The building, though lacking all unity, is attractive: an elaborate late 15C square tower contrasts with a small 12C one built of iron agglomerate, surmounted by a more recent spire. Beautiful modern statues stand in niches between the windows of the south nave added in the 16C.

Inside, two 16C stained glass windows (right of the chancel and first window, south aisle) complement a fine contemporary series, while a Renaissance aisle is decorated with graceful hanging keystones.

"Juin 44: Bataille de Normandie" Museum.—*Open 9 a.m. to noon, 2 to 7 p.m.; 3 F.*
Waxworks of the major personalities involved, with contemporary recordings and maps.

ENVIRONS

St-Sulpice-sur-Rille.—*2 miles—3 km—by the N 830.*
This church, adjoining an old 13C priory which was partially reconstructed in the 16C, contains a 16C tapestry, a 17C canvas of St. Cecilia, statues of St. Avertin and St. Anne and two stained glass windows, one 13C, the other 14C.

ALENÇON *—Michelin map ⑥⓪ ③—local maps pp. 41 and 87—pop. 33,388—*Place to stay (see p. 37).*

Alençon, on the Upper Sarthe, is the principal market of a fertile country region (see p. 12), and also, through horse dealing, has connections with the neighbouring Perche Region.

It was a key town in the Mortain-Falaise pocket battle during the war (see p. 25).

Memories of the childhood of St. Theresa of the Child Jesus attract pilgrims.

Lace.—Lace began to be manufactured in Alençon in 1665 in competition with the current craze for Venetian lace.

The town, already known for its fine needlewomen and lacemakers, had a stitch of its own which, by the end of the 17C, had become highly prized by the fashionable.

Modifications in manufacture in the 18C and later mean that Alençon lace today—available from the School of Lace in the town—appears as minute bunches of flowers upon a background of rectangular needlework stitches (see also the Art Gallery p. 40).

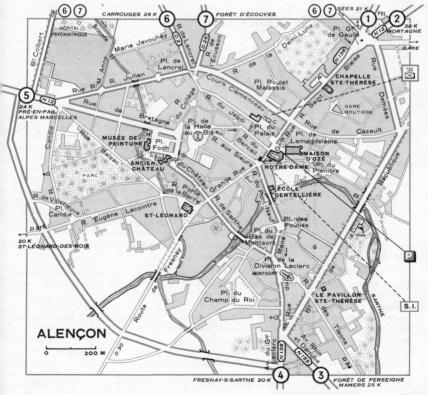

ALENÇON

CHURCH OF OUR LADY* Notre Dame—(tour: about ¼ hour)

This beautiful 14C Flamboyant Gothic monument was completed in 1444—the tower, transept and chancel being reconstructed in the 18C.

The most elegant three-sided **porch**** in Flamboyant style by Jean Lemoine took from 1490 to 1506 to build. Among the decoration, which is concentrated in the upper part, a Transfiguration in the centre of the central gable shows Christ surrounded by prophets and apostles among whom John may be seen standing, unusually, with his back to the street.

Inside, the sweeping lines of the nave converge in the decorated liernes and tiercerons of the pointed vaulting. The lines of the clerestory merge successfully with those of the upper lights of the tall windows which, in the nave, contain **stained glass*** from about 1530 (some are being restored).

Thérèse Martin was baptised in the chapel closed by the modern grille with symbolic roses.

ADDITIONAL SIGHTS

Art Gallery*.—In the town hall. Open 10 a.m. to noon, 2 to 6 p.m. (4 p.m., 30 September to 15 March). Closed Mondays and 1 May: 1 F. Lace making and design; also 17 and 19C paintings.

Old Castle.—The 14 and 15C castle—much restored—was originally built by Jean Le Beau. 1st Duke of Alençon. It now serves as a prison.

St. Leonard's.—The interior of this church, which was rebuilt between 1489 and 1505, has an elegant nave without a triforium, and is an example of the Flamboyant style at its best.

School of Lace (Ecole de Dentelle).—Exhibition and sales galleries open 15 May to 30 September, 10 a.m. to noon, 2 to 6 p.m.—Sundays and Mondays 3 to 6 p.m.; 1 October to 14 May, 10 to 11.30 a.m., 2 to 5 p.m.—closed Sundays and Monday mornings. ℘ 26 27 26; recorded commentary; 2.50 F; the workshops are not open. Alençon and other lace is displayed.

Ozé House.—Same times, etc., as for the Art Gallery. This beautiful, restored, 15C house contains the local museum including Gallo-Roman antiquities and Cambodian items.

SAINT THERESA'S CHAPEL AND HOUSE

St. Theresa Chapel.—If closed ring at No. 42 Rue St. Blaise.

A double staircase opposite the prefecture (a fine 17C building and former military headquarters) leads to the chapel which adjoins the house in which the saint, Thérèse Martin, was born on 2 January 1873. Her room can be entered from the chapel. (See also p. 110.)

ENVIRONS

Perseigne Forest*.—Tour of 33 miles—53 km—about 2 hours. Some forest roads are narrow.
The forest, which lies between the Perche and Mancelle Champagne, covers a well defined crest massif deeply cut by picturesque valleys. The itinerary passes south before penetrating the heart of the mixed oak, beech and fir forest beyond Aillières-Beauvoir.

Alençon*.—Description p. 39.
There are views from the D 19, beyond the Champfleur road and before you reach Ancinnes, of the Ecouves and Multonne Forests and the cone shaped Chaumont Hillock.

PERSEIGNE FOREST

The road, beyond Ancinnes, runs beside Lake Vaubezon and, by way of Neufchâtel-en-Saosnois, arrives at St-Rémy-du-Val.

Our Lady of Succour Chapel (Notre-Dame de Toutes-Aides).—This graceful pilgrim chapel contains a 17C altarpiece surmounted by an Assumption; above is a picture of the Annunciation.

Remarkable views into the heart of the forest from the D 116 begin between the D 116/N 155 crossroads and Villaines-la-Carelle.

At the D 116/D 3 crossroads bear left into the D 234 to go through the twin villages of Aillières-Beauvoir and into the forest proper. The road drops to follow the picturesque Enfer or Hell Valley and its stream. (Belvedere: 2 F; 5 miles—8 km—of marked paths enable walkers to circle the belvedere and penetrate deep into the valley.) At the Trois-Ponts crossroads on the edge of the forest, turn sharp right up another valley of fine oaks, beeches and firs.

Rond de Croix-Pergeline.—Bear right until you come to the D 236 when you turn sharp left for the hamlet of Le Buisson. The N 155 returns you to Alençon.

The Mancelle Alps*.—Tour of 51 miles—82 km—about 3 hours. The designation Alps seems a little exaggerated, nevertheless the Sarthe Valley has a considerable appeal, being deeply enclosed between granite walls covered in heath and broom.

Alençon*.—Description p. 39.
Leave Alençon by ⑤ the N 12. At the place known as Lentillière, turn left into a narrow surfaced road with good open views south of the Pail Forest.

Mount Avaloirs*.—The road to the beacon branches off the road linking the D 144 and the N 12. A metal belvedere marks the "summit" which at 1,368 ft.—417 m—makes it, with the Ecouves Forest beacon (see p. 87), the highest point in western France. The vast panorama extends northwest over the Monaye Forest, further right, to the long crestline of the Ecouves Forest, the sharp outline of the Chaumont Hillock, the round denuded summit of Mount

Souprat, the Alençon countryside, the Perseigne Forest Massif and the hills of the Perche Region and the Mancelle Alps on the horizon.

Cross the D 144 to take the D 204 on the left and, after 1,500 yds., the D 255, on the right. Beyond St-Julien-des-Eglantiers, follow the D 245 uphill to the N 23 *bis* on the right.

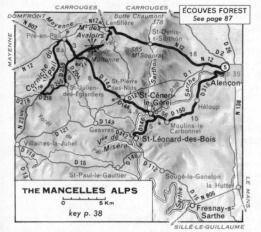

The Pail Corniche.—On a clear day, as the road cuts across the hillsides, there are wide **views*** over the Upper Mayenne Basin and, against the background of Andaines Forest, Domfront belfry standing close by the arresting conical outline of Mount Margantin. At Pré-en-Pail turn right (D 144) for St-Pierre-des-Nids.

St-Céneri-le-Gérei.—A Romanesque church and an old bridge over the Sarthe stand surrounded by old houses in this picturesque small village. Beyond St-Céneri-le-Gérei turn right into the D 146 from which, as it climbs, a view opens out to the north of the Sarthe Valley and higher points of the Multonne Forest.

Bare valley slopes contrast with lush river banks as you descend to St-Léonard-des-Bois.

St-Léonard-des-Bois*.—This small town of 639 inhabitants, in an enclosed bend in the Sarthe beneath steep heath covered hills, is the best situated touring centre for the Mancelle Alps.

The Misère Valley*.—*Walk: 1 hour Rtn.* Start from the church square in St-Léonard and take the path from the corner by the Bon Laboureur Hotel. This passes in front of the town hall and continues straight uphill at the crossroads marked by a stone cross.

Go right through the hamlet of Le Champ-des-Pas before turning left and continuing to a crossroads from which a path marked in blue bears off to the right. **Views*** appear of the wild Misère Valley, particularly from a rocky promontory on the right. Later, from a bench, you can see St-Léonard, and a little apart, downstream, Linthe Manor. Left is the Multonne Forest. The path behind the bench will bring you out on to a cart track which you soon leave to take a downhill path on the right to the crossroads marked by a stone cross and, finally, the car. Returning along the D 146 you get a last glimpse of the picturesque St-Céneri-le-Gérei before joining the D 56. After Héloup, a town well sited at the top of the long ridge which overlooks the Sarthe Valley, the view includes Multonne Forest with Mount Avaloirs on the left and, slightly to the right, Mount Souprat. Further right the Chaumont Hillock and Ecouves Forest again come into view, and as you drop down, the Perseigne Forest Massif, to the east.

ANDELLE Valley—Michelin maps 55 ⑦ ⑧, 97 ② ③.

The lovely, swift running Andelle rises in the Bray Region depression. Although industrialised, particularly downstream, it and its tributaries, the Héronchelles and the Crevon, remain rural in character.

FROM FORGES-LES-EAUX TO THE AMFREVILLE LOCKS

30 miles—49 km—about 1½ hours—plus ½ hour sightseeing

Forges-les-Eaux.—*Description p. 98.* A few miles from Forges, a hill, on which the village of La Ferté stands perched, precedes the main rim of the Bray "button hole" (*see p. 54*) which the Andelle and its early tributaries have cut into hill blocks with distinct, symmetrical outlines.

La Ferté.—*Excursion of 1 mile—1·5 km—from the N 321.* View of the Bray Region depression within its clearly defined rim as you walk up to the church.

Le Héron.—Pleasant shady village with an old castle.

Héronchelles Valley.—*Excursion of 5 miles—7·5 km—from Le Héron to Yville.* The drive along the D 46 is delightful from Héronchelles village to Yville where the houses have overhanging thatched roofs.

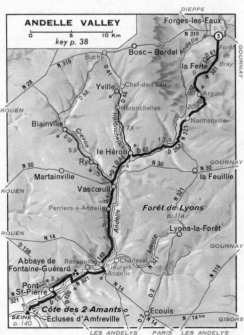

ANDELLE Valley (concluded)

Vascœuil.—The tomb of the 12C blessed Hugues de Saint-Jovinien lies in the church.
Vascœuil Castle, a little below where the Crevon joins the Andelle, again has a traditional Norman setting since half-timbered thatched cottages have been reconstructed around it. *Open 1 July to 31 October, 10 a.m. to noon, 2 to 6.30 p.m. (7.30 p.m. Sundays and public holidays). Admission: 5 F.*
The valley below Vascœuil is industrialised although fine houses in their own grounds do much to maintain the country atmosphere.

> **Crevon Valley.**—*Excursion of 5 miles—8·5 km—from Vascœuil to Blainville. The D 12 goes up this delightful valley enabling one also to see* **Ry** *and* **Blainville** Churches (*descripton p. 134*).

Fontaine-Guérard Abbey*.—*Tour ½ hour. Description p. 98.*
The road continues beyond Fontaine-Guérard Abbey beside the ruins of a surprising mill erected in the "troubadour" style early this century.

Pont-St-Pierre.—The town which stretches across the Andelle Valley owes much to its 12-18C château (*not open*) and surrounding park which can be seen through a gap in the main street. The 11 and 12C church is rich in **woodwork***, the old complemented by modern additions largely from the abbey close to Fontaine-Guérard. A 14C Virgin in the chancel has a dress incrusted with cabuchon stones.
The great Crucifix between the Virgin and St. John on the right in the porch is 15C.

Amfreville Lock*.—The lock, which lies just upstream from the Andelle Valley and below the Côte des Deux Amants, constitutes, with the Poses Dam, the main water flow control of the Seine, dividing the canalised from the free flowing stretch affected by the Channel tides.
Leave the D 19 by the last house in Amfreville-sous-les-Monts and turn towards the Seine; park the car by the barracks. (*Tour: ¼ hour.*)
The big lock is 722 ft. long by 56 ft. wide—220×17 m. Take the footbridge across the Amfreville Lock before walking over the Poses Dam and downstream along the left bank to see the full force of the water.

Les ANDELYS **—Michelin maps ⑤⑤ ⑰, ⑨⑥ ①, ⑨⑦ ⑬ ⑭—local map p. 143—pop. 7,438.—*Place to stay (see p. 37).*

Les Andelys, dominated by the impressive ruins of Gaillard Castle, has one of the loveliest settings along the Seine.

The King of England's Fortress.—Richard Lionheart, King of England and Duke of Normandy, decided, in 1196, to bar the King of France's way to Rouen along the Seine Valley by building a massive fortress on the cliff commanding the river at Andely. Work progressed rapidly so that within the year Gaillard Castle was erect and Richard able to cry aloud "See my fine yearling!"

Philippe Auguste, though bold, did not at first dare to attack so formidable a redoubt. But when Richard I was succeeded by King John he decided to try and starve it into surrender. By the end of 1203 the castle had been isolated by a double moat reinforced by wooden watch towers. In February, however, the French king learned that the defenders had commons for another year and he decided, therefore, to take the castle by storm.

The King of France's Attack.—The first obstacle was the triangular redoubt guarding the vulnerable approach across the isthmus. The 45 ft.—15 m—deep moat was, therefore, partially filled in and a corner tower mined by the attackers to force the outer strongpoint to fall. On 6 March the French entered the main defence through the latrines and let down the drawbridge to the lower courtyard. The assailants swarmed in. Repeated ramming soon breached the next line, forcing the garrison to surrender.

Three months later Rouen, too, had fallen to the French king.

GAILLARD CASTLE** (tour: ¾ hour)

Take the D 1 out of Grand Andely and at the top of Cléry Hill turn right into Roi de Rome Avenue. Leave the car in a park (*1 F*) from which there is an outstanding **view** of the Seine, Les Andelys and Gaillard Castle. Walk along the footpath on the left.

Guided tours, Easter to 15 September, 10 a.m. to 12.30 p.m. and 2.30 to 6 p.m. Closed on Tuesdays and Wednesday mornings. Admission: 1 F.

The fortress consisted of two parts: the main fort towering above the Seine and the advanced redoubt (*see above*).

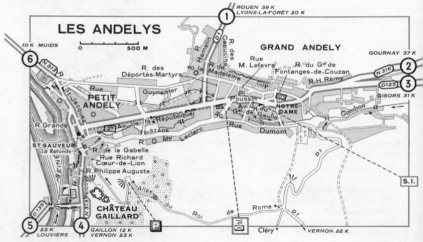

The Redoubt.—The redoubt, separated from the main fort by a moat, possessed five towers of which only one, the tallest, remains. It was the one attacked by Philippe Auguste and is encircled by a narrow slippery path overlooking the perpendicular walls of the moat.

The Main Fort.—Enter the courtyard between the redoubt and main defence and follow the wall round to the left, passing before the keep foundations which were cleverly cut into the rock. The view at the end is sheer and uninterrupted.

Return along the bottom of the moat passing, on your right, casemates dug as food stores out of the rock. Enter the main defence by way of the footbridge which has replaced the drawbridge. The keep, straight before you, has walls 16 ft.—5 m—thick. The inner diameter is 26 ft.—8 m; formerly it was three storeys high with removable inner wooden ladders.

The ruins, to the right, were the governor's lodge.

Coming out through the perimeter wall one can continue to the edge of the rock escarpment from where there is a commanding view up and down the Seine Valley.

ADDITIONAL SIGHTS

Church of Our Lady★.—A well balanced façade of twin towers flanked by a square staircase tower fronts this church in which the 16C south side is a good example of Flamboyant Gothic and the 16 and 17C north side is Renaissance with round arches, Ionic pilasters, balustraded roofs, caryatids and Antique-style statues.

Inside, the well proportioned nave is 13C; the delicately ornamented triforium and tall windows were remodelled in the 16C; the organ★ and loft are Renaissance. The fine stained glass★ in the south aisle is 16C, that at the east end is modern (Gaudin). The Entombment in the south aisle beneath the tower is 16C, the Christ in the Tomb, 14C.

St. Saviour's.—St. Saviour's is Greek cross in ground plan and Gothic in style; the chancel is late 12C, the nave early 13C. The wooden porch stands on an early 15C stone foundation.

Inside, twin bays in the triforium are separated by slender columns which begin above the capitals of the main arches and rise to the roof.

ARGENTAN —Michelin map ⑥⓪ ② ③—local map p. 44—pop. 15,269.

This peaceful small town, badly damaged during the Mortain-Falaise pocket action (see p. 25), has two fine churches.

In 1874 some 18C patterns were recovered which has enabled Argentan lace to be made once more in the town.

ST. GERMANUS★

(**St. Germain**—tour: about ½ hour)

The 15–17C church was badly damaged by shelling in 1944.

Exterior.—The best view of the church is from the Place St-Germain bordered on its south side by the remains of the 14C castle of the Dukes of Alençon. The belfry, left, was given its dome and turret in 1631; the transept lantern is Renaissance.

Go round the 16C east end to the base of the belfry where there is a fine Flamboyant porch★ opening on to the Rue St-Germain.

Interior.—The whole is Flamboyant Gothic with a most unusual four-sided apse and transepts also ending in apses. The triforium is Flamboyant except for the Renaissance decoration on the walls of the apse. The gallery beyond the second ambulatory and the apsidal chapels have hanging keystones.

ADDITIONAL SIGHTS

St. Martin's.—The war damaged church is dominated by an octagonal tower surmounted by a decapitated spire. The church is Flamboyant but having been built early in the Renaissance there are some innovations, especially in the nave and chancel clerestories and the glazing of seven windows in the chancel with fine 16C stained glass.

The Argentan Lace Stitch, Benedictine Abbey, 2 Rue de l'Abbaye.—There are no workshops but one can ask to see (2.30 to 4 p.m. except Sundays and holidays) specimens illustrating steps in the working of Argentan lace and old and modern needle-point lace.

The ARGENTAN Region —Michelin map ⑥⓪ ② ③.

The Argentan Region is virtually a plain bordered to its north by the Ecouves Forest ranges and to the south by the Gouffern woodlands. In August 1944, the German 7th Army, in retreat up the Dives Valley, was annihilated as it was finally caught here between the Americans and the French in the south and the Canadians and the British in the north (p. 24).

EXCURSIONS FROM ARGENTAN

Ecouché; Ménil-Glaise★.—Tour of 20 miles—32 km—about 1 hour. Leave Argentan by ④, N 24 bis.

Ecouché.—A tank from the French 2nd Armoured Division stands at the crossroads entrance

The ARGENTAN Region (*concluded*)

to the town in commemoration of the battles of liberation of 13/20 August 1944. The impressive 15 and 16C church was never completed and the 13C nave, now in ruins, has never been rebuilt, but inside is a good Renaissance triforium.

Take the D 29, Falaise road, and after the second bridge over the Orne, the central road at a road fork; half a mile further on—1 km—bear left.

Ménil-Glaise*.—The **view*** from the bridge takes in the rock escarpment crowned by a castle on the left bank of the Orne. At the top of a steep and narrow uphill road turn sharp right (leave the car after the tennis courts, left). Terrace view of the Orne winding on its way. Turn and go straight ahead to rejoin the N 24 *bis* for Argentan.

St-Christophe-le-Jajolet.—*7 miles—11·5 km—by the N 158. Description p. 155.*

ARGENTAN REGION

key p. 38

The Vaudobin.—*7 miles—11·5 km—plus ¼ hour's walk Rtn along slippery paths.* Leave Argentan by ①, the N 816. Turn left in Villedieu-lès-Bailleul at a café-grocer's; go right through La Londe to a five roads junction and take the second road on the left. Leave the car in front of a house with a wrought iron gate 750 yds. along the road and walk past a quarry. The footpath to the left of the quarry entrance leads to the Meillon stream which you cross over a stepping stone near an open washing place. Continue left round a large rock and uphill, past a rock bearing fossil imprints said locally to be those of oxen. Climb to the top of the mound for a view of the Meillon Gorge and the Upper Dives Valley.

FROM ARGENTAN TO SEES by the Le Pin Stud
27 miles—43 km—about 1½ hours—plus ¾ hour sightseeing

The D 113 leaves Argentan to approach and cross the heights of the Gouffern Forest. The route then descends into the wide depression drained by the Upper Dives.

Argentan.—*Description p. 43.*

Chambois.—A stele near a central crossroads recalls the joining up of Polish (1st Canadian Army) and American troops on 19 August 1944, cutting off the retreat of the German 7th Army. The huge rectangular **keep**, quartered by four towers which served as buttresses, is a good example of 12C military architecture.

Le Bourg-St-Léonard.—The Louis XV château appeals through the elegance of its lines, the harmony of its design. *The interior is being restored.*

There are superb views of the forest setting of the Le Pin Stud from the N 24 *bis*.

Le Pin Stud*.—*Tour ½ hour. Description p. 125.*

> **Exmes.**—*Excursion of 2 miles—4 km—from Le Pin-au-Haras.* Exmes, former historical capital of the Argentan Region and then known as Hiémois, is now a well known archaeological site. From the Butte du Cavalier, a hillock built up at the time of the Gauls (east of the church), there is a view of Exmes and its valleys carpeted with apple orchards, and beyond, west, of Argentan, Ecouché and the Gouffern Forest. North lie the Upper Dives Valley and the Falaise area, southwest the Ecouves Forest.

Almenêches.—The Renaissance church in which the altars are adorned with terracotta low reliefs was formerly the church of a Benedictine abbey.

Médavy.—Two free-standing towers crowned by lantern domes before the sober early 18C château recall the town's one time fortifications.

Ô Castle.—*Tour ½ hour. Description p. 123.*

Sées*.—*Description p. 139.*

ARQUES-LA-BATAILLE **—Michelin map ⑤② ④—5 miles—8·5 km—southeast of Dieppe—pop. 2,813.*

Arques-la-Bataille, now a small industrial town, recalls by its name and castle ruins the famous battle in which **Henri IV**, still a king without a kingdom and with only 7,000 men, vanquished 30,000 men of the Catholic League in 1589 (Monument: *see p. 45*).

SIGHTS

Castle*.—Starting from the Place Desceliers, turn second right into a steep uphill road (1:7—14%. 3 tight bends). Leave the car 30 yds. from the castle entrance.

The castle, one of the most interesting remaining feudal ruins in Normandy, is built on a rock promontory with the keep perched on the highest point. One can still walk round the old ramparts which command a good view of the valley. (*Interior unsafe.*)

Church of Our Lady.—The church, rebuilt in about 1515, was given the belfry in the 17C.

Look first at the façade with its twin turrets and pierced buttress before walking round the building to see the gallery encircling the apse.

Inside, the nave was roofed in the 18C with wood cradle vaulting on pendentives; the chancel and transept, a fine Flamboyant group, are separated from the nave by a 17C rood screen. The apse windows are 16C (restored). A chapel to the right of the chancel with 16C woodwork contains a small bust of Henri IV and an inscription commemorating the battle.

The Lady Chapel, to the left of the chancel, has 17C panelling and other woodwork.

ENVIRONS

Arques Forest.—*Tour: 22 miles—36 km—about 1 hour—plus ¼ hour on foot Rtn.* The tour described below starting from Arques can equally well be made from Dieppe. Leave Arques by the D 56 which skirts the forest.

St-Nicolas-d'Aliermont.—St-Nicolas, like other villages on the narrow Aliermont Plateau and along the D 56 is a "street-village", a type developed in 12–13C as road communication improved. The town is now a precision goods centre manufacturing alarm and electric clocks, meters, fishing tackle and telephone parts.

Envermeu.—The Gothic church, although incomplete, has several features: a remarkable **chancel***, an apse in which the roof ribs are most successfully light and elegant and, finally, skilfully carved spiral columns. The N 320, the N 25 and ① bring you to Dieppe.

Dieppe★★.—*Description p. 82.*
Leave Dieppe by ②, the D 1, which goes up the Arques Valley.

Martin-Eglise.—*Place to stay (see p. 37).* The village, on the edge of the forest, is famous for trout.
Turn left into a narrow road immediately after the bridge over the Eaulne. 650 yds. further on turn right before a house into a forest road which runs by the forest edge providing attractive glimpses of the Arques Valley.

Battle of Arques Monument.—*¼ hour on foot Rtn.* Leave the car on the grass in a sharp left bend. A path leads off on the right to the obelisk erected as a tribute to the victory won by Henri IV on this field. Arques-la-Bataille, commanded by its castle, stands on the far side of the valley. The road enters the forest. After Rond Duquesne you will see the St. Barbara beech tree on your left as you turn into the pretty winding descent to the D 56 for Arques.

ARROMANCHES-LES-BAINS —Michelin map 54 ⑮—local map p. 62—pop. 339 —*Place to stay (see p. 36).*

Arromanches, a modest seaside resort, owes its fame to the fantastic "Mulberry" operation which was an integral part of the Allied Landing in Europe in June 1944.

THE ARTIFICIAL PORT

"If we want to land, we must take our harbours with us" was the conclusion of a British officer even before it had been decided to use the Calvados Coast as the beachhead.

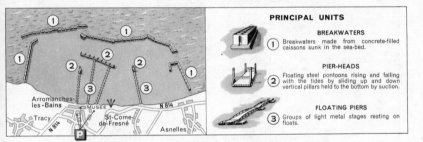

PRINCIPAL UNITS

BREAKWATERS
① Breakwaters made from concrete-filled caissons sunk in the sea-bed.

PIER-HEADS
② Floating steel pontoons rising and falling with the tides by sliding up and down vertical pillars held to the bottom by suction.

FLOATING PIERS
③ Groups of light metal stages resting on floats.

The artificial port of Arromanches in June 1944

The Mulberries.—Arromanches harbour was chosen as the landing point for Mulberry B for British troops (*p. 62,* Mulberry A for the Americans was taken to Omaha Beach—see *p. 123).* The establishment of these artificial ports meant the laying of 146 Phoenix caissons, representing 600,000 tons of concrete, 33 jetties and 10 miles of floating "roads". All this was towed across the Channel at just over 4 m.p.h.

Mulberry B at Arromanches enabled 9,000 tons of material to be landed each day—more than 500,000 tons had been so landed by the end of August when the return to service of Cherbourg and Antwerp and the rapid sanding up of the artificial port subsequently ended the harbour's part in the war.

Invasion Museum (Musée du Débarquement).—*Open 9 a.m. to noon, 2 to 7 p.m. (winter 6 p.m.); 3 F.* Models, dioramas, equipment and a Royal Navy film of the Landing.

The AUGE Region ★—Michelin map 55 ② to ④ and ⑫ to ⑭.

The Auge Region provides a wonderful hinterland to the beaches of the Côte Fleurie (see *p. 73),* with pasturelands, thatched cottages, manor houses, cider (see *p. 21)* and cheeses.

The Region's Riches.—The Auge has an unusually wooded appearance, greenery largely hiding the variations in relief brought about by the raising, in the west, of the chalk foundation which ends abruptly in a cliff a hundred feet high overlooking the Dives Valley and the Caen area (*map p. 13).* This cliff is known to geographers as the Auge "coast".
Fame has come through cider, *calvados* and cheeses: *Camemberts, Pont-l'Evêques Livarots.*

Marie Harel.—Marie Harel was the woman who at the beginning of the 19C perfected the making of the creamy cheese now universally known as *Camembert* after the village 3 miles—5 km—southwest of Vimoutiers (90% of all cheese now made in Lower Normandy).

The Manor Houses.—Auge farms stand at the centre of their apple orchards. The half-timbered buildings around the farmhouse contain the oven, the ciderpress, the apple barn and the cow byre. The dairy, the farmer's wife's preserve, is always well placed.
Much of the region's charm derives from its manor houses which are more or less rural, more or less harmonious architecturally and always completely right in their own setting.

45

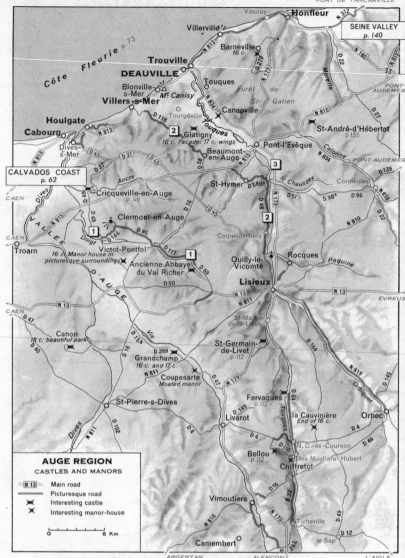

SEINE VALLEY
p. 140

CALVADOS COAST
p. 62

AUGE REGION
CASTLES AND MANORS

N 13	Main road
	Picturesque road
✕	Interesting castle
✕	Interesting manor-house

0   6 Km

---

1 FROM LISIEUX TO CABOURG by the Auge Coast

27 miles—44 km—about 1½ hours

This route affords wide views of the countryside—a rare occurrence in Normandy.

Lisieux**.—*Description p. 110.*

    Clermont-en-Auge*.—*500 yd. walk from the D 146—by a narrow path off the Beuvron road on the right, 100 yds. from the Forges de Clermont crossroads—plus ¼ hour on foot Rtn.* Leave the car at the start of the beech avenue leading to the church. From the east end there is an extensive **panorama*** of the Dives and Vie Valleys while in the distance the Caen countryside can be seen, bounded on the horizon by the dark line of the Bocage hills.
On the way down from Clermont-en-Auge to Beuvron-en-Auge there are several good views of the Dives Valley and the Caen countryside.

Cricqueville-en-Auge.—The castle, completed in 1584, and its three main buildings with vast roofs, remains typically mediaeval while its chequered stone and brick decoration makes it also characteristically Norman (*not open*).
A good panorama of the Calvados coast on either side of the mouth of the Orne opens out on the descent between Sarlabot and Dives.

Dives-sur-Mer.—*Description p. 55.*

Cabourg**.—*Description p. 55.*

---

2 FROM VILLERS-SUR-MER TO LISIEUX

22 miles—36 km—about 1¼ hours

On this drive there are wide views over the Lower Touques Valley and pleasant glimpses of traditional Normandy.

Villers-sur-Mer**.—*Description p. 74.*

    St-Pierre-Azif Church.—*Excursion of 1 mile—1·5 km—starting from the D 118 by a narrow low-lying road.* Turn left opposite the village hall into a road with a cement wall along its right side.

If you want to go into the church which stands isolated and perfectly placed and contains interesting pictures, ask for the key at the grocers. (A Van Helmont *St. Jerome*, a Jordaens *Jesus and Mary*, two portraits of nuns by Van Cleef and a triptych by Lucas Van Leyden.)

Beaumont-en-Auge.—This small town, remarkably situated on a spur commanding the Touques Valley, was the birthplace of the mathematician and physicist Laplace (1749–1827). Take the D 58, N 815 and D 280A on the right to St. Hymer.

St-Hymer.—The village, picturesquely set in a valley, has a 16C church with traces of Romanesque in its style. It served as the priory chapel to one of the last Jansenist centres in the 18C and the belfry is a replica of that of Port-Royal-des-Champs. Inside, there is fine 17 and 18C woodwork and 14C stained glass.

The sometimes winding road from St-Hymer to Ouilly-le-Vicomte is particularly pleasant in the spring when the tall hedges are in flower and the orchards in blossom. There are several attractive half-timbered farms visible from the road. Continue along the D 280A.

Pierrefitte-en-Auge.—The wooden beams over the nave in the 13C church are adorned with camaïeu paintings.

Ouilly-le-Vicomte.—The church, which includes remains from the 10 and 11C, is one of the oldest in Normandy. It contains a carved wood Renaissance altar, modern glass by Grüber and a 17C *pietà. Ask for the key at the presbytery, 200 yards to the north, beside the railway line.*

Lisieux.**—*Description p. 110.*

---

3 FROM LISIEUX TO TROUVILLE-DEAUVILLE by the Touques Valley

17 miles—28 km—about 1 hour

The N 179 and N 834 are fast roads and carry heavy traffic in summer. As the N 179 rises and falls a little above the valley floor you get many glimpses of the Touques Valley and the fertile east bank with its alternating orchards and pastures. Most of the town names recall the time of the early invasions of Normandy.

Lisieux.**—*Description p. 110.*

> **Alternative road by Rocques.**—*Extra distance: 1 mile—2 km. The D 263 northeast out of Lisieux and D 262, back to the N 179, are narrow and hilly.*
> The solid country church in the centre of its old burial ground is preceded by two juxtaposed wooden porches. The chancel and tower go back to the 13C. Inside note the torches of the Brotherhoods of Charity (*see p. 27*) and several polychrome wood statues.

Good view from the hilltop on leaving Manneville-la-Pipard.

Pont-l'Evêque.—*Description p. 125.*

Canapville.—The 13–15C manor house built of wood for the Bishops of Lisieux is one of the most delightful in the Auge (*not open*).

Touques.—From its past as a river mouth port, Touques retains some old houses beside the Ouyes stream and the 11C Church of St. Peter (now secularised). Only a few small ruins remain of William the Conqueror's castle at Bonneville-sur-Touques. *Open Sundays and holidays, 2 to 6 p.m. (5 p.m., 1 November to 31 March). Admission: 2 F.*

Deauville***.**—*Description p. 81.*

Trouville**.**—*Description p. 115.*

AVRANCHES *—Michelin map 59 ⑧—pop. 11,102—*Place to stay (see p. 37).*

St. Aubert, Bishop of Avranches in the 8C, founded Mont-St-Michel and the two centres are, therefore, linked not only geographically but also historically.

In more modern times, it was from Avranches on 31 July 1944 that General Patton began the terrific advance which smashed the German Panzer counter-offensive from Mortain (*see map p. 24*). This, the Avranches breakthrough, marked the beginning of the attack which was to take the American 3rd Army right through to Bastogne in Belgium.

The town was fortunate not to be in the line of destruction.

The outline of Mont-St-Michel can be seen from the Botanical Gardens.

HISTORICAL NOTES

A Norman Doubting Thomas (8C.).—When St. Michael appeared twice before **Aubert** and commanded him to raise a chapel in his honour on the rock then called Mount Tombe, a dense forest covered Mont-St-Michel Bay.

Although sanctuaries to St. Michael were built by tradition upon high rocks, the Bishop of Avranches doubted his visions and prevaricated. St. Michael settled the matter by reappearing and digging an imperious finger into the doubting crown. Aubert could delay no longer—and his holed pate remains for all to see in the treasure of the St. Gervase Basilica.

Murder in the Cathedral.—Relations between Henry Plantagenet and his Archbishop, Thomas of Canterbury, having become particularly bitter, the King cried one day "Is there no one who will rid me of this insolent priest?" Four knights took the words as a command and, on 29 December 1170, Thomas Becket was murdered in Canterbury Cathedral. The pope excommunicated Henry, who pleaded innocence of the crime and begged absolution.

Robert of Torigni, Abbot of Mont-St-Michel, obtained permission to hold a council attended by the king at Avranches and so it was that at the cathedral entrance (*collapsed in 1794—see The Platform p. 48*), Henry II, barefoot and dressed only in a shirt, made public penance on his knees on 22 May 1172 for the death of his archbishop.

The Barefoot Peasants' War.—The imposition of the Salt Tax in western France in 1639 brought about a revolt by the Avranches saltworkers. Insurrection spread rapidly throughout Normandy; armed bands led by Jean Quétil, known as John Barefoot, pillaged towns and countryside. Repression followed other manifestations of Normandy's native spirit of independence.

MAIN SIGHTS (tour, about ¾ hour)

Botanical Gardens★.—*Open until 11.30 p.m., 1 June to 1 October (illuminations and commentary)*. The garden, on the gentle slope of the spur on which the town stands, includes a waterfall, heliotrope, a cedar of Lebanon and other trees. From the viewing table on the terrace there is a wonderful **panorama★★** of Mont-St-Michel Bay—particularly by moonlight.

The Platform.—On the small square, the site of the former cathedral, and known locally as the Platform, the paving stone can still be seen on which Henry II kneeled in public penance. The **panorama★** of Mont-St-Michel from the terrace at the end of the square is less typical than that from the Botanical Gardens.

The Avranchin Museum (M on the map), Place St-Avrit.—*Open Easter to 30 September, 9 a.m. to noon, 2 to 6 p.m.; closed Tuesdays. Admission: 2 F.*

The museum possesses outstanding 8 to 15C **manuscripts★★**, largely from Mont-St-Michel Abbey, and precious incunabula. Avranches being known in the Middle Ages for its learning, there are the Chronicle of Robert of Torigni on the foundation of Mont-St-Michel, Romanesque illuminated MSS, a Mont-St-Michel missal and cartulary, Abelard's *Sic et Non* and 16, 17 and 18C bindings.

ADDITIONAL SIGHTS

St. Gervase and St. Protase Basilica.—*Treasure open 9 a.m. to noon, 2 to 4 p.m. (winter), 7 p.m. (summer); closed Sunday mornings. Apply to the sacristan in the church.* St. Aubert's head is the outstanding relic.

Patton Monument.—The monument stands on the exact spot where General Patton stayed before the offensive; the square in which it stands is now American territory—the soil and trees were brought from the U.S.

BAGNOLES-DE-L'ORNE ★★—Map 60 ①—pop. 642—*Place to stay (see p. 37).*

Bagnoles-de-l'Orne, with Tessé-la-Madeleine (*see below*) is the largest spa in western France (*season: 22 April to 30 September*).

The town's attraction for the tourist, however, lies in its excellence as an excursion centre and in its original **setting★** on a lake. This is formed by the Vée, a tributary of the Mayenne, before it glides into a deep gorge cut through the range of hills covered by the Andaine Forest. The site can be best seen by walking from Tessé-la-Madeleine to the Roc au Chien.

HISTORICAL NOTES

Horse medicine.—Hugues de Tessé, rather than kill his horse, Rapide, when it got old, abandoned it in the forest. Some time later he was surprised to see Rapide return to the stable in fine fettle. He tracked the hoof marks to a spring where the horse had bathed, and bathed in it himself, with similar rejuvenating effect.

The local peasants flocked to see and a Capuchin, cured of his ills, fulfilled a vow by making a gigantic leap of 13 ft.—4 m—from one to the other of the rock spikes high above the spring —since when the spot has been known as the Capuchin's Leap (Saut du Capucin).

The Heroic Bathers.—The first bathing establishment was rudimentary in the extreme. Wooden boards protected three pools through which the water passed successively first to the men, then the women and finally the poor. The desire for a cure made people brave the brigands and wolves of the Andaine Forest and the far from hygienic or comfortable conditions.

SIGHTS

The lake★.—The white walls of the casino stand reflected in the lake.

The Spa Building Park★.—The Dante Avenue, on the left bank of the Vée and often crowded with bathers, leads to the spa building which is in the Vée Gorge.

The waters come exclusively from the Great Spring which gushes forth at the rate of 11,000 gallons—50,000 l.—an hour at a temperature of 81°F.—27°C. It is the only hot spring in western France. Treatment is for circulation and glandular disorders.

Alleys in the park wind towards the Capuchin's Leap and former Janolin Shelter.

Tessé-la-Madeleine.—Walk from the houses and scattered villas of the town which forms one with Bagnoles, to the **Roc au Chien★** (¾ hour on foot Rtn) to see the setting. Go up the beautiful Château Avenue from the church to pass through a gateway and enter the park of Tessé Château, now the town hall. Take the avenue on the right which overlooks Bagnoles Gorge and will bring you to the rocky promontory, the Roc au Chien, from which there is the **view★** of Bagnoles.

ENVIRONS

Bonvouloir Beacon; St. Genevieve Chapel.—Tour: 13 miles—21 km. Leave Bagnoles by the D 235 going northwest. As you descend towards Juvigny take the road which branches off to the right at the end of an estate wall and ends at the farm where the beacon stands.

Bonvouloir Beacon.—The beacon, a strange elongated observation tower, stands beside a more massive tower. The older farm buildings such as the dovecote and the ruins of an old wall create a certain atmosphere.

Return to the D 235. Before entering Juvigny-sous-Andaine, bear right and at the next crossroads, at Blutel, bear right again into a road rising towards the Andaine Forest.

St. Genevieve Chapel.—The chapel dominates a rolling expanse of hills from a secluded spot. At the Etoile d'Andaine crossroads take the D 335, right, through the forest for Bagnoles.

Couterne Castle.—1 mile—1.5 km. Leave Bagnoles by the D 335 going south. Park the car by the bridge over the water in which is reflected the massive brick and granite castle (shut).

Cour Valley.—Tour: 7 miles—11 km—Leave Bagnoles by the N 816 going north, the D 387 right, and the D 20. Place to stay (p. 37). The pool in the forest is a favourite spot.

BALLEROY ★—Michelin map 54 ⑭—pop. 757—Place to stay (see p. 37).

Balleroy Castle, built between 1626 and 1636 by François Mansart, has been owned for three centuries by the Marquises of Balleroy, descendants of Jean de Choisy who had it built.

The plain edifice majestically prolongs the village's single wide street which forms an avenue of approach; symmetrical annexes behind formal flowerbeds designed by Le Nôtre and a terrace flanked by twin pavilions complete the whole. The park greenery fills in the background.

Castle★.—Open 9 a.m. to noon, 2 to 6 p.m. Closed on Thursdays. Admission, 4.50 F; time: ½ hour.

The castle's exterior gives no hint of its rich **interior decoration★**. The State Drawing Room has a French style painted ceiling and a remarkable series of portraits by Mignard of Louis XIII, Condé, Madame de Montespan and her four children, the Great Mademoiselle and Louis XIV with his brother, Philip of Orleans and his mother, Anne of Austria.

Parish Church.—Former castle chapel attributed to Mansart.

BARNEVILLE-CARTERET ★—Michelin map 54 ①—local map p. 79—pop. 1,924

—Place to stay (see p. 36).

Carteret★.—A magnificent rock headland to the north, protects the Gerfleur estuary and the delightful small beach of Carteret, making it one of the pleasantest seaside resorts on the Cotentin Peninsula. The harbour is the nearest to Jersey (access: see Michelin Red Guide France).

Walk round the headland★★.—¾ hour on foot Rtn. Leave the car at a roundabout overlooking the beach. Take the Customs Officers' Path (Sentier des Douaniers) on the left which becomes very narrow as it follows the line of the headland. The view alters all the time on the way to Carteret's second beach which is entirely natural.

Return up the path. For an overall view either bear right into the road going up to the **lighthouse★** (open 9 a.m. to noon, 2 to 7 p.m.) or take the road on the left, the Avenue de la Roche Biard, to a viewing table—in which case the walk will take a couple of hours.

Alternatively continue straight over the crossroads to return to the car.

Barneville.—The 11C church was given a fortified tower in the 15C. Inside, the Romanesque arches are beautifully **decorated★**, particularly those with carved animal capitals.

The monument on the way out of Barneville commemorates the Cutting of the Cotentin Peninsula on 18 June 1944 (see p. 24).

ENVIRONS

Masse de Romond.—1 mile—2 km—plus ½ hour on foot Rtn. Leave Barneville-Carteret by the N 804 going towards Cherbourg; at the top of the hill, in a bend, take the right hand road towards a Cross, where you leave the car. Turn towards the ruins of an old mill when you come out on the grass covered hillock and you will see a rolling, hilly, landscape and the coastline from Sénequet Lighthouse in the south to Cape Flamanville in the north.

Portbail; Mount Castre★.—18 miles—29 km—about 1¾ hours—plus ½ hour on foot Rtn. Leave Barneville-Carteret by the Coutances road. At La Picauderie, bear right into D 50.

Portbail.—Place to stay (see p. 36). The small harbour and the fine sand beach a mile away enable Portbail to describe itself as one of the Cotentin's modest seaside resorts. The fortified tower on the Church of Our Lady is 15C though the church itself is older, dating back to earliest Romanesque times. One of the main attractions inside are the 16 capitals carved with interlacing and animals. Excavations are taking place in the nave (closed).

An ancient baptistry was uncovered in 1956, 150 yds. from the church. Apply at the town hall or tourist office.

Take the D 15 and N 803 to La Haye-du-Puits and on to Carentan.

Mount Castre★.—½ hour Rtn. Turn right off the N 803, 1,600 yds. beyond the first railway crossing after La Hay-du-Puits. Pass in front of a crushing mill and bear right to come to the church ruins and an old cemetery. A path leads to the ruins of a Roman watchpost—still a strategic point in July 1944, see map p. 24—from which the **view★** extends across the Cotentin.

Bayeux Cathedral continues, as it has done for 900 years, to stand guard over the old Bessin capital. It was the first town in France to be liberated—7 June 1944—and suffered no damage in the process. The tapestry draws crowds as always.

HISTORICAL NOTES

The Cradle of the Dukes of Normandy.—Bayeux, Gaulish capital of the Bajocasses, a Roman town and an important episcopal city, was subsequently captured by assault by the Bretons, the Saxons and the Normans.

Rollo, the famous Viking, married Popa, the daughter of Count Béranger, governor of the town. In 905 they had a son, the future William Longsword, making the town the cradle of the dynasty of the Norman Dukedom (see genealogical tree p. 22). When Rouen became French, Bayeux remained Scandinavian and the people continued to speak Norse.

The Oath of Bayeux.—Edward the Confessor, King of England, remained childless, and it seemed therefore, since he had lived much of his life in Normandy, that his cousin, William the Bastard, would be his chosen heir. Harold went to Normandy to tell William the news and swear fealty. But, on his deathbed, the Confessor named Harold his heir and, above all, the Witan preferred the strong man, son of the Earl Godwin, to be their king. Harold foreswore the promise he had made to William Duke of Normandy and grasped the crown. The epic which was to give William his appellation of the Conqueror and which was later to be so minutely embroidered on the tapestry was about to begin (see p. 73, the Conquest).

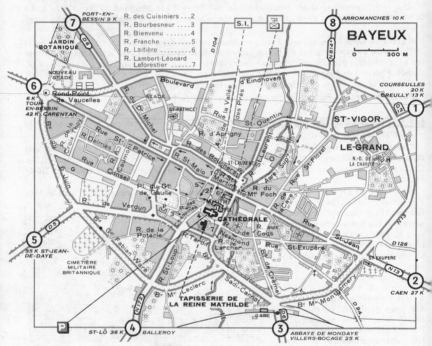

MAIN SIGHTS (tour: about 1¼ hours)

Cathedral of Our Lady**.—The cathedral is a fine edifice in the Norman Gothic style. Only the façade towers and the crypt remain of the church completed in 1077 by Bishop Odon of Conteville, William's turbulent companion in arms, who he was finally compelled to lock up.

Exterior.—The east end is graceful; flying buttresses support the chancel which is flanked by two bell-turrets. The central tower is 15C but the top, known as the bonnet, was rebuilt most regrettably in the 19C.

The south transept is pure in style; on the doorway tympanum the story of Thomas Becket's murder in Canterbury Cathedral is graphically portrayed. Above, radiating tracery is surmounted by a highly ornate gable.

Further along on the south side there is a delicate small 12C porch.

The two Romanesque towers of the façade must have had buttresses added in the 13C to help support the Gothic spires. Only the tympana of the two intermediary doors are interesting—on the left, the Passion (read from bottom to top), on the right, the Last Judgment (top to bottom).

Interior.—Open: 8 a.m. to noon and 2 to 7 p.m. (8 or 9 p.m. from July to October). The nave, which is light, is a harmonious blend of Romanesque and Gothic. The tall windows and vaulting are 13C but the wide arches are in the best 12C style and their justly famous decoration is typical of Norman Romanesque sculpture (details p. 17): on an interlaced or knotted ground, low reliefs on the corner stones clearly show the oriental influence handed down by illuminators.

The three storey chancel is a magnificent example of Norman Gothic architecture. The wide arches are divided by pierced rose windows above an intricately ornate triforium. The stalls were carved by a late 16C artist from Caen while the high altar is 18C as are the six candelabra, the tabernacle and the Cross by Caffiéri the Elder. Portraits (restored) of the early bishops of Bayeux may be seen on the chancel vaulting.

The ambulatory adorned with blind arcades lies below the chancel separated from it by fine wrought iron grilles. The 3rd and 4th ambulatory chapels on the right contain 15C frescoes.

To see the treasure, crypt and chapterhouse, apply to the sacristy off the north transept. Guided tours 1 May to 30 September, 2 to 6 p.m. Admission: 1 F.

The **treasury***, abutting on the ambulatory, is a fine 13C construction. The interesting items are on the first floor and include a great 13C cupboard now used for relics.

The 11C **crypt** beneath the chancel is divided into three equal sized rooms: the recumbent statue of a canon (left) is 15C as are the frescoes.

The **chapterhouse** is a beautiful late 12C Gothic building where the vaulting, reconstructed in the 14C, rests on consoles decorated with grotesques or monsters. A graceful blind arcade adorns the lower walls, while the pavement of 15C glazed bricks is designed at the centre as a labyrinth.

The **central tower** (354 steps—*possibly closed*) commands a fine panorama of the Bessin.

Leave the cathedral through the small doorway in the south aisle. Opposite, on the far side of the street is the one time bishopric which now houses the tapestry.

The Bayeux Tapestry***.—*Open: Easter to October, 9 a.m. to noon, 2 to 6.30 p.m. October to Easter, 9.30 a.m. to noon, 2 to 5 p.m. Closed Christmas and 1 January; 3 F. including the Baron-Gérard Museum. Recorded commentary in English: 1 F.*

Go up to the 1st floor by an 18C staircase rebuilt in its present position to enable the full length of the building to be used to display the tapestry which is 231 ft. long by 19½ in. deep—70.34×0.50 m.

The origin of the tapestry, which is, in fact, an embroidery of coloured wool on linen, is not definite, but it was almost certainly commissioned in England shortly after the Conquest by Odon of Conteville, Count of Kent and Bishop of Bayeux, from the then famous school of Saxon embroiderers. The work was intended to adorn the cathedral he had just had built in Bayeux and is mentioned in the cathedral records of 1476.

It was in the 18C that the tapestry was wrongly attributed to Queen Mathilda—the name has stuck in France where it is known as La Tapisserie de la Reine.

The work is the most precise and living document to come down to us from the Middle Ages giving graphic details of the clothes, ships, arms and the customs of the period. The rivalry between Harold and William is shown as well as preparations for the conquest, the battle and the final victory, in 58 dramatic scenes. Latin captions spelt in the Saxon manner run below the pictures while the upper and lower edges are embroidered with fantastic animals or motifs relating to the principal events. The most outstanding scenes are Harold's embarkation and crossing (4–6), the audience with William (14), the crossing of the Couesnon (17), Harold's oath (23), the death and burial of Edward the Confessor (26–28), the appearance of a comet (32), the building of the fleet (36), the crossing of the Channel and the march to Hastings (38–40), the bivouac (41–43) and the battle (51–58). The English can be identified by their moustaches, the Normans by their shaven necks.

ADDITIONAL SIGHTS

Baron-Gérard Museum (M on plan).—*Open 16 March to 15 October, 9 a.m. to noon, 2 to 6.30 p.m.; 16 October to 15 March, 10 a.m. to noon, 2 to 5 p.m.; entrance: Place des Tribunaux; 3 F. including Tapestry Museum above.*

The outstanding exhibits in this old bishopric—one room has a beautiful 18C fireplace and woodwork—are 17C tapestries, Italian primitives, old Rouen ceramics and Bayeux porcelain.

Bayeux lace—old and new—and pillow lace are also displayed.

Law Courts.—Also in the old bishopric (J on plan—*apply to the caretaker*).

Old Houses.—No. 6, **Rue St-Martin**—a 17C mansion; on the corner of the Rue des Cuisiniers—a 14C house; No. 4, **Rue St-Malo**—15–16C Fresne Mansion, take a look at the inner courtyard; No. 10 **Rue Bourbesneur**—the governor's house, 15–17C; No. 6 **Rue Bienvenue**—attractive wooden house; No. 5, **Rue Franche**—15C turreted manorhouse and No. 7, the 18C Crespillière Mansion.

ENVIRONS

The Bessin Coast*.—*Tour, 21 miles—34 km—about an hour—plus ¾ hour on foot Rtn.* Leave Bayeux by ⑧, the N 814B.

Arromanches-les-Bains.—*Description p. 45.*
In Arromanches cut back for ½ mile to take the road on the right to Port-en-Bessin. In Longues-sur-Mer turn right into the D 104 towards the sea; ½ mile further on a path branches off left (¼ *hour on foot Rtn*) to the powerful German battery silenced for ever at 6.20 a.m. on 6 June 1944 by shells from the British cruiser *Ajax*.

The Chaos.—½ *hour on foot Rtn.* Leave the car at the cliff edge and continue on foot down the steep path (*dangerous by car—falling rocks*). View from Cape Manvieux to Percée Point.
From the foot of the cliffs the soft marl subsoil and rock chaos are clearly visible. The cliff-face has worn away into a chaos of tumbled rocks.

St. Mary's Abbey.—*Open Thursday afternoons, other days by permission.*
Of the abbey buildings there remain the entrance and ruins of the 12C church cloister, chancel and transept. In the refectory are the tombstones of Lords of Argouges and an attractive collection of coloured tiles from the Pré-d'Auge (*see p. 20*).
Turn round; at the Longues war memorial bear left for Port-en-Bessin.

Port-en-Bessin*.—*Description p. 64.*
There is a good view on your return to Bayeux along the D 6, from the Aure bridge, of the 15–18C **Maisons Château** surrounded by a river fed moat.

Balleroy*; **Cerisy-la-Forêt.**—*Tour: 29 miles—46 km—about 1½ hours—plus 1 hour sightseeing.* Leave Bayeux by ④, the N 172.

St-Loup-Hors.—The 12–13C church still has its Romanesque tower.

Noron-la-Poterie.—Well known salt glaze ware centre (*see p. 26*) where one can visit the Dubost pottery: *open in July and in September, Monday afternoons and Friday mornings*. In La Tuilerie take the D 73, left, to Castillon and on to reach Balleroy.

BAYEUX** (concluded)

Balleroy*.—*Description p. 49.*
On leaving the castle bear left into the D 13 and across the N 172 into the D 8 through the forest.

Cerisy-la-Forêt.—*Description p. 69.*
Return to Bayeux by the D 8, the D 13E and the N 172.

St-Gabriel-Brécy.—Leave Bayeux by the D 126. At Vieux Pont turn left into the D 35. The former **Priory of St. Gabriel** (now a horticultural college), founded in the 11C and entered through a monumental 12C doorway, is built round a central courtyard. Visitors see the great vaulted refectory, the prior's lodging and the chapel's still extant 11 and 12C chancel which is magnificent in both line and decoration.

Mondaye Abbey.—*7 miles—11 km—about ¾ hour.* Leave Bayeux by ③ the D 6. Bear right into the D 33 after 5 miles—8 km—and at Couvert take the D 178 to the abbey.
The abbey and parish church has a classical unity no doubt due to one man, Canon Eustache Restout of the Premonstratensians, being both architect and decorator. The lines of the façade are worth noting as are, inside, the organ loft—restored—the high altar, stalls and chancel woodwork and finally the large terracotta group in the Lady Chapel.

BEC-HELLOUIN **—Michelin maps 54 ⑲, 55 ⑮—*Place to stay (see p. 37).*

The importance of Bec-Hellouin Abbey as a mediaeval religious and cultural centre can still be seen, in spite of mutilation to the building. Two great Archbishops of Canterbury came from it.

The Anchorite Knight.—In 1034 the knight **Herluin** abandoned his charger for a donkey and vowed to devote himself to God. Others followed his example and by 1041 there were 32 monks in the "Bec" community.

Lanfranc the Illustrious.—One day in 1042 as Herluin was mending the bread oven a stranger appeared. It was the Italian clerk, Lanfranc, who had been teaching at Avranches, and, tired of his success, had left and come to Bec, drawn by the monastery's obscurity.
He stayed for three years before Herluin persuaded him once more to take up his teaching.

The Faithful Counsellor.—It was during his siege of Brionne from 1047 to 1050 *(see p. 55)* that the young Duke William got to know Lanfranc who subsequently became his most trusted adviser—Lanfranc was the monk sent as emissary to Rome to get the interdict raised which had weighed on Normandy since William's marriage to Mathilda *(details p. 56)*.
In about 1060 Herluin moved the community further up the valley.
Then Pope Alexander II, who had been one of Lanfranc's students at Bec, appointed his former teacher Archbishop of Canterbury, a position which made him virtual regent of England whenever William returned to Normandy. On Lanfranc's death in 1093, Anselm, the philosopher and theologian who had come from Aosta and was by now Abbot of Bec, was transferred to Canterbury. Bec Abbey long continued as a major intellectual centre.

The Maurists.—In the 17C, Bec, which was the second abbey to accept the Maurian reform, found a new lustre with Guillaume de la Tremblaye (1644-1715). The great master builder of the congregation and one of the greatest sculptors and architects of his period *(see Abbaye aux Hommes, Caen, p. 57)*, made his profession of faith there in 1699.
The monks were driven out during the Revolution and the abbey church, one of the largest in Christendom, demolished under the Empire. In 1948 the site was restored to the Benedictine Order and on 29 September of that year mass was celebrated once more.

THE ABBEY** *(tour: ½ hour)*

Open daily, except Tuesdays, 9.30 a.m. to noon, 2.30 to 6 p.m.; no visiting Sundays and feast days during services (10.30 to 11.45 a.m., 4 to 4.40 p.m.). Admission: 3 F.

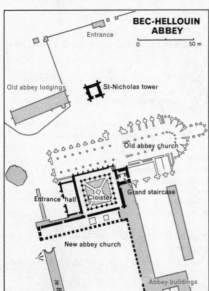

BEC-HELLOUIN ABBEY

Entrance
0   50 m

Old abbey lodgings
St-Nicholas tower
Old abbey church
Entrance hall
Cloister
Grand staircase
New abbey church
le Bec
Abbey buildings

Entrance Hall.—The former library contains portraits and documents.

New Abbey.—The New Abbey is in what was the former Maurist refectory, a majestically proportioned vaulted hall. The statue of the Virgin at the entrance is 14C, the Fathers of the Church all 15C; the Italian marble altar was presented in 1959 by Aosta, birthplace of Bishop Anselm; before the high altar lies the 11C sarcophagus of Herluin, founder of Bec.

Old Abbey.—Only the column foundations remain to give an idea of its size.

Cloister.—A monumental 17C grand staircase (modern banister) leads to the cloister. A good 13C Gothic doorway in the northeast corner has a tympanum with a Virgin in Majesty.

St. Nicholas' Tower.—The 15C tower is the most important remainder of the Old Abbey Church, although it stood apart from it. The spire has disappeared. A plaque recalls the Abbey's ties with England in the 11 and 12C.
The **view*** from the tower summit *(201 steps)* includes the Bec Valley.

BELLÊME—Michelin map ⑥⓪—north of ⑭ ⑮— local map p. 122—pop. 1,740—*Place to stay (see p. 37).*

Bellême, capital of the Perche region, groups its houses at the top of a small spur of 738 ft.—225 m—which overlooks the forest and beautiful Perche countryside. The town had a particularly turbulent history in the Middle Ages when, among other events, the fortress was taken by assault in 1229 by Blanche of Castile and the future St. Louis.

TOUR (about ½ hour)

From the Place de la République make for the fortified gate known as the Porche.

The Walled Town.—The **Porche,** flanked by two reconstructed towers, and some towers now incorporated in domestic buildings, are the only remains of the 15C ramparts which were, in turn, built upon 11C fortress foundations. Note the portcullis grooves.

The Rue Ville-Close, on the site of the former citadel, is lined with fine 17 and 18C Classical style houses. Outstanding are No. 24, the governor's house, and No. 26,

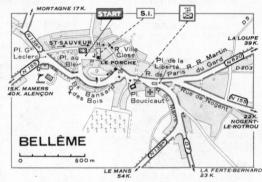

BELLÊME

the **Bansard des Bois Mansion,** whose elegant façade can be seen from beside a stretch of water, once the castle moat.

St. Saviour's.—This late 17C purely Classical church has a richly decorated interior.

BELLÊME FOREST★

Tour: 17 miles—28 km—about 1 hour—plus ¼ hour on foot Rtn

This national forest of just over 9 sq. miles of majestic oaks and beeches is very beautiful. Leave Bellême by the N 138 *bis* from which there is a pretty view of the town.

La Herse Pool.—*A path circles the pool.* The calm waters reflect the surrounding greenery.
On the northern edge of the forest take the forest road on the right (*not surfaced*) which winds along to the Etoile de la Reine Blanche, where you turn right. The road crosses the N 138 *bis* before reaching the Carrouge crossroads where you turn left and then first right for the Montimer crossroads. Turn left into a downhill road and, after 450 yds., you will come to the **Ecole Oak Tree** which stands 118 ft. tall—36 m.
Return to the Montimer crossroads and bear left for La Perrière.

La Perrière.—One of the best **panoramas★** of the Perche countryside, including to the west also the Perseigne Forest and, further off, the Ecouves Forest, can be seen from the cemetery path near the church.
Return to the forest road which crosses the Bellême Forest from west to east and passes through the delightful Creux Valley.
At the Rendez-Vous crossroads take the D 310 on the right, which goes through **St-Martin-du-Vieux-Bellême,** where the houses stand grouped round the church. The road joins the N 155 for Bellême town.

BERNAY—Michelin maps ⑤④ ⑲, ⑤⑤ ⑭ ⑮—local map p. 69—pop. 10,776.

Bernay developed rapidly round an abbey founded early in the 11C by Judith of Brittany, wife of Duke Richard II (*see genealogical table, p. 22*). It was at Bernay in the 12C that the troubadour Alexandre of Bernay composed the long poem, the *Romance of Alexander* in 12 syllable lines known subsequently as alexandrines.

Promenade des Monts★.—*About ¼ hour.* Beech avenue on the hillside: good views.

Town Hall.—The former Bernay Abbey. The 17C buildings are Maurist in style (*p. 20*).

Former Abbey Church.—*Possibly closed for restoration.*
The church, begun in 1013 by Gugliemo da Volpiano (*see p. 95*), called from Fécamp by Duchess Judith, has domed vaulting, restored in the 17C as were the few remaining capitals.

St. Cross Church.—The church, begun in the 14C and considerably restored, contains fine works of art principally from Bec Hellouin. A 16C gilded wood low relief on the reverse of the main door shows the carrying of the Cross.
Large 14C statues of the Apostles stand against the columns of the nave and chancel; abbots' tombstones face the pillars supporting the organ loft, others have been placed in the south transept and left of the sacristy door is the most outstanding of all, the **tombstone★** of Guillaume of Auvillars, Abbot of Bec (1418). (The gold highlights and colours are 19C.)

Notre-Dame-de-la-Couture Basilica.—*Access by the Rue Kléber Mercier.* This 15C church, raised to the status of a basilica in 1950, has an entirely wooden roof. A 16C statue of Our Lady the Seamstress stands in the north transept; there are also two good (restored) stained glass windows.
Brothers of Charity (*see p. 27*) take part in the Whit Monday pilgrimage.

Museum.—*Open 2 to 6 p.m. (summer), 4 p.m. (winter); closed Mondays; apply to the caretaker (public garden side); 1 F.* The museum in the old abbot's lodge has a fine collection of Rouen, Nevers and Strasburg china and Norman furniture.

ENVIRONS

Broglie.—*16 miles Rtn—24 km—by the D 33.* The small town by the Charentonne River, took its name from the Piedmontese family whose fief it became in the 18C.
The centre of the **church** façade, the lower part of the belfry and the upper area of the nave are in a red ironstone agglomerate (*see the Ouche Region, p. 12*), the remainder is in a white stone; the crossed Romanesque blind arcades date from the 11C. Inside, the massive pillars on the north side and the chancel are Romanesque, all else is 15 and 16C.

The Bray Region, a green oasis in the centre of the bare vastness of the Caux Plateau, has a landscape of more clearly defined outlines than any other area in Normandy. It exists because of that geological accident known as the "buttonhole".

GEOGRAPHICAL NOTES

The movement of the earth's crust which brought about the raising of the Alps in the Tertiary Era had repercussions as far as the Paris Basin. The shocks which disturbed the ancient shelf (*see Composition of the Terrain p. 11*) formed ridges in the upper layers deposited in the Secondary Era. Wide and deep undulations were formed in a southeast–northwest direction. One of these swelled into a large dome with a steep northeast face of some 3,000 ft. —nearly 1,000 m.

Ceaseless erosion wore away and cut into the dome exposing subjacent Jurassic soil in considerable geological variety. This cut, with its clearly defined rim, is known as the "Bray buttonhole". Its south-west edge is

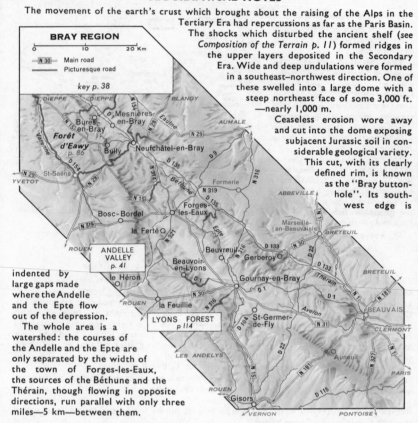

indented by large gaps made where the Andelle and the Epte flow out of the depression.

The whole area is a watershed: the courses of the Andelle and the Epte are only separated by the width of the town of Forges-les-Eaux, the sources of the Béthune and the Thérain, though flowing in opposite directions, run parallel with only three miles—5 km—between them.

RICHES OF THE BRAY REGION

With the development of transport in the 19C, Bray became the Paris larder. Today 40 million gallons of milk and 220 thousand gallons of cream are sent annually to the capital. Dairy farming—almost the sole type in the region—is centred on Gournay-Ferrières where prodigious quantities of double cream and *demi-sel* cheeses are produced although the cylindrical Neufchâtel *bondon* still holds its own with connoisseurs.

Production of dessert apples and cider have recently been increased.

Recently the region's geological structure has attracted the attention of oil prospectors.

*TOUR STARTING FROM NEUFCHÂTEL-EN-BRAY

31 miles—50 km—about 1½ hours—plus ¼ hour sightseeing

The tour, not confined to a geographer's true Bray, has the attraction of a hilly landscape.

Neuchâtel-en-Bray.—*Description p. 121.*

From the N 314, going north through a strangely denuded landscape on the northeast slope of the buttonhole, there are ever more extensive views of the Béthune Valley before you cross the Hellet Forest (D 56) to come out at Croixdalle. There turn left, D 77, first, to descend into the Béthune Valley and then, beyond Osmoy-St-Valery, climb out of it, up its southwest slope by what is virtually a pass into the Mesnil-Follemprise Valley, which you leave by a second pass. Once more the view opens out and you see farming country on the chalklands, the Bures-en-Bray belfry, the Hellet Forest and Mesnières Castle. Take the D 298 and D 12.

Bures-en-Bray.—The church, partly 12C, was damaged in 1944 but not the bold twisted wooden spire. Inside, behind the modern porch and brick façade, is a 16C Entombment.

The D 114 follows a terrace which marks the rising level of the springs and also the line along which the villages at the foot of the southwest face of the buttonhole have been built.

In Fresles take the D 97, on the left.

Mesnières-en-Bray.—The **castle★** (*guided tours for groups by appointment on Sundays only*), which is the most majestic civil monument in the Bray Region, and is now an ecclesiastical college, started to be built in the late 15C as a Renaissance building flanked by powerful although purely ornamental, machicolated towers. The main central building has steep roofs, an arcaded gallery and all the Classical adornment of superimposed orders, ornamented dormer windows and Antique-style busts. The grand staircase to the main courtyard is 18C, the right wing 19C. The tour includes the gallery adorned with carved stags and other richly decorated rooms. The 16C castle chapel has an axe-shaped roof.

Return to Fresles and take the D 114.

Bully.—The church has a 13C Gothic chancel and inside, a 16C Entombment and keystones.

Return to Neufchâtel-en-Bray by the D 48.

BRICQUEBEC—Michelin map ⑤④ ②—pop. 3,267—*Place to stay (see p. 37).*
  Bricquebec, in the heart of the Cotentin Peninsula, is known for its old castle and its Trappist Monastery.

  Castle.—Enter the inner courtyard which has a surrounding wall and is picturesque.
  Guided tours, 9 a.m. to noon and 1.30 to 7 p.m.; 10 a.m. to 12.30 p.m. and 2 to 7 p.m., Sundays and public holidays; 10 a.m. to noon and 2 to 5 p.m. out of season. Closed in February. Admission: 1 F (tower) and 0.50 F (crypt). Apply to the caretaker, at the south entrance of the castle.
  The 14C **keep★**, which stands upon a mound, is a fine polygonal tower 75 ft.—23 m—high. The four storeys which once existed have fallen in but the upper platform (*160 steps*) can still be climbed and commands a view of the town, the countryside and the monastery.
  The **clock tower** contains a small musuem (*0.50 F.*) of furniture, medals and mineral specimens.

ENVIRONS

Our Lady of Grace Abbey or Bricquebec Trappist Monastery (Abbaye Notre-Dame-de-Grâce ou Trappe de Bricquebec).—*2 miles—2·5 km—by the D 121 and left path before the Calvary. Only men may enter the Trappist monastery, founded in 1824—daily, except Sundays and feast days, at 3 p.m. Women may enter the church. Service times weekdays and Sundays respectively: mass, 8.15 a.m. and 11 a.m.; compline 6 and 3.30 p.m.; vespers 8 p.m.—all subject to alteration.*

BRIONNE—Michelin maps ⑤④ ⑲, ⑤⑤ ⑮—pop. 4,493—*Place to stay (see p. 37).*
  Brionne in mediaeval times was a stronghold commanding the Risle Valley and in the 11C had close ties with the monastery in the neighbouring Bec Valley. It was in fact when William of Normandy was besieging the Duke of Burgundy in Brionne from 1047 to 1050 that he first came in contact with the Bec-Hellouin monastery which was to have such influence subsequently on his political actions and religious life generally in England (*see p. 52*).

SIGHTS

  Keep.—$\frac{1}{4}$ *hour on foot Rtn.* Leave the car in the Place de Frémont-des-Essarts. Take the Rue des Canadiens and, after 50 yds. the "Sente du Vieux Château" on the right. This leads steeply uphill to the early 12C castle ruins—a rare and good example of the square Norman keep. From the base of the keep there is a pleasant view over the town and along the Risle Valley.

  St. Martin's.—The nave is 15C, the chancel and Gothic wood vaulting above, 14C, the marble altar and altarpiece 17C and both from the Bec-Hellouin Abbey. The stained glass, which is modern, is by Gabriel Loire of Chartres.

ENVIRONS

Bec-Hellouin★★.—*4 miles—6 km—by the N 138 and D 39 on the left. Description p. 52.*

Harcourt★.—*4 miles—7 km—by the D 26 and D 137. Description p. 121.*

Tour in the Lieuvin.—*17 miles—28 km—about 1 hour.*
The D 38 goes up the green Livet Valley.

Livet-sur-Authou.—The church, the castle and park form a delightful scene.

St-Benoît-des-Ombres.—Beyond the miniature town hall look out, on the right, for the chapel hidden in the greenery which has a porch crowned by a great 15C statue of St. Benedict.
The roofs of Launay Château appear straight ahead as you reach the bottom of a steep hill. Continue up a beech avenue where the branches meet overhead.

Launay Château.—Turn off right into the castle approach. From the main gate there is a good view of this attractive well kept Louis XV building, supported by beautiful pavilion wings and half-timbered outbuildings including dovecotes (*not open to the public*). Return to Brionne by way of St-Georges-du-Vièvre along the D 137 from which there is a view of the Risle Valley.

CABOURG ★★—Michelin maps ⑤④ ⑯ ⑰, ⑤⑤ ②—pop. 3,067—*Place to stay (see p. 36).*
  Cabourg was created as a seaside resort at the time of the Second Empire and although now very much larger, retains all its former elegance.
  French literature owes *Within a Budding Grove (A l'Ombre des Jeunes Filles en Fleurs)* to Marcel Proust's stay in the town—his descriptions of Albertine playing with her *diabolo* on the breakwater, the girls on their *jokari* and many others, evoke a clear picture of life in a seaside resort at the turn of the century. Names and entertainments have changed but Normandy beaches still please.

THE RESORT

  The town has a geometrical symmetry. The Casino and Grand Hôtel (not a commercial hotel) stand together facing the sea and forming the focal point from which streets radiate, linked at their perimeter and two intermediary points by concentric semicircular avenues. The avenues and streets are, in many cases, lined by attractive houses set in shaded gardens.
  The Boulevard des Anglais, a terrace running the full length of the immense fine sand beach, makes a magnificent promenade with a view extending from Riva-Bella to Houlgate with Trouville as background and Cape La Hève on the horizon.

Dives-sur-Mer.—It was from Dives that William of Normandy set out for England in 1066 (*see p. 73*).
  Dives, a town of 6,500 inhabitants, faces Cabourg from across the river of the same name, its one time port now silted up. Today it is known for its large copper-alloy foundry and works, the Société Tréfimétaux, which is now turning also to plastics.

Our Lady of Dives.—The massive former pilgrimage church is 14 and 15C except for the transept crossing which is 11C, dating from an earlier sanctuary.
  Inside, the elegance of the 15C nave is in sharp contrast with the massive pillars and the plain Romanesque arches of the transept crossing. The transepts themselves, the chancel and the beautiful Lady Chapel were built in the Radiating Gothic style of the 14C.

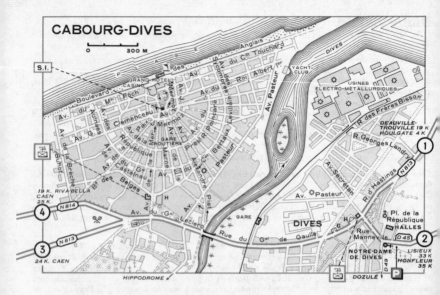

Before leaving the church look on the back of the west wall at the list carved in 1862 of the names of William's companions in arms on his expedition to England. Many have a familiar ring.

The Covered Market.—The magnificent timber roof of the 15 and 16C market is in good condition still.

The 16C Bois-Hibou manorhouse can be seen from the end of the Place de la République.

ENVIRONS

Bellengreville.—Zoo. *Open 8 a.m. to nightfall; 2·50 F.*

Troarn.—13C abbey ruins.

CAEN ***—Michelin maps ⑤④ ⑯, ⑤⑤ ⑪ ⑫—local maps pp. 61 and 62—pop. 114,398.

Caen, capital of Lower Normandy, industrial city, France's ninth port, cultural centre, was three-quarters destroyed in 1944 but has risen like a phoenix with a new-found vitality to rebuild with Caen stone to modern city plans. The churches and abbeys founded by William the Conqueror and Queen Matilda were spared war damage and still delight.

HISTORICAL NOTES

William the Bastard and Proud Matilda (11C).—Caen developed from the island at the confluence of the Rivers Orne and Odon which was fortified very early by the Normans but only grew in importance in the 11C. Then it became the favourite town of Duke William who was to leave his imprint on it for all time.

After his victory at Val-es-Dunes (commemorative column on the D 41 1 mile—1·5 km—west of Bellengreville) over the rebel barons of the Cotentin and Bessin Regions, William, now assured in his own Duchy, demanded the hand in marriage of Matilda of Flanders. The duke's cousin was not flattered at his proposal; "I would rather take the veil than be wed to a bastard," she replied (*see p. 94, the Beautiful Arlette*). The duke swallowed the insult, but later, mad with rage and love, rode straight to Lille and forced his way into the palace of the Count of Flanders. According to the Chronicler of Tours, he seized Matilda by her plaits, dragged her round the room, kicked her fiercely and leaving her gasping for breath, rode off at full gallop.

Matilda, beaten, consented to marry the duke and the marriage was celebrated in spite of the opposition of the pope who objected to the cousins' distant kinship. In 1059, Lanfranc (*see p. 52*) had the excommunication, which weighed heavily upon the duke, lifted. William and Matilda, in penance, founded two abbeys—the Abbaye aux Hommes and the Abbaye aux Dames, making Caen virtually a Benedictine city—and four hospitals.

When William left for England (*details p. 73*), the faithful Matilda assumed the regency for the Duchy of Normandy. Two years later, in 1068, she was crowned Queen of England at Westminster. When she died, in 1083, she was buried in the Abbaye aux Dames.

The Caen Battle.—The battle for Caen lasted for more than two months. Bombs poured down on 6 June 1944; the city was set alight and fire raged for eleven days. The central area was burnt out.

On 9 July the Canadians, who had taken Carpiquet airport, entered the town from the west, but the Germans who had fallen back to Vaucelles on the right bank of the Orne began to shell it in their turn.

Throughout the battle the citizens of Caen sought refuge in their famous buildings: 1,500 homeless camped out in the Abbaye aux Hommes; the Malherbe Lycée refectory was used as a hospital operating theatre and the dead were buried in its courtyards; the Good Saviour Hospice sheltered 4,000. The Allies were informed through the Resistance and the buildings were not bombed. The largest shelter was provided in the Fleury Quarry a mile south of the town where families remained in the underground passages until the end of July.

The final liberation ceremony took place at Vaucelles on 20 July, although another month was to pass before the last German shell had fallen on Caen.

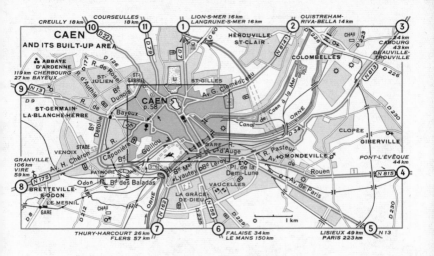

CAEN'S EXPANSION

A new town.—The destroyed central area has been entirely rebuilt since 1944, the more important historic buildings such as St. Peter's and St. John's Churches being safeguarded and others, such as the castle, being cleared of disfiguring surroundings.

The new university, which is modern and vast, has been erected north of the castle. New built up areas have sprung up all round the city outskirts while factories which were bombed out have been reconstructed in a designated area between the Orne, the Caen Canal and the sea and also outside the city.

The town, which is a good bit more healthy and much more open than it was, retains contact with the country through the Prairie, a wide area of greenery which juts deeply into the town.

Caen's Steel Industry.—Caen is the natural outlet for the iron ore mines of Lower Normandy which, with an annual production of over 3 million tons (the grades of ore being about 45%), are the second largest in France. This mineral wealth encouraged the establishment of heavy industry on a considerable scale locally just before the First World War.

The works and surrounding town of Mondeville-Colombelles were destroyed in 1944 and have since been entirely rebuilt on modern lines. The first blast furnace was relit on 11 December 1950 and production capacity is now 780,000 tons of steel a year.

The Seaport of Caen.—While it is the Orne that has made Caen a seaport since the beginning of time, it is Baron Cachin who, in the middle of the 19C, gave Caen its true seaport character. To link the town with the sea he had a canal nearly 9 miles—14 km—long dug parallel with the Orne, constructed a series of locks along it and converted Ouistreham into an outer port. Since it was first constructed, work has never ceased on the canal, deepening and widening it and adding new basins to keep pace with the requirements of the ever expanding steel industry.

Today the port of Caen with an annual traffic of nearly 2½ million tons chiefly derived from imports of coke, wood, hydrocarbons and exports of steel and food products, has four main docks—the St-Pierre, the Nouveau Bassin, the Calix and the Hérouville.

A dock 738×98 ft.—225×30 m—has been built at Ouistreham, and the sea channel deepened so that barges of up to 15,000 tons loaded with ore and ships of up to 580 ft.—180 m—in length will be able to sail up to Caen.

MAIN SIGHTS (tour: about 2 hours)

Abbaye aux Hommes**.—St. Stephen's Church and the abbey buildings, although different in style, form a single unit historically and even architecturally and should be seen together.

St. Stephen's** (Eglise St-Etienne).—St. Stephen's is the original church of the abbey founded by William the Conqueror (*details p. 56*) and of which Lanfranc was prior before becoming Archbishop of Canterbury (*details p. 52*). It was probably he who inspired the plans for the abbey which was begun in 1066 and solemnly consecrated before King William and Queen Matilda in 1077.

The church, which was badly damaged during the Wars of Religion, was well restored in the 17C by the then prior. It has been a parish church since the Concordat of 1801.

EXTERIOR.—Romanesque art has produced few more striking works than this completely unadorned façade of a gable wall, flanked by twin buttresses, pierced by three plain Romanesque doors and ten windows beneath rounded arches. All the severity of line of Ravenna and Lombardy it would appear were transmitted to the building by Lanfranc. But, in fact, the façade's austerity is countered by the glorious upward sweep of the tall and slender towers on either side. The first level is ornamented with plain blind fluting, the two above are pierced. The spires are Gothic and later—13C. (The turrets of the right tower have a typically Norman Gothic decoration—*details p. 18*.)

INTERIOR.—*Restoration work in progress.* The vast nave with wide rounded arches has little ornament. The construction of the sexpartite vaulting in the 12C modified the lines of the high windows.

The early 13C chancel with elegant central arches was the first to be built in the Norman Gothic style although the decorative motifs had been seen in the duchy for over a century.

William the Conqueror's tomb before the high altar is marked by a stone bearing his epitaph. The sarcophagus containing his body, which was buried beneath the lantern tower,

57

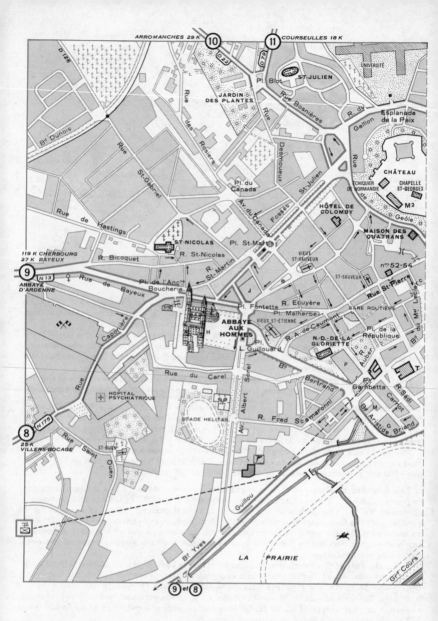

was desecrated when the Huguenots sacked the church in the 16C and his remains were thrown in the river during the Revolution.

The Paschal candelabrum to the left of the altar is 18C; the names and coats of arms on the wrought iron grille dividing the chancel from the nave are those of former abbots and priors.

There is a large 18C clock encased in wood on the first floor in the north transept.

Abbey Buildings*.—*Open 9 a.m. to noon and 4 to 7 p.m.; closed Tuesdays and one winter month; 1·50 F.; apply to the caretaker.*

The beautiful abbey buildings, reconstructed in the 18C by Brother Guillaume de la Tremblaye, master-builder of the Congregation of St-Maur (*see pp. 20 and 52*), now house the town hall and attendant offices.

The **woodwork**** inside is magnificent and from the cloister there is a very good view of the church towers and its south wall (*illustration p. 17*).

The tour begins in the parlour, a large room covered with an elliptical vault and with 18C panelled doors. The cloister has ribbed vaulting decorated, where the arches meet, with octagonal coffering. The west gallery leads to the former guests' wing.

The refectory, now a reception chamber, has broken barrel vaulting and rich oak panelling. The bold lines of the main staircase are enhanced by a magnificent wrought iron banister of 1760–1764.

From the great east court there is a good view of the abbey's long façade bordered with formal gardens laid out exactly as they were in the 18C.

The former chapterhouse, now the council chamber, has light panelling and the chapel sacristy, which is reached through a vestibule with a staircase with another wrought iron banister, has panelling in oak.

Returning to the cloister, you will get a wonderful **glimpse**** from the corner by the south and east galleries of St. Stephen's towers. Note, as you pass, the old board of monks' observances on the service room door leading into the church.

At the end of the tour you will see the west façade, which was never completed, and "Duke William's palace", one of the few traces remaining, though much restored, of the mediaeval abbey.

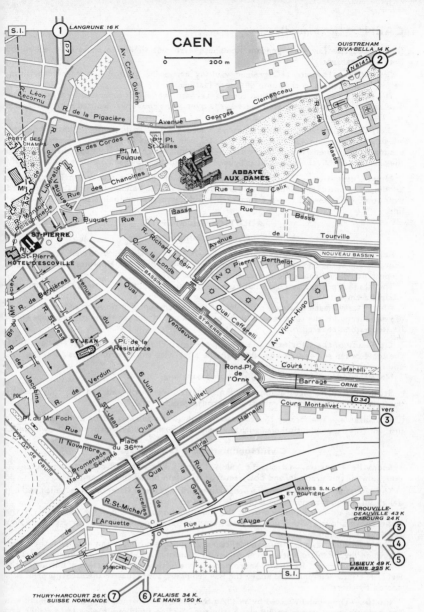

St. Peter's★★ (Eglise St-Pierre).—This parish church which the rich merchants of Caen endowed so often and so liberally is in striking contrast to the great abbeys. Its famous belfry, erected in 1308 through the generosity of a single parishioner, fell during the battle of 1944, but has since been rebuilt and is known once more as the king of all Norman belfries.

The façade is preceded by a Flamboyant porch.

The **east end**★★, which was built between 1518 and 1545, is a famous example of Renaissance architecture in which the richness of the ornament with pinnacles in tiers, urns and massive scrollwork balustrades is outstanding, following on the late Gothic which had become anaemic.

Inside, the architect grafted on to the Gothic ambulatory an opulent decoration which becomes ever more ornate as it approaches the chancel. The five radiating chapels form a delicately ornamental group of which the first chapel on the right is the most remarkable. The hanging keystones, in some cases deeply carved, appear almost to have the fragility of stalactites, although the one above the major altar supports a statue of St. Peter which weighs three tons.

Abbaye aux Dames★★.—The Abbaye aux Dames was founded by Queen Matilda (*details p. 56*), to complement the Abbaye aux Hommes.

The old abbey buildings, rebuilt in the Classical style in the 17C, were more severely damaged by the war than those of the Abbaye aux Hommes whose spires can be seen from the west front, rising in the distance above the far end of the Rue des Chanoines.

Church of the Holy Trinity★★.—The church, a squat Romanesque building, was largely completed by the end of the 11C. The spires, which should have given it a more graceful appearance, were destroyed during the Hundred Years War and were replaced in the early 18C by a clumsy balustrade.

NAVE.—The vast nave of nine bays is a good example of Romanesque architecture with round arches decorated with banded archivolts and a blind arcade encircling the triforium. The upper parts of the church were rebuilt when it was given pointed vaulting in the 12C.

TRANSEPT.—The transept crossing, which opens on to the nave beneath a round arch, is very wide. The beautiful chapel off the south transept, now serving as a chapterhouse, is 13C.

(It replaced two former dependant Romanesque chapels similar to those now leading off the north transept.)

CHANCEL.—The late IIC groined vaulting above the chancel has magnificent lines; below, in the centre, is the tomb of Queen Matilda.

The two storey apse is later than the chancel from which it is separated by a great beam. The historiated capitals are well carved; the oven vault above was painted with a fresco in the 17C.

CRYPT**.—*Go down a staircase (lower your head) from the south transept chapel.* The crypt, which was dedicated to St. Nicholas in the IIC, is in a remarkable state of preservation. The unsupported groined vaulting rests on sixteen columns which stand close together and divide the chamber into five. An attempt at figured decoration may be seen on some of the capitals.

New University.—The University is both one of the most modern in France by its buildings and one of the oldest by its foundation in 1432. The buildings, which are now spread over some 80 acres—33 ha—are remarkable architecturally for their size and simplicity of line.

ADDITIONAL SIGHTS
Religious Buildings

St. Nicholas' Church and Cemetery*.—*The church, now deconsecrated, is closed.* The church, built at the end of the IIC by monks from the Abbaye aux Hommes, has never been reconstructed, and therefore retains all its original style.

The façade is pierced by a beautiful Romanesque door with, most unusually for Normandy, a triple archivolt.

An old **burial ground** (*entrance to the left of the church—opening times according to the time of year*) surrounds the church enabling one to walk round and see the magnificent apse with its steep stone covered roof.

Our Lady of the Gloriette.—In this former Jesuit church, built between 1684 and 1689, the Ionic order reigns supreme, although the altar with the ciborium dates from the 18C and comes from the Abbaye aux Hommes.

Note the wrought ironwork and the wood panelling.

St. John's.—The picturesque St. John's quarter was burnt out and the church badly damaged. It has been totally rebuilt and reconsecrated.

St. Julian's.—The former church destroyed in 1944 was replaced by a modern building in 1958. This has an elliptical plan with the main wall forming a latticework of dark windows.

Civil Monuments and Old Houses

Escoville Mansion.—Nicolas Le Valois d'Escoville, a rich and ostentatious merchant, built himself this gracious, and now restored, mansion between 1535 and 1540.

The **courtyard*** has a harmony of proportion and a grace in its decoration which make it delightful—even if some of the façades have had to be rebuilt.

A beautiful dormer window crowns the main building at the end of the courtyard; to the right, above a loggia with a fine staircase, are two very pleasing lantern turrets resembling small circular temples.

The right wing has an unusual and felicitous arrangement of bays and windows; the niches at ground level contain statues of Judith and Holofernes, and David and Goliath; above are low reliefs of Perseus' Rescue of Andromeda on the left and the Abduction of Europa on the right. The intercolumniations above the low reliefs are adorned with the Escoville arms supported by cherubs.

Castle.—The citadel erected by William the Conqueror, which suffered considerably in the last war, now stands boldly alone, the surrounding buildings having been either destroyed or removed.

Enter up the approach ramp, which starts from below St. Peter's, and through the main gate. The uphill path immediately to the right leads to the site of Queen Matilda's Tower.

The platform commands a good view of the town while the Field Gate (Porte des Champs) is an interesting example of 14C military architecture.

Inside the walls the St. George Chapel, now a memorial to those killed in action in Normandy, is open (*10 a.m. to noon and 2 to 5.30 p.m.*) as are the Norman Exchequer, an example of architecture in William's time, and the **Fine Arts Museum** (M 1—*open 16 March to 30 September, 10 a.m. to noon, 2 to 6 p.m.; 1 October to 15 March, 10 a.m. to noon, 2 to 5 p.m. Closed Tuesdays, 1 January, Easter and Ascension Days, 1 May, 1 November and 25 December. Admission: 2 F*) and the Normandy Museum.

Normandy Museum (M 2).—*Same hours of opening as the Fine Arts Museum except closed also on public holidays; 1.50 F.*

This historical and ethnographic museum is in the governor's old lodging. Particular emphasis is laid on Normandy's development in the 19C.

Colomby Mansion, 6 Rue des Cordeliers.—Louis XIII mansion with a watch tower.

Nos. 52 and 54, Rue St-Pierre.—The finest wooden houses in Caen.

Quatrans House, 31 Rue de Geôle.—Picturesque front on the road.

ENVIRONS

Other tours: the Côte Fleurie (p. 73), Calvados Coast (p. 62), the Auge Region and Suisse Normande.

Churches and Castles in the Caen countryside

Ardenne Abbey*.—*4 miles—6 km—see map p. 61.* Leave Caen by ⑨, the N 13. Turn right in the abbey road and park the car in front of the 12C, restored, main gate on the right. Ardenne Abbey, founded in the 12C by the Premonstratensians, fell into ruin in the 19C and was further damaged during the war. The buildings now belong to two agricultural institutes

—*apply to each in turn to enter.* At the end, on the left of the first courtyard, is a very big tithe barn now covered by a single asymmetrical vaulted wooden roof.
The nave of the 13C **abbey church**—damaged outside—is a good example of pure Norman Gothic. *Restoration in progress.*

Biéville-sur-Orne; la Délivrande.—*Tour: 19 miles—31 km—about 1 hour.* Leave Caen by ① and at the top of the hill turn right into the D 60. After a right turn there is a panoramic view of Caen and its towers and further on of the Mondeville blast furnaces (*see p. 57*).

Biéville-sur-Orne.—The church façade with its blind arcades and oculi recalls those of Tuscany. Further on from a hilltop you will see the sea and seaside resorts, Ouistreham belfry and the spires of Our Lady at La Délivrande. Turn left into the D 35 before Hermanville.

La Délivrande.—*Description p. 63.*
Come out of La Délivrande by the D 7.

Epron.—Village reconstructed from the proceeds of a collection organised by French radio of old bank-notes.
At sunset, the view of Caen, as you drop down to the city, is wonderful.

Lasson; Rots; Secqueville-en-Bassin.—*Tour: 19 miles—31 km.* Leave Caen by ⑨, the N 13, the Bayeux road. Take the Rots road on the right.

Rots.—The Romanesque church has an attractive façade, though the door is 19C.
Continue along the D 170. Bear left in Rosel, at a road junction which has a farm on the right. Go through the village and turn right at the second bridge.

Lasson.—Lasson Castle consists of two Renaissance wings (*not open*).
Turn to continue straight on along the D 126.

Secqueville-en-Bassin.—The 11C church has a fine three-storey belfry with a 13C spire. The pure style nave and transept are decorated with blind arcades.
Return to the entrance to Secqueville and turn right into the D 93 and the N 13.

Cintheaux.—*9 miles—15 km—south of Caen along the N 158,* ⑥ *on the map.*
The village, known for its late 12C church, stands on the southern border of the Caen countryside, mining country with an occasional isolated slagheap.
The road from Caen to Falaise, beyond Cintheaux, passes through the terrain fought over by the Canadian 1st Army and its Polish units from 8 to 17 August 1944 (Caumensnil and Langannerie Cemeteries respectively—*see the Battle of Normandy p. 24*).

The Battlefields

The natural vigour of Normandy soon hid the scars of battle and few traces remain except at Omaha Beach (*see p. 123*) and the Le Hoc Point (*see p. 64*).
The tour takes one to the scenes of bitter fighting which took place southwest of Caen from 26 June to 4 August 1944.

Tour of the Odon.—*21 miles—33 km—about 1 hour.* Leave Caen by ⑨, the N 13. Take the D 9 on the left which goes through the village of Carpiquet and then beside the airfield, bitterly fought over by the Canadian 3rd Division and the German 12th SS Panzers. Continue a further 2 miles—3 km—along the D 9 before bearing left into the D 170 to Chaux. Turn left in the village after the church, into the D 89 which you follow through Tourville and across the national highway. You will then be in the line of the British thrust, which began at Tilly-sur-Seulles on 26 June in pouring rain, with the River Orne, to the southeast, as its objective. A monument to the Scottish 15th Division stands on the right.

Just as one expects to reach the floor of the Odon Valley the road turns sharply into a rocky ravine, hitherto camouflaged by thickets; the river has cut a kind of second valley within the valley. This second valley, with its obvious defensive advantages, proved cruelly difficult to take with the British advancing under heavy German fire from the far side of the valley. The crossing of the Odon finally cost more British lives than the crossing of the Rhine.

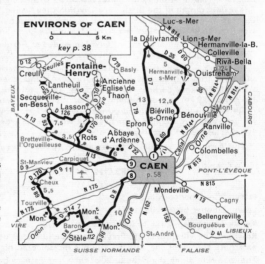

The road climbs the far slope.
At the top, turn left at a crossroads and go through Baron village. Turn right beyond a small stone monument surmounted by an iron cross (on the right) into William the Conqueror's Road, a raised and ancient Roman road. Near the D 8 crossroads, a stele has been erected in memory of the battles fought by the 43rd Wessex Division. **Hill 112** is also clearly visible—a strategic objective through the ages.
Take the D 8, left, towards Caen. The monument at the D 36 road junction recalls the operations of July 1944 which were marked by savage armoured fighting—the night attack of 15 July was made by the light of an artificial full moon produced by reflecting searchlight beams on low clouds. The D 8 and the N 175 bring you into Caen by ⑧.

The CALVADOS Coast *—Michelin map 54 ③ ④ and ⑭ to ⑯.

Calvados gets its name from a ship of the Spanish Armada, the *Salvador*, which was running for home after the defeat of 1588 and sank on the underwater rocks off Arromanches. Over the years the ship's name became so distorted as to be virtually unrecognisable.

The variety of the Calvados coastline reflects the hinterland: the open farmlands of the Caen countryside are edged by a perfectly flat shore, the undulating Bessin pasturelands by the indented coast west of Asnelles marked by low and often crumbling cliffs (*see p. 13*).

The coast between the Orne and the Vire, the **Côte de Nacre** or Mother of Pearl Coast, coast of the **D-Day* beaches** of June 1944, is described below. The Côte Fleurie, east of Cabourg, will be found on p. 73.

THE D-DAY LANDING

The Dawn of D-Day.—The formidable armada of 4,266 barges and landing craft and the accompanying warships and naval escorts, preceded by minesweepers, set sail from the ports and harbours of southern England on the night of 5 June 1944 (*for preparation for the Invasion and the Battle of Normandy see p. 24*). Above the ships, on which no light showed, airborne troops were flown out and landed in two detachments at either end of the invasion front. The British 6th Division charged with guarding the left flank of the operation quickly took the Bénouville–Ranville Bridge, since named Pegasus Bridge (*see below*) after the airborne insignia, and stirred up trouble in the enemy positions between the Orne and Dives Rivers, so preventing enemy reinforcements approaching from the east and south. West of the Vire the American 101st and 82nd Divisions attacked important positions such as Ste-Mère-Eglise (*details p. 138*) or cleared the Utah Beach units.

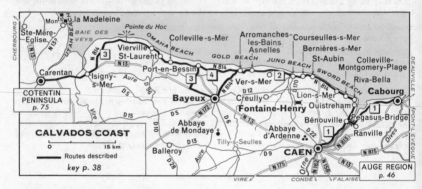

The British Sector.—Preliminary bombing and shelling, without destroying Hitler's Atlantic Wall completely, succeeded, and this was what counted, in totally disorganising the German defence. The land forces, mostly preceded by Commandos, charged with destroying the most dangerous pockets of resistance, were therefore able to make contact with their objectives, scattered along the three beachheads. The hastily prepared German counter-attacks were crushed under naval bombardment. The destruction of enemy strongpoints —Douvres resisted until 17 June—was the major objective immediately following the landing.

Sword Beach.—The Anglo-French Commandos landed at Colleville-Plage, Lion-sur-Mer and St-Aubin and after taking the Riva-Bella strongpoint and the more obdurate ones at Lion and Langrune (captured only on 7 June) linked up with the airborne troops at Pegasus Bridge. The main strength of the British 3rd Division then landed. This zone, clearly exposed to the German long-range guns at Le Havre, became the real hinge of the front. No major Allied attack was launched against the right bank of the Orne until 18 July.

Juno Beach.—The Canadian 3rd Division landed at Bernières and Courseulles and reached Creully by 5 p.m. A month later they were the first to enter Caen.

Gold Beach.—The British 50th Division landed at Ver-sur-Mer and Asnelles in the morning and, by a flanking movement, had captured Arromanches by the afternoon, enabling the artificial Mulberry harbour to be brought into position. The 47th Commando advanced 12½ miles—20 km—through enemy territory and took Port-en-Bessin on the night of 7 June. On 9 June the British linked up with the Americans from Omaha Beach and, on 12 June, with the taking of Carentan, the final link with the US troops at Utah Beach was made, thus establishing a solid beachhead.

The American Sector.—The **Omaha** and **Utah** landings are described on pp. 123 and 76.

① FROM CABOURG TO CAEN

16 miles—26 km—about 1 hour

Cabourg**.—*Description p. 55.*

Leave Cabourg by ④, the N 814.

Merville-Franceville.—*Place to stay (see p. 36).*

Ranville.—The village was the first place to be liberated on French soil, being captured by parachute troops of the 13th Battalion, Lancashire Fusiliers, at 2.30 a.m. on 6 June 1944.

The road runs along the right bank of the Orne Estuary before crossing the river and then the canal over Pegasus Bridge.

Pegasus Bridge.—The two Ranville–Bénouville Bridges were taken after a brief engagement on the night of 5/6 June by the British 5th Paratroop Brigade; the canal bridge, to commemorate the feat, was renamed Pegasus Bridge.

The road continues down the left bank.

Bénouville.—*Description p. 63.*
There is a good view of the Colombelles steel complex before you reach Caen.

Caen***.—*Description p. 56.*

2 *FROM CAEN TO BAYEUX along the Coast

35 miles—56 km—about 1¾ hours

Caen***.—*Description p. 56.*

The road from Caen to Riva-Bella (N 814A) lies west of the canal, following the course of the Lower Orne. There is a good view of the steel complex of Colombelles on the far bank.

Bénouville.—Bénouville Château is an imposing and well preserved 18C edifice with a characteristic porticoed façade overlooking a court and a monumental grand staircase.

A small monument, typical of many right along the coast where the D-Day landings took place, commemorates in this instance the capture of the town hall (at the crossroads near Pegasus Bridge) by the 5th Paratroop Brigade at 11.45 p.m. on 5 June 1944.

Ouistreham*.—*Description p. 124.*

Riva-Bella.—*Description p. 124.*

The N 814 follows the shoreline of the Côte de Nacre from Riva-Bella to Asnelles.

Colleville-Montgomery-Plage.—The 4th Anglo-French Commando landed on this beach at dawn on 6 June; in honour of the commander of the British forces, the town added his name to its own and erected him a statue.

Hermanville-la-Brèche.—*Place to stay (see Hermanville-sur-Mer, p. 36).* The old French battleship *Courbet* was sunk off the beach to act as blockship or primitive sea wall to protect Sword Beach at the time of the 1944 landing.

Lion-sur-Mer—*Place to stay (see p. 36).* This family seaside resort has a **castle** built in the 16 and 17C now surrounded by a park (*not open*) and a church with an early 12C Romanesque tower and fine capitals of the same date.

Luc-sur-Mer.—*Place to stay (see p. 36).* This seaside resort, which is known for its bracing air —the rocks at low tide are covered with seaweed—has a spa establishment offering hydro-sodium-iodate cures and a marine zoology laboratory. The **Municipal Park*** (35 Rue de la Mer—*open 9 a.m. to noon, 2 to 7 p.m.*) provides an oasis of greenery. The local "sight" is the skeleton of a whale washed up on the beach in 1885.

> **La Délivrande.**—*Excursion of 1 mile—2 km—by the D 83.*
> The tall spires of the **Basilica of Our Lady of La Délivrande** mark from far across the Caen countryside the oldest Marian pilgrimage in Normandy.
> The 19C Neo-Gothic edifice contains a highly venerated Black Madonna. The largest of the pilgrimages are on the feast days to the Virgin (15 August and 8 September) and on the Coronation of the Virgin of La Délivrande (Thursday following 15 August).
>
> The **Convent of the Faithful Virgin** (last house on the Cresserons road, D 35. *Ring at the second door—offering*) has a chapel successfully furnished and decorated with 1931 Lalique chromium and glass, also a shrine to the African St. Florida and a modern lacquer Stations of the Cross.

Langrune-sur-Mer.—*Place to stay (see p. 36).* The resort's name has the same derivation from the Scandinavian as Greenland: *land groen*—given possibly on account of the seaweed exposed on the rocks at low tide.

The 13C **church** has a beautiful two-storey belfry reminiscent of that of St. Stephen's in Caen.

St-Aubin-sur-Mer.—*Place to stay (see p. 36).* Bracing seaside resort.

Bernières-sur-Mer.—*Place to stay (see p. 36).* The French Canadian "Chaudière" Regiment landed on this beach. It was also where the press and radio reporters came ashore.

The church's 13C **belfry*** with three levels and a stone spire is justly famous, standing 220 ft. tall—67 m. The nave and aisles are Romanesque—the vaulting has been reconstructed—and the raised chancel 15C.

> **Alternative road* by Thaon and Fontaine-Henry.**—*7 miles less—11 km—along the D 22 and D 170, but reckon an extra hour's walking and sightseeing. Leave Caen by ⑩ the D 22.*
> **Thaon Old Church*.**—*½ hour by a downhill path off the D 170, 500 yds. from Thaon Parish Church or 1,200 yds. from Fontaine-Henry Church. Ask for permission to visit the church, accompanied, except on Mondays, at the house at the bottom of the valley (tip).* The small 12C Romanesque church (deconsecrated) stands out well against the valley greenery and running spring. Outside, the flat east end is decorated with blind arcades, the main building all round with a modillioned cornice. The belfry, with a pyramid roof and deep wide bays, is one of the most original in Normandy.
> Inside, the nave and chancel, in which blind arcades are the only decoration, have great purity of line and the capitals of the main arches (now bricked up) are intricately carved.
> **Fontaine-Henry**.**—The **château**** (*open Thursdays, Saturdays and Sundays, 2.30 to 6.30 p.m.; 2·50 F.; time: ½ hour; ring*) was built in the 15 and 16C on the foundations of a 13C fortress and is a fine example of Renaissance architecture (*illustration p. 19*).
> An immense steeply sloping slate roof, deeper than the building is tall, covers the main construction which stands on the site of the old keep. The decorated pepperpot tower is 15C. The wing is 16C and appears almost chiselled so detailed is the stonework.
> Inside, the most remarkable items are the François I staircase and the sculpture, though there are besides furniture, pictures and mementoes. The chapel is 13C.
> The 13C **parish church** has beautiful blind arcades.

Courseulles-sur-Mer.—*Description p. 79.*

Ver-sur-Mer.—This minute resort—pop. 580—was the focal point in the main beachhead for the British forces in the Gold Beach sector—a fact commemorated in the monument at the coast and village crossroads.

The village has a **church** with a massive 11C Romanesque **tower***, four storeys high which is original (the rest has been rebuilt) and a **lighthouse and radio beam** (*open 1 April to 30 September, 9 a.m. to noon and 2 to 7 p.m.; 1 October to 31 March, 10 a.m. to noon and 2 to 4 p.m.* Approach along a road off the D 112). The light with a beam of 28 nautical miles works in conjunction with the Cherbourg and Nab Tower (Isle of Wight) lights guiding Channel shipping.

After Ver-sur-Mer the view opens out to include the Arromanches cliffs.

The CALVADOS Coast* (concluded)

Asnelles.—This small seaside resort found itself at the eastern end of the artificial harbour constructed at Arromanches in 1944 (see *diagram p. 45*). There is a good view of Arromanches, cliffs and roadstead from the rebuilt sea wall promenade.

The road rises between Asnelles and Arromanches, to the eastern edge of the Bessin Plateau, when the Romanesque Church of St. Como comes into view.

Arromanches-les-Bains.—*Description p. 45.*

The road goes through the Bessin pasturelands between Arromanches and Bayeux.

Bayeux**.—*Description p. 50.*

③ *FROM BAYEUX TO CARENTAN by Omaha Beach

36 miles—58 km—about 1¾ hours—plus ½ hour on foot Rtn

The D 100 is liable to be flooded by the River Aure in winter, in which case take the D 6 out of Bayeux.

Bayeux**.—*Description p. 50.*

Leave Bayeux by ⑥, N 13, turn right into the D 100.

Tour-en-Bessin.—The church has a 12C doorway and an early 13C tower surmounted by a spire above the transept crossing. Inside, the beauty of the early 15C Gothic chancel is very striking, as are the graceful lines of the apsidal chapels with their slender columns around the central stained glass window. Scenes depicting the months of the year can be seen carved on the right on the small columns of the blind arcades.

The D 100 crosses the Aure Valley at Port-en-Bessin where the river disappears into the Fosses de Soucy marshes.

Escures Tower.—¼ *hour on foot Rtn. Leave the car on the D 100 and walk along a private path.* Good view from the tower of the rolling Bessin countryside.

Port-en-Bessin*.—*Place to stay (see p. 36).* "Port", as it is known locally, lies hidden in a hollow in the marl cliffs, a lively and picturesque small seaside resort.

The **harbour*** consists of an inner basin enclosed by two semicircular granite jetties. Fishing boats set out for the waters off Devon and Cornwall and in 1968 returned with some 9,000 tons of fish. This is auctioned very early on Mondays, Wednesdays and Thursdays. From the end of one of the jetties you can see the crumbling cliffs of the Bessin coast from Cape Manvieux to the Percée Point. There is a 17C Vauban defence tower on the west cliff in the far distance.

The road continues beyond Port-en-Bessin to Grandcamp through the Bessin meadows divided by trees and hedges.

Omaha Beach.—*Description p. 123.*

Le Hoc Point.—The point is one of the few places in Normandy which still gives the impression of having been a battlefield. To reduce a German battery which would have been particularly dangerous to troops landing on Omaha Beach, the American commander ordered a naval bombardment from the American warship *Texas*. After 600 salvoes of 14-inch shells the 2nd Rangers Battalion climbed the cliffs with rope ladders and took the position by assault at dawn on 6 June. A granite stele at the edge of the cliff marks the **battlefield** (*approach by the Le Hoc Point road, branching off the N 814, coming from Bayeux*).

The view opens out over Les Veys Bay and the east coast of the Cotentin Peninsula as you approach Grandcamp.

Grandcamp-les-Bains.—*Place to stay (see p. 36).* Fishing port and seaside resort with a sand and shingle beach.

Isigny-sur-Mer.—This milk and butter centre which has been famous since the 17C was badly damaged in 1944. *The Isigny Milk Cooperative is open 15 June to 15 September at 10 and 11 a.m. (the best times) and 2.30 and 3.30 p.m. except Sundays and holidays; time: about ½ hour.*

Carentan.—*See p. 155.*

CAROLLES
—Michelin map ㊾ ⑦—7 miles—11 km—south of Granville—local map p. 119—pop. 653—*Place to stay (see p. 36).*

Carolles, a small village with a sand beach at the bottom of the cliff, lies on the last headland on the west coast of the Cotentin Peninsula. On the far side of the headland is Mont-St-Michel Bay with immense stretches of sand at low tide and the island on the horizon.

ENVIRONS (ask the way locally)

The Pignon Butor*.—½ *mile—1 km—or 1 hour on foot Rtn.*
The **view*** from the edge of the cliff extends, north, along the coast to Granville Rock and, west, in clear weather, to the Grouin Point and Cancale in Britanny.

Vauban Hut* (Cabane Vauban).—½ *mile—1 km—plus ¼ hour on foot Rtn.* View of Mont-St-Michel.

The Painters' Valley (Vallée des Peintres).—¾ *hour on foot Rtn.* A small green valley.

The Lude Valley.—1 *hour on foot Rtn.* The small valley flows out into a lonely rock surrounded bay, the Port du Lude.

CARROUGES Castle
*—Map ㊿ ②—south of Carrouges—*Place to stay (see p. 37).*

This immense castle belonged, until 1936 when it was bought by the nation, to the Le Veneur de Tillières, a famous Norman family, and local lords of Carrouges, who had owned it since the 12C.

Castle*.—*Open 1 May to 30 September, 9 a.m. to noon, 2 to 6 p.m.; 1 October to Easter, 10 a.m. to noon, 1.30 to 4 p.m.; closed Tuesdays; time: about ¾ hour; 2 F.*

The lodge or redoubt is 16C. The castle, itself surrounded by a moat, was constructed largely during the reign of Henri IV in the late 16C, early 17C, to replace a fortress built above the village at the top of the hill. Although the new site appears of little military value, it in fact gave a better command of the road up the Maine Valley (now the D 16).

The first floor contains the state rooms where fine Renaissance and Classical style decorations provide a background to rich furnishings. The **portrait gallery** is particularly interesting.

Caudebec, which for many years enjoyed the status of being capital of the Caux Region, has
been built in the form of an amphitheatre facing the Seine where the Ste-Gertrude Valley runs
into the river.

It lies at the place where the tidal bore (*details p. 140*), driven further upstream by the
Seine embankment, is highly spectacular at times.

The fine Church of Our Lady was virtually undamaged by the fire which swept the town in
June 1940. Also preserved were the three old houses to the left of the church which give an
idea of what Caudebec must once have looked like.

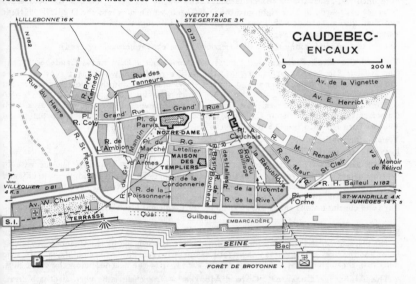

CHURCH OF OUR LADY* (tour: ¼ hour)

Leave the car on the Place du Marché, except on Saturdays when the market, which has
been held on the same spot since 1390, is in full swing.

This fine Flamboyant edifice which Henri IV described as ''the most beautiful chapel in the
kingdom'' was built between 1425 and 1539.

Exterior.—The belfry adjoining the south wall has a delicately worked upper part surmounted by a stone tiara shaped spire which had to be restored in the 19C after being struck
by lightning.

The west face is pierced by three beautiful Flamboyant doorways and, above, a remarkable
rose window surrounded by small statues.

Interior.—Immediately noticeable are the general inner proportions, the lack of transept
and the triforium and tracery which are the areas most characteristically Flamboyant.

The 17C font, on the left, is decorated with intricately carved panels; the great 16C organ
has never been put back in its original setting.

The stained glass windows are 16C, the most outstanding being those of St. Peter beside
Christ Crucified, on the left above the high altar, and, on the right, the Coronation of the
Virgin and St. Paul. Some attractive old
statues which have been cleaned and now
appear in all their original colouring and
character may be seen in the side chapels.

Go, right, round the chancel.

Chapel of the Holy Sepulchre.—The chapel
inspired Fragonard to paint a picture of
it. Beneath the 16C baldachin a recumbent Christ, carved in incredible detail,
faces some very large stone statues—all
come from Jumièges Abbey. The *pietà*
between the windows is 15C.

Lady Chapel (axial chapel).—The chapel
is famous for its **keystone***, a 7 ton monolith, upheld only by the dependent
arching and forming a 13 ft.—4 m—
pendentive. This feat by the architect
Guillaume Le Tellier, who lies buried in
the chapel, is commemorated in a plaque
beneath the right window.

ADDITIONAL SIGHT

The Templars' House.—*Open from
June to the end of August, 2 to 5 p.m.,
Sundays only.*

This precious specimen of 13C civil
architecture retains its two original gable
walls intact—the interior has been considerably restored.

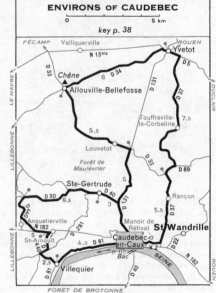

ENVIRONS OF CAUDEBEC

CAUDEBEC-EN-CAUX★ *(concluded)*

ENVIRONS

Ste-Gertrude; Villequier★.—*Tour: 13 miles—21 km—about ¾ hour. The trip to Villequier can also be made by boat (Sundays and holidays only out of season); apply at the Caudebec landing stage, Quai Guilbaud; ☏ 124.* Leave Caudebec by the Yvetot road and bear left into the D 40.

Ste-Gertrude.—The small church, which was consecrated in 1519 and is Flamboyant in character, stands in picturesque surroundings. Inside, is a rare 15C stone tabernacle.

Continue along the D 40, the D 30 on the left and next the D 440 going towards Anquetierville until you reach the N 182 crossroads. Take the N 182 going left and just before the entrance to St-Arnoult bear right into the D 440 again which runs into the D 281. Turn right and then into a steep downhill road on the left to Villequier.

Villequier★. *Description p. 154.*

Return to Caudebec along the D 81 *(described in the opposite direction p. 144).*

Tour of the Caux Plateau★.—*19 miles—30 km—about 1 hour.* Leave Caudebec by the Rue St-Clair and, bearing right, turn into the Rétival road from which, as it runs along the top of a low escarpment, there are good brief views of the bend in the river. At the bottom of a steep descent, turn left into the D 37, which goes up a delightful small **valley★** with scattered thatched farmhouses, now, in some cases, converted into country houses. Rich Caux farmsteads, half hidden in the trees, can be seen between Touffreville-la-Corbeline and Yvetot. Turn left into the D 5 to enter the town where you turn left.

Yvetot.—*Description p. 68.*

Leave Yvetot by the D 34 which goes to Allouville-Bellefosse.

Allouville-Bellefosse.—The village is well known for its **oak tree★**, the most famous tree in Normandy and at 1,000 years, one of the oldest in France. To keep it standing the trunk and biggest branches have had to be supported. Two superimposed chapels have been built into the hollow trunk. *To visit apply at the Gros Chêne Café—guide.*

Turn and continue along the D 33; after Louvetot turn right into the D 131 for Caudebec.

The CAUX Region ★—Michelin map 52 ② to ⑤ and ⑪ to ⑮.

The plateau, which is monotonous but prosperous, is bordered by the Channel, the Lower Seine and the Bresle Valley. It is known for its impressive coastline where holidaymakers, who delight in the region's natural beauty, return each year to the beaches below the chalk cliffs.

The Alabaster Coast or "Côte d'Albatre".—The chalk cliffs with alternate strata of flint and yellow marl are worn away ceaselessly by the combined action of the tides and the weather. The Etretat needle rocks and underwater shelves a mile from the present shore indicate the former coastline. At the particularly exposed point of the Cape de la Hève erosion is 6 ft. a year—2 m; the water is milky with chalk, and flints are pounded endlessly upon the beaches. The **valleuses** or dry hollows cut into every cliff top as far as the eye can see are dry valleys, which, overcome by the retreating coastline, are now isolated and hang more or less suspended in mid-air; only abundant water courses actually reach the sea. Ports and harbours have been constructed from the natural inlets and seaside resorts use the hanging valleys as means of access to beaches and the sea.

The Caux Farmsteads.—Seen from a distance, the farms appear as green oases but as you approach the plan becomes evident: 6 ft. high embankments topped by a double row of oaks, beeches or elms protect the **farmstead** from the wind. This comprises a meadow of some 5 to 7 acres—2 to 3 ha—planted with apple trees in the centre of which stand the half-timbered farmhouse and other buildings. The entrance is often through a monumental gateway. Farms have their own ponds, wells and cisterns although with mains water the latter have now often been replaced by water-towers.

Caux cattle-raising procedure is nothing if not unusual, including putting cattle and horses out on a tether in spring. Milk—the chief source of income—is sent to the towns of the Lower Seine or the butter and cheese factories in the valleys.

1 FROM LE TRÉPORT TO DIEPPE

21 miles—33 km—about 1 hour

Le Tréport*.—*Description p. 150.*

Mers-les-Bains. *Place to stay (p. 36).* Twin resort with Le Tréport on the north bank of the Bresle.

Criel-Plage.—*Place to stay (p. 36).*

Biville.—While hiding in a local farm after being hoisted up the cliffs the Royalists plotted unsuccessfully to kidnap Napoleon in 1803.

Bracquemont.—The church of this small village has a brilliantly coloured series of stained glass windows by Henderycksen.

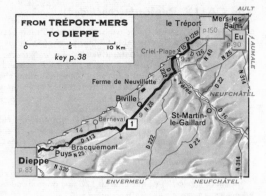

FROM TRÉPORT-MERS TO DIEPPE
key p. 38

Puys.—*Place to stay (see p. 36).* This pleasant resort was launched by the son of Alexander Dumas who had died there in 1870. A monument on the beach recalls one of the most bloody episodes in the Dieppe raid of 19 August 1942 (see p. 82) when the Royal Regiment of Canada landed and was massacred before reaching its objective.

From the Chapel of Our Lady of Succour (N.D. de Bon Secours): good view of Dieppe.

Dieppe**.—*Description p. 82.*

2 *FROM DIEPPE TO ÉTRETAT by the coast road

58 miles—93 km—about 3 hours—plus 1¾ hours sightseeing

The winding road (best light in the morning) passes by a whole string of beach resorts built at the mouths of small coastal streams or hidden away in deep suspended valleys. *There are long stretches of winding road and hidden turnings—narrow in Senneville.*

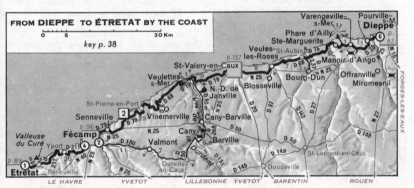

FROM DIEPPE TO ÉTRETAT BY THE COAST
key p. 38

Dieppe**.—*Description p. 82.*

Pourville-sur-Mer.—*Place to stay (see p. 36).* This seaside resort, pleasantly situated near jagged cliffs, has re-arisen from the ruins resulting from the commando raid of 19 August 1942 (*details p. 82*) when a Canadian Regiment and the Cameron Highlanders landed to the sound of the pipes, inflicted severe damage on the enemy and under cover of the navy and through the sacrifice of their own rearguard, re-embarked early in the afternoon.

Varengeville-sur-Mer*.—The village houses lie scattered in small groups along the deeply embanked roads in a true Norman countryside which has always attracted painters.

The church, dating from the 11, 13 and 16C and decorated with a stained glass window of the Tree of Jesse by Georges Braque (buried in the cemetery), has a beautiful **site***.

> **Ango Manor*.**—¼ mile—0·5 km—from Varengeville. Description p. 84.

> **Ailly Lighthouse*.**—Excursion of ½ mile—1 km—from the D 75—plus ¼ hour sightseeing. Open 8 a.m. to 1 hour before the light is lit—guided tour; tip. From the lighthouse upper platform, there is a 40-mile **view*** along the cliffs.

Ste-Marguerite.—*Place to stay (see p. 36).* The 12C church, which has no transept, was considerably remodelled in the 16C. Inside, four of the original **arches*** remain on the north side; those on the south date from 1528. The second column on the right is twisted and scattered with shells; the high altar dates from 1160 and is one of the very few to exist still today.

> **Bourg-Dun.**—2 miles—3·5 km—by the D 237 starting from St-Aubin. The Church of Our Lady is a vast composite edifice, outwardly remarkable for its **tower*** built on a massive square 13C base. The hatchet shaped roof is 17C. Go through the Renaissance door into the south aisle. Only the base of the roodscreen remains to support statues of St. Anthony and St. Sebastian. Beneath Flamboyant vaulting in the south transept are a Renaissance bay and piscina; the beautiful south aisle through three wide bays off the chancel was added in the 14C. The font in the north aisle is Renaissance.

Veules-les-Roses.—*Place to stay (see p. 36).* The seaside resort lies sheltered in a small valley which is particularly attractive higher up. **St. Martin's Church** in the town itself is 16 and 17C with a 13C lantern. Inside are five 16C twisted, carved limestone columns and ancient statues.

> **Blosseville.**—1 mile—2 km—by the D 37. The church, surmounted by a 12C belfry, possesses beautiful Renaissance stained glass windows and some old statues.

St-Valery-en-Caux.—*Tour: ¼ hour. Description p. 137.*

Veulettes-sur-Mer.—*Place to stay (see p. 36).* The 11 and 13C church stands halfway up a hill overlooking the seaside resort in the wide green valley below.

The CAUX Region* (concluded)

Senneville.—The drive's finest panorama is to be seen between Senneville and Fécamp from a belvedere with a viewing table by Our Lady of Salvation (N.D. du Salut—see p. 96).

Alternative route* by the Durdent Valley.—*Extra distance: 2 miles—3 km.*
Between Veulettes and the junction of the D 268 and D 131, follow the route indicated below through the Durdent Valley. Continue along the D 50 to Ourville where you take the road which follows the Valmont Valley to Fécamp.

Valmont*.—*Guided tours, 10 a.m. to noon and 2 to 6 p.m., except Sundays during the season and Thursdays. Time: ¼ hour. Admission: 1.50 F.*
Valmont Abbey, founded in the 12C was entirely rebuilt in the 16C and then reconstructed in the 18C by the Maurists after a fire. Of the old abbey there remain only the Renaissance chancel, and it has no roof, and the **Lady Chapel***, which is intact. The chapel is beautifully graceful with highly ornate but still delicate vaulting and five 16C stained glass windows depicting the Life of the Virgin. Above the altar is a tiny and exquisite room in which hangs an Annunciation. To the right a low relief illustrates the Baptism of Christ. The altar cross is 12C and once stood in the monks' burial ground.

Fécamp**.—*Tour: 1½ hours. Description p. 95.*

Yport.—*Place to stay (see p. 36).*

The Curé Valleuse*.—The *valleuse* or suspended dry valley is the most typical of the Caux Region (see p. 66 on suspended valleys). At high tide, the sea breaks against the foot of the cliff, making a thunderous noise in the tunnel hollowed out originally as a way down to the beach at low tide—*access to the tunnel no longer allowed.*

Etretat**.—*Description p. 88.*

③ FROM ÉTRETAT TO LE HAVRE by the Lézarde Valley
21 miles—33 km—about 1 hour

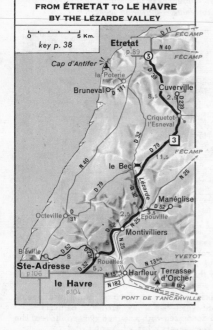

FROM ÉTRETAT TO LE HAVRE
BY THE LÉZARDE VALLEY

key p. 38

Étretat**.—*Description p. 88.*
The road goes inland up a small valley on to the plateau.

Cuverville.—*Excursion of 2 miles—2·5 km— by the D 239 from Criquetot-l'Esneval.* The writer, André Gide, is buried in the small church cemetery.
The road drops again, along the pleasant Lézarde Valley.

Bec Castle.—*Not open.* The 12–16C castle has an enhancing setting of trees and still waters.

Manéglise.—*Excursion of 2½ miles—3·5 km —by the D 52 starting from Epouville.* The small church is one of the most graceful examples of Romanesque architecture in Normandy. In spite of its minuteness, the 12C nave is flanked by aisles.

Montivilliers.—*Description p. 155.*
The road runs away from the Lézarde by cutting through the small Rouelles Valley.

Alternative route** by Ste-Adresse.—*Extra distance: 2 miles—3 km.* Starting from Rouelles make for Ste-Adresse by way of the D 231 and D 52 through Bléville.

Ste-Adresse**.—Turn sharp right immediately after the post office into the Rue de Vitanval which enables you to join the itinerary described on p. 106.
You come into Le Havre by the Ingouville Hill. The Rue du 329ᵉ and Rue Félix-Faure afford views of the harbour.

Le Havre**.—*Description p. 102.*

④ *THE DURDENT VALLEY, from Veulettes to Yvetot
20 miles—32 km—about 1 hour

The Durdent, which flows into the sea at Veulettes, has cut a wide valley across the plateau.

Veulettes-sur-Mer.—*Description p. 67.*

Janville Chapel.—*Excursion of ½ mile—1 km—from Paluel by the D 68—plus ¼ hour on foot Rtn.* Continue beyond a sharp right turn along the D 68 and after Viard farm bear left to the Chapel of Our Lady of Janville, isolated on the edge of the plateau. Inside this old pilgrimage church are a wrought iron chancel grille and some small painted panels.

Cany-Barville.—The church, on the left bank, rebuilt in the 16C in its original pointed arch style, has a 13C belfry. Two 16C **carved panels*** at the entrance show the Virgin of the Seven Swords and St. Martin.

Barville.—The small church has a delightful **setting*** between two arms of the River Durdent. The drive is particularly pleasant between Cany-Barville and Grainville-la-Teinturière when the road runs through a beech avenue and you get a close view of Cany Château, a lovely late Louis XIII building (*not open*).

The valley keeps its rural character despite the factories between Grainville and Héricourt.

Yvetot.—Yvetot, the legendary capital of an imaginary kingdom made famous in a song by Béranger, is, in fact, a large market town on the Caux Plateau. Its church, **St. Peter's**, is particularly outstanding for the huge **stained glass windows**** by Max Ingrano which form the walls and are dazzling. The colours, soft at the entrance, become brilliant at the centre where the Virgin and Apostles can be seen around the Crucified Christ. Other panels show the saints of France, founders of religious orders and great saints of the Rouen diocese.

CERISY-LA-FORÊT —Michelin map ⑤④ ⑭—5 miles—8·5 km—west of Balleroy.

The old 11C abbey at Cerisy is a remarkable example of Norman Romanesque architecture.

Abbey Church★.—*Tour: ¼ hour. Son et Lumière performances 14 July to 31 August on Saturdays, 10 p.m. in July, 9.30 p.m. in August.*

The nave, although now comprising only three bays where once it had seven, still has a remarkable elevation: a gallery runs above the main arches; rounded arcs crown the upper windows; the chancel and apse continue the lines of the three levels of the nave giving the vessel unity. The chancel has a wooden roof, the apse groined vaulting with fine ribs.

Turn right as you come out of the church and go through a small door to see the abbey from an unusual and attractive angle: the flat east end with its steep roof, the massive but low belfry and the apse quartered by turrets.

Conventual Buildings.—Restored. *Guided tours, Easter to 11 November, Sundays and holidays, 2.30 to 7 p.m.; 1 July to 15 September, weekdays, 10 a.m. to noon and 2.30 to 7 p.m. Admission: 2.50 F; leaving through the tunnel: 1 F.*

Monks' Parlour.—Remains of a dungeon, at the back on the left, with 15 and 16C graffiti.

Abbots' Chapel.—The chapel built in the 13C from a gift by St. Louis is a good example of Gothic architecture. There is a piscina beneath twin rounded arches, on the right.

Presidial.—The room, still called the Judgement Room, contains furniture, documents, MSS.

CHARENTONNE VALLEY —Michelin maps ⑤⑤ ⑭ ⑮, ⑥⓪ ④.

This swift running river, which is a tributary of the Risle and full of fish, winds, sometimes solitary, through the damp valley grasslands.

FROM LA RIVIÈRE-THIBOUVILLE TO ST-ÉVROULT-NOTRE-DAME-DU-BOIS
34 miles—54 km—about 1½ hours—plus ¼ hour sightseeing

As you come out of La Rivière-Thibouville, the Nassandres sugar beet factory adds a touch of modern industry to the Risle Valley landscape.

St. Eligius' Chapel (St-Eloi).—*Excursion of 1 mile—2 km—by the D 46 from Nassandres. Access and description p. 126.*

Serquigny.—The church, with a chequered façade of black flint and white stone, has a Romanesque doorway. Inside, on the left, are a Renaissance chapel with stained glass windows of the same period; four massive round pillars which support the belfry; modern stained glass in the right chapel and chapel off the chancel; old wooden statues in the nave.

The road from Serquigny to Anceins often approaches the river and as it runs beside it you get glimpses of local castles and the sharply pointed belfries of country churches.

Fontaine-l'Abbé.—The church, next to the Louis XIII castle in this attractive Norman village, contains two carved and painted Renaissance panels on either side of the choir and some colourful banners of the local Brotherhood of Charity (see p. 27).

Menneval.—The village lies in one of the most attractive folds in the valley and the church is delightful. The Brotherhood of Charity is the oldest in the region, dating from 1060 (see p. 27).

Bernay.—*Tour: ¼ hour. Description p. 53.*

Broglie.—*Description p. 53.*

Alternative road by St-Denis-d'Augerons.—*Extra distance: 4 miles—7 km.* The road, the D 107, does not cross the river but goes up the green Guiel Valley to Montreuil-l'Argillé, St-Denis-d'Augerons, St-Aquilin-d'Augerons, and back to Montreuil-l'Argillé.

St-Denis-d'Augerons.—From the war memorial, near a beech wood, there is an attractive view of the Norman countryside highlighted by the two village churches of St-Denis-d'Augerons and St-Aquilin. The road continues from Montreuil-l'Argillé, rejoining the D 33 on the far side of the river.

St-Evroult-Notre-Dame-du-Bois.—The town, which lies near the source of the Charentonne, is named after the most famous abbey of the Ouche Region.

The abbey, founded by St-Evroult in the 6C, laid waste by the Normans in the 10C, rearose to find its greatest glory in the 11C when it became an influential centre of learning. In the 13C it was rebuilt in the Gothic style and today is once more a ruin. A statue was erected on the church site in 1912 to Orderic Vital, one of the abbey's great men and a historian and chronicler of Normandy in the 12C (1075–1141).

Go through the late 13C porch behind the monument to see the abbey ruins on the left (*restoration in progress since 1966*).

CAMPING AND CARAVANNING

The Michelin Guide **Camping-Caravaning en France**

revised each year and published in March lists more than 2,500 camping sites with details of their facilities and charges, outlook and, by means of an atlas and local maps, their exact situation.

CHAUSEY Islands *—Michelin map ⑤⑨ ⑦.

The Chausey Islands, a day excursion particularly popular with those staying in Granville, make up a small archipelago of granite islands, islets, and reefs, which according to legend were once part of the ancient Scissy Forest (see p. 119), submerged by the sea in 709.

The islands, with the exception of the Great Island on which a hundred people, mostly fishermen and their families, now live, are uninhabited and the quarries which supplied the brown granite for such edifices as Mont-St-Michel, no longer worked.

Access.—*See current Michelin Red Guide France.*

THE GREAT ISLAND* (La Grande Ile)

The island, one mile long by 700 yds.—2 km by 700 m—at its widest point, is the largest and the only one accessible to visitors.

Lighthouse.—*Apply to the keeper.* From the top (79 steps) of the lighthouse which stands 121 ft.—37 m—above the sea, there is a **view*** of the archipelago both above and below sea level. The beam carries 28 miles—45 km.

Fort.—The fort was built between 1860 and 1866 against British attack—but has never been used.

Castle.—*Not open.* The castle, rebuilt by Louis Renault in 1928 on the remains of a fort constructed in 1528, commands the island's western shore, particularly the Eboulis Beach where the tide sometimes recedes as much as 45 ft.—14 m.

The Monks (Moines) and the Elephant.—These rocks, evocative both in shape and colour, can be reached at low tide.

Church.—The small fisherman's church is decorated with six modern stained glass windows of fishing life. To the left of the altar there is a model of a fishing boat.

An aileron from an American plane shot down on 8 June 1944 stands as a memorial to the Normandy liberation.

CHERBOURG *—Michelin map ⑤④ ②—local maps pp. 77 and 78—pop. 40,333—*Place to stay (see p. 36).*

Cherbourg, primarily a naval base, has also developed, because of its position, into a transatlantic passenger port. The capture of Cherbourg on 26 and 27 June 1944 marked a decisive stage in the Battle of Normandy since it allowed for the future landing of heavy equipment on a large scale.

HISTORICAL NOTES

Titanic Undertakings.—Vauban, in the 17C, was the first person to see the possibilities of Cherbourg as an Atlantic port. But the sea washed and swept away all the underwater constructions placed on its bed for three-quarters of a century, and so though work began in 1776, the port of Cherbourg was not opened until 1853; the naval base planned by Napoleon I was only opened by Napoleon III; the first transatlantic passenger ship—of the Hamburg Amerika Line—did not berth there until 1869.

Frogmen at Work.—When the American 7th Corps took Cherbourg they found the harbour completely devastated and mined. In record time they got it back into working order, clearing it of mines and wrecks with the aid of frogmen, so that the Mulberry Harbour at Arromanches could be run down, and Cherbourg could become the port of supply for the Allied armies. This role of single supply port was stepped up during the Ardennes offensive when Cherbourg was handling twice the tonnage a month that New York had been in 1939. The undersea pipeline PLUTO (Pipe Line Under The Ocean) from the Isle of Wight also emerged at Cherbourg, bringing petrol to the Allies from 12 August 1944.

CLIMB TO THE ROULE FORT
¾ hour approach and sightseeing by car

A road winds up to the fort on the top of the Roule Hill (alt. 367 ft.—112 m) which was the main point of German resistance in 1944. Turn left at the fort. The terrace commands a good **panorama*** of the town, the harbour station, the arsenal, the vast harbour (nearly 6 sq. miles—1,500 ha) and the breakwaters which divide it from the sea.

War and Liberation Museum.—*Open 1 April to 30 September, 9 a.m. to noon, 2 to 6 p.m.; 1 October to 31 March, 9.30 a.m. to noon and 2 to 5.30 p.m.; closed Tuesdays; 1 F.*

The **map room** illustrates the progress of the war from the Allied landings on 6 June 1944 to the final German capitulation on 7 May 1945.

ADDITIONAL SIGHTS

Harbour Station—Roadstead.—Open; entrance: north of the Quai de France.

Outer Harbour (Avant Port).—The attractions in summer are the pleasure boats and yachts, largely British, and the fishing fleet.

Thomas Henry Fine Arts Museum, in the town hall.—*Open 10 a.m. to noon, 2 to 6 p.m.; Admission: 1 F.*

A panel by Fra Filippo Lippi, canvasses and drawings by Millet, a local artist (see p. 77) and 18C works.

Emmanuel-Liais Park.—*Guided tours 2 to 4 p.m.; closed Saturdays and Sundays.*

The park, created by the naturalist and astronomer (1826–1900) after whom it is named, is famous for its tropical plants which flourish because of the proximity of the Gulf Stream.

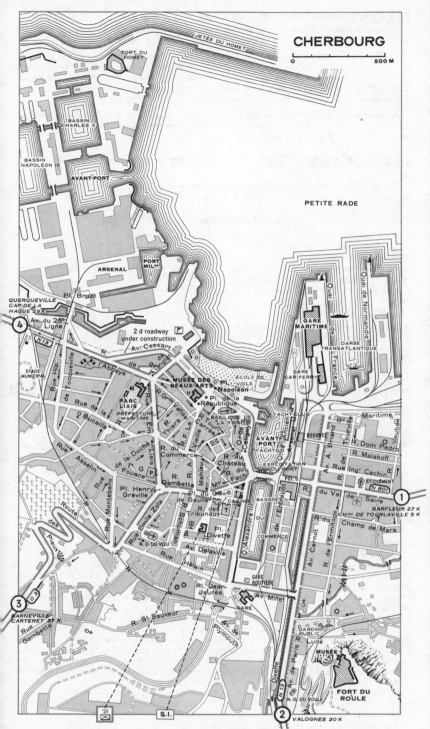

ENVIRONS

Tourlaville Château*.—*3 miles—5 km. Park open 2 to 6 p.m. (summer), 5 p.m. (winter);*
0·50 F. Leave Cherbourg by ①, the N 801. At Tourlaville-Place, a crossroads before the
Terminus Hotel on your right, turn second right into the D 63—Rue des Alliés; at a second
crossroads, 850 yds. further on turn right again; leave the car at a crossroads triangle and
continue on foot to the château (left).

The **park*** round the Renaissance château, has picturesque tropical vegetation, beech trees
and stretches of water.

Querqueville.—*4 miles—7 km.* Leave Cherbourg by ④, the N 801, and continue along the
La Hague road (*description p. 77*) to Querqueville. In the village, turn left at a crossroads and
then immediately right into the uphill Rue de l'Eglise. Leave the car 30 yds. from the entrance
to the church cemetery and go in. To the left of the parish church stands the small 6–8C
St. Germanus' Chapel, the oldest religious edifice on the Cotentin Peninsula and possibly in
western France. The plan is trefoil in outline; the walls have a "fish-bone" motif decoration. Walk between the chapel and the parish church to get an interesting view of the great
Cherbourg roadstead and its quays and a panorama stretching from Cape Lévy, in the east,
to Jardeheu Point in the west.

CLÈRES *—Michelin maps 52 ⑭, 55 ⑥, 97 ① ②—pop. 1,055.

Clères Château, a 14C castle considerably reconstructed in the 19C, has had a zoo occupying part of its park since 1920. It is one of Normandy's great attractions.

Zoo*.—*Open 9 a.m. to nightfall; 4 F.; children: 2.50 F.; time: 1 to 2 hours.* The zoo specialises in birds, although there are some animals—antelope, kangaroos and deer—wandering at liberty in the inner area. There are pink flamingoes, duck and oriental geese in the garden, and, in the zoo area, storks and peacocks and 120 species of waterfowl. There are also indoor and outdoor aviaries of tropical and other birds.

Normandy Car Museum.—*Open 8 a.m. to 8 p.m. in summer; 9 a.m. to 7 p.m. in winter; 2 F.* The oldest machine in this fine collection is a steam fire engine of 1876. Bicycles of pre-1900 vintage are also on display. All exhibits are in running order.

CONCHES-EN-OUCHE *—Michelin maps 55 ⑯, 97 ⑫—pop. 3,534—*Place to stay* (see p. 37).

The town of Conches, bordering on the woodlands which mark the northern limits of the Ouche Region, is remarkably situated on a spur encircled by the River Rouloir.

TOUR (about ½ hour)

Start from the square on the south side of St-Foy's. Go up the Rue Ste-Foy and turn left in the first dead end street on the left. Go through the town hall's Gothic doorway—the gate through the old castle walls—to the garden in which stands the ruined keep surrounded by several 12C towers.

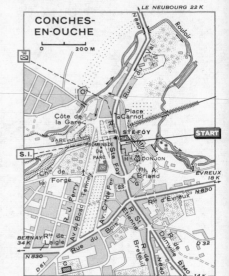

St-Foy's Church*.—Roger de Tosny, a local lord, who had been fighting the Moors in Spain in 1034, returned by way of Aquitaine and a pilgrimage to Conques from which he brought back the relics of St. Foy. Roger dedicated a church to the young martyr which was replaced by the present building at the end of the 15C.

The Flamboyant apse is the most elegant part of the church.

Walk along the nave, of which the vaulting was never completed, to the west front. The south tower is crowned by a tall spire of wood and lead, a copy of the one blown down in a storm in 1842. The fine carved panels of the façade doors are early 16C.

Enter the church where you will see a naïve statue of St. Rock in the uniform of a 17C musketeer, facing the organ at the end of the south aisle.

The Stained Glass Windows*.—The Renaissance windows, dating from the first half of the 16C, have retained their unity in spite of restoration. Those in the north aisle depict the life of the Virgin. The second window shows the Virgin between St. Adrian, on the left, and St. Romanus, on the right, and, dating from 1510, may have adorned the original church. Its pair, John the Baptist Preaching, is some twenty years earlier—both are considerably older than the windows which follow.

The seven 34 ft.—10·50 m—windows in the chancel are divided into two by a trilobed transom, the upper part being given to the illustration of the Life of Christ, the lower to that of St. Foy and portraits of the donors. The whole magnificent series, inspired by German master engravers such as Dürer and Aldegrever, is said to be by Romain Buron, a pupil of Engrand le Prince of Beauvais.

The windows in the south aisle were made in either the Ile-de-France or at Fontainebleau. The Mystical Wine Press, 4th window, is the best known.

An **alabaster triptych*** beautifully carved by English craftsmen in the 15C to illustrate scenes from the Passion stands on the side altar at the end of the south aisle. A second alabaster triptych showing the Holy Trinity by the same craftsmen stands in the north aisle.

The houses facing the church are 15 and 16C.

ENVIRONS

Rouloir Valley.—*Tour: 6 miles—10 km—along narrow roads.* Leave Conches by the Evreux road, the N 830.

After a couple of miles—3 km—turn left at a crossroads into a surfaced road which goes steeply downhill beneath the trees. Beyond Croisille turn into the first tarred road on the left, and ½ mile—1 km—further on, at a crossroads, bear left into a downhill road which reaches the bottom of the Rouloir Valley in the pleasant setting of St-Elier Church.

Return along the river from which you will get one of the best views of Conches.

For other drives in the Risle Valley starting from Conches, see p. 126.

The Côte Fleurie, which extends from Honfleur round to Cabourg, is known for its beauty and its clear light—several of the Impressionist painters returned for years to its beaches and waterways. The hinterland is divided into small lush patches of green (see the Auge Region p. 12) in complete contrast to the infinite horizons of the sea. The area is easily accessible from Paris and, in less than a century, has become one of the most popular in France with a tide of visitors sweeping in each weekend throughout the summer. It retains its character and beauty nevertheless.

THE CONQUEST OF ENGLAND

In 1066, Dives, then a large port, saw the departure of what was one of the most amazing expeditions of the Middle Ages, the force which was to conquer England.

William the Diplomat.—When William of Normandy learnt of Harold's ascent to the throne of England (see p. 50) in January 1066, he sent emissaries to remind him of his former promises. Harold, named as heir to the throne by the dying Edward the Confessor and approved by the English barons, ignored the envoy.

The Duke then called on Rome and the Pope, recognising the justice of William's complaint, commanded him to chastise the English, sent him a consecrated standard and relics of St. Peter and excommunicated Harold.

William needed the consent of his barons before he could lead an expedition overseas and an extraordinary council was therefore convened at Lillebonne. There the Duke, a tenacious character and clever politician, won over the barons and enthusiasm began to mount.

Preparations for the invasion included a diplomatic tour de force: William assured himself of the neutrality in the affair of the rest of France, that his neighbours would not attack Normandy while he was away, and persuaded Norway to undertake a second front against England.

Meanwhile a fleet was equipped and troops mustered—paid for from the treasuries of Rouen and Caen.

At Easter a comet "whose tail illuminated almost half the firmament" sowed terror in England but in Normandy was interpreted by the duke's astrologer as a good augury for the future king.

William the Conqueror.—Duke William resided in Bonneville Castle above Touques from where in less than seven months, he had completed his political and military plans.

The main fleet was gathered ready at Dives but had to await a favourable wind. The duke, an amazing man of many parts, personally imposed strict discipline on the troops.

Finally on 12 September, under the Pope's standard, some 12,000 knights and foot soldiers embarked in 696 ships followed by boats and skiffs which brought the overall number of vessels afloat to 3,000. The fleet made for St-Valéry-sur-Somme to pick up reinforcements.

Meanwhile Harold was forced to break up the armed watch he was keeping on the south coast against the expected Norman armada and hurry off north. At Stamford Bridge the English cavalry and foot soldiers under Harold utterly destroyed the Viking host, but in Normandy the wind had changed and three days later, on 28 September, William was landing at Pevensey. Harold and his knights rode south, reaching London on 6 October and determined to give battle immediately and on 14 October the armies clashed.

Harold had chosen a position on an isolated spur 6 miles—9 km—northwest of Hastings. The armies were similar but employed different tactics: the English left the cavalry in the rear and fought on foot, using the Danish battle-axe which Harold himself plied manfully in his last fight; the Normans fought from the saddle with spear and sword, supported between charges by bowmen from the rear. The English, on their hill, resisted the cavalry but were shot down by the archers. By nightfall Harold and all his house earls lay dead on the hilltop.

William celebrated his victory by founding Battle Abbey upon the hilltop in Sussex.

The Bayeux Tapestry graphically records the events of the Conquest (see pp. 50, 51).

William, Duke and King.—William occupied Dover after his victory and then Canterbury, where the prosperous London merchants, fearful of civil war, sent him a delegation. Realists to a man, they offered their support in exchange for confirmation of their privileges; in their turn, the bishops and the army made their submission. With the consent of the Norman barons, William, Duke of Normandy, accepted the crown.

The coronation took place in Westminster Abbey on Christmas Day. The new king swore to maintain the laws and customs of the kingdom. The acclamation of the sovereign was so loud that the guards posted outside suspected a revolt and rushed into the abbey.

The King rewarded his companions in arms liberally with land and offices and kept for himself 1,422 manor-houses and all forts and forests.

In the spring he returned to celebrate Easter in Normandy—it was the apotheosis to an expedition conceived only some fifteen months earlier.

Nine centuries later an invasion in the opposite direction was to land on the Coast of Calvados, and conclude equally victoriously.

FROM HONFLEUR TO TROUVILLE by the Normandy Corniche
9 miles—15 km—about ½ hour

There are glimpses in the course of the drive, through the lush vegetation, of the Seine Estuary, and of the large estates which line the road at intervals.

The N 813 is narrow, winding and rounded between Honfleur and Pennedepie with hidden turnings and further narrow stretches as far as Villerville. There is heavy traffic during the season.

Honfleur**.—Description p. 107.
There is a good view of the Seine Estuary and Le Havre as you reach the lighthouse between Honfleur and Vasouy and again between Vasouy and Pennedepie.

Alternative route by the Côte de Grâce (recommended to those going in the Trouville–Honfleur direction).—Extra distance: 1 mile—2 km.
Take the D 62 at Pennedepie, then after 1½ miles—2·5 km—the D 279 and after a further mile—2 km—the D 62. Description of the Côte de Grace p. 108.

After Pennedepie the road turns inland up several small valleys.

The CÔTE FLEURIE** (concluded)

Cricqueboeuf.—The 12C church, its ivy covered walls reflected in a pond, may be familiar from travel posters.

Villerville*.—*Place to stay (see p. 36).* From the terrace overlooking the beach of this lively seaside resort, there is a view in the distance of Le Havre and Cape La Hève. At low water the Ratier Bank lies exposed to mussel gatherers.

There is a view from the top of the hill beyond Villerville back over the Seine Estuary, with its oil refineries, to Le Havre, away on the left.

As you approach Trouville ever more substantial villas line the road.

Trouville**.—*Description p. 151.*

Deauville***.—*Description p. 81.*

FROM TROUVILLE-DEAUVILLE TO CABOURG along the coast

12 miles—19 km—about ½ hour—plus ¼ hour on foot Rtn

Along this busy coast road you see the resorts which have made the Côte Fleurie famous.

Trouville**.—*Description p. 151.*

Deauville***.—*Description p. 81.*

Bénerville and Blonville-sur-Mer.—*Place to stay: see under Blonville p. 36.* The towns form a single resort at the foot of Mount Canisy—the long gently sloping sand beach is ideal for children.

Villers-sur-Mer**.—This elegant seaside resort is known for its immense three-mile beach which extends from Blonville to the **Vaches Noires Cliffs** (*see below*) and is separated from the town by a promenade wall (*viewing balcony*). At the back lies a countryside of woods and hills.

Vaches Noires Cliffs*.—*½ hour's walk Rtn starting from the D 163.* Leave the car on the road to the church and walk straight along the path (difficult in wet weather) to the first cliff edge.

This site, where the Auberville Plateau ends in a ravined cliff crumbling into the sea, is a local landmark, known also for the many fossils to be found in its strata of clay and dark marls. The cliffs can be approached at low tide from either Houlgate or Villers along the beach (*about 2 hours on foot Rtn in either case*) where the blocks which have separated from the chalk face are now covered in seaweed and the "Black Cows" proper, can be seen from close to. One mile—1·5 km—before Houlgate along the D 163, is a lay-by terrace from which you can see the Drochon Valley as it enters the sea and the coast from the mouth of the River Dives to that of the Orne.

A vast panorama spreads out before you from a hairpin bend at the entrance to Houlgate.

Houlgate**.—*Description p. 109.*

The drive's best panorama occurs between Houlgate and Dives when, from a pine avenue on the D 45A, you can see the Dives Valley, Dives-Cabourg town, the coast on either side of the mouth of the Orne and, in the far distance, the countryside around Caen.

Dives-sur-Mer.—*Description p. 55.*

Cabourg**.—*Description p. 55.*

COTENTIN Peninsula **—Michelin map 54 ① to ③ and ⑪ to ⑬.

The pronounced thrust of the Cotentin Peninsula into the Atlantic corresponds with an equally uncharacteristic landscape: the austerity around La Hague is less a reminder of Normandy than a foretaste of Brittany, and even bleaker, if that were possible.

The wooded hinterland, the cradle of a race who for a time controlled the fortunes of countries of the central Mediterranean, deserves to be better known.

GEOGRAPHICAL NOTES

In addition to the typical Norman woodlands (see p. 12), there are three distinct geographical areas in the peninsula.

The Cotentin "Pass".—The lower plain, watered by the converging Vire, Taute and Douve Rivers, resembles an open parkland where cows, whose dairy products are sold in the wholesale market at Carentan, graze placidly.

Towns and villages crown the lowest hills or stand upon the alluvial plateau of Ste-Mère-Eglise, the horse and cattle breeding area for which Normandy is famous (see p. 14).

The area includes marshlands which extend to the centre of the peninsula: if the sea were to rise by 30 ft.—10 m—the Cotentin Peninsula would once again become an offshore island.

Peat has brought new life to Baupte—the 50,000 tons cut annually being used as fuel for thermal electric power and the manufacture of fertilisers. A large seaweed factory, recently erected, now extracts the industrial colloids required in the manufacture of plastics.

The marshes are also grazed and attract waterfowlers.

The Val de Saire.—The name applies not only to the delightful Saire Valley but to the whole of the northeast of the peninsula.

From the top of the Gatteville lighthouse you can see clearly the granite plateau which gradually dips beneath the sea, the dense woods inland and the busily picturesque small harbour towns of St-Vaast and Barfleur, which make the area so attractive. The mild climate enables cattle to be left out of doors for nine months of the year and early vegetables to be grown along the coast.

La Hague Point.—This granite spine becomes more and more rugged and wild the closer you get to Auderville and Jobourg—grandiose end-of-the-world places. On the far side of the frightening Alderney Race, where the current often runs at more than 8 knots, lie the Channel Islands which, only a short time ago geologically speaking, were part of the mainland (see map p. 11).

HISTORICAL NOTES

The Normans as Kings of Sicily (11 and 12C).—Many Cotentin Normans decided at the beginning of the 11C to escape the heavy authority of the then duke. They took to the roads leading to the Holy Places, their devotion to St. Michael leading some to Mount Gargano in southern Italy, where the feudal barons were in a perpetual state of war. A system of troop raising was thereupon instituted—the Cotentin was both poor and overpopulated—for the benefit of such as the lord of Apulia when he sought to rise against Byzantium.

The exploits of three sons of Tancrède de Hauteville, a small baron from the Coutances area, aroused great enthusiasm. The eldest William, known as Iron Arm, profited from the local imbroglio to chase away those who had summoned him and become William of Apulia in 1042. His two brothers, however, were the true founders of Norman power in the Mediterranean: Robert Guiscard de Hauteville and, even more, his younger brother Roger, who became one of the strongest Christian monarchs. The reign of Roger II from 1101 to 1154 surpassed that of all others in brilliance and display. The last Norman King of Sicily was Manfred who was killed at Benevento in 1265 by Charles of Anjou, brother of St. Louis, and whose tragic fate was sung by Dante, Byron and Schumann.

The Naval Battle of La Hougue (1692).—James II of England when deposed by William of Orange in 1688 sought refuge in France where Louis XIV supported his dreams of restoration.

In 1692 a plan was formulated to invade England with the aid of Irish troops gathered at St-Vaast. The French Admiral of the Fleet was commanded to proceed to La Hougue with 44 ships to protect the operation.

But at dawn off Barfleur the French met the combined Anglo-Dutch fleet of 99 vessels under Admirals Russell, Rooke and Van Allemonde. After a terrific battle which lasted all day the French broke away to escape encirclement; the plan by which the undamaged ships were to run for Brest and those damaged were to use the Alderney Race to speed them to St. Malo miscarried. The English set fire to the pride of the French navy (2 to 5 June 1692) and James's last hopes of restoration went up in the flames.

The War of the Hedgerows.—For the American soldiers of 1944, the Cotentin campaign —the advance to Cherbourg and the Battle of St-Lô (*details p. 24*)—is summed up in the description "the war of the hedgerows".

Hedges and sunken roads such as those that divide the Normandy Bocage are unknown in America and came as an unpleasant surprise, for as a place for defensive warfare or guerilla tactics the countryside offered unending opportunities.

Modern arms were not much help: 4-inch shells scarcely shook the tree covered embankments which constituted natural anti-tank barriers; armoured vehicles moved with difficulty along the roads; only the foot soldier could fight successfully in this "hell of hedges".

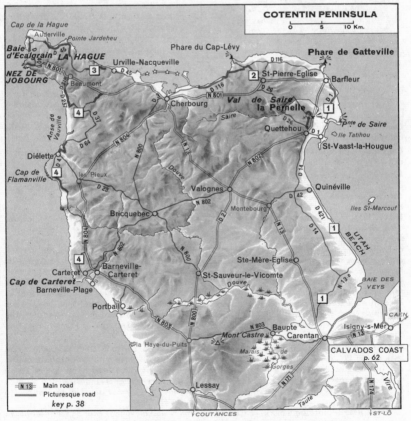

1 ***FROM CARENTAN TO BARFLEUR by Utah Beach**
47 miles—75 km—about 2½ hours—plus ¼ hour walking and sightseeing

Carentan.—*Description p. 155.*
The road between St-Côme and Ste-Marie-du-Mont crosses the marshland area of Ste-Mère-Eglise.

Ste-Marie-du-Mont.—One's first sight of the impressive Church of St. Mary is of its square 14C tower of which the top storey is a Renaissance addition (restored in 1843 after a storm). The nave is early 12C, the transept and chancel 14C, also the nave's windows and vaulting. Inside, are a late 16C figured pulpit and in the chancel, on the left, a funerary statue of Henri Robert aux Espaulles carved in the early 17C.

FROM **CARENTAN**
TO **BARFLEUR**

0   5 km

key p. 38

The Magdalene Monument.—This former German blockhouse has been transformed into a monument to the Americans of the 1st Engineer Brigade (see *p. 124 for the role of the special units*). From the top there is a view of the coast while to the north the blockships sunk off the Calvados Coast may still be seen at low tide (*see p. 63*).

One of the Liberty Way milestones stands nearby; another can be seen in Ste-Mère-Eglise. The road from La Madeleine to Quinéville is separated from the sea for the most part by a line of sand dunes although there are a few stretches, as between Les Gougins and Quinéville, where the view opens out along the coast from the Grandcamp Cliffs to the fort at La Hougue and the Saire Point.

Low granite houses with slate roofs indicate you have reached the Val de Saire and the first palm trees and mimosa bushes that the local climate is exceptionally mild.

Utah Beach.—Although the 7th Corps of the 4th American Division was subjected to murderous fire from the German coastal batteries when it landed on 6 June 1944 at the approaches to the Magdalene Blockhouse and Les Dunes-de-Varreville, they were able to link up with the airborne troops of the 82nd and 101st Divisions dropped round Ste-Mère-Eglise. Three weeks later the Cotentin Peninsula was completely liberated. *Commemorative exhibition open: Easter to All Saints Day 9 a.m. to noon, 2 to 7 p.m.; All Saints Day to Easter, 10 a.m. to noon, 2 to 6 p.m. Sundays and holidays only. Admission: 2.50 F.*

Les Dunes-de-Varreville Monument.—*100 yds. from the Route des Alliés, in an opening in the dunes. A rose granite stele in the form of a ship's prow and bearing the cross of Lorraine commemorates the landing of the 2nd French Armoured Division under General Leclerc on 1 August 1944.*

Quinéville.—*Place to stay (see p. 36).*—There is a good view of the St-Vaast roadstead from the church cemetery.

Quettehou.—The church on a height is flanked by a tall 15C belfry. From the cemetery there is a view of Morsalines Bay, the La Hougue Fort, St-Vaast town and the Saire Point.

Val de Saire★★.—The tour described below starting from Quettehou (*although it can be joined at any point according to whether one is coming from Cherbourg, Barfleur or Valognes*) goes through a green countryside and affords good views of the east coast of the Cotentin Peninsula.

Leave Quettehou by the N 802 going north, turning left, shortly, into the D 26 which climbs through apple orchards to the pretty village of Le Vast where you turn right. The countryside with its rolling woodlands and well kept pastures in the valleys is reminiscent, in places, of England. Turn right into the D 125 at a crossroads at the entrance to Valcanville. As you emerge from the trees you see the sea and, on the left, the tall white candle of Gatteville lighthouse.

At a crossroads 200 yds. before a Calvary on your right, bear left into the signposted **La Pernelle** road, from which you turn off right after 300 yds. Beyond the rebuilt church of La Pernelle is a former German blockhouse which commands a **panorama★★** (*viewing table*) extending from the Gatteville lighthouse to the Grandcamp Cliffs and, in clear weather, the Percée Point, by way of the Saire Head, Réville Bay, Tatihou Island, the La Hougue Fort and the St-Marcouf Islands.

St-Vaast-La-Hougue.—St-Vaast is a picturesque small fishing port with fortifications which date back to the 17C just after the naval victory by the English off La Hougue; a lighthouse on the end of a 400 yd. long granite jetty commanding distant views both to north and south; a mariners' chapel with an apse painted white to act as a navigational landmark; and a beach over a mile in length along the isthmus which now links the former island of La Hougue to St-Vaast.

    Saire Head (Pointe de Saire).—*Excursion of 3 miles—5 km—plus ¼ hour on foot Rtn.* Leave St-Vaast by the Réville road. Turn right immediately beyond Saire Bridge and, at the next crossroads, right again. After 500 yds. opposite an oratory, bear right.

    From the top of an old blockhouse there is a good circular view of the Saire Head promontory, Tatihou Island and St-Vaast in the background.

To the left of the road between St-Vaast and Barfleur is La Crasvillerie, a beautiful 16C manor. Further on, again to the left, is **Montfarville Church,** an 18C granite building with a chapel and belfry dating back to the 13C. The bare granite walls inside give it a special character; the paintings on the vaulting are by a local 19C artist.

As you approach Barfleur, the countryside develops Armorican characteristics—sombre granite houses, rocky bays and trees bent by the wind. Gatteville lighthouse stands to the north.

Barfleur.—*Place to stay (see p. 36).* Barfleur, once a famous fishing port, is now a seaside resort, its harbour filled with pleasure craft. The squat and sombre 17C **church** contains a 16C *pietà*.

Gatteville village and lighthouse**.—*Excursion of 2 miles—4 km—from Barfleur, plus ½ hour sightseeing.* Leave Barfleur by the D 116.

The church, rebuilt in the 18C, still has its original 12C belfry. Inside, in a chapel to the right off the chancel, a 14C medallioned ciborium is surmounted by a 16C Trinity. The Mariners' Chapel, in the square, is built over a Merovingian necropolis and has a Romanesque apse.

Turn right into the D 10 by the war memorial; leave the car at the near end of the jetty. *Lighthouse open 8 a.m. to one hour before sunset; apply to the keeper.*

The **lighthouse*** is 233 ft.—71 m—high and one of the tallest in France. The light can be seen for 35 miles—56 km—and, with its radio signal, serves to guide ships into Le Havre. From the top there is a **panorama**** stretching over the east coast of the Cotentin Peninsula, the St. Marcouf Islands, Veys Bay and, in clear weather, Grandcamp Cliffs. But the most astonishing sight is the granite tableland of the Saire gradually disappearing beneath the sea in the foreground. The shallow waters and the swiftness of the currents have made many ships founder, including the historic *White Ship* in 1120, with Henry I's heir, William Atheling, one of his daughters and 300 high born Anglo-Normans, aboard.

② **FROM BARFLEUR TO CHERBOURG by the Corniche Road
18 miles—29 km—about 1 hour

The Fermanville–Bretteville Corniche Road should be taken slowly to be appreciated.

Barfleur.—*Description above.*

Gatteville Lighthouse**.—*Excursion of 2 miles—4 km—from Barfleur. See above.*

Tocqueville.—Alexis de Tocqueville (1805–1859) the far-seeing historian, author of *Democracy in the United States* and the *Ancien Régime and the Revolution*, lived in the château.

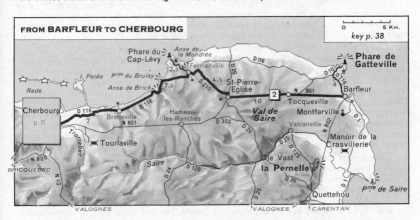

FROM BARFLEUR TO CHERBOURG

St-Pierre-Eglise—The 17C church has a 12C Romanesque doorway.

Between St-Pierre-Eglise and Fermanville the view soon extends to La Mondrée Bay.

Cape Lévy Lighthouse*.—*Excursion: 2 miles—2·5 km—from Fermanville; ¼ hour sightseeing.* The **lighthouse*** is an elegant modern construction with curved walls commanding from its lantern tower (113 steps) a **panorama**** of Cherbourg roadstead and Cape La Hague.

Views of Brulay Point and Brick Bay from the Fermanville–Bretteville *corniche*.

As you approach Cherbourg you can see the roadstead and Pelée Island which serves as an anchor for the mole which, with the great breakwater, divides the harbour from the sea. To the left is the sandstone bank crowned by Roule Fort.

Cherbourg*.—*Description p. 70.*

③ ***FROM CHERBOURG TO BEAUMONT by Cape La Hague
29 miles—47 km—about 1½ hours—plus ½ hour on foot Rtn

On leaving Cherbourg, the road skirts the main harbour, then, after Querqueville, turns inland. Beyond Landemer it goes up the Habilland Ravine from which there emerges a view from Cape Lévy lighthouse to Jardeheu Point.

Gréville.—It was in Gruchy (*see below: Castel-Vendon Rock*), a part of this parish, that the painter Millet was born and it was in this setting that he began to observe and make his first drawings of peasant life (*see p. 20*). The small squat church must often have served as his model.

Castel-Vendon Rock*.—*Excursion of 1 mile—1·5 km—from Gréville, plus ¼ hour on foot Rtn.* Go by the D 237 to Gruchy where Millet's birthplace stands abandoned although marked with a plaque.

Leave the car by a public wash-house on the left and continue straight ahead on foot by a poor sunken road which improves into a footpath along the right hand side of the valley. From a rocky promontory, there is soon a **view*** of the coast from Cape Lévy to the Jardeheu Point. In the foreground stands the granite rock spine surrounded by deep ravines, known as the Castel-Vendon Rock.

The sea reappears during the long hydrangea bordered descent to Omonville-la-Rogue. After Omonville the road skirts the St-Martin Bay almost at sea level before rising to St-Germain-des-Vaux from where the minute Port-Racine can be seen. The landscape is now a moorland broken by rock spikes.

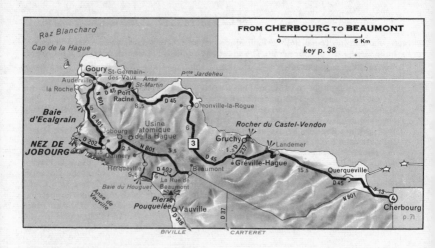

FROM CHERBOURG TO BEAUMONT

St-Germain-des-Vaux.—*Place to stay (see p. 36).*

At the entrance to **Auderville** (*place to stay: see p. 36*) a road down to Goury enables you to explore the north end of Cape La Hague. Beyond the foam lined shore are the island light-house of La Hague and, in the distance, the steep cliffs of Alderney.

Goury*.—The small harbour, only refuge for fishermen caught in the Alderney Race (*see p. 75*), is an important life-saving station. Two slipways enable the lifeboat to be launched from its octagonal station at either high or low tide (*admission free: offering*).

Take the D 401 on the right on leaving Auderville, which brings you to **Ecalgrain Bay**** where the desolate strand is surrounded by heathland. Guernsey and Sark can be seen on the horizon to the left of Alderney and, in the far distance, the west coast of the Cotentin Peninsula. Make for the Nez de Jobourg from Dannery along the D 202.

Nez de Jobourg***.—*½ hour on foot Rtn. Leave the car at the end of the D 202.*

Walk the old beacon road, the crest and then left round the beacon. The Nez de Jobourg appears, a long escarped and rugged promontory, encircled by reefs and separated from the Nez de Voidries, on which you are standing by the small but steep sided Sennival Bay. The setting is spectacular with Vauville Bay curving round in the distance to the Flamanville Cliffs.

From the end of the Voidries "Nose" a second view includes Ecalgrain Bay, La Hague Light-house and promontory and the Channel Islands. Sea bird reserve on the Nez de Jobourg.

After Dannery take the N 801 to Beaumont. On the left is the La Hague plutonium atomic power station.

> **Recommended alternative route** by Herqueville.**—*Extra distance: 2 miles—2·5 km; take the D 403 opposite the power station. Although excellent, the road is difficult between Herqueville and Beaumont.*
>
> Leave the car in a lay-by in a bend beyond Herqueville to look at the splendid **vista**** across Vauville Bay and over the Flamanville Cliffs. The descent continues with the small and rocky Houguet Bay on the right and the road at one point coming within walking distance of the shore.

④ ** FROM BEAUMONT TO BARNEVILLE-CARTERET

29 miles—46 km—about 1½ hours

From the inland road which crosses a less hilly countryside than previously, there are distant views of the Channel Islands and the rugged coast.

> **Pierre-Pouquelée*.**—*¾ hour walk Rtn starting from the D 318.*
>
> Leave the car 200 yds. before the first houses of Vauville and walk inland up a steep path on the right. When it reaches the plateau turn left towards the enclosed meadows which you go round by the right to the covered way leading to the almost totally ruined Pierre-Pouquelée. Continue right to a small rise from which there is a magnificent **panorama*** of the coast from the Nez de Jobourg to the Flamanville Cliffs. In clear weather you can also see Alderney and, inland, Jobourg village and the Beaumont belfry.

Vauville.—The country church and Renaissance manorhouse, nestling in a hollow of the wild bay to which the village gave its name, are most attractive. Standing upon a height is the recently built priory of St-Hermel, originally erected by a companion in arms of William the Conqueror, Richard de Vauville, an ancestor of Field-Marshal Lord Wavell (1883–1950). From a steep hill after the village of Petit-Thot, there is a grand **view*** of the barren countryside around Vauville Bay. Gliding enthusiasts have used Camp Maneyrol since 1923.

> **The Dunes Calvary*.**—*¼ hour on foot Rtn from the D 237 before entering Biville.*
>
> The **panorama*** from the foot of the Calvary includes the coast from the Nez de Jobourg round the barren Vauville Bay to the Flamanville Cliffs in the foreground, and out to sea, in clear weather, the Channel Islands.

Biville*.—The restored 13C chancel of the village church, which is adorned with small 15C low reliefs, contains a marble sarcophagus enclosing the glass coffin of the blessed Thomas Hélye (1187–1257), a native of Biville. The recumbent figure on the right is from the original tomb. A popular pilgrimage to the church occurs for the midnight Mass of his anniversary on 18 and 19 October.

The road returns to the dunes and the sea at Siouville-Plage.

Diélette appears closely hugging its sombre cliff.

Diélette.—The small port of Diélette is the only refuge between Goury and Carteret. As the tide goes out, a beach of fine sand appears between its two breakwaters.

From the road which skirts the granite quarries to go to the old iron mines (*1 mile—1·5 km—poorly surfaced*) and forms a sort of boulevard-promenade, there is a view north to the Nez de Jobourg. (The ore strata were under the sea.)

Flamanville*. — The village of Flamanville on the granite promontory of the same name is distinguished by its mid-17C **castle** (*only the park is open: apply to the gardener, to the right of the entrance gate*). The buildings of granite are grouped round a main courtyard, the wings on either side being prolonged by galleries ending in pavilions, of which one is a chapel. This homogeneous building is surrounded by a shaded park in which palm trees stand reflected in the lakes.

Cape Flamanville*. —*1 mile Rtn —2 km.* Starting from the castle entrance and turning your back on the village, follow the castle wall round to the right. At the next corner, turn left and 300 yds. later, right into a path above which runs a telephone line. 300 yds. further on leave the car by a wooden barrier and walk to the edge of the cliff. From the cliff edge, 285 ft.—90 m—above the sea, there is a **view*** south over **Sciotot Bay** and Le Rozel Point to Cape Carteret and on the horizon, in clear weather, of the Channel Islands with Alderney as the most northerly followed by the Casquets reef and lighthouse, Guernsey, Sark, Jersey and the Ecrehou Islets.

Between Flamanville and Le Rozel the *corniche* road overlooks **Sciotot Bay**, which is less wild than those further north.

Carteret*. —*Description p. 49.*

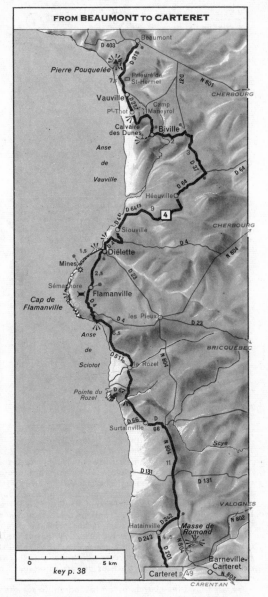

FROM BEAUMONT TO CARTERET

key p. 38

COURSEULLES-SUR-MER —Michelin maps ⑤④ ⑮, ⑤⑤ ①—local map p. 62—pop. 1,938—*Place to stay (see p. 36)*.

Courseulles, a modest seaside resort famous for its oysters, is situated in what was the Canadian sector of Juno Beach at the time of the Allied Invasion in June 1944 (*see p. 62*).

The Seulles river mouth shelters a small port which was extremely useful to the British and Canadian forces until Mulberry Harbour had been established off Arromanches (*see p. 45*).

The resort's west beach was the place Winston Churchill landed on 12 June 1944, General de Gaulle on 14 June and King George VI on 16 June to see the high command and the troops.

Oyster Beds. —The flat Breton or Portuguese oysters from the Ile de Ré are matured in the beds. *To visit apply to the Maison Héroult, Place du 6-Juin, or at the Domaine de l'Ile de Plaisance.* For information about oyster farming visit the oyster museum on the right of the N 814 going towards Arromanches. *Open Easter to the end of September, 10 a.m. to noon, 2.30 to 6.30 p.m.; 1 F.*

COUTANCES **—Michelin map ⑤④ ⑫—pop. 10,993.

Coutances, the religious centre of the Cotentin Peninsula, is perched on a hillock crowned by the town's magnificent cathedral. This escaped damage when the town suffered in 1944.

CATHEDRAL OF OUR LADY*** (tour: about ½ hour)

Start from the Place du Parvis, a square which was rebuilt after the war in such a way as to enhance the cathedral. This, through the felicity of its proportions and the purity of its lines, is one of the most successful of Norman Gothic buildings (*see p. 18*).

The construction. —Geoffroy de Montbray—one of those great prelate knights Duke William drew around him before he went to England—completed the first nave in 1056. Then, thanks to the generosity of the sons of Tancrède de Hauteville whose amazing Mediterranean adventure had just began (*see p. 74*), he had the chancel, transept and central tower of the façade built, flanked by twin octagonal towers reminiscent of those at Jumièges.

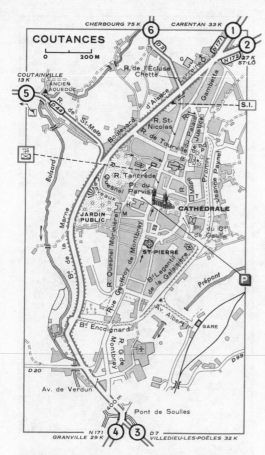

COUTANCES

CHERBOURG 75 K — CARENTAN 33 K
27 K ST-LÔ
R. de l'Écluse Chette
COUTAINVILLE 13 K
ANCIEN AQUEDUC
R. de St-Malo
Boulevard d'Alsace
R. St-Nicolas
R. de Tourville
S.I.
R. Tancrède
Pl. du Fesnel Parvis
JARDIN PUBLIC
CATHÉDRALE
ST-PIERRE
Bd Legentil de la Galaisière
Prépont
P
Av. Albert
GARE
Bd Encoignard
R. Gde Montbray
Av. de Verdun
Pont de Soulles
GRANVILLE 29 K — VILLEDIEU-LES-POÊLES 32 K

In 1218, after the town had been burnt down, a new Gothic cathedral was literally mounted on the remains of the 11C church, involving prodigious adaptations of style as can be seen from the way the Romanesque towers of the old façade were incorporated in a new rectangular face and surmounted by spires.

Interior.—Pause at the beginning of the nave for a remarkable general view of this singular building with its upswept lines: to right and left wide arcades are lined above by galleries where the lower windows, surmounted by blind rose windows, have been blocked up; above again, on a level with the tall windows, a second balustrade of a different design, lines the walls.

In the transept, two massive pillars which formed part of the original Romanesque building were ornamented in the Gothic period with graceful upsweeping columns. Dominating the transept crossing is the octagonal, lead covered, **lantern tower***. It is 135 ft. high—41 m—at its apex and the best example of its type in Normandy. Below, but above the triforium, is a gallery supporting the columns from which spring the ribs of the pointed arching and tall windows between the columns.

The north transept contains the oldest, 13C (restored) stained glass windows; the south, a 14C window, in sombre tones, of the Last Judgment.

The chancel, with the same architectural simplicity as the nave, is later in date and wider.

As you walk round the two ambulatories, which are of different height, note the false triforium formed from two arches each covering twin bays. The radiating chapels are shallow and the ribs of their vaulting combine with the corresponding ambulatory bay rib to form a single arch. The central apsidal chapel, known as the Circata, which was rebuilt and enlarged in the second half of the 14C, contains the beautiful and deeply venerated 14C statue of Our Lady of Coutances. Leave the cathedral by the main door.

Above the great window a beautiful gallery crowns the façade while on either side rise the towers (*the one on the left is under restoration*), quartered at their highest, octagonal level, by graceful elongated pierced turrets (*illustration p. 18*). The profusion of ascending lines, so remarkable in their detail, perhaps detract somewhat from the flight of the spires which rise to 256 ft.—78 m.

Go left round the church, past a 13C porch, to see the apse, rising from a surge of flying buttresses and, higher still, the lantern tower circled by a single balustrade.

ADDITIONAL SIGHTS

Public Gardens*.—*Open in summer 8 a.m. to 9 p.m., in winter 9 a.m. to 5 p.m.*

From the end of the vast terraced promenade which traverses the sloping gardens look right towards the Bulsard Valley where three arches remain of the old 13C Coutances aqueduct. Son et Lumière *performances in summer on Thursdays, Saturdays, Sundays and holidays.*

St. Peter's.—This fine 15 and 16C church was given a lantern tower over the transept crossing which, in accordance with Renaissance custom, was decorated ever more richly the nearer the ornament was to the summit. The interior is plainer, although the graceful Flamboyant balustrade to the gallery adds a light touch. The inside of the lantern tower above the crossing is a happy adaptation of the Renaissance to the style of the cathedral.

ENVIRONS

Tourville-sur-Sienne; Coutainville; Gratot. *Tour of 17 miles—28 km.* Leave Tourville by ⑤, the D 44.

Tourville-sur-Sienne.—The statue beside the road is of the unfortunate Admiral de Tourville who lost the battle off Cape de la Hougue (*see p. 75*). From the cemetery (road from the statue) there is a good view of Regnéville harbour, Montmartin belfry and the Granville Rock. Continue along the D 44 to Coutainville.

Coutainville.—Coutainville, built among the sand dunes, forms, with the neighbouring parish of **Agon**, the best equipped seaside resort on the west coast of the Cotentin Peninsula between Carteret and Granville. The beach is scattered with curious straw bathing huts.

Take the D 272, the D 68 and turn off right for Gratot.

Gratot.—Go behind the church and through the north wall of the cemetery to the ruined buildings of the former Argouges manor where twin towers still flank the main façade. *Open: 10 a.m. to noon (1 July to 1 September) and 2.30 to 6.30 p.m. on Sunday afternoons only out of season. Admission: 2 F.*

Deauville is world famous: its dazzling luxury, its variety of entertainment—racing, regattas, car rallies, galas, tournaments—make it a favourite international resort.

THE RESORT

High season in Deauville opens in July and closes on the fourth Sunday in August with the Deauville Grand Prix. Racing takes place alternatively on the La Touques (flat) and Clairefontaine courses (flat and steeplechase) and it is at Deauville that the international yearling sales are held (in August).

The coming and going of everyone on the **Planches**—a wooden plank promenade which runs the length of the beach—is the special characteristic of Deauville beach life. As a background, on the far side to the beach with its vividly coloured tents, the *planches* are lined by elegant buildings such as the Pompeian Baths and the Soleil Bar where celebrities enjoy being seen.

The yacht basin on the Touques River, the Yacht Club and such boulevards as the Eugène-Cornuché give the resort an air which over the years has earned it the homonym of the Plage Fleurie.

In 1970 a vast new construction project was conceived: the Port Deauville or a marina extending from the mouth of the Touques, from which breakwaters would be built out into the sea, to the east end of the *planches*. When complete the yachts moored to the quay will add still further distinction to this already distinguished resort.

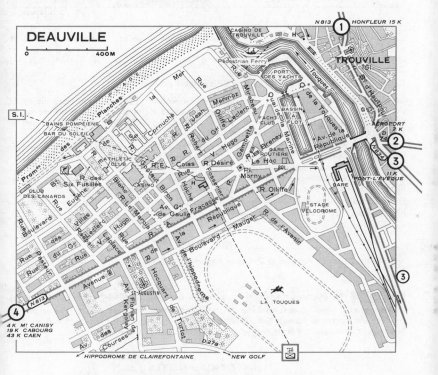

ENVIRONS OF DEAUVILLE-TROUVILLE
Distances from the Touques Bridge

Mount Canisy*.—*Tour of 7 miles—11 km—plus ½ hour walking and sightseeing. Narrow roads.* Leave Deauville by ④, the N 813. Turn left up the hill in front of Bénerville Church and, after 200 yds., left again opposite the town hall. At the top, bear right into a road to Mount Canisy. Leave the car by the blockhouses and continue on foot for a **view*** which extends from the La Héve Cape to the Orne Estuary.
Walk back to the car and turn round, taking the road on the right. The road, after going through Canisy town, drops rapidly to the St-Arnoult crossroads where you turn left for Deauville along the D 278.
To visit the **St-Arnoult Chapel** turn sharp left after 850 yds. into an uphill road. The chapel, which was formerly the goal of a popular pilgrimage, stands in a picturesque setting. *To see inside apply to M. Auger in front of the door.*

The Côte Fleurie**; Caen***.—*Tour of 54 miles—87 km—about 3 hours—plus 2 hours sightseeing.* Leave Deauville by ④, the N 813; follow the Trouville–Deauville road to Cabourg (*described p. 74*), then the Cabourg–Caen road (*described p. 62*). *Description of Caen p. 56.* Leave Caen by ③, the N 813. At Varaville turn right into the D 27 and after Tourgéville, always bearing left, return to Deauville along the D 278.

Honfleur**; the Normandy Corniche**.—*Tour of 21 miles—34 km—about 1 hour—plus ¾ hour sightseeing.* Leave Trouville by ③, the N 834. On coming out of Touques, turn left into the D 288; at the David crossroads bear sharp left into the D 279.

Barneville.—The church, hidden in greenery, stands beside the magnificent castle park.
Drive along the D 62 and at a crossroads turn left into the D 279 again. Turn left, by a castle, into the Côte de Grâce road. *Description of Honfleur p. 107.*
Return from Honfleur to Trouville-Deauville by the road described on p. 73.

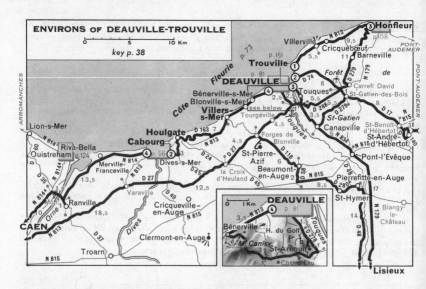

ENVIRONS OF DEAUVILLE-TROUVILLE

key p. 38

Lisieux★★; the Auge Region★.—*Tour of 42 miles—68 km—about 2 hours—plus ¼ hour sightseeing.* Leave Deauville by the D 278, south on the map. Bear right into the D 27; at the Forges de Blonville crossroads turn left into the Villers–Lisieux road (*described p. 46*). *Description of Lisieux p. 110.*

Return from Lisieux along the Touques Valley (*route described p. 47*).

St-André-d'Hébertot★.—*Tour of 25 miles—40 km—about 1¼ hours.* Leave Trouville by ②, the D 74, and continue along the D 17 to the St-Benoît-d'Hébertot crossroads where you go straight ahead, D 140, and at a second crossroads 1,250 yds. further on, turn left towards St-André-d'Hébertot Castle (*description p. 135*).

After seeing the castle continue along the road for 300 yds. before turning left where, in front of the St-Benoît-d'Hébertot Church, you rejoin the road you came out on. Return up it until you come to St-Gatien Church and after a further 425 yds. turn left into the D 279. There are attractive views of the Touques Valley from the downhill road before it reaches Canapville where you take the Lisieux-Trouville-Deauville road (*p. 47*).

Other beautiful tours from Deauville-Trouville would be up the Seine Valley (see p. 140), the Risle Valley (p. 126) and in the Auge Region (p. 45).

AIR TRIPS

Apply to the Deauville Air Club at St-Gatien Airport—☎ 88 00 52.

DIEPPE ★★—Michelin map ⑤② ④—local map p. 67—pop. 30,404—*Place to stay (see p. 36).*
   Dieppe, the beach closest to Paris, is the oldest French seaside resort; the harbour is modern but many old corners and alleys remain, making it one of the most unusual towns in Normandy. The town's past is evoked in its churches, castle and museum.

HISTORICAL NOTES

Jean Ango and the Privateers' War (16C).—In the 16C the Portuguese treated as pirates any ships venturing off the coast of Africa but François I decided that reprisals should be undertaken and issued letters of marque. The master mariners of Dieppe, who were already known for their voyages of exploration, retaliated with the shipbuilder and maritime counsellor to King François, Jean Ango, constructing for the purpose, a fleet of privateers "such as would make a king tremble". Among the mariners were the brothers Parmentier who in 1529 when crossing the equator had thought up the ducking ceremony, still practised, when crossing the line; another outstanding figure was **Verrazano**, the Florentine who, in April 1524, discovered the site of New York to which he gave the name Land of Angoulême.

   Ango's fleet captured more than 300 Portuguese ships in only a few years and the King of Portugal, fearful for his merchant fleet, was compelled to intrigue for the withdrawal, at a price, of the letters of marque. Finally, in 1530, Jean Ango gave up the war and built himself a splendid palace of wood in Dieppe and, at Varengeville (*see p. 67*), a less sumptuous but equally sure styled country residence. In 1535 the King appointed him Governor of Dieppe and in 1551 he died and was buried in the chapel he had had built in St. James's Church.

   The Canadian Commando Raid of 1942.—On 19 August 1942, Operation Jubilee was launched with Dieppe as the primary objective; 7,000 men, mostly Canadians, were landed in this first Allied reconnaissance in force on the coast of Europe. Landings were made at eight points between Berneval and Ste-Marguerite but the only German strongpoint to be taken was the battery near the Ailly Lighthouse (*see p. 67*); the Churchill tanks floundered hopelessly on the beach under intense fire and were finally sacrificed to protect the re-embarkation. 5,000 men were killed or taken prisoner; the Allies learned that German defences were concentrated round the ports and, as naval losses were small, that amphibious operations on a larger scale might be successful; the Germans felt convinced that future Allied attacks would be directed particularly at the ports.

DIEPPE VIEWPOINTS

Boulevard de la Mer (view* of the town and the beach).—*Telescope: 0.20 F.; English commentary: I F.* The point can be reached either by car from the Pourville-sur-Mer road (a detour recommended to those arriving or leaving Dieppe by the D 75) or on foot along the Chemin de la Citadelle.

Chapel of Our Lady of Succour (N.D. de Bon Secours—view* of the town and harbour).— Approach the chapel from the D 113, the Puys road.

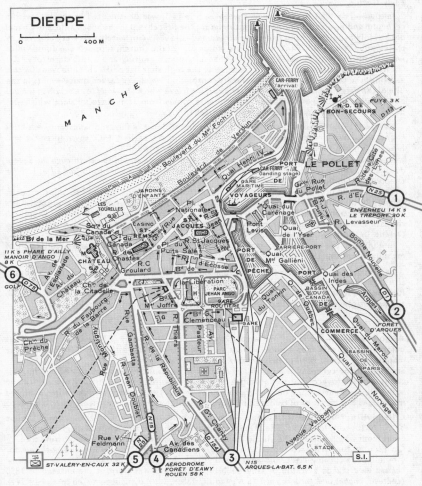

THE PORT

Dieppe port is interesting for its variety.

Passenger Port (Outer harbour).—This is the most unusual part of Dieppe harbour with tall, dark stone buildings, surrounding the basin where the Newhaven–Dieppe ships moor. The coming and going beneath the arcades and around the fish market add to the old shipping harbour atmosphere.

Dieppe is one of France's larger passenger ports: in 1971 half a million passengers used the Newhaven–Dieppe line alone.

Fishing Port.—The fishing fleet brings in primarily the higher grade fish (turbot, brill, bass and sole). The early morning bustle of the fish auction is full of local colour. The fishermen, who live mostly in the old Le Pollet quarter on the right bank of the river, landed 20,000 tons of fish in 1968 and a further 2,291 tons of scallops, for which Dieppe is known and is the major harbour in France.

Commercial Port.—The principal commodities handled are bananas from the Antilles (half the islands' production) and fruit and early vegetables from Morocco and the Canaries— Dieppe is France's main banana and its second largest fruit port. Handling equipment, heated and refrigerated warehouses line the Morocco Quay.

THE BEACH

The Maréchal Foch boulevard runs the length of the shingle beach which gets ever more crowded as you approach the west end where the castle stands out high on the cliff top. On the town side are gardens and sports areas and a second parallel avenue, the Boulevard de Verdun. Near the casino can be seen the west harbour gateway, a part of the 14C town defences and now known as Les Tourelles. Below the castle and west cliff a monument in the Square du Canada commemorates the Dieppe explorers of Canada in the 16, 17 and 18C and a plaque recalls the 1942 Commando Raid.

THE TOWN AND ITS MONUMENTS

The busiest part of Dieppe and the most interesting, apart from the streets around the exchange and the fish market, is the Puits-Salé Square where six roads meet and the Café des Tribunaux pediment stands.

St. James'★ (**St-Jacques**).—*Restoration in progress.* Begin by going round the outside which has been considerably rebuilt over the centuries. The 14C central doorway is surmounted by a fine rose window; the façade tower is 15C, the east end and radiating chapels are 16C; the south transept, on the other hand, has been left untouched, and is a good example of Early Gothic.

Interior.—The well proportioned nave, which is 13C, was ornamented in the 14C with a triforium and given tall windows a century later. The first chapel in the south aisle, the Chapel of the Holy Sepulchre, has a fine stone screen and is 15C. The other chapels were all given by the shipbuilders of old. The transept, the oldest part of the church, supports the dome which was rebuilt in the 18C while above the chancel are star vaulting and a 16C clerestory.

The Sacred Heart Chapel on the right facing the high altar has original Flamboyant Gothic vaulting; the centre chapel is known for its consoles on which are carved major events in the Life of the Virgin. Left, above the sacristy door, is a frieze which shows a file of Brazilian Indians and recalls the voyages of Dieppe explorers. It comes from Jean Ango's Palace which was destroyed by British naval bombardment in 1694.

Castle (15C).—Dieppe Castle, faced with alternate blocks of flint and sandstone, was built round a massive circular tower which formed part of the earlier, 14C, town fortifications. 17C curtain walls link the castle to the square St-Rémy tower.

Museum.—*Open always over the drawbridge, Rue de Chastes and in season through the Square du Canada; 10 a.m. to noon 2 to 6 p.m.; closed Tuesdays, 15 September to 15 June; 1 F. (2 F for temporary exhibitions).*

The museum, in addition to sculpture, local archaeological finds, 18 and 19C ships' models, 16 and 17C maps and navigation instruments, and pre-columbian Peruvian pottery, possesses a unique collection of **Dieppe ivories**★. These were made by craftsmen who came to Dieppe in the late Middle Ages to carve on the spot the ivory being imported from Africa and the Orient. In the 17C there were 350 ivory carvers in the town; today there is one.

In addition, the museum has many 19C Dutch and French paintings and a collection of mementoes of the 19/20C composer Saint-Saëns (1835–1921).

St. Rémy.—The chancel is the most remarkable part of the church, since its style is Gothic, although it was built during the Renaissance. There is an attractive wall decoration in the Renaissance style in which a savage appears armed with an assegai, a bow and an arrow, above the ambulatory on the left between the St. Catherine and Guardian Angel Chapels.

ENVIRONS

Ango Manor★.—*6 miles—9 km—about 2 hours.* Leave Dieppe by ⑥, the D 75; turn off left before Varengeville into a double avenue of beech trees. Leave the car 150 yds. from the manorhouse (*open 1 April to 10 November, 2.30 to 6.30 p.m.; 3 F.*).

Standing at the centre of the vast inner courtyard, surrounded by steep roofed buildings, is the seignorial dovecote—its importance further emphasised by the intricacy of its brick and stone facing. Four arches on the ground floor level of the manor's south wing, sculpted medallions and patterns of coloured brickwork provide the basic ornament which is perfect.

Offranville; Miromesnil Château.—*Tour of 14 miles—22 km—about 1 hour.* Leave Dieppe by ⑤, N 25; turn left, D 55. The drive to Offranville includes an avenue of magnificent beech trees from which you see the village church and beside it its thousand-year-old yew tree.

On leaving, turn left into the D 54 and cross through St-Aubin-sur-Scie and continue for ½ mile before turning right, and after 1,500 yds., right again. At the boundary of **Miromesnil Château Park** stands a statue of Guy de Maupassant who was born in the château in 1850 (*château, chapel and gardens open 15 May to 1 October, 2 to 6 p.m.; apply to the caretaker; 3 F.*). The excursions starting from Argnes can be made equally from Dieppe: see p. 45.

DOMFRONT ★—Michelin map ⑤⑨ ⑩—pop. 4,264—*Place to stay (see p. 37).*

Domfront (meaning Saint Front, or Frontius) lies spread along a rock crest, **a site★** commanding from some 200 ft.—70 m—the gorge through which the Varenne River pierces the last line of hills of Lower Normandy, and the Passais.

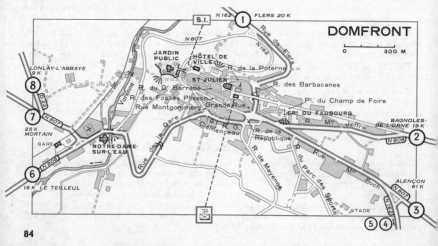

Public Garden round the Keep*.—Cross the bridge over the old moat to the garden laid out on the site of the fortress which was razed. There remain two majestic walls of the square keep. **Panorama*** of the Passais countryside from the terrace (*viewing table*).

Our Lady by the Water* (N.-D.-sur-l'Eau).—Stand on the Varenne River bridge to view this Romanesque church with its low central belfry and east end radiating chapels.

North Terrace on the Ramparts.—From the terrace there is a restricted but interesting view of the deep Valley of the Varenne known here as the Valley of the Rocks.

St. Julian's.—This 20C church, dominated by a tall cement belfry, has an interior plan in which an octagonal dome rests on four wide circular arches intersecting to form a square.

209 steps lead to the top of the belfry (closed for restoration).

ENVIRONS

Lonlay-l'Abbaye; La Fosse-Arthour.—*21 miles—33 km—about 1 hour. The small roads suggested, particularly those from Lonlay-l'Abbaye to the N 807, are narrow but beautiful.*
Leave Domfront by ①, the N 162, bearing left after 500 yds. into the Haute-Chapelle road

from which, at the start, there is an excellent view of Domfront. Go through La Haute-Chapelle and turn right into the D 22. Turn left after 5 miles—8 km—to Lonlay-l'Abbaye.

ENVIRONS OF DOMFRONT

Lonlay-l'Abbaye.—The church (*restoration in progress*), once part of an 11C abbey, has a pleasant country setting. The 15C portal opens directly on to the transept in which the south arm is typically Romanesque. The chancel, with granite pillars, is Gothic.

La Fosse-Arthour.—The most interesting part of the drive is between the two bridges. From a rock height on the left there is a view of the setting in which La Fosse-Arthour lies with the Sonce running swiftly between two steep sandstone banks and opening out into a pool before continuing on its way in a series of small cascades.
Return by way of the D 134 and N 807 (left).

DUCLAIR—Michelin maps ⑤④ ⑩, ⑤⑤ ⑥, ⑨⑦ ①—local map p. 145—pop. 2,705.
Duclair has developed on the outer side of a bend on the Lower Seine where the Ste-Austreberthe flows into the main river. The Liberation Quay, shaded by lime trees, makes a good spot from which to watch cargo boats, seemingly so out of place in this country setting, moving upstream to Rouen.

St. Denis'.—The church, though restored last century, has retained its 12C belfry which was crowned in the 16C with a spire. The first two round arches, through which the nave opens on to the aisles, rest on four half columns of Gallo-Roman marble.

The bay beneath the belfry, bounded by circular relieving arches, has the original early 12C vaulting still. The two stone panels with many small figures, leaning against the pillars, are late 14C.

The wooden Trinity placed on high is 14C as are the Crucifix with the Virgin and St. John in the lower nave, and the eleven large stone figures of the Apostles in the north aisle which came originally from Jumièges Abbey. Some of the windows are wholly or in part 14C; the east window dates from 1968.

The Catel Promenade.—Leave the car where the road to the cemetery joins the road overlooking the Seine so that you can turn round. Walk right, along the path bordered by a rail on the cliff side where after 150 yds. you can view the Seine below Duclair.

EAWY Forest **—Michelin map ⑤② ⑭ ⑮.
Eawy Forest—a name of German origin meaning wet pastureland and pronounced Ee-a-vi—covers a jagged crest 25 sq. miles in area—6,500 ha—bordered by the Varenne and Béthune Valleys. Eawy Forest, with that of Lyons, is the most beautiful beech woodland in Normandy. A straight divide, the Allée des Limousins, cuts through it, crossing deeply shaded valleys.

**FROM DIEPPE TO NEUFCHATEL-EN-BRAY through the forest
37 miles—60 km—about 3 hours

The forest roads suggested are often narrow and some are dirt roads only.

Dieppe**.—*Description p. 78.*
The N 15 crosses the plateau between the Varenne and Scie Rivers. From the D 107 after Le Bois-Robert there are views of the wooded crest between the Varenne and a tributary. The D 149 and D 154 go up the quiet Varenne Valley scattered with small brick manorhouses and where, on the left bank, the beeches of Eawy Forest grow ever more densely. The road turns into the forest at St-Hellier and, passing beneath the trees, goes up a valley to what is known as the Réformation crossroads where you turn right. At the Le Châtelet crossroads you find yourself in the Allée des Limousins, a firebreak 66 ft. wide—20 m—and nearly 9 miles long—14 km. The road continues, swinging from side to side across the Allée.

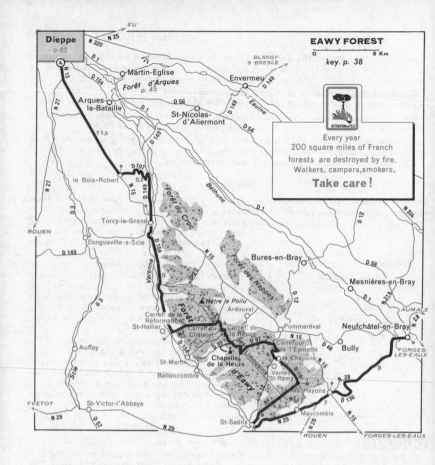

EAWY FOREST

key. p. 38

ATTENTION au FEU

Every year
200 square miles of French
forests are destroyed by fire.
Walkers, campers, smokers,
Take care!

La Heuze Chapel.—*Excursion of ½ mile—I km—from the La Heuze crossroads, by the D 99, the Grande-Heuze road (left) and second turning left, signposted by a ring of stone posts.*
The chapel, dedicated to St. Christopher, blends well in a group of old farm buildings. Drivers come in pilgrimage to the chapel on the Sunday preceding or following 26 July.

The Limousins Alley opens out in a new valley reached by the road in a wide bend. Turn sharp left into the D 97 aptly called the Road of the Long Valleys. At the Epinette crossroads, take the D 12 on the right which emerges into a wide clearing which you cross by the D 118 on the left. Continue to the St-Saëns road on the right. From this second straight cut through the forest you will get attractive views of the small town of St-Saëns. The N 29, beyond St-Saëns, goes up a valley, wooded, on the far side, by Eawy Forest.
Immediately beyond the Les Hayons crossroads, turn right into the D 136 which drops down in a great curve to the Bray Depression (*see p. 54*), which you can see well from the road.

Neufchâtel-en-Bray.—*Description p. 121.*

ECOUIS *—Michelin maps ⑤⑤ southeast of ⑦, ⑨⑦ ③—pop. 870.

The village of Ecouis in the Normandy Vexin Region centres round the twin towers of its old collegiate church. This was built between 1310 and 1313 by Enguerrand de Marigny, Superintendent of Finances to Philip the Fair. His life ended tragically upon the gibet only two years later but how his politics have been outlived by his policy of local artistic patronage may be seen from the works of art in the church.

The Collegiate Church*.—*Tour: about ½ hour.* The sombre building—the roof was replaced by the present brick and stone vaulting at the end of the 18C—would be disappointing but for the collection of 14C **statues*** inside.

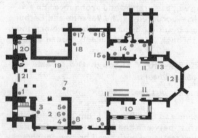

6) 17C Altarpiece of the Assumption.
7) Our Lady of Ecouis (14C).
8) 14C Statue of St. Margaret.
9) Funerary statue of Jean de Marigny, brother of Enguerrand and Archbishop of Rouen at his death in 1351.
10) St. John's Chapel—the wooden vaulting gives an idea of the original roof over the nave.
11) 14C choirstalls; 16C doors and panelling.
12) Monumental door, once part of the roodscreen.
13) 16C Christ in his shroud.
14) North side chapel: 14C St. Lawrence; 14C St. Denis; St. Martin; St. Cecilia.
15) 14C Royal Madonna.
16) 14C St. Agnes.
17) 14C St. Veronica.
18) 15C *Ecce Homo* in wood.
19) 15C Annunciation group: a group of delightful cherubs reading prophecies of the Incarnation support the Virgin, whose face and hands, and the face of Archangel Gabriel, are in marble inlaid into the stone.
20) 14C John the Baptist.
21) 17C organ case.

1) 14C Statue of Alips of Mons, wife of Enguerrand de Marigny.
2) 16C Chapel of the Immaculate Conception with beautiful vaulting and hanging keystones.
3) Early 15C Crucifix.
4) 14C St. Nicasius.
5) 14C St. Anne and the Virgin.

ÉCOUVES Forest ** —Michelin map ⑥⓪ ② ③.

This forest with its deep glades of oak, beech, Norman and woodland pine, and spruce, sheltering deer and roe-buck which are hunted in winter, extends for some 58 sq. miles— 15,000 ha—covering the eastward foothills of Lower Normandy. The tallest of the hills is the Ecouves Beacon, which with that of the Avaloirs (see p. 40) reaches an altitude of 1,368 ft.—417 m— making it the joint highest point in western France.

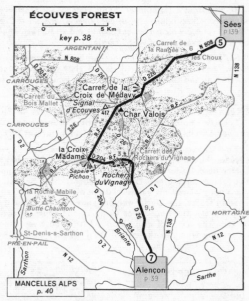

**FROM SÉES TO ALENÇON through the forest

18 miles—29 km—about 1½ hours— plus ¾ hour on foot Rtn

Sées*.—*Description p. 139.*

The N 808 enters the forest at Les Choux. At the top of a rise, at the La Rangée crossroads, bear left into the D 226 from which you will glimpse the Argentan.

The Croix de Médavy Crossroads.—This major viewpoint is marked by an old octagonal milestone carved with the old road names. The tank commemorates the part played by the French 2nd Armoured Division commanded by General Leclerc in clearing the forest of Germans on 12/13 August 1944 (see p. 25).

The Croix-Madame Crossroads.—This crossroads too is marked with an ancient milestone and also by a magnificent clump of Normandy Pines.

Several attractive walks can be made from the crossroads including that along Sapaie Pichon path on the left. Follow the yellow blazes through the tall and closely planted pines through which you will get occasional glimpses of the woodland countryside. *Time: about 1¼ hours.* Return and drive, to the left of the Sapaie Path, down the D 204 from which there is a beautiful view, to the Vignage Rocks crossroads where you bear right into the D 26 and again right into a forest road where you park the car.

The Vignage Rocks*.—¾ hour on foot Rtn. The path, marked with yellow blazes, leaves the forest road to turn back, right, to a low rock crest from which there are outstanding views over the forest. The path returns higher up to the forest road.

Continue along the D 26 towards Alençon. The monument on the edge of the forest is to the French 2nd Armoured Division.

From the road there are views of the conical Chaumont Mound, Mount Souprat in the distance and later of the Alençon countryside edged by the Perseigne Forest.

Alençon*.—*Description p. 39.*

ELBEUF —Michelin maps ⑤④ ②⓪, ⑤⑤ ⑥, ⑨⑦ ①—pop. 19,827.

Elbeuf, which was formerly one of France's major textile centres, now finds itself a general industrial agglomeration, numbering, with the adjoining towns of St-Pierre, Caudebec, St-Aubin and Cléon, some 40,000 inhabitants. Chemical, electrical, engineering and metallurgical plants and car factories, including Renault, have been built close to the older mills.

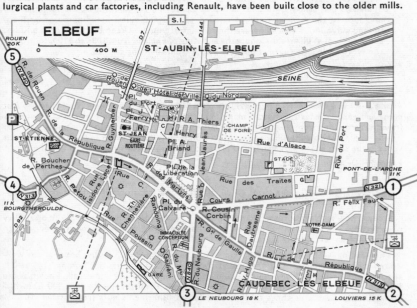

SIGHTS

St. Stephen's (St-Etienne).—This Flamboyant Gothic church possesses 16C stained glass windows (Crucifixion, Life of the Virgin), and an 18C glory beam at the entrance to the chancel (*possibly hidden by scaffolding*) and a 13C recumbent figure of Our Lord (north aisle), both good examples of wood carving.

St. John's (St-Jean).—The interest of this Gothic church with its Classical ornament and furnishings lies in its original stained glass windows—1st, 3rd, 4th and 5th windows in the north aisle and the 1st in the south aisle which all date from 1500.

EPTE Valley—Michelin maps **55** ⑧ and ⑱, **96** ②, **97** ③ ④ and ⑭.

The River Epte, which rises in the Bray countryside crosses the Vexin Plateaux and enters the Seine on its north bank, has played an important part in Norman history.

The Creation of the Duchy of Normandy.—It was at St-Clair-sur-Epte in 911 that Charles the Simple—a patronymic meaning sincere and honest and not in the least pejorative —met **Rollo**, leader of the Normans. The Normans camped on the right bank of the river, the French on the left. Dudon St-Quentin, the first chronicler of Normandy, recalls how the Viking placed his hands in those of the King of France and without there ever being a written treaty, the Duchy of Normandy was created and the Epte and Avre Rivers declared, respectively, the boundaries to north and south of the Seine. The Epte line was later to become the scene of many bloody battles between the Kings of France and the Dukes of Normandy when, at the end of the 11C, they became Kings of England (*see p. 73*).

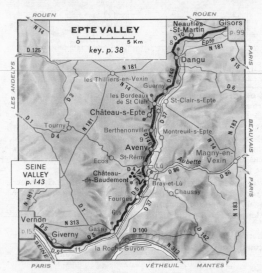

FROM GISORS TO VERNON

25 miles—41 km—about 1 hour

The road along the right bank of the Epte is often deeply shaded. Prosperous small villages and fortresses, now in ruins, dating back to the Franco-Norman wars add interest to the drive.

Gisors★.—Description p. 99.

Neaufles-St-Martin.—The village is dominated by a keep upon a perfectly preserved artificial mound. The only remaining walls are those facing France.

Dangu.—The main feature of the Gothic church (*closed on Sunday afternoons in winter*) are the 18C woodwork and painted panelling in the chancel, the 16C Montmorency Chapel in which a monotone window above the altar shows St. Denis, St. Lawrence and, on his knees, William, fifth son of Anne of Montmorency, High Constable of France. Near the pulpit is an 18C Beauvais tapestry of the Crucifixion and at the end of the church a fine wood carving of the Annunciation.

Château-sur-Epte.—*Excursion of ½ mile—1 km—from the D 146. Open 1 April to 30 September, Thursdays and Sundays: 10 a.m. to 6 p.m.* Leave the car in front of the fortified 13C entrance to the farm and ask permission to visit the ruins. Standing on an artificial mound surrounded by a moat, are the remains of a massive keep built by William Rufus, second son of William the Conqueror and King of England from 1087 to 1100, to protect the Norman frontier against possible attack from the King of France.

Aveny.—15C bridge.

Baudemont Castle.—*Excursion of ½ mile—1 km—from Bray-et-Lû.* Castle ruins and good view of the valley.

Giverny.—Claude Monet lived in the village from 1883 until his death in 1926. His house (*not open*) and garden, which possessed many more flowers in the lifetime of the artist and his friends, can be seen from the D 5^E. On the far side of the road Monet had the pool dug which he was to plant with waterlilies and paint so wonderfully, particularly in the great *Nymphéas* series to be seen at the Orangerie and Marmottan Museums in Paris.

Vernon★.—Description p. 153.

ÉTRETAT ★★—Michelin maps **52** ⑪, **54** ⑧—local maps pp. 67 and 68—pop. 1,472. *Place to stay (see p. 36).*

Etretat, now an elegant resort, has always had a great reputation because of the originality of its setting. The usual gentle Normandy beach scene here gives way to the grandeur of high cliffs and, often, of crashing waves.

The setting.—The shingle beach, skirted by a sea wall promenade, lies between the well-known cliffs—to the right the Amont or Downstream Cliff with its small chapel; to the left the Aval or Upstream Cliff with its monumental arch or cut through the chalk, known as the Porte d'Aval, the Upstream Gateway. Offshore stands a solitary needle rock 200 ft. high— 70 m. On the beach are three traditional thatched fishermen's huts (reconstructed).

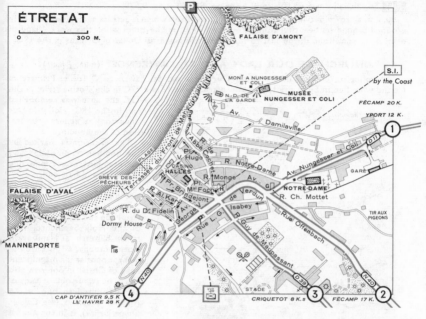

SIGHTS

Church of Our Lady.—The Romanesque doorway of the church was unfortunately spoiled last century by the addition of a tympanum, but inside the first six bays of the nave, dating from the 11C, can be seen in all their purely Romanesque decoration of geometric motifs and godroon adorned capitals. The rest of the building, including the lantern, is 12C.

Covered Market.—The reconstructed market adds character to Maréchal Foch Square.

ENVIRONS

Aval Cliff★★★ (Falaise d'Aval)—*1 hour on foot Rtn. See above. The path has no hand rails.*
Climb the steps at the west end of the promenade to the path which scales the cliff face. Walk along the edge of the cliff to the Porte d'Aval crest. There is a wonderful view of the Manne Gate on the left and the needle rock. Walk on round the bay to the Manne Gate where the view extends to Cape Antifer. A more direct path back skirts the golf course.

Amont Cliff★ (Falaise d'Amont).—*Access: see above.* Leave the car by the Nungesser and Coli Monument—a memorial to the first, and unsuccessful, attempt made on 8 May 1927 to fly the Atlantic *(museum open: 15 June to 15 September, 10 a.m. to noon, 2 to 7 p.m.; 2 F.)*

Fécamp★★.—*Tour of 23 miles—37 km—about 1 hour—plus 1½ hours sightseeing.* Leave Etretat by ② and continue along the N 40 to Fécamp. Return by the Dieppe–Etretat road *(p. 67).*

Le Havre★★.—*Tour of 40 miles—64 km—about 2 hours—plus 2½ hours sightseeing.* Leave Etretat by ③, the D 39, and follow the Etretat–Le Havre road *(described p. 68)* taking in the alternative route through Ste-Adresse. Return to Etretat by the N 40.

Cape Antifer; Bruneval.—*4 miles—7 km—from Etretat to Cape Antifer, plus 3 miles—5 km— from Cape Antifer to Bruneval.* Leave Etretat by ④, the N 40, turning right into the D 111, right again at the church in La Poterie and right once more in front of the Café du Phare.

Cape Antifer.—*Lighthouse—open 1 April to 30 September, 2 to 6 p.m.; 1 October to 31 March, 2 to 4 p.m.*
There is an extensive view of the coast south to Cape La Hève from the top of the lighthouse which stands on a promontory 334 ft.—102 m—above sea level.
Turn round and at La Poterie take the D 111 on the right.

Bruneval.—A German radar installation not far from the beach was the objective of an Allied raid on the night of 27/28 February 1942 when three detachments of British parachutists landed and, after destroying the enemy position, re-embarked almost without loss. The monument, up from the beach, on the left, commemorates the part played by the French Resistance and the British Paratroops.
Other drives starting from Etretat can be made into the Caux Region (see p. 66) and in the Seine Valley (see p. 140).

Eu, a small town between the sea and the forest from which it gets its name, lies peacefully grouped around its beautiful collegiate church built in the times when this was a "land of princes"—from Rollo in the 11C to the last of the powerful Dukes of Orleans in the 19C.

CHURCH OF OUR LADY AND ST. LAWRENCE* (tour: ½ hour)

The collegiate church, dedicated to Our Lady and St. Lawrence O'Toole, Primate of Ireland who died in Eu in the 12C, was erected in the 12 and 13C in the Gothic style. In the 15C the apse was remodelled and in the 19C, Viollet-le-Duc undertook a general restoration of the building.

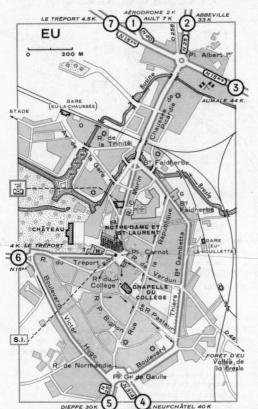

The exterior is marked by the number of pinnacled and turreted buttresses supporting the aisles and east end.

The **interior** is striking in size and harmonious proportions. The second ambulatory chapel on the right, the Chapel of the Holy Sepulchre, contains, beneath a Flamboyant Gothic canopy, a 15C Entombment; opposite is a magnificent head of Christ in Sorrow, also 15C. The statue of Our Lady of Eu, attributed to one of the Anguier brothers (see College Chapel below), is in the absidal chapel, while in the north transept chapel is a 15C low relief in wood of the Nativity.

Crypt.—Open 9.30 a.m. to noon, 2 to 6 p.m.; closed Tuesdays and Wednesday afternoons from 15 September to 1 May; 1 F.; apply at the sacristy.

The then Duke of Orleans, and future King Louis-Philippe (who reigned from 1830 to 1848 when he abdicated and fled to England where he died —at Claremont in Surrey—in 1850) restored the crypt in 1828. The 12/13C recumbent statue against the north wall is of St. Lawrence.

ADDITIONAL SIGHTS

Castle.—Open 1 April to 31 October, 10 a.m. to noon, 2 to 6 p.m. Admission: 2 F.

Eu Castle, a huge building without much character, was begun by Henri of Guise in 1578 and has obviously been restored several times since. It passed to the Orleans and, in time, became Louis-Philippe's favourite residence. The castle is now owned by the town; its contents are primarily of interest as mementoes of the Orleans princes.

College Chapel.—Closed for restoration.

The college, founded by Henri of Guise in 1573, bears the name of the 17C Anguier Brothers, one time students and gifted sculptors. The chapel was built in 1620 by Catherine of Cleves, Henri's widow, to whom she brought the County of Eu as a dowry in 1570. The Louis XIII façade is harmonious.

In the chancel are the two magnificent 17C marble **mausoleums*** of the Duke of Guise, assassinated at Blois on the orders of Henri III, King of France in 1588, and of his Duchess.

EU FOREST

35 miles—57 km—about 2 hours—plus ¼ hour on foot Rtn

Leave Eu by the D 49. At Incheville turn right into the D 58 which enters the forest. When, beyond the St. Martin's Priory Chapel on your left, you reach the Hêtre des Princes crossroads turn into the winding road beneath the trees which brings you to the Montauban crossroads and, after a dead straight section of road lined by very tall trees (D 278) and a forest lodge, to St. Catherine's Post where you turn right for the forest lodge.

St. Catherine's Viewpoint.—¼ hour on foot Rtn. Drive past the lodge (on your left) and park the car on the edge of the forest. Walk beneath the trees to a point from which you can see the peaceful countryside of the Yères Valley.

Return to St. Catherine's Post and continue along the road by which you came.

The Bonne Entente.—20 yds. off the road to the right. This Real Agreement has arisen from an oak and a beech growing so close together that, as the trunks have enlarged, they appear to spring jointly from a single bole.

At the St-Rémy Post, turn sharp right into the D 149 which brings you out of the forest and affords a view of the Yères Valley along which you drive, D 16, to St-Martin.

St-Martin-le-Gaillard.—The 13C church, altered in the 16C, has a slender slate belfry. Inside, the capitals are carved with humorous figures.

The road passes through Criel-sur-Mer from which you return to Eu along the N 25.

The Eure Valley, although not to be compared with the Seine, runs through a countryside between Dreux and Louviers which is most attractive. The green river banks below bare hill slopes hold many delightful surprises.

FROM DREUX TO PACY-SUR-EURE by way of Anet

29 miles—46 km—about 1½ hours—plus ½ hour sightseeing

Dreux*.—*Description p. 155.*

Leave Dreux by ①, the N 828, before bearing left into the D 16¹. The aqueduct across the valley takes water from the River Avre to Paris; the woodlands on the far bank form part of Dreux Forest; the outline which appears through a gap in the park wall a little before St-Georges-Motel is of the 17C Motel Castle.

> **Breuil-Benoît Abbey.**—*Excursion of ½ mile—1 km—from the D 143. Not open.* The monks who founded the Grande Trappe, mother house of the Cistercian Order, came from this now ruined abbey in the 11C. Beyond the castle stands the 12 and 13C church, its transept now collapsed, and the 16C abbot's lodge.

Just before Ezy-sur-Eure, the old humpback bridge of St-Jean links Saussay to the left bank where the bare slopes, hollowed out here and there into caves, become steeper.

Ezy-sur-Eure.—*Place to stay (see p. 37).* The town's speciality is the manufacture of combs, once made of horn.

Anet*.—*Tour: ½ hour. See p. 155.*

Ivry-la-Bataille.—*Place to stay (see p. 37).* The town possesses a restored 16C church which is remarkable for its tower and particularly its south door—now walled up—attributed to the 16C architect of the Tuileries in Paris, Philibert Delorme.
The battle in the town's name is the one in which Henri IV defeated the Ligueurs of Mayenne in 1590. The victory is commemorated by an **obelisk**, erected in 1804 by Napoleon, 4 miles away—7 km—northwest upon the plateau and approached through Couture-Boussey. The village has been famous since 1707 as a major centre for the making of reed instruments.

FROM DREUX TO PACY VIA ANET

0 — 5 Km.

key p. 38

Folletière Castle, an impressive late 16C brick edifice standing in a park, can be seen from the road between Neuilly and the Merey mills.
From the N 836, between Chambines and Pacy-sur-Eure, there are good views down to the river as it winds between green fields.

Pacy-sur-Eure.—The monument at the entrance to the town is of Aristide Briand (see *Cocherel, below*) who was greatly attached to the area.
The **Church of St. Aubin,** a fine Gothic building, remodelled in the 16C, has a nave remarkable for its symmetry and unity of style. The modern ornaments include four glass powder paste low reliefs round the altar and amber coloured stained glass windows by Decorchemont of the Ascension. There is also a beautiful 16C stone statue of the Virgin and Child.

FROM PACY-SUR-EURE TO LOUVIERS

21 miles—34 km—about 1 hour

Pacy-sur-Eure.—*See above.* Leave Pacy by the N 836 going north.

Cocherel.—The exploits of a man-at-arms and an apostle of peace have between them brought fame to Cocherel.
A pyramid beside the Jouy-sur-Eure road, the D 57 west from Cocherel, commemorates the victory of Bertrand Du Guesclin in this spot over the Anglo-Navarre forces in 1364.
From 1908 until his death in 1932, **Aristide Briand,** statesman and "apostle of peace" spent all his leisure time in three houses which he owned successively in Cocherel. He lies buried in the local cemetery beneath a massive dark granite stone. A statue, *Meditation*, on the far bank of the Eure, is also in his memory. Continue along the N 836.

La Croix St-Leufroy.—The church has a carved Renaissance font and an interesting collection of pictures from the former Abbey of Croix-St-Ouen.
The drive, which is attractive between Cocherel and Chambray-sur-Eure, becomes even more so along the left bank between Crevecœur and Cailly-sur-Eure where the river is lined by fine estates.

Acquigny.—There is a good view of the late 16C castle from the bridge over the Eure.

Louviers*.—*Description p. 112.*

Evreux, the religious and administrative capital of the Eure, standing on the River Iton which here divides into several arms, is the great agricultural market for the surrounding regions (see p. 12).

A French City throughout the Wars of History.—Evreux's story, like that of many towns in France, is a lengthy chronicle of fire and destruction:

5C.—The Vandals sacked Old Evreux, a prosperous market town on the plateau going back to the time of the Gauls.

9C.—The Normans destroyed the fortified town established by the Romans on the present site beside the Iton.

1119.—Henry I, King of England, set fire to the town when fighting the Count of Evreux who was supported by Louis VII.

1193.—King Philippe-Auguste, betrayed here by King John of England, fired the city in reprisal.

1356.—Jean the Good, King of France, laid siege to Evreux in his struggle against the House of Navarre, and set fire to the town.

1379.—Charles V besieged the town which suffered cruelly.

June 1940.—Following Germain air raids the centre of the city burned for nearly a week.

June 1944.—Allied air raids razed the quarter round the station.

After each disaster the people of Evreux have rebuilt their town from the ruins and worked to restore its prosperity.

Evreux today.—The opportunity was taken when the city centre was rebuilt after 1945, to provide attractive settings for the last of the town ramparts, the old bishopric, the cathedral and the 15C belfry, all of which remained undamaged. Gardens and a walk have been laid out at the foot of the Gallo-Roman ramparts beside the Iton. A ring road is planned to divert the N 13, Paris–Deauville, traffic from the city centre.

PRINCIPAL SIGHTS (tour: about 1 hour)

Cathedral of Our Lady⋆⋆.—The great arches of the nave are the only part remaining of the original church, which was rebuilt between 1119 and 1193, and once more set on fire. The chancel was built in 1260; the chapels added in the 14C.

Following the fire of 1356 the church was not repaired for two centuries when the lantern tower and the Lady Chapel were added.

At the beginning of the 16C the master builder Jean Cossart devised the magnificent north transept façade and doorway. The reconstruction was completed by remodelling the south tower in the Henri II style and the termination, in the 17C only, of the north tower.

It was the upper parts of the cathedral which suffered in the 1940 conflagration: the "silver belfry", a lead spire above the transept lantern tower, melted, and the west façade towers lost their coronation. (Reconstruction work in progress.)

Exterior.—Walk along the north side where the aisle windows were redesigned in the 16C in the Flamboyant style. The north door is a perfect entity in which all the richness of Flamboyant Gothic, then at its height, can be seen. Enter through the north door.

Interior.—The **stained glass⋆** and the **carved wood screens⋆** of the ambulatory chapels are outstanding.

Stand in the transept, between the pillars supporting the graceful lantern tower on Flamboyant pendentives. The nave—with one bay still to be restored—has the original massive Romanesque arches and, above, an elegant triforium of Gothic bays. The monotone glass dates from 1400.

The light chancel is closed by a superb 18C wrought iron grille and is very beautiful. The apse windows have been declared the most beautiful, the most limpid, of the 14C.

Fine wood screens dating from the Renaissance mark the ambulatory entrance in which the first chapel on the right, the Treasury Chapel, is entirely enclosed in a 15C wrought iron grille bristling with spikes and hooks. The screen to the 4th chapel is a masterpiece of imagination and execution, particularly the lower figures; the chapel glass is early 14C.

The central or Lady Chapel, given by Louis XI, has 15C windows of considerable documentary interest. The upper parts, including fleurs de lys, depict the peers of France at the king's coronation; the central window has a Tree of Jesse in which the Virgin is surrounded by a crowd of people. Two windows further on is Louis XI himself. On the altar is the venerated and delightful statue of Our Lady which is said to be late 15C.

The 3rd, 4th and 6th chapel screens are the oldest and purely Gothic—note the fantastic animals at the base of the 6th screen.

St. Taurinus' (St-Taurin).—This former abbey church dedicated to the first bishop of Evreux dates back to the 14 and 15C. A beautiful Romanesque blind arcade runs along the foot of the north aisle to the Renaissance font. The well proportioned 14C chancel is lit by superb 15C windows. Three windows in the apse trace the life of St. Taurinus.

St. Taurinus' Shrine⋆⋆.—Apply at the sacristy in the south transept, or at the presbytery, 2 Place St-Taurin. This masterpiece of 13C French craftsmanship was given by St. Louis to the abbey to contain St. Taurinus' relics and was certainly made in the abbey workshops. The silver gilt reliquary enriched with enamel (the best are low down) is in the form of a miniature chapel and even shows St. Taurinus with his crozier.

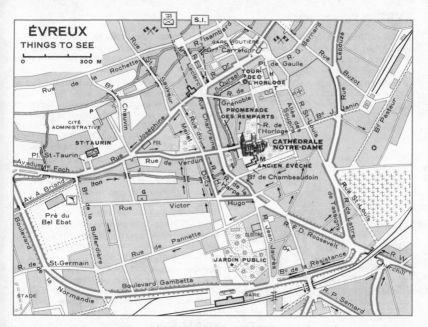

ÉVREUX
THINGS TO SEE

0 _____ 300 M

ADDITIONAL SIGHTS

Former Bishopric.—The 15C façade on to the cathedral has a fine Flamboyant air with dormer windows, ornamented window pediments and a staircase tower. The museum is inside.

Museum*.—Open, 10 a.m. to noon and 2 to 5 p.m. Closed on Tuesdays, 1 October to 15 March, 1 and 11 November, 25 December, 1 January, 1 May. Admission: 1 F.

Of the four galleries two are devoted to prehistoric Gallo-Roman archaeology—note a bronze *Jupiter Stator* and a late 2C or early 3C glass bowl—and two to the Middle Ages.

Clock tower.—An elegant 15C tower.

ÉVRON *—Michelin map 60 ⑪—pop. 4,977.

Évron, a small town at the foot of the Coëvrons, possesses one of the finest churches in the Mayenne Department. In the 19C the town flourished from its linen mills; now it is more generally industrialised—cheese, clothes, large scale animal slaughter.

Basilica of Our Lady*. *Tour: about ½ hour.* A massive square 11C tower, embellished with corner buttresses and turrets, links the Romanesque part of the nave to the abbey buildings which are a reminder that Évron was the seat of an abbey a very long time ago—the present buildings are 18C.

The nave's four original bays are Romanesque in contrast to the remainder of the building which was rebuilt to an enlarged plan in the 14C in Radiating Gothic style.

Enter through the south door. The bare Romanesque bays heighten the sense of space.

At the transept crossing the pointed arches rest on attached carved bell capitals. At the end of the north transept the polychrome stone *pietà* is 14C.

Chancel*.—Slender columns, pure lines and subtle decoration give the chancel, encircled by seven richly decorated radiating chapels, considerable elegance.

Chapel of Our Lady of the Thorn**.—The 12C chapel opens left off the ambulatory. Above is plain broken barrel vaulting supported by ceiling beams; in the chancel, oven vaulting. Christ is shown in a mandorla surrounded by the symbols of the Evangelists.

The chapel contains many works of art including Aubusson tapestries, three 17C terracotta statues, a large 13C statue, at the altar, of Our Lady of the Thorn in wood plated with silver. Beneath a remarkable 13C Crucifix on the left a glass contains the **treasure**** (open, 10 a.m. to noon and 2.30 to 6 p.m.; 1 to 5 p.m., on Sundays. Closed on Mondays. Apply to the presbytery) which includes plate, a delightful 15C silver Virgin and 16C reliquary.

ENVIRONS

Montaigu Mound*; Le Rocher Castle*.—*Tour of 20 miles—32 km—about 1 hour—plus ½ hour on foot.* Leave Évron by the N 23 bis, north on the map. As the road starts the climb towards the Coëvrons the views extend west over woods and lakes; to the east is Mount Rochard (1,171 ft.—357 m). The road drops down into Bais where, before the bridge, you turn left into the D 241 which skirts **Montesson Castle** with its curious convex roofs. Turn left, opposite the church, in Hambers, into the D 236.

1½ miles—2·5 km—further on bear left again into the narrow road to the Montaigu Mound.

Montaigu Mound*.—The mound, crowned by an old chapel dedicated to St. Michael, is only 952 ft. high—290 m—but, because of its isolation, makes an excellent viewpoint from which to see the Coëvrons rising in the southeast, Évron, Ste-Suzanne on its rock spike, in the south, Mayenne and the forest to the northwest and the Andaines forest in the distance.

Return to the D 236 and bear left and continue through Chellé to the D 7 where you turn left again until at the entrance to Mézangers village you turn right to Le Rocher Castle.

Le Rocher Castle*.—½ hour on foot Rtn. Leave the car at the entrance. Exterior and park only open: 15 June to 15 October, weekends, Mondays, Thursdays, 10 a.m. to noon, 3 to 6 p.m.

A gallery of five low rounded arches runs the length of the Renaissance façade. The 15C front, which is reflected in the lake, is more austere although harmonious, with a granite façade lightened by tall windows and three towers with pepperpot roofs.

Return to the D 7 and bear right for Évron.

EVRON* (concluded)

La Roche-Pichemère; La Chapelle-Rainsouin; Montecler.—*Tour of 22 miles—36 km— about 1 hour.* Leave Evron by the N 805, west on the map. Just after Brée turn right into the D 557 and continue to the entrance of St-Ouën-des-Vallons where a road on the right leads to La Roche-Pichemère Castle.

La Roche-Pichemère Castle.—Enter the park but don't cross the moat. The castle is made up of two main Louis XIII wings built at right angles and covered with the deep French style slate roofs. Massive square pavilions project from each corner adding considerable dignity to the building which stands on a grass mound. Make for the D 129 towards Montsûrs and from there, the N 162 *bis* to La Chapelle-Rainsouin.

La Chapelle-Rainsouin.—A room off the church chancel contains a beautiful 16C polychrome stone **Entombment***. The church itself has an unusual glory beam (*ask Mme Gélinier, in the house facing the east end of the church for the key; light switch on the right at the entrance*). The N 23 *bis* goes through the Vallons woods to Châtres-la-forêt where you take the D 562 on the right. A further road on the right brings you to Montecler Castle.

Montecler Château.—*Do not go beyond the moat.* The castle, built at the very beginning of the 17C, stands in sober dignity at the end of a vast courtyard. The remaining sides of the court are framed by unadorned annexes, built at right angles to the main wing, and an attractive chapel. But, in fact, the castle's most eye-catching building is the drawbridge lodge with ivy covered walls and a rounded roof crowned by a lantern turret. Return to the N 23 *bis* and Evron.

Montecler Château

FALAISE *—Michelin map ⑤⑤ ⑫—local map p. 148—pop. 7,599—*Place to stay (see p. 37).*

The attractive small town of Falaise, the proud birth place of William the Conqueror, suffered cruelly in the war since it lay in the direct path of the Germans as they tried to escape the Allied advance of August 1944 (*see map p. 24*).

The town's setting in the Ante Valley, a ravine marked by scattered rock spurs, is hard and rough and made even more mediaeval by being dominated by the enormous fortress haunted by the memory of Arlette and her victorious son William the Bastard.

The Beautiful Arlette (1027).—One evening on returning from the hunt, Robert, younger son of King Richard II, was struck by the beauty of a girl, her skirts drawn high as she worked with her companions washing clothes at the stream.

He was 17, watched for her daily and desired her. Arlette's father, a rich tanner, let her decide for herself and she, refusing all secrecy, entered the castle over the drawbridge on horseback and finely apparelled. Then, as the chroniclers of the time wrote, "When Nature had reached her term, Arlette bore a son who was named William."

Falaise is a good excursion centre for the Suisse Normande (p. 147).

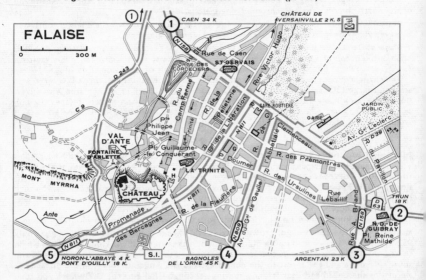

THE CASTLE** (tour: ½ hour)

An equestrian statue of William the Conqueror with the first six Dukes of Normandy on the pedestal stands in the Place Guillaume-le-Conquérant.

Guided tours: 16 May to 15 September, 8 a.m. to noon, 2 to 7 p.m.; 16 September to 15 May, 9 a.m. to noon, 2 to 6 p.m., closed Tuesdays, Fridays and 10 to 25 January; 1 F.; apply to the keeper.

Inside the castle perimeter follow the ramparts, once flanked by fourteen towers. The fortress stands at the end of a spur, facing Mount Myrrha and commanding the Ante Valley.

Keep.—This square building, standing on rock and dating from the 12C, is amazing in size and still appears redoubtable with great flat buttresses indicating where the walls stood until razed in the 18C. Inside, the guide points out the window through which Robert is said to have watched Arlette. Next door is a space said to have been the room in which William was born. A "little keep" guards the main entrance against possible attack.

Talbot Tower.—This impressive round tower 115 ft. tall—35 m—with walls 12 ft. thick—4 m—was built in the 15C and linked to the little keep by means of curtain walls.
In the St. Prix Chapel, the former garrison chapel, a memorial bears the names of 315 of William's companions-in-arms at the Battle of Hastings—the names have a familiar ring.

ADDITIONAL SIGHTS

Holy Trinity Church*.—*The chancel is being restored.*
The west front has a triangular Gothic porch; the east end Renaissance flying buttresses which were highly ornate (*restoration in progress*). Enter through a Renaissance porch with a coffered vault. The 15C pillars in the nave are quartered by slender engaged columns.

St. Gervase.—Building continued from the 11 to the 16C before St. Gervase was finished; the lantern tower is 12C. Inside, the contrast between the two architectural styles is striking: the right is Romanesque, the left Gothic. Modern glass in the nave and transept.

Our Lady of Guibray.—The apse and absidal chapels are pure Romanesque.

Arlette's Fountain.—The view is impressive towards the vast dominating castle.

ENVIRONS

Mount Myrrha*.—¼ *hour on foot Rtn. See map p. 94.* Drive to Mount Myrrha by way of the panoramic D 243 and the C 9 on the left. Leave the car at the top of the hill. Walk along a path to the left, over the plateau to a limestone escarpment overlooking the Ante Valley. Follow the crest line, left, to its end from where you will get a close-up view* of the castle.

The Devil's Breach** (Brèche au Diable).—*Tour of 16 miles—26 km—about 1 hour—plus ¼ hour on foot Rtn.* Leave Falaise by ①, the Caen road.

Aubigny.—At the entrance to the village, on the left, stands a Louis XIII castle and its even older annexes. In the parish church statues of six lords of Aubigny may be seen kneeling in the chancel in the sequence in which they lived, providing interesting details of contemporary dress.
Continue up the N 158, leaving the tall 13C belfry of Soulangy on your left and turning right into the D 261 from which you turn off left after 1½ miles—2·5 km—just beyond a rise. Go past the Mont-Joly Inn, skirt a small cemetery and park the car in a field.

Devil's Breach*.—Walk towards a rock outcrop topped by a spinney marking the tomb of Marie Joly, an 18C actress, whose husband was inconsolable if one is to believe the tearful lines upon the tombstone. From the escarpment edge you will see the Brèche au Diable or Devil's Breach, a gorge hollowed out by the Laison through limestone crests, typical of the Falaise countryside (*see p. 12*). A steep path to the left leads to the gorge.
Return past the Mont-Joly Inn and at the next crossroads turn left. Turn right at Ouilly-le-Tesson and at the next crossroads, right again.

Assy.—A magnificent avenue on the left leads straight to Assy Château, a beautiful 18C mansion, considerably enhanced by a portico of tall and elegant Corinthian columns.
Return to the road juncture and turn right and later left into the D 91.

Soumont-St-Quentin.—The church is 13, 14C; the belfry Romanesque below, Gothic above.
Return to Falaise along the N 158.

Versainville.—*2 miles—2·5 km.* Leave Falaise by the north. The château, completed in the 18C (*not open*) has a peristyled central wing linked by a gallery to a monumental pavilion.

Noron-l'Abbaye. *2¼ miles—4 km.* Leave Falaise by ⑤, the N 811; bear right in the D 243. 13C village church with two storey Romanesque belfry.

FÉCAMP **—Maps ㊹ ⑫, ㊻ ⑧—local map p. 67—pop. 21,745—*Place to stay (see p. 36).*
Fécamp is known today as a fishing port—it is France's fourth largest and her most important for cod, landed from the boats which sail regularly to the Newfoundland banks. The town is also famous as the home of Benedictine—a link with its monastic past when it was one of the more glorious religious centres of mediaeval Normandy.
Guy de Maupassant lived in the town, which figures in several of his works.

The Heavenly Gate.—From the 7C there was always a monastery in Fécamp to shelter the relic of the Precious Blood which had descended on the town (*see p. 97*).
Richard II, whose father, not content with having rebuilt a magnificent church to the Holy Trinity, had made him promise to found a Benedictine abbey, was much struck by the reformed Cluny style which he saw in several monasteries in Burgundy. These Cluniac reforms had been instigated by the Abbot of St-Bénigne at Dijon, **Guglielmo da Volpiano**, who was persuaded by Richard in 1003 to move with his monastic following to Fécamp.
The new abbey assumed considerable importance and its influence was felt throughout the duchy. Until the advent of Mont-St-Michel, Fécamp was the leading pilgrimage in Normandy with the dukes traditionally coming there at Easter; from the 11C, troubadours and minstrels, particularly favoured by the abbots, helped to spread the renown of the Precious Blood and the Holy Trinity Church. The Bishop of Dol was to write of this centre which attracted both religious and popular devotion and added prestige to the dukes of Normandy that "The monastery can be compared to a heavenly Jerusalem: it is called the Heavenly Gate, the Palace of Our Lord. Gold, silver and silken ornaments shine everywhere."

FÉCAMP VIEWPOINTS**

For a general view, make for the Senneville road, the D 79, northeast on the map. A mile from the village—2 km—as the road descends towards Fécamp, a valley widens and the view opens out to include the town, the cliffs and the sea. To the right is the path to the

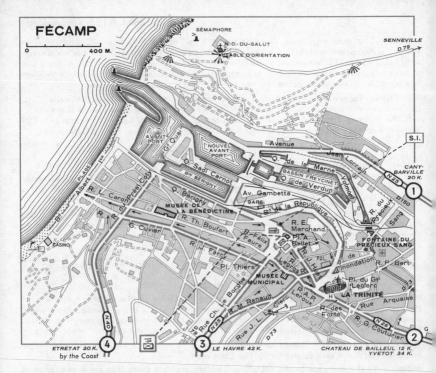

```
FÉCAMP

0          400 M.

SÉMAPHORE
N·D·-DU-SALUT
TABLE D'ORIENTATION
SENNEVILLE  D 79

S.I.
CANY-
BARVILLE
20 K.

AVANT
PORT
NOUVEL
AVANT
PORT

Avenue
Jean Lorrain
Q. de la Marne
BASSIN FRÉYCINET
Q. de Verdun
Av. Gambetta
GARE
Bd de la République
R. du Précieux Sang
FONTAINE DU
PRÉCIEUX SANG

MUSÉE DE
LA BÉNÉDICTINE

MUSÉE
MUNICIPAL
LA TRINITÉ
Rue Arquaise

CASINO

ETRETAT 20 K.
by the Coast          LE HAVRE 42 K.

CHATEAU DE BAILLEUL 12 K.
YVETOT 34 K.
```

Chapel of Our Lady of Safe Return (Notre-Dame-du-Salut), a seamen's pilgrimage church. Good walkers will advance beyond the beacon and the Crucifix, to the cliff edge where there is a view along the coast (*viewing table opposite the chapel on the D 79*).

As the road drops you can see along the cliffs to the Porte d'Amont at Etretat, until after a left-hand bend, the view changes to Fécamp town and harbour.

THE TOWN

Fécamp, a hardworking industrial town, takes on a lighthearted air in summer when it also becomes a seaside resort with tourists crowding its beach and historic buildings.

MAIN SIGHTS (tour: about 1½ hours)

Holy Trinity Church★★.—Pilgrims flock on the Tuesday and Thursday following Trinity Sunday to venerate the Precious Blood relic within this ancient abbey which is equally interesting for its contents as for its architecture.

Richard I's church, which was struck by lightning, was rebuilt in the 12 and 13C and reconstructed several times between the 15 and 18C. The town hall abutting on the north wall is in what were formerly monastic buildings of the latter period.

Exterior.—In length—416 ft.—127 m—the cathedral is one of the greatest in France. The Classical façade does not go well with the rest of the building, and the walls of the nave are severe. Walk along the south wall to a porch restored in the 19C and where an inner door has a tympanum which is a good example of Norman Gothic decoration (*details p. 18*). The square lantern tower rising 210 ft.—65 m—over the transept evokes, though on a grander scale, the typical Norman belfry. Enter through the west door.

Interior.—The majestically proportioned nave of ten bays but little adornment ends at the transept where the lantern tower rises in a sweep to 125 ft.—40 m.

The south transept contains a beautiful late 15C **Dormition of the Virgin★** (1). On the right of the altar is the Angel's Footprint. In 943, when the reconstructed church was being consecrated before William Longsword, an angel pilgrim appeared before the bishops deliberating on the church's patronage and commanded them to dedicate the sanctuary to the Holy and Indivisible Trinity. Before disappearing in a blaze of light, the angel left his footprint on the stone for all to see for ever.

The chancel's dimensions make it magnificent. The stalls (2), baldachin and high altar (3) are all good 18C works by the Rouen artist, De France. A Renaissance altar (4), commissioned by Abbot Antoine Bohier from Girolamo Viscardo, stands behind the high altar. The altarpiece is adorned with five low reliefs—the abbey's two benefactors, Richard I and Richard II, are depicted at either end.

The chapels off the chancel aisles and radiating chapels were given wonderful **carved screens★** in the 16C through the munificence of Abbot Antoine Bohier. The frieze of small Romanesque low reliefs (5) below the window in the 3rd chapel, were taken from an ancient 12C shrine. The **tomb★** (6) in the next chapel of Abbot Thomas of St-Benoît who died in 1307 is decorated with scenes from the abbey's history on its base. The radiating chapel (7) contains abbots' tombs.

The Lady Chapel★, rebuilt in the 15C on a crypt of the same dimensions, forms a separate group in Flamboyant Gothic. The wood

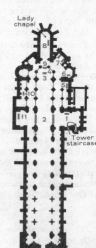

Lady
chapel

Tower
staircase

96

medallions, of which the fourth panel shows the veiled Christ (8), are 18C; the windows are 13, 14 and 16C. Facing the chapel is the white marble **tabernacle*** of the Precious Blood (9) by Viscardo.

The two following radiating chapels are the only remains of the earlier Romanesque church destroyed by lightning. From the first a door leads to the crypt below the Lady Chapel which served as a charter library. The door itself is surmounted by a Flamboyant decoration in which the donor's initials, R.C., can be seen intertwined with thistles—his name was Robert Chardon, the French for thistle.

The 17C tomb (10) in the Chapel of the Sacred Heart belongs to the Blessed Guglielmo da Volpiano, first Abbot of Fécamp, who returned to the abbey he had founded to die in 1031.

The north transept contains fragments of the former roodscreen (11) and a 17C timepiece showing the tides and phases of the moon.

The Benedictine Distillery and Museum*, 110 Rue Alexandre-Le-Grand.—*Open 9 to 11.30 a.m., 2 to 5.30 p.m.; closed Saturdays, Sundays and public holidays, 15 November to Palm Sunday. Admission: 1 F.*

In 1510, a monk by the name of Vincelli had the idea of distilling a liqueur from the aromatic plants which grew on the cliff: *Benedictine* was born. The Gothic and Renaissance style buildings were erected in the late 19C. To the **museum's*** original collection from the celebrated Fécamp Abbey—remains of the roodscreen, statues, charters, books and church ornaments—have been added enamels, ivories and wrought iron. The tour of the distillery and museum is accompanied by synchronised lighting and sound commentary (in several languages).

ADDITIONAL SIGHTS

Municipal Museum, Centre des Arts, Rue Alexandre-Legros.—*Open 10 to 11.30 a.m., 2 to 5.30 p.m.; closed Tuesdays; 1 F.* The museum has specialised in the town's history as an abbatical city and life in the Caux Region.

Fountain of the Precious Blood, inner courtyard to the right of No. 12, Rue de l'Aumône.—The fountain, which is of no artistic interest, was built round the spring rising on the spot where, according to tradition, the hollowed out trunk of a fig tree containing the relic of the Precious Blood came to rest. The relic, again according to tradition, was "entrusted to the sea and the Grace of God" by Isaac, nephew of Joseph of Arimathea.

THE PORT

Fécamp is primarily a deep sea cod fishing port and as such landed 25,271 tons in 1968—53% of the French total; in addition 4,770 tons of frozen fillets (37% of French production) were produced, giving an overall total of about 90,000 tons. Inshore fishing—herring and mackerel—is relatively unimportant. The Freycinet Basin is the liveliest: the Marne Quay is used for landing fresh fish, the Verdun Quay for salt and other fish. Trawlers with both fresh and salted fish come into the Sadi-Carnot Quay in the Bérigny Basin.

Associated industries are to be found all round: cod drying plants, herring curing works, canning factories, fish meal fertiliser works, rope and net works, shipyards.

The pleasure harbour, which is being enlarged already has moorings for 210 boats.

ENVIRONS

Bailleul Castle.—*Tour of 15 miles—24 km.* Leave Fécamp by ②, the Yvetot road. Turn right into the D 28 which goes up the pleasant Ganzeville River Valley.
When you reach the plateau a little before Bénarville, bear right into the D 11, and right again at Angerville village. Leave the car on the track before the castle entrance.
Open Easter to 30 June, 10 a.m. to noon, 2 to 6 p.m.; 1 July to 30 September, Thursdays, Sundays and holidays only from 2 to 6 p.m.; 1 October to All Saints Day, 10 a.m. to noon, 2 to 6 p.m.; 5 F.
Bailleul Castle has all the appearance of a highly original 16C building as you see it first, set in its beautiful park. Walking round you will discover an unexpected contrast between its main façade, where Renaissance fantasy has run free, and the lateral façades almost without windows or other openings and still positively mediaeval. The guardroom, the reception room and a state room are open.
Continue along the D 11 and return to Fécamp by way of Epreville and the N 25.

La FERTÉ-MACÉ—Michelin map ⑥⑩ ① ②—pop. 7,136.

La Ferté-Macé, situated next to Bagnoles and a spa which has known considerable changes in fortune, remains a stolid commercial and industrial regional town. It has a certain gastronomic renown for tripe, which is cooked on skewers, and holds a large market on Thursday.

Church.—The modern church has an 11C Romanesque tower, now the sacristy, and a carillon of 16 bells.
The **Municipal Museum**, in the town hall (*open on Thursdays and Saturdays from 2.30 to 4.30 p.m.*), contains works by the local artist, Léandre de La Touche.

FILIÈRES Castle—Michelin map ⑤⑤ ④—½ mile—1 km—northeast of Gommerville.

The castle can be seen at the end of the avenue leading to the main courtyard which is surrounded by a moat. All around is a park landscaped by Le Nôtre in the 17C.
The castle, which is built of white Caen stone, is in two very distinct parts—the left, 16C, wing and the central and right wings which date from the 18C. The plain classical façade of this later addition is ornamented with a pediment bearing the arms of the Mirvilles who built the castle and whose descendants still own it.
Open Easter to All Saints Day, Thursdays, Saturdays, Sundays, 2 to 7 p.m.; 3 F.; ½ hour.
The collections include Oriental porcelain and wall hangings, mementoes of the kings of France (Sèvres biscuit medallions), furniture, Fragonard lithographs, a good portrait of Louis XV by Van Loo and a *Yellow Lady* by Nattier.
Return to the courtyard and turn right for the **cathedral**, a magnificent avenue, set a little apart in the park, where the branches of seven rows of beech trees meet overhead.

Flers has managed both to modernise itself and remain true to the Normandy Bocage industrial tradition. Small ironworks were replaced as long ago as 1860 by cotton mills and today by components and electro-mechanical equipment factories.

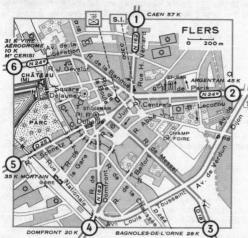

The Castle

The park is open from 1 April to 30 September, 7 a.m. to nightfall; 1 October to 31 March, 7 a.m. to 7 p.m.

Flers Castle, its 16C towers reflected in the moat and pool, is an unusual and somewhat bizarre building with a Classical main façade.

The park is pleasantly shady.

Museum.—*In the castle: open Easter to 30 September, 2.30 to 6 p.m.* The ten galleries are devoted to 17 and 19C paintings, weaving, and local paleontology and mineralogy.

ENVIRONS

Mount Cerisi*; Les Vaux.—*6 miles*—*10 km.* Leave Flers by ⑥, the N 24 bis.
Turn right at La Fontaine, into the D 229. Note the two giant yews in the old cemetery near the church as you go through La Lande-Patry.
Turn left into the surfaced D 18.

Mount Cerisi*.—Turn left by a petrol station in the village of Cerisi-Belle-Etoile.
A road—toll for its upkeep: 2 F. for cars—bordered by huge clumps of rhododendrons (*in flower: May–June; all flowers protected on Mount Cerisi*), rises up the slopes of Mount Cerisi, affording ever more extensive views over the Bocage. Finally you reach the castle which commands a **view*** of the last foothills of the Suisse Normande.
Return to the D 18 and continue along it.

Les Vaux.—Turn left immediately after a bridge over the Noireau and a dairy, into a narrow road. This follows the left bank of the river getting ever more enclosed by Mount Cerisi on the left and the St-Pierre Rocks on the right. Les Vaux is this enclosed beauty spot.
You can turn 800 yds. further on in a quarry or continue on foot.
Return to Flers by the D 18.

FONTAINE-GUÉRARD Abbey *—Michelin map ⑤⑤ ⑦—local map p. 41.

The ruins of the 12C abbey, standing isolated on the right bank of the Andelle, are both evocative and moving, so menacing is the threat of flood by the river.

Guided commentaries 2 to 6 p.m. (7 p.m. Sundays and holidays). If closed apply to the office at Radepont Castle (Salvation Army), ½ mile—1 km—away up the valley; 1 F.; time: ½ hour.

As you walk up the path you will see first, St. Michael's Chapel, built in the 15C over vaulted cellars. An underground passage links these with the abbey storerooms.

Straight ahead lie the ruins of the abbey church, consecrated in 1218. The flat east end with its many elegant windows remains as does a part of the absidal vaulting.

To the right, abutting on the now vanished cloister, is the chapterhouse, a most attractive room and fine example of Norman architecture of the first half of the 13C, with three aisles divided by a double row of small columns with crocheted capitals.

Further on is a second vaulted chamber, possibly the monks' workroom which resembles the knights' room in Mont-St-Michel Abbey. Go up a staircase to the monks' sleeping quarters on the storey above.

FORGES-LES-EAUX—Michelin maps ⑤② ⑯, ⑤⑤ ⑧, ⑨⑦ ③—local map p. 41—pop. 3,258.—*Place to stay (see p. 37).*

Forges-les-Eaux, a town where metal was worked until the 15C, is today a spa resort and an extremely pleasant place in which to relax, set in the green depression of the Bray Region (*see p. 54*) where this opens out to its fullest extent.

As you approach the entrance to the spa park along the Avenue des Sources, immediately beyond the railway bridge on the left, there is a 17C façade which once formed part of the Carmelite Convent of Gisors. Another beautiful façade overlooks the park, that of a hunting pavilion formerly erected near Versailles, which belonged to Louis XV.

The Spa Park.—The spa—the waters are only used for drinking (at a *buvette* at the park entrance) —offers, in elegant modern surroundings, all the distractions proper to a watering place. As you walk through the park, on your left is the "grotto" where Louis XIII, his queen and Richelieu took the waters. You come after a short while on to the pool formed by the Andelle.

ENVIRONS

Beauvoir-en-Lyons*.—*10 miles—16 km.* Leave Forges by ③, the N 321 and follow the route described on p. 41 along the Andelle Valley as far as Fry. Take the D 1 on the left before the church which brings you to the southwest Bray escarpment, massive bare mounds crowned, in the case of Mount Robert and a few others, with spinneys.

Beauvoir-en-Lyons*.—Park the car beyond the town hall and walk up the street on the left to the church. From the east end there is a **view*** of the green depression of the Bray Valley cutting away in a straight line, southeast. In clear weather you can see Beauvais Cathedral.

FRESNAY-SUR-SARTHE —Map ⑥⓪ ⑫ ③—pop. 2,615—*Place to stay (see p. 37).*

This small picturesque village perched above a curve in the Sarthe is a pleasant place in which to stay and a favourite with anglers and those wishing to explore the Mancelle Alps (*p. 40*).

The Setting.—To get a good view of Fresnay's setting stop near the bridge over the River Sarthe on the N 805 coming from Sillé-le-Guillaume.

Church of Our Lady.—The church is 12C and dominated by a remarkable octagonal belfry. The Romanesque doorway surrounds beautiful carved doors dating from 1528; on the left is the Tree of Jesse, on the right, Christ Crucified with the 12 Apostles in the fan and the Virgin in the architrave above.

Town Hall Terrace.—A public garden has been laid out in the castle's former precincts; from the terrace there is a pleasant view down to the river.

Headdress Museum (Musée des Coiffes).—*Open 1 March to 30 September (every day in July and August; on Sundays only, the rest of the year), 9 a.m. to noon and 2.30 to 7 p.m. Admission: 2 F. Apply to M. Chéreau, 1 rue de la Basse-Cour, ℡ 220.* Headdresses of the provinces of France are displayed in one of the old castle towers.

GISORS *—Michelin maps ⑤⑤ ⑧ ⑨, ⑨⑦ ④—pop. 7,660.

Gisors, a one time frontier town in the possession of the Dukes of Normandy, is the capital of the Normandy Vexin (*see p. 12*). Although badly battered in 1940, the town has retained considerable historical character.

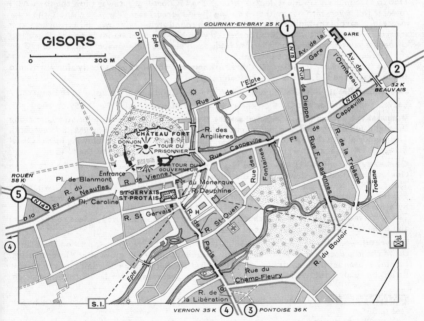

TOUR (about 1 hour)

Castle**.—*The precincts are open. Guided tours of the castle proper, 1 May to 30 September, 9, 10, 11 a.m., 2, 3, 4 p.m. (and 5 p.m. Sundays); 1 October to 30 April, 10 and 11 a.m., 2, 3, 4 p.m.; closed Tuesdays; 1 F.*

This magnificent group of 11 and 12C Norman military architecture dominates the town and commands a view of it, including the Church of St. Gervase and St. Protase, built, as can clearly be seen, throughout many different architectural periods.

The 11C **keep,** on its 65 ft.—20 m—artificial mound in the centre of the fortified perimeter and surrounded now by a public garden where once there was a moat, is flanked by a watch tower. This, and a solid surrounding wall, were added by Philippe-Auguste at the end of the 12C (*possibly closed for restoration*).

The most massive of the eight perimeter towers, known as the **Prisoner's Tower** and three storeys high, was also probably constructed by Philippe-Auguste. Access to the pointed arched chambers is by a curtain wall at the third storey level. There one sees built into the thickness of the walls both a chimney, with its open oven, and a well. The chamber below is adorned on its walls, where these receive the light, by prisoners' graffiti.

GISORS* (concluded)

St. Gervase and St. Protase*.—The oldest parts of the church go back to the 12C but construction continued to the end of the 16C as is evident both outside and inside. The Gothic chancel was completed in 1249; the side chapels which form the ambulatory were added in 1498 and 1507 and are immediately noticeable outside by their pointed gables well separated from the main east end which they nevertheless surround. The remarkable transept doors are 16C and Gothic as is the very tall nave. Finally the monumental west front is Renaissance: the doorway is delicately carved and flanked by two towers, that on the north being built in 1536 in François I style and crowned by a cupola, that on the south in Henri II style and left unfinished in 1591.

In spite of the mixture of architectural style the church as a whole appears perfectly harmonious, particularly inside. Enter through the south transept and you will see how the uncluttered light walls add to the architectural lines and richness of the carved decoration. The large monochrome window in the north chapel is 16C.

GOURNAY-EN-BRAY —Michelin maps ⑤②⑯, ⑤⑤⑧, ⑨⑦ ③ ④—local map p. 54— pop. 6,040.—*See town plan in the Michelin Red Annual Guide* France.

Gournay and Ferrières are the busiest towns in the Bray Region (*see p. 54*): the local dairy industry supplies the major part of the fresh cheese consumed in France.

In 1850 a local farmer's wife, helped by a Swiss cowherd, had the idea of mixing fresh cream with curds before these had been broken. The *Petit Suisse* knew instant success; today the Gervais-Danone works at Ferrières-en-Bray (*not open to the public*) treat more than 44,000 gallons of milk a day in the production of *suisses, carrés, double-crème, demi-sel* and "*Gervita*".

St. Hildevert's.—The church, which is largely 11C, has withstood several wars but the late 12C doors have suffered from overmuch restoration.

Inside, the massive columns are surmounted by capitals interestingly carved with animal and plant motifs. The oldest and most worn, at the end of the south aisle, are amongst the earliest examples of attempt at human portrayal and date from the Romanesque period.

ENVIRONS

St-Germer-de-Fly*.—*Tour of 23 miles—37 km—plus ¼ hour walking or sightseeing.* Leave Gournay-en-Bray by ② on the map in the *Michelin Guide* France, the N 31; after 4 miles— 6 km—turn right into the D 129.

St-Germer-de-Fly*.—The vast church, completely dominating the humble village crouched at its feet, is the finest religious edifice in the Bray. It was an abbey church and was built from 1150 to 1175 in Early Gothic style. Go through the 14C fortified gateway (now the town hall) to enter the nave which was mutilated during the Hundred Years War. The chancel, the most interesting part of the building, has galleries with round arched windows and a triforium with square lintels. A Romanesque altar decorated with blind arcades stands in one of the absidal chapels; a vaulted passage from the apse leads to an elegant Holy Chapel built in the 13C on the model of the famous Paris original.

Take the D 104 to Neuf-Marché; there turn left into the N 15 and shortly afterwards into the D 1ᴬ and the D 3, on the right to Mainneville.

Mainneville.—Beautiful 14C statues of the Virgin and Child and of St. Louis in the church.

Leave Mainneville by the D 14 on the right and at Martagny take the D 659 on the right.

Monument to the Rouge-Mare Engagement and the Flemings.—Rouge-Mare hamlet stretches along the right side of the road, the monument is on the left (¼ *hour on foot Rtn along a forest path*). The memorial is to those who prevented a German pioneer group from blowing up the Oissel Bridge over the Seine in 1914. Return to Gournay by Neuf-Marché and the N 15.

Gerberoy*.—*7 miles—11 km—by the N 30 and the surfaced Gerberoy road on the left.* Leave Gournay by ① on the town plan in the *Michelin Guide* France.
This fortified town, perched on its mound, had been forgotten since the 17C when the painter Le Sidaner (1862–1939), attracted by its character, came to live in it. He was followed by others who have restored the old houses and given it new life.
There is a modest 16C collegiate church (through the gate which used to lead to the castle) and a shaded walk where the moat once was.

Beuvreuil.—*5 miles—7.5 km.* Leave Gournay by ⑥, the N 316, going north on the plan in the *Michelin Guide* France. Continue straight ahead into the D 8 at a fork after a level crossing, turning subsequently first left into the D 84. After the Epte Bridge bear left into the narrow Beuvreuil road. A 16C wood and glazed brick porch precedes the small 11C country church.

GRANVILLE *—Michelin map ⑤⑨ ⑦—local map p. 119—pop. 13,967—*Place to stay* (*see p. 36*).

Granville, dominated by its rock, is a busy commercial port and lively seaside resort with a small beach. The Upper Town, encircled by ramparts, still has considerable character.

THE SETTING*

Roc Point, or la **Pointe du Roc,** which marks the northern limit of Mont-St-Michel Bay is linked to the mainland only by a narrow rocky isthmus which, in 1439 was captured by the Norman-English as a counter to Mont-St-Michel, the last French stronghold in the area. In 1440 a citadel was built more or less where the ramparts are now, and the English Trench or Tranchée aux Anglais dug. Two years later, nevertheless, the knights of Mont-St-Michel captured Granville.

The port has developed on the south side of the promontory, protected naturally from the north winds. The military installations remain on the promontory tip; the Lower Town, partly built on reclaimed land, is the business and bustling resort area.

THE UPPER TOWN—La Haute Ville

This Upper Town concentrates within its walls all Granville's military and religious past. The tourist with little time can content himself with views from the ramparts.

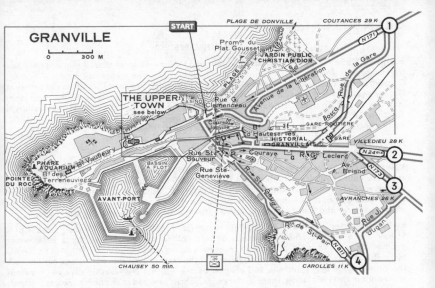

TOUR OF THE RAMPARTS* (about 1 hour)

Start from the square in front of the Casino.

Go along the Rue Georges-Clemenceau and the Rue des Juifs, from which there are views of the roadstead and harbour.

Go through the Main Gate (Grande Porte), on the right, and over the drawbridge, into the Upper Town. Turn right up the steps of the Rue Lecarpentier to follow the south rampart to the Place de l'Isthme. The view* from the enormous square extends, on a clear day, to the coast of Brittany (*viewing table*).

Continue along the inside of the ramparts by the Rue du Nord —where the town and the landscape are at their most severe but where the view is spectacular in stormy weather. The Chausey Islands lie to the northwest and in clear weather you can see Jersey.

There is an old house at No. 3 Rue St-Jean. Bear left by the Church of Our Lady into Rue Notre-Dame which brings you back to the Place de l'Isthme where you descend the main steps to the Casino.

ADDITIONAL SIGHTS

Old Granville Museum.—In the Main Gate building. *Open in the Easter school holidays and 1 April to 31 October, 10 a.m. to noon, 3 to 5 p.m. (1 April to 1 June, 15 September to 31 October Thursdays and Sundays only); closed at other times; 1 F.* Local history and headdresses.

Church of Our Lady.—The oldest parts of this massive granite edifice with a tower over the meeting point of the nave and chancel, go back to the 15C. The nave itself and west front, adorned with monolithic columns, were erected in the 17C.

Inside, since granite lends itself ill to sculpture, there are only a few carved capitals around the chancel which has interesting modern stained glass windows. The 13C statue, in the north chapel, of Our Lady of Cape Lihou—the traditional name for the tip of the Rock Point—is honoured in the Great Pardon of the Corporations and of the Sea (see p. 27).

The Lighthouse.—*Open 10 a.m. to noon, 2 to 6 p.m.* The **panorama*** from the lantern platform extends, in clear weather, from Cape Fréhel to Cape Carteret and includes the Chausey Islands, Jersey and the tip of Mont-St-Michel Abbey spire above the Carolles cliffs.

Aquarium.—*Open Easter to 30 October, 9 a.m. to noon, 2 to 7 p.m.; 4 F.* Sea lion pool.

THE LOWER TOWN—La Basse Ville

The old quarters now merge with later buildings centred on a main crossroads known as the Pont. From the Pont run the Rue Lecampion, over land reclaimed in 1835, to the harbour and the shopping street, the Rue du Docteur-Paul-Poirier to the Casino and the beach by way of the former and now enlarged Tranchée aux Anglais.

The Beach.—The narrow beach at the foot of shaly cliffs surrounding the bay is overlooked by the Plat-Gousset breakwater promenade. (Steps at northeast end at a public garden.)

Christian Dior Garden.—The garden belonged formerly to the couturier's family.

From the upper terrace you look down on the Granville promontory. Fifteen minutes' walk along the cliff path bring you to the vast beach at Donville, the complement to Granville's.

Granville Historical Waxworks Museum, 79 Rue Couraye.—*Guided tours 1 July to 15 September, 9 a.m. to noon, 2 to 7 p.m.; 3 F.*

GRANVILLE* (concluded)

ENVIRONS

Hambye Abbey**; Mount Robin*.—*Tour of 55 miles—88 km—about 3 hours—plus ½ hour sightseeing and walking.* Leave Granville by ①, the N 171, the Coutances road.

Go from Bréhal to Gavray by way of the D 13, D 33 (through Vey) and D 7. Cross the bridge at Gavray and 100 yds. further on bear right into the D 38. After 1½ miles—2.5 km—turn right into the D 238 towards La Baleine before continuing along the D 398 to Hambye church. Take the D 13, off which you turn right into Hambye town and right again into the D 51. At the bottom of a hill turn left, before a bridge over the Sienne, into the D 258.

Hambye Abbey**.—*Description below.*
Continue along the D 258.

Mount Robin*.—Leave the car by a barrier on the left and walk across a field to the Calvary at the summit at 905 ft.—276 m. There is a **panorama*** looking east of the Suisse Normande, northwest (from a little to the right of the Cross) of Coutances' Cathedral spires, and, on a very clear day, of the Channel Islands out to sea. Return to the N 799 from which you turn off left to Percy and Villedieu-les-Poêles to return to Granville directly by the N 24 *bis*.

St-Pair-sur-Mer.—*2 miles—3.5 km. Place to stay (see p. 36).* Leave Granville by ④, the N 811. St-Pair has a perfect children's beach of safe golden sands bordered by a breakwater promenade and a very old church said to have as its original a monastery founded in the 6C by St. Pair and St. Scubilion, local evangelists. Of the early church there remains a bay beneath the Romanesque belfry and the 14C chancel before which a Neo-Gothic nave and transept were built in the 19C. Inside, there is a large 16C Christ in wood in the north transept chapel; an old font in the baptistry, a 14C tomb of Sts. Pair and Scubilion in the old chancel behind the high altar (the recumbent figures are modern), and, in the north chapel, a 15C Virgin and the chasuble of St. Gaud, Bishop of Evreux in the early 7C.

HAMBYE Abbey **—Michelin maps ❺❹ south of ⑬, ❺❾ north of ③—2½ miles—4 km —south of Hambye (*place to stay: see p. 37*).

Hambye Abbey whose plainly majestic and serene ruins punctuate the green Sienne Valley was founded in about 1145 by the local lord, Guillaume Paisnel.

Guided tours (1 hour), 10 a.m. to noon and 2 to 7 p.m. (5 p.m., 1 November to Easter). Closed on Tuesdays out of season. Admission: 2.50 F. The approach, off the D 258, passes beneath a monumental gateway into the monastery.

Abbey Church**.—The abbey's very disposition makes it impressive even though it lacks its west front, the first bay of the nave and its roof. The Romanesque nave is narrow and without aisles; the appearance severe but for a romantic note given by slender lancet windows.

Above the transept a two storey lantern rests on pointed arches, its paired windows beneath semicircular transoms so placed as to light the chancel to full advantage.

The Gothic chancel, with sharply pointed arches, an ambulatory and radiating chapels is exceptionally large. In the centre, two 15C tombstones mark the sepulchre of the last member of the abbey founder's family.

Conventual Buildings.—*Under restoration.* A visit includes rooms off the old cloister: the sacristy, a narrow corridor with cradle vaulting where a 16C polychrome *pietà* is to be seen; the typical Norman Gothic chapterhouse; the small frescoed Hall of the Dead; the library; the kitchen with a monumental chimney; the guests' dormitory with walls hung with 17 Norman tapestries and furnished with period pieces.

Le HAVRE **—Michelin maps ❺❷ ⑪, ❺❹ ⑦, ❺❺ ③—local maps pp. 68 and 144—pop. 200,940.

Le Havre, a great seaport and the final milestone along the beautiful Seine Valley, spreads its modern installations to the edge of the furthest Caux promontory. In 1945 Le Havre bore the least enviable title of Europe's worst damaged port; today it is once more France's greatest transatlantic harbour. Two car ferries also operate to England and Ireland.

Le Havre town, including the residential area of Ste-Adresse and the old port of Harfleur, is a remarkable example of large scale reconstruction and successful town planning.

HISTORICAL NOTES

The port, created on the decision of a king in the 16C, has been repeatedly enlarged and modernised by the industry and tenacity of the local Havrais.

A Judicious Choice.—In 1517, François I ordered the construction, to replace Harfleur which was silted up, of a harbour—*havre*—and fortification on the Grâce coast. The marshy site chosen did not look promising except that the floodwaters of high tide remained there for two hours or more and this, in fact, proved decisive in Le Havre's development.

In 1518 the first flagship entered the Bassin du Roi; the king bestowed his name, provisionally, on the town and his arms: a salamander on a red field . . . which it retains.

Gateway to the Ocean.—Le Havre's present importance as a trading and transatlantic port began during the American War of Independence when it supplied the "rebels". All produce such as cotton, coffee, sugar, tobacco and exotic woods from the one time colony were distributed from Le Havre to all parts of Europe, bringing considerable prosperity to the town. The exchange was founded in 1784. Le Havre is a close parallel to Liverpool in many senses, particularly cotton, both being traditional ports of entry with a textile industry founded close by, and each having a cotton exchange closely in touch with the other.

In the 19C relations with New York grew even closer: in 1850 the vessel *Franklin*, using sails and paddles, crossed the ocean in a fortnight; in 1864 came the first steamship, the *Washington*. The Place du Havre became a synonym for the powerful international commercial and banking organisation which had developed in the town.

Le Havre during the War.—Le Havre suffered 146 raids, more than 4,000 killed, 9,935 dwellings totally destroyed and 9,710 partially destroyed. The town's siege began on 2 September 1944—the Battle of Normandy was over and Paris liberated, but Le Havre was still occupied.

Allied air raids went on ceaselessly for eight days from 5 September; the Germans determined to blow up any port installations still in existence. On 13 September 1944 Le Havre was liberated. It took two years, even with the Allied aid, to clear the destruction and reconstruction was, therefore, able to begin only in 1946.

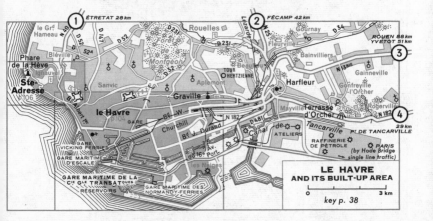

LE HAVRE AND ITS BUILT-UP AREA

key p. 38

THE PORT

The **port**** consists of three distinct areas:

the tidal docks, used by ships of all sizes but principally intended for ocean liners, tankers and cargo ships with rapid turn round;

the wet docks, serving merchant ships only;

the closed docks where the water level is constant and, finally, beyond the refinery, the Tancarville Canal which handles river traffic.

The present traffic is eight times pre-war—Le Havre has become a considerable oil port, with petrol representing 80% of the merchandise handled. In 1969 traffic reached 51 million tons, making Le Havre France's second port after Marseilles; nearly 450,000 passengers passed through its six harbour stations.

The opening of Tancarville suspension bridge connecting the Havre region with the areas on the left bank of the Seine has rapidly brought the anticipated additional traffic to the town.

The Port in the Future.—The alluvial land along the north bank of the Seine which extends to Tancarville affords excellent possibilities for extending the port so enabling it to receive even larger ships.

A new tidal basin has been built to take merchant ships, tankers and ore carriers. A **lock** at the end of the basin will control the water level in a second closed dock which in turn will connect with a maritime canal along which factories will ultimately be built. Ships of more than 200,000 tons will be able to come up the canal and discharge directly to the factories in the industrial zone.

An artificial island is also to be built up offshore to afford a harbour for giant tankers.

TOUR (*about an hour excluding any visit to a liner*)

Trips round the harbour begin at Easter; apply for information to the Syndicat d'Initiative, Place de l'Hôtel-de-Ville, ☎ *42 57 49.*

Start by car from the Port Autonome du Havre building between the Citadelle Basin and the inner port. (*Information on liner sailings available from the reception of the Port Autonome or harbour master's office.*) Go along the Lucien-Corbeaux Avenue.

Port Authority Harbour Station (Gares Maritimes du Port Autonome).—A lively congress hall when a boat docks or sails.

Compagnie Générale Transatlantique Harbour Station.—The Joannès-Couvert Quay can be reached on foot except when a liner is actually docking or sailing. On the far side of the Théophile-Ducrocq Tidal Basin are refineries and tanker moorings.

Tour of a liner.—*Visits to transatlantic liners—date of stay in port to be found in the press— 8 to 11.45 a.m. or 4.30 p.m. Advance booking compulsory at the Service de la Compagnie Générale Transatlantique, 89 Bd. de Strasbourg.*

Continue along the Lucien-Corbeaux Avenue, turning right when you see the power station.

Go past the Normandy Ferries Harbour Station and along the north quay of the central jetty of the Théophile-Ducrocq Dock. After looking at the passenger ships moored at the Transatlantique quay return to the power station.

Power Station.—The present capacity of 850,000 kW will rise to 3,250,000 kW by 1980 (Battersea 1971: 473,000 kW). The station will be one of the largest in Europe, spreading over an area of 80 acres—32 ha—and ultimately with three chimneys each rising 787 ft.— 240 m.

Cross the Lucien-Corbeaux Avenue and the railway. On your right is the longest cotton warehouse in Europe: 820 yds. from end to end (750 m). Facing the cotton warehouse is the tropical wood landing quay. By way of Bridge No. 4 (Pont no. 4), the Saône Quay, Rue de l'Amiral Courbet and the Rue Marceau, you will come to the Vauban Dock where you turn left and, at the end, left again before the Citadelle Basin to regain the Port Authority building.

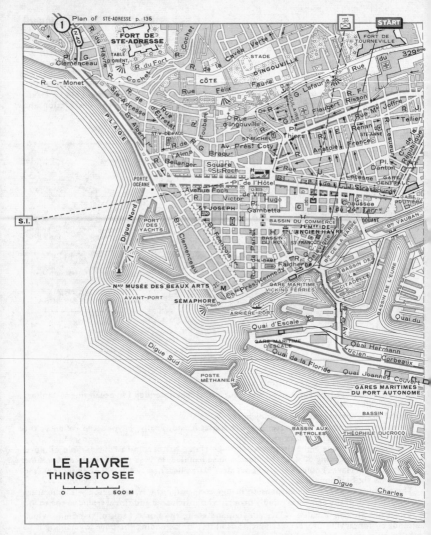

Plan of STE-ADRESSE p. 135

LE HAVRE
THINGS TO SEE

0   500 M

ADDITIONAL SIGHT

Signal Station (Semaphore).—The signal station (radar, radio, telegraph) is also the pilot and tugboat station—the tugs are known as *abeilles* or busy bees. From the end of the jetty you will get a good view particularly of the methane gas tankers in the outer harbour.

THE TOWN

The interest in a visit to Le Havre lies in seeing large scale postwar town planning.

The Reconstruction.—The old town, which had been planned on a chessboard principle by the Italian architect, Belarmato, in 1541 was virtually wiped out in 1944. A new town was therefore planned keeping the chessboard concept but including wide vistas to balance the huge groups of buildings that would continue Le Havre's commercial tradition.

The Commercial Dock (Bassin du Commerce), now reserved for yachts and the sailing school, has been made the focal point for the new central quarter with a new Chamber of Commerce on one side, surrounded by business houses. A cycle and foot tunnel 650 yds. long has been constructed beneath the Cours de la République; the Place de l'Hôtel de Ville and Avenue Foch so reconstructed that they look out to sea, the vista enhanced by the new town hall in the square and the Porte Océane (see p. 106) at the end.

TOUR *(about 1½ hours by car)*

Modern Quarter★★.—Start from the Town Hall Square.

Place de l'Hôtel-de-Ville.—The square, as designed by Auguste Perret, is one of the largest in Europe. Three storey buildings with flat roofs line the sides, the horizontal lines being broken by six ten-storey tower blocks. The town hall itself, also by Perret, is a plain building with good lines.

The Rue de Paris, Le Havre's finest street in the 18C, leads off the square opposite the town hall, the **Avenue Foch**, a magnificent modern street and Le Havre's Champs Elysées, west to the sea.

Turn left in the Boulevard François I for St. Joseph's.

St. Joseph's★.—*Best in a clear light.* This modern church is by Auguste Perret and is regarded as one of his major accomplishments. The structure is of reinforced concrete including the 348 ft. high belfry—106 m—which dominates the exterior. **Inside★★** a strikingly monumental effect has been gained by grouping four clusters each of four square pillars to support the 260 ft. high lantern—80 m. Light pours through coloured glass inset into the church walls.

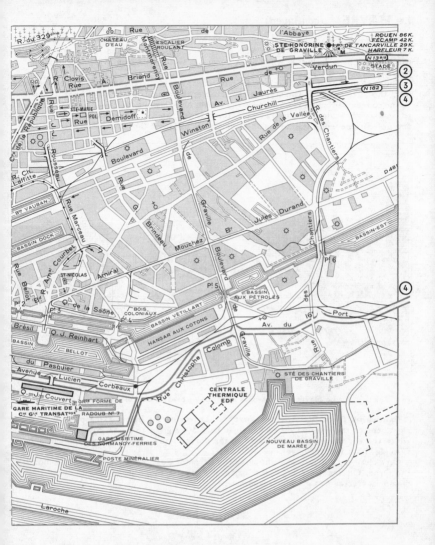

Continue along the Boulevard François Ier, the Chaussée Président-Kennedy—Fine Arts Museum on the corner—and the Boulevard Clemenceau to the beach.

Return along the Avenue Foch to the town hall then take the Avenue Président-Coty, the Rue d'Ingouville and, on the right, the Rue Georges-Lafaurie.

Côte d'Ingouville.—This quarter has, since the beginning of the 19C when rich shipbuilders and others built fine houses on the hillside, been *the* residential area of Le Havre.

From the end of the Rue Georges-Lafaurie there is a good **panorama of the town★★**.

Return along the Rues Félix-Faure (from which you will get good occasional glimpses of the town, the port and the estuary), Foubert and Georges-Braque to the town hall.

ADDITIONAL SIGHTS

Old Havre Museum.—*Open 10 a.m. to noon, 2 to 6 p.m.—closed Tuesdays, 11 November, 25 December, 1 January and 1 May. Admission: 1 F.*

The museum, which possesses plans and engravings relating the town's history from its foundation in 1517 to the end of the 19C, is in a restored 17C house which in itself gives a good idea of urban life in Normandy at that time. Displays of model ships and china, porcelain and glass.

Fine Arts Museum.—*Open 10 a.m. to noon, 2 to 6 p.m.; closed Tuesdays, 11 November, 25 December, 1 January and 1 May; 1 F.*

The building, officially opened in 1961 and facing the open sea, is built entirely of glass and steel. The roof, designed to provide the best possible light to the galleries inside, is highly original. It consists of six sheets of glass covered by a horizontal slatted aluminium sun blind through which natural light passes together with electric light which is subsequently filtered through clear or opaque ceiling lights. The galleries are linked on different levels by gangways similar to those on the outside of the building and reminiscent of those on board ship.

French, Italian, Dutch and Flemish schools are represented. There is an outstanding **collection★ of works by Eugène Boudin,** painter of the Normandy beaches of the last quarter of the 19C (see p. 20) and of **canvases★ by Raoul Dufy.**

Ste-Honorine de Graville Church.—*Enter if possible from the Rue de l'Abbaye—leave the car by the gate to the cemetery (if closed enter by the footpath on the far side of the abbey).*

A sanctuary was erected in the 6C on this spot to shelter the relics of St. Honorine. These, however, were later removed to Conflans near Pontoise to preserve them from the "fury of the Normans".

Le HAVRE** (continued)

A monumental Black Madonna stands at the Rue de l'Abbaye entrance, placed there after the Franco-Prussian War of 1870. Walk along the cemetery path and round the church to the right to the old cloister which is in a pleasant setting and from which you can see out over the Seine Estuary.

The present church (*possibly closed for restoration*) was formerly the abbey church and dates from the 11 to the 13C. The crypt is remarkable; the capitals in the nave most unusual.

The conventual buildings now house the **Graville Abbey Museum** which is principally devoted to lapidary and sculptural art—12 to 16C tombstones, capitals, stone statues, also low reliefs and polychrome wood statues (*same opening times as for the Old Havre Museum*).

(After Galf photo, Paris)

Le Havre.—The Avenue Foch looking towards the Porte Océane

Panorama from Ste-Adresse Fort.**—Leave the car in a parking place by a sharp right bend on the way up by the Chemin du Fort. Steps go up to a grass covered terrace from which there is a wonderful **panorama**** of the port, the town, the estuary, Honfleur and the Côte de Grace (*viewing table*).

On a clear day you can see right along the Calvados Coast on either side of the mouth of the Orne. On the far side of the Ignauval Valley is the Pain de Sucre—Sugar Loaf—a memorial erected as a mariner's landmark.

STE-ADRESSE

(about 1 hour)

Ste-Adresse**, a town once limited to the Ignauval Valley, has expanded to form a continuous whole with Le Havre.

La Hève Lighthouse (1951).—*Open 8 a.m. (10 a.m. in winter) to 1 hour before sunset.*

The **view*** from the second platform from which the light flashes a white beam visible at night for 31 miles—50 km—includes the Seine Estuary, the Côte Fleurie and Le Havre port.

Extensive views also from the **viewing table*** and telescope on the Boulevard du Président-Félix-Faure.

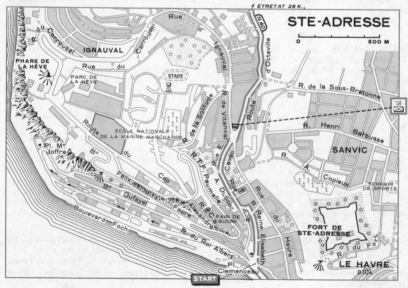

HARFLEUR

Harfleur, once a port in its own right at the mouth of the Lézarde Valley, has retained a certain character, in spite of now being at the centre of Le Havre's industrial zone.

St. Martin's.—The church's 272 ft. belfry—83 m—has been famous in the Caux Region since the 15C. Inside, the pillars on the north side have foliated capitals, those in all other parts of the church rise in a single sweep. The first chapel on the south aisle contains an 18C altarpiece and a 14C tombstone of a local lord and lady.

View from the Bridge.—Go from the church along the Rue des 104 and Rue Gambetta, on the right, to the bridge over the Lézarde from which you will get a good view of the church belfry.

ENVIRONS

Orcher Terrace*.—*2 miles—3·5 km—plus ¼ hour on foot Rtn.* Leave Harfleur by the Gonfreville–l'Orcher road; turn right 100 yds. after Gonfreville church. Park the car 50 yds. further on in front of Orcher Castle gate. *Apply for permission to park the car from the keeper (on the right).*
An alley leads to the shaded west end of a long **terrace*** situated some 300 ft.—90 m—above the Seine. The view includes the oil refineries, the estuary, Honfleur, the Côte de Grâce and, further to the right, Le Havre.

HONFLEUR **—Michelin maps ⑤⑷ ⑧, ⑤⑤ ③ ④—local map p. 144—pop. 9,207—*Place to stay (see p. 36).*

Honfleur on the Seine Estuary, at the foot of the Côte de Grâce hill, is a delicious town. Its old dock, its church and old streets combine in singular harmony.

HISTORICAL NOTES

Honfleur, an important strongpoint until the 15C, acquired true glory through the part played by its mariners in the 17C Norman voyages of discovery.

Canada, a Norman Colony.—Ever since the beginning of the 16C, navigators had been anchoring briefly along the coast of a land named Gallia Nova by Verrazano, the discoverer of the site of New York (*see p. 82*); in 1534, however, **Jacques Cartier** stepped ashore and claimed the territory in the name of France. He named it Canada, the Huron word for village. François I, however, was disillusioned as the explorer brought back no spices, no gold, no diamonds. Canada was left unexplored until the 17C when the experienced navigator, **Samuel Champlain**, received orders to colonise this vast territory. He set sail from Honfleur, and in 1608 founded Quebec.

As a result of Louis XIV's interest, on Colbert's advice, Canada was rapidly developed into virtually a Norman and Percheron colony populated by more than 4,000 peasants who emigrated across the Atlantic. Fishing, hunting, fur trading and agriculture flourished.

The Iroquois Indians, however, bitterly opposed the French colonists and by 1665 these had to appeal to France for aid against mounting attacks. A thousand soldiers arrived; simultaneously a decree was published compelling each to marry within a fortnight one of the "king's daughters" dispatched from France to help increase the sparse population.

From Canada, **Cavelier de la Salle** journeyed south to explore and colonise Louisiana in 1682 and establish the communication route along the Ohio Valley which was to lead to war with the British and finally the loss by the French of Canada in 1760. *See map (p. 23).*

Honfleur, the Artists' Paradise.—The character, the atmosphere of Honfleur have inspired painters, writers and musicians. At a time when the coast of Normandy was in fashion with the Romantics, Musset came to stay on St-Gatien and Honfleur began to fill with painters and not only those who were Norman born such as Boudin, Hamelin and Lebourg but also Paul Huet, Daubigny, Corot and others from Paris and foreigners such as Bonnington and Jongkind.

It was in the small St-Siméon Inn, at Mère Toutain's that the Impressionists (*see p. 20*) first met. Artists have continued ever since to visit Honfleur.

Baudelaire, who stayed in the town with his mother in her old age, declared "Honfleur has always been the dearest of my dreams" and while there wrote his *Invitation au Voyage.*

Other Honfleur citizens include the composer Erik Satie (1866–1925), the poet and novelist Henri de Régnier (1864–1936) and Lucie Delarue-Mardrus.

THE TOWN

PRINCIPAL SIGHTS *(tour: about ¾ hour)*

Start from the Place de la Porte-de-Rouen.

The Old Dock**.—The quaysides are picturesque and lined along one side by tall slender houses. Slate reigns, darkening all roofs and sometimes facing the walls. The governor's house, at the end, completes the scene.

Walk along the St-Etienne Quay to look across to the tall façades on St. Catherine's Quay reflected in the water. The Old Dock provides moorings for pleasure craft and fishing boats.

St. Stephen's Church (14 and 15C) on the right has now been incorporated into the Ethnographic and Norman Folk Art Museum (see p. 108). Cross the swivel bridge.

The Governor's House (La Lieutenance).—Only a relic now remains of the 16C house in which the king's lieutenant, Governor of Honfleur, once lived. The Caen Gate, once part of the town ramparts, has been inset between two wicket gates in the façade overlooking the square while that on the harbour bears a plaque commemorating the sailing of Samuel Champlain for Canada. From the corner of the passenger quay you get a good view of the house, the Old Dock and, on the other side, the outer harbour.

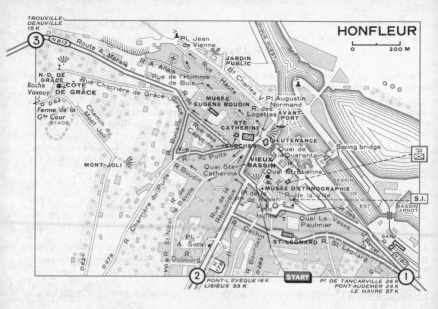

Take the Rue des Logettes which comes out on the Place Ste-Catherine where the market is held and which is one of the most attractive spots in the old town.

St. Catherine's Belfry*.—*Open Easter to 15 October, 10 a.m. to noon, 2 to 6 p.m.; closed Tuesdays; 2 F., ticket valid also for the Eugène-Boudin Municipal Museum.*

The belfry, a building covered in chestnut weather boarding, stands apart from the church on a large foundation which contained the bellringer's dwelling. A visit inside discloses the fine timberwork.

St. Catherine's*.—This church is a rare example in western Europe of a building constructed, apart from the foundation, entirely of wood. After the Hundred Years War all masons and architects were employed on the inevitable postwar reconstruction, but the Honfleur "axe masters" from the local shipyards determined to thank God immediately for the departure of the English and built a church by their own skill.

The interior has twin naves and side aisles, the timber roof over each nave being supported by wooden pillars. The carved panels ornamenting the gallery are 16C, the organ 18C. There are also many statues, both old and new, of wood.

Return to the Governor's House: view of St. Stephen's from St. Catherine Quay.

ADDITIONAL SIGHTS

Eugène-Boudin Museum, Rue Albert Iᵉʳ.—*Open Easter to 15 October, 10 a.m. to noon, 2 to 6 p.m.—closed Tuesdays, 1 May, 14 July; 2 F., ticket also valid for the St. Catherine Belfry.*

The museum is primarily devoted to the Honfleur school of painting and works by painters of the Seine Estuary. Two galleries contain oils and pastels by Eugène Boudin and his friends, Isabey, Huet, Courbet, Monet, Jongkind and others. Dufy, Marquet and Villon and their contemporaries are to be found elsewhere in the museum.

There is also an excellent **display of Norman costumes and headdresses***.

Ethnographic and Norman Folk Art Museum.—*Guided tours 10 a.m. to noon, 3 to 6 p.m.; closed 15 January to 15 February; 3 F. During the season enter through St. Stephen's Church, at other times by the door at the end of the alley to the right of the church.*

St. Stephen's now contains mementoes of the town and local celebrities.

The old houses in the Rue de la Prison adjoining the church have been reconstituted and as one walks through them, one gets a good idea of life in a 16C Norman town.

Old Streets.—All Honfleur's old quarter is picturesque. The Rue Haute, formerly the Chemin de la Grève, outside the fortifications is particularly characteristic, being the street where many rich shipbuilders lived. Erik Satie was born in No. 90.

The Rue de l'Homme-de-Bois and the Rue de la Ville are where the salt warehouses were.

St. Leonard's.—The church's façade associates, in bizarre amalgam, an ornate Flamboyant doorway and a 17C belfry tower. Inside are two immense shells which have been converted into fonts, two wooden statues of St. Peter and St. Paul at the entrance to the nave and an 18C copper lectern from Villedieu-les-Poëles in the narthex.

THE CÔTE DE GRÂCE**

The hill's serene beauty makes it dear to all who know Honfleur.

The Calvary.—There is a good **panorama**** from the Cross of the Seine Estuary, the Le Havre roadstead and Tancarville Bridge. *Telescope.*

Chapel of Our Lady of Grace.—In the centre of the esplanade beneath tall trees, stands the small Chapel of Our Lady of Grace and within it the statue after which it is named. This graceful 17C building which has replaced a sanctuary, said to have been founded by Robert the Devil in the 11C, is visited by pilgrims throughout the year (see p. 27).

Mont-Joli Viewpoint.—The view complements the one from the Calvary: in the foreground is the town and to the east the semicircle of hills.

HOULGATE★★—Michelin maps ❺❹ ⑰, ❺❺ ②—pop. 1,741—*Place to stay (see p. 36).*

Houlgate is the perfect type of Normandy resort where the coast and the surrounding countryside are equally lovely. The shady avenues, the houses and gardens all add to the attraction of the green Drochon Valley in which the resort is set.

The magnificent fine sand beach is bordered by a breakwater promenade which extends to the foot of the Vaches Noires Cliffs (*see p. 74*). Bathers congregate on the beach section of the promenade; anglers and those in search of shellfish at the end beneath the jagged cliffs.

JUBLAINS Roman Ruins—Map ❻❶ ⑪—9 miles—14 km—northwest of Evron.

The ruins of the Roman Fort of Jublains—Neodanus—lying south of the village along the Montsûrs road, afford the best local evidence of the Gallo-Roman period. Coins, figurines and jewellery discovered during excavations would seem to indicate that the fort was built in the first half of the 3C. Jublains camp appears to have been not only a citadel but also, to judge by the number of roads meeting there, a stage post with houses, shops, officials and police.

Entrenched Camp.—*Open 9 a.m. to noon, 2 to 7 p.m.; 1 F.; time: ½ hour.*

The camp, enclosed by a thick stone wall with brick courses, is a quadrilateral, 138 yds. long by 126 yds.—!26 × 115 m—flanked by nine towers.

Within the walls can be seen traces of the public baths and a massive construction with four buildings at right angles, possibly food shops, in which the basements and one doorway are constructed of squared granite blocks laid in a complicated style.

In the centre is the impluvium, a sloping paved court to catch the rain.

JUMIÈGES★★★—Michelin maps ❺❷ ⑬, ❺❹ ⑩, ❺❺ ⑤—local map p. 145—pop. 1,305—*Place to stay (see p. 37).*

Jumièges, in a splendid setting on the Lower Seine, is one of the greatest ruins in France.

The Jumièges Almshouse.—In the 10C Duke William Longsword rebuilt Jumièges on the ruins of the former abbey founded in the 7C by St. Philibert and destroyed by the Vikings (*details p. 141*). The new Benedictine abbey soon became popularly known through its benefactions as the Jumièges Almshouse. But charity did not preclude learning and Jumièges also became widely recognised as a centre of scholarship and wisdom.

The large abbey church was consecrated in 1067 in the presence of the Conqueror.

The Black Band.—The last monks dispersed at the Revolution and in 1793 the abbey was bought at a public auction by a timber merchant from Canteleu who undertook to make use of Jumièges as a stone quarry and to that end blew up the lantern in the church. A new proprietor in 1852 set about saving the ruins which now belong to the nation.

THE ABBEY★★★ *(tour: ½ hour)*

Open 1 May to 30 September, 9 a.m. to noon, 2 to 6 p.m.; 1 October to 30 April, 10 a.m. to noon, 1.30 to 4 p.m.; 2 F., including the museum—half price Sundays and holidays. Enquire about Son et Lumière performances.

Church of Our Lady.—The entire nave, which rises to a height of 89 ft.—27 m—together with part of the transept and chancel, remain. Twin towers, square at the base, octagonal above, rise 141 ft.—43 m—on either side of the main door. Inside, backing on the façade, a wide gallery overlooks the nave of which one of the features which makes it outstanding is the arrangement of massive square pillars quartered by columns alternating with slender piles of single columns. On either side are galleries covered with groined vaulting. The transept was largely destroyed in the 19C and only the west wall of the lantern remains, supported with great effect still by a high and sweeping arch.

The original chancel, around which traces of an ambulatory have been discovered, was enlarged in the 13 and 14C but today all that remains are two vaulted chapels.

A covered passage, named the Charles VII Passage after the king's visit, leads from the major church to the smaller St. Peter's.

St. Peter's.—The porch and first bays of the nave are Carolingian, the remaining ruins 13 and 14C.

The porch, pierced by an arch, is flanked by two small doors behind which are steps to the towers and galleries. The first two bays are a rare example of 10C Norman architecture; the rounded hollows above the semicircular arches were once covered in frescoes. Above, a gallery opens on the nave through small twin bays with rounded arches.

Chapterhouse.—In accordance with monastic tradition, the chapterhouse, which is early 12C, opened on the cloister. The square bay and apse were covered by pointed arches which are amongst the oldest known examples of this type of vaulting.

An ancient yew tree marks the centre of the square cloister with its 26 bays.

Storeroom.—The west wall of the very large storeroom, which dates from the late 12C, is decorated outside with bays encircled by arcades or surmounted by trilobed tympana.

Museum.—The museum in the former abbot's lodge contains keystones, abbots' tomb-stones, the Enervés tomb, a fine example of 13C sculpture, the gravestone of Agnès Sorel, favourite of Charles VII, and numerous capitals and statues from the abbey.

ADDITIONAL SIGHT

Parish Church.—The nave is 11 and 12C. In the 16C a vast chancel and ambulatory were added with the idea of the new church's replacing the abbey. A few works of art—altarpieces, 15 and 16C stained glass, etc.—were brought from the abbey to the church at this time.

LASSAY—Michelin map 60 ① —pop. 1,806.

Lassay Castle, dominating the village with its towers with their pepperpot roofs, was built in 1458 in place of an older building which had been dismantled in 1417. The later castle is a prime example of military architecture of the reign of Charles VII.

CASTLE★ (tour: ½ hour)

Guided tours 8 to 11.30 a.m., 1.30 to 8 p.m. Leave the car on the castle esplanade approached from Bagnoles by the Sept-Forges road, the right turn at the main town crossroads. Cross the bridge over the moat and ring; 2 F.

One enters the inner courtyard, surrounded by high walls, through the barbican, a fortified construction protecting the true entrance to the castle over the drawbridge. The two towers guarding the bridge were linked by living quarters which now contain 16 and 17C furniture. A curious "Chinese oven" in which porcelain was fired, is to be seen in one of the towers—the Duke of Brancas Lauragais produced the first porcelain objects to be made from Alençon kaolin in this stove in the 18C. One of the tower staircases leads to the curtain walls from which you can see the casemates at the foot of the barbican.

ENVIRONS

Bois-Thibault Château.—*½ mile—1 km—along the D 216 and 650 yds. beyond the town along a road on the left. Ask M. Brochard in the shoeshop at the start of the castle road near Lassay central crossroads, for the key before setting out.* The Renaissance château ruins are a striking contrast with the severity of Lassay Castle.

LESSAY ★—Michelin map 54 ⑫—pop. 1,375.

Lessay, a small town, bordered to the south by moors (*landes*) of the same name whose harsh beauty has been sung by the poet Barbey d'Aurevilly, comes vividly alive in September at the Holy Cross Fair (see p. 27).

Abbey Church★★.—The magnificent Romanesque church of the abbey founded in 1056 by the La Haye-du-Puits barons was badly damaged in 1944 but has since been repaired from existing materials and is once more one of the most perfect examples of Romanesque architecture in Normandy (see p. 17).

Exterior.—The full beauty of the lines of the apse abutting on a flat gable, can best be seen from the war memorial square. The square belfry is also worth noting.

Interior.—The overall plan, the tones of the stone, the pure lines of the nave and chancel, are immediately apparent as you enter through the south door. The nave, with seven wide arched bays has pointed vaulting, as has the transept, while the aisles are groined. A gallery encircles the entire building, passing through the thickness of the walls and before the upper parts of the tall windows. In the oven vaulted apse the windows are divided into two tiers. The furnishings are plain : the high altar a monolithic slab upon two massive supports, the white font, another monolith set upon shingles in the 15C baptistry chapel to the right of the chancel. The font cover is of incised bronze.

Barbey d'Aurevilly deplored the abbey's plain glass in 1864; the new glass is coloured, the design inspired by Irish Celtic manuscripts as are motifs to be seen on the capitals.

Zoo.—*Guided tours: 5 F.*

LILLEBONNE—Michelin maps 52 ⑫, 54 ⑨, 55 ④ ⑤—local map p. 144—pop. 9,758.

The small industrial town of Lillebonne was once a capital city. After the conquest of Gaul by Julius Caesar, the military camp of Juliobonna, named in honour of the proconsul, became a major port with 25,000 inhabitants on Bolbec Bay. It is now silted up.

Roman Theatre.—*To visit, apply to the Café de l'Hôtel de Ville.* From the main square you can see plainly the layout of this 2C theatre which could hold 3,000 spectators.

Castle.—*The keep is open, 9 a.m. to 5 p.m.; closed Sundays and holidays. Entrance, 46 Rue Césarine (small wooden door): 2 F. Apply by the east steps of the castle.* There remains of this fortress (rebuilt in the 12 and 13C) where William the Conqueror assembled his barons before invading England, one wall of an octagonal tower and, on the left, a bold round tower which one can still climb (109 steps).

Church of Our Lady.—The sweeping spire, doorway and the first three bays of the nave go back to the 16C.

Museum.—*In the town hall opposite the Roman Theatre. Open 10 a.m. to noon and 2 to 6 p.m.; apply to the keeper.* Local archaeological finds, furniture and documents.

LISIEUX ★★—Michelin maps 54 ⑱, 55 ⑬—pop. 25,223.

Lisieux has become the most important commercial and industrial town in the prosperous Auge Region.

Old Lisieux, apart from the cathedral which was untouched, was totally destroyed in 1944.

The town's renown centres today on the "Lisieux of St. Theresa" which did not perish and which dominated replanning to facilitate the town's role as a place of pilgrimage.

ST. THERESA OF LISIEUX

An Early Calling.—Born on 2 January 1873, to a well-to-do and very religious family in Alençon, Thérèse Martin was an eager and sensitive child, who soon showed intelligence and will power. At the death of her mother, M. Martin brought the family to Lisieux where they lived at Les Buissonnets. Thérèse grew up in an atmosphere of kindness and piety and at nine years felt the call of the Church. Notwithstanding her father's permission on Whit Sunday 1887 that she might join her sister at the Carmelite Convent, the authorities felt she was too young, and it was only in April 1888, after a pilgrimage to Rome and a request to the Holy Father, that she entered the Order finally at the age of 15¼ years.

"Little Theresa".—"A soul of such quality should not be treated as a child; dispensations were not intended for her", said the prioress of the new postulant who undertook the severe life of a Carmelite. Leading a solitary life in the cloisters where she had come "to save souls

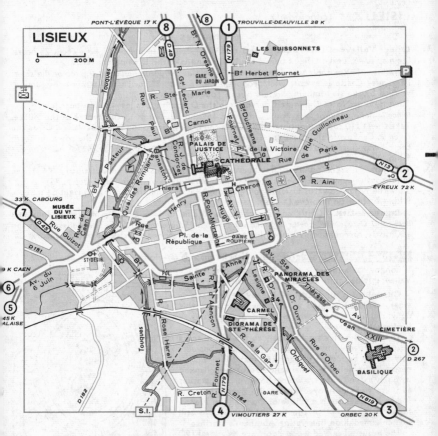

and, above all, to pray for the priests'', Sister Theresa of the Infant Jesus, with humility and courage, mounted the difficult path to perfection. Her gaiety and simplicity cloaked a consuming energy. She wrote the story of her life, *History of a Soul*, finishing the last pages only a few days before entering the Carmelite hospital in which, after a slow and agonising illness, she died. She was beatified in 1923 and canonised on 17 May 1925.

ST. PETER'S CATHEDRAL** *(tour: ¼ hour)*

The cathedral was begun in 1170 and only completed in the middle of the 13C.

Exterior.—The façade, raised above the ground on stone steps, is pierced by three doors and flanked by towers. The one on the left is beautiful with bays and quartering columns, that on the right was rebuilt in the 16C in the Romanesque style and in the 17C was given a spire.

Walk round the church by the right to the south transept so called Paradise Door. The massive buttresses linked by an arch surmounted by a gallery were added in the 15C.

Interior.—The transept is extremely elegant with the lantern rising in a single sweep at the crossing. The nave has great unity with a blind triforium and robust round pillars surmounted by circular capitals supporting its wide arches. Walk to the right, round the 13C chancel, to the huge central chapel which was remodelled in the pure Flamboyant style on the orders of Pierre Cauchon, Bishop of Lisieux after the trial of Joan of Arc *(details see p. 127)*.

ADDITIONAL SIGHTS

Law Courts.—The courts are in the old Louis XIII style bishop's palace. Go through the main gate into the Cour Matignon.

The **Gold Chamber**, the bishop's robing room, decorated with gilded pannelling and a remarkable coffered ceiling is open *(9 a.m. to noon, 2 to 6 p.m.; apply to the court usher—tip)*.

Old Houses.—No. 34, Rue du Dr-Lesigne, Rue Henry-Chéron and Rue P.-Banaston.

Old Lisieux Museum.—*Guided tours 2 to 6 p.m.; closed weekends in winter; 1.50 F.*
Pré-d'Auge pottery, old costumes, Gallo-Roman coins and Roman pottery.

THE PILGRIMAGE**

(Lisieux's major religious festivals are listed on p. 27)

Les Buissonnets.—The saint's family house. *Park the car: Bd. Herbert-Fournet. Open Easter to 30 June, 9 a.m. to noon, 2 to 5.30 p.m.; 1 July to 30 September, 9 a.m. to noon, 2 to 6 p.m.; 1 October to 2 November, 10 a.m. to noon, 2 to 5 p.m.; 3 November to Easter, 10 a.m. to noon, 2 to 4 p.m.*

Carmelite Chapel.—The saint's shrine is in the chapel on the right.

Reliquary Chamber.—*Open 7 a.m. to noon, 2 to 7 p.m. Entrance to the left of the sacristy.*

St. Theresa's Basilica.—*Enquire about* Son et Lumière *performances.* This impressive basilica was consecrated on 11 July 1954. Inside is an immense nave built to accommodate pilgrim crowds; the **crypt** *(entrance outside, beneath the galleries)* is more inviting. The **dome** is open: *9 a.m. to noon, 2 to 6 p.m.; 1 F.*

Display: St. Theresa's Life as a Carmelite, north cloister.—*Permanently open: 1 F.*

Diorama: St. Theresa's Life, 57 Rue du Carmel.—*Open 1 March to 15 December; 1.50 F.*

Panorama: the Saint's Miracles, Rue du Dr-Lesigne.—*Open 1 March to 30 November; 1 F.*

LISIEUX★★ (concluded)

ENVIRONS

Upper Valleys of the Touques and the Vie.—*Tour of 44 miles—71 km—about 2½ hours. See map p. 46.* Leave Lisieux by ④, the N 179, and take the D 64 on the left.

Fervaques.—*To see the castle (exterior only), apply at the aerium office at the top of the steps.* Fervaques Castle is a vast, well proportioned 16 and 17C brick and stone construction, washed by the slow moving waters of the Touques.

Turn right at Notre-Dame-de-Courson into the D 4; after 2 miles—3 km—bear left.

Bellou.—Bellou Manor, a graceful timbered 16C house, stands in the centre of the village. Take the D 110 to Les Moutiers-Hubert and the D 64 again up the Touques Valley. Cross the river at Canapville and make for Ticheville along the D 33. Go through the town, beneath the railway (just beyond the station), across the N 179 and along the D 242 for half a mile— 1 km. At the first fork, bear right for Vimoutiers.

Vimoutiers. This great butter and cheese making centre has been rebuilt since 1944. Three miles south—5 km—lies the village of Camembert, home of Marie Harel (see p. 45).

Take the N 179 towards Lisieux, going through Livarot, before turning off right 5½ miles— 9 km—further on into the D 268A.

St-Germain-de-Livet.—*Castle and gardens open 10 a.m. to noon, 2 to 6 p.m.; closed Thursdays between 1 October and Easter and for 1 month from 15 December; 1.50 F.* This delightful 15 and 16C castle, surrounded by a moat, has a highly original stone and brick chequered decoration.

LONGNY-AU-PERCHE—Michelin map ⑥⓪ ⑤—local map p. 122—pop. 1,572.

Longny has a pleasant setting in the green Jambée Valley; it is also quite near the forest of the same name.

Chapel of Our Lady of Mercy (Notre-Dame de Pitié).—There is a good view of the town from this delightful 16C chapel where an important stairway leads up to the apse.

The square belfry set obliquely to the façade and a buttress crowned by an open pinnacle add considerably to the building's design. The main door is surmounted by delicate Renaissance decoration flanked by finely carved pilasters which, however, lack statues as these were destroyed during the Revolution.

Above the lintel is a statue of Our Lady of Mercy, higher is the head of the Eternal Father, and still higher a medallion illustrating Abraham's sacrifice.

The beautiful carved wood doors are by a local 19C artist: the Visitation and Annunciation are shown on the west door panels; the Virgin in Sorrow and Christ Crucified in medallions on the north and south doors which both open beneath low arches.

The nave has pointed arching with liernes, tiercerons and hanging keystones; two side chapels at the beginning of the chancel form a false transept. The

(After A. Edeline photo)
Longny-au-Perche
Chapel of Our Lady of Mercy:
Ecce Homo

miraculous statue of Our Lady of Mercy (pilgrimage: 8 September), stands upon the high altar.

St. Martin's.—The façade of this late 15C, early 16C church is flanked by a square belfry supported by sculpture ornamented buttresses and a staircase tower.

The belfry's great blind window frames three statues. Above, in a niche, St. Martin on horseback can be seen, dividing his cloak.

ENVIRONS

Tour in the Normandy Perche★.—*71 miles—115 km—about 3 hours.* This drive, described on p. 122, as departing from Bellême, can be made equally well from Longny.

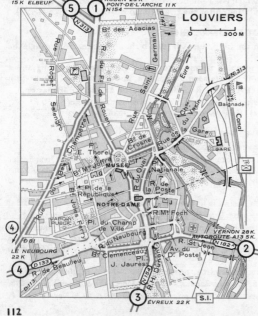

LOUVIERS ★ — Michelin maps ⑤⑤ ⑯ ⑰, ⑨⑦ ⑬—local map p. 143—pop. 15,726.

The small industrial but tranquil town of Louviers, bathed by the many arms of the Eure and closely skirted by its forest, makes an interesting stop on the drive from Paris to Rouen or Paris to Deauville.

Modern light industries in the industrial area north of the town have replaced the woollen textile industry traditionally associated with Louviers since the 13C.

Church of Our Lady★.—*Tour: ½ hour.* This plain 13C church was renovated at the end of the 15C in a Flamboyant style which brought it local renown.

Exterior.—The **south wall★** is the most astonishing part of the church for it is there that the exuberance of the Flamboyant style appears at its most involved with pointed gables, openwork balustrades, pinnacles and gargoyles; the **porch*** (on the south side) has been described as more closely resembling silver work than masonry. The door panels are Renaissance.

A beautiful 15C Virgin stands at the 14C west door.

Interior.—The 13C nave, flanked by double aisles on either side, has a considerable elegance and contains numerous **works of art***.

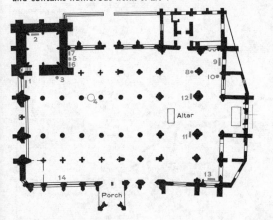

1) Late 15C Entombment in a bay;
2) 16C group of Salome and her two sons;
3) 15C statue of Our Lady of Succour between St. Denis and St. Honorius;
4) 18C pulpit;
5) Above the altar, three 15C statues: Christ in the Wilderness, the Virgin and St. John;
6 and 7) 14C sculptured panels of the Swooning of the Virgin and the Centurion at Calvary;
8) Alabaster Descent from the Cross;
9) Altar decorated with 16C sculptured panels illustrating the Life of the Virgin;
10) Alabaster Crucifixion;
11 and 12) Paintings by the early 17C Louviers painter, Jean Nicolle, of the *Nativity* and the *Adoration of the Magi*;
13) Late 15C mausoleum of the Lord of Esternay;
14) Baptistry chapel with restored Renaissance windows.

Museum.—*Open 2 to 7 p.m.*
Beautiful **Rouen faïence**. *Continuous programme of special exhibitions.*

LUCERNE Abbey—Michelin map 59 ⑦ ⑧—7 miles—12 km—southeast of Granville.

Lucerne Abbey stands in a green setting in the wide secluded valley of the Thar. It was founded in 1143 by a great-nephew of Duke William. It prospered, at one time owning three manors near Chichester, but fell into ruin in 1789. It is now being restored.

Abbey Church.—*Open 9 a.m. to 12.30 p.m., 2 to 7 p.m.; time: about ½ hour; 2 F.*

The church was built between 1164 and 1178 at the instigation of the Blessed Achard, Bishop of Avranches, who was later buried within it. The façade, in which the Romanesque doorway is ornamented with figures in relief in the archivolts, is 12C and, with the south arches and one north arch, the only parts of the nave to remain. The transept crossing (*being restored*) supports a fine tall Gothic tower which is late 12C and is pierced on each of its four square walls by three tierspoint bays. The windows in the chancel rise to a surprising height.

Cloister and Conventual Buildings.—There remain ten arches of the cloister in the northwest corner, the 12C lavatorium, in the southwest corner near the doorway to the former refectory, and the arches at the entrance to the chapterhouse.

The abbot's palace (*private*) with a Classical façade, stands apart on the far side of the expanse of water.

The judgment rooms above the 12–15C almonry door, are used for temporary exhibitions.

LYONS Forest **—Michelin maps 55 ⑦ ⑧, 97 ② ③.

The Lyons Forest, favourite hunting ground of the Dukes of Normandy, has been considerably reduced over the centuries but it still extends for more than 40 square miles—10,700 ha —principally in the Eure Department. Its particular glory is that it is a beech forest.

① FROM LES ANDELYS TO LYONS-LA-FORÊT
by the Fouillebroc Valley (*15 miles—24 km*)

Les Andelys.—*Description p. 42.*
Leave Les Andelys by ① on the map, the D 1, later joining the D 2 to Lisors.

Lisors.—The church contains a 14C crowned Virgin found buried in 1936.

Mortemer Abbey.—*Guided tours 1 April to 15 November, 2 to 6 p.m. Admission: 2 F.*
Take a downhill road, opposite a farm, to the property where the 12 and 13C ruins of the Cistercian abbey stand in a woodland setting.

Source Ste-Catherine.—A signpost points the way beside a wall to the oratory where young girls come to pray for a husband.

At **Sources du Fouillebroc**, a pleasant forest setting, bear left into the D 6 for Lyons-la-Forêt.

Lyons-la-Forêt*.—*Description below.*

② FROM LYONS-LA-FORÊT TO FLEURY-SUR-ANDELLE
through the forest (*11 miles—18 km*)

Lyons-la-Forêt*.—*Description below.*

The Great Oak.—A signpost points to where the 300-year-old oak stands (220 yds. to the left of the road). A little further on a second signpost indicates a group of four oaks (Quatre Chênes).

Croix-Vaubois Crossroads.—The plain memorial is to the foresters who died in the Resistance.

God's Beech (Hêtre à Dieu).—The beech is 275 years old and its trunk measures 14 ft. 8 ins.— 4·50 m—in circumference.

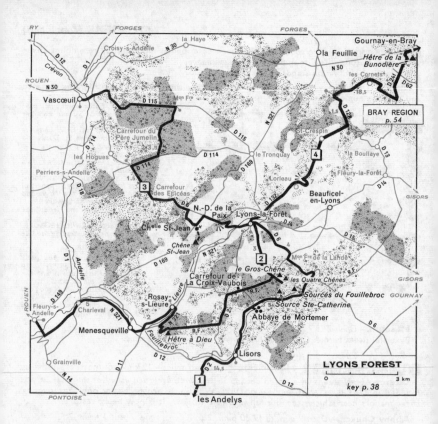

Rosay-sur-Lieure.—The small church surrounded by a well kept burial ground is in a pleasant setting. Inside is a lovely 13C Virgin with a mysterious smile.

Menesqueville.—The small 12C country church, which has been cleverly restored, contains some very old statues. The Canticle of Canticles is the theme of the stained glass windows by Decorchemont.

The N 321 brings you to Fleury-sur-Andelle.

③ FROM LYONS-LA-FORÊT TO VASCOEUIL (N 30)
through the forest (9 miles—15 km)

Lyons-la-Forêt*.—Description below.

Notre-Dame-de-la-Paix.—Good **view*** of Lyons in its setting from the approach to the statue.

St. John's Chapel.—The 17C chapel has a modern window by Decorchemont. A path at the back of the chapel leads to a tree known as St. John's Oak with a circumference of 16 ft. round the trunk—5 m—3 ft. 6 in. above the ground—1·30 m.

Vascoeuil.—Description p. 42.

④ *FROM GOURNAY-EN-BRAY TO LYONS-LA-FORÊT (17 miles—27 km)

Gournay-en-Bray.—Description p. 100.
Leave Gournay by ⑤ on the map in the Michelin Guide *France*.

La Bunodière Beech*.—This magnificent tree which is 138 ft. tall—42 m—stands near the Câtelier reserve where all the trees are over 100 years old and is indicated by a signpost on the left as you leave the N 30 to enter the forest.

Lyons-la-Forêt*.—Description below.

LYONS-LA-FORÊT *—Michelin maps ㉟ ⑧, ㊲ ③—local map above—pop. 880—
Place to stay (see p. 37).

The village of Lyons, lying in the heart of the forest, is a beautiful, tranquil place to stay.

    Covered Market.—The market is covered by a fine 18C timber roof. Nearby is a house with unusual window supports.

    Church.—The church is 15C—the timber belfry and great wooden statues very apt in this woodmen's village.

ENVIRONS

Notre-Dame-de-la-Paix.—¾ hour on foot Rtn along the D 6. Good **view*** of Lyons in its woodland setting.

Beauficel-en-Lyons.—2 miles—3·5 km—along the D 14. The church, preceded by a 17C porch, contains good statues, particularly a 13C Virgin in polychrome stone inlaid with glass.

MAMERS—Michelin map ⑥⓪ ⑭—local map p. 40—pop. 6,325.

Mamers lies in a hollow in the Dives Valley, the capital of the Saosnois, a small transitional area between the Perche hills and the flat countryside of the Mans.

It is a prosperous small town as can be seen from its well kept spacious squares and old covered market; large fairs are held there regularly. The manufacture of household and camping equipment and trimming materials has replaced the traditional net making.

Church of Our Lady.—The church, which was founded in the 12C as part of a Benedictine priory was almost entirely rebuilt in the 16C.

The nave has an unusual triforium within wide mullioned bays. At the back of the façade, on the left, there is a 16C terracotta study of the Dormition of the Virgin.

ENVIRONS

Chèreperrine.—2 miles—4 km. Leave Mamers by the Rue Coru and then the D 276 going east towards Origny-le-Roux. Turn right on crossing a bridge at the entrance to the village.

Chèreperrine Château.—You get a good view from the entrance of the elegant 18C white stone and brick château in which the living areas are set at right angles to the main building, forming an elongated square. The terrace balustrades, the mansard roof of the main building and the tall windows add a Classical distinction.

Perseigne Forest*.—Tour of 35 miles—57 km—about 2 hours. The circular tour described on p. 40 starting from Alençon can be equally well made from Mamers. Take the D 3 going north to Aillières-Beauvoir or the N 155 west and bear left when this crosses the N 805.

MAYENNE—Michelin map ⑤⑨ ⑳—pop. 12,315.

Mayenne is a bridge town whose strategic importance has been demonstrated throughout history, including the last war. The town was partly destroyed in an air raid but the bridge remained and, thanks to the heroism of an American sergeant, Mack Racken, fell intact into the hands of the Allies. The path was then clear, over the old bridge across the Mayenne to Maine. The town has been spaciously rebuilt over the hillsides running down on either side to the River Mayenne.

War and diplomacy.—In 1573 the marquisate of Mayenne was raised to the status of a dukedom for the benefit of Charles of Lorraine, second son of François of Guise. The young duke, aged fifteen, had already seen battle in the struggle against the Huguenots. He next went to offer his services to the Venetian Republic in their war against the Turks. On his return he took part in the siege of La Rochelle and was subsequently appointed commander of the royal army.

On the assassination of Henri III, Mayenne resisted pressure from the Guises to ascend the throne of France; instead he undertook a war against the semi-independent state of Béarn, controlled by the House of Navarre. In the six years which followed, fighting was interspersed with passionate religious and political embroilments and diplomatic intrigue. After the conversion of Henri IV to Catholicism, Mayenne signed a treaty ending the civil war and retired from political life.

The Mayenne as a Waterway.—Cardinal Mazarin had no sooner acquired the Duchy of Mayenne in 1654 than he undertook to make the Mayenne River navigable as far as the town. After 150,000 livres had been spent, construction materials could be brought up as far as the town by barge. However, the course and installations were not maintained and the river again fell into disuse.

New projects were studied and in 1852 45 locks were constructed to enable boats to ascend the 177 ft.—54 m—from the Laval to the Mayenne River. By 1874 barges were calling regularly at the recently completed quays, but later came the railway and the river traffic died finally.

TOUR (about ½ hour)

Old Castle.—Possibly closed for restoration. The castle, abutting on rock escarpments, stands on the hill on the right bank of the river. It was built in the 11C by Juhel I, Lord of Mayenne, and was one of the major local strongpoints undergoing frequent siege.

The perimeter wall remains complete, giving the castle a truly feudal appearance. It commands an attractive view* of the town with the river flowing through it between the granite quays.

Basilica of Our Lady.—This early Gothic church has been remodelled several times. The pillars and arches in the nave are 12C, the transept walls and windows 16C; the windows throughout are modern; the reconstruction undertaken at the end of the 19C in the transitional style sought to enlarge the ground plan.

ENVIRONS

Jublains.—6 miles—10 km. Leave Mayenne by the N 823 going southeast. Turn right as you come out of Aron village into the D 7 for **Jublains** (description p. 109).

Fontaine Daniel; Mayenne Forest.—Tour of 31 miles—50 km—about 1 hour. Leave Mayenne by the D 104, going southwest.

Fontaine Daniel.—The sight at Fontaine Daniel of a lovely pool overlooked by an attractive modern chapel, well kept houses and an old Cistercian abbey makes the drive highly popular. A sheet and ticking mill continues the linen weaving tradition that flourished in the 18C. The D 104 advances beneath a group of oaks.

   Tourists with little time should turn left immediately after La Tervionière into the D 510 to return to Mayenne by way of Contest, St-Baudelle, so well sited by the river, and the N 162 (mileage reduction 19 miles—30 km).

Continue along the D 104 and D 123 to St-Germain-le-Guillaume where you take the D 165 to Chailland. At Chailland turn into the narrow road on the right past the church perched on a spur and once past La Touche Castle, bear right again to go through **Mayenne Forest** which is largely oak and elm. The N 12 on the right will return you to Mayenne.

Mont-St-Michel, that "wonder of the western world", leaves an indelible memory on every visitor, so individual is its setting, so rich its history and so perfect is its architecture.

Visitors able to do so should try to see the feast of the Archangel Michael on the Sunday nearest to 29 September. Another spectacle is the flooding in of the particularly high tides round the island twice a month—at the new and full moon—and, in even greater force, at the spring and autumn equinox.

HISTORICAL NOTES

A Masterpiece.—The abbey's origin goes back to the beginning of the 8C when the Archangel Michael appeared before Aubert, Bishop of Avranches, who founded an oratory on the island, then known as Mount Tombe. This was replaced, on what had been renamed Mont-St-Michel, first by a Carolingian abbey and then, until the 16C, by a series of Romanesque and Gothic churches, each more splendid than its predecessor. The abbey was fortified but never captured.

The construction is a masterpiece of skill: granite blocks had to be brought from either the Chausey Islands or Brittany and hauled up to the site which at its crest was so narrow that supports had to be built up from the rocks below.

Pilgrimages.—Pilgrims flocked to the Mont even during the Hundred Years War, the English, who held the surrounding region, granting safe conduct, on payment, to the faithful. Nobles, rich merchants and beggars, who were given free shelter by the monks, all flocked to the great Almshouse.

Hoteliers and souvenir craftsmen prospered even then: pilgrims bought emblems bearing the effigy of St. Michael and lead caskets which they filled with sand from the beach. Crossing the bay had its perils and there were deaths among the multitudes of pilgrims by drowning and sinking into the quicksands so that the mound became known as St. Michael in Peril from the Sea.

Decadence.—The abbey declined into a commandery and discipline among the monks became lax—under this system abbots were not necessarily churchmen and did not always supervise the abbey although they took the stipends. In the 17C, the Maurists (see p. 20) were charged with reforming the monastery but in fact only made superficial architectural changes.

The conversion of the abbey into a prison in the late 18 and early 19C brought it even lower—the museums listed on p. 118 evoke complacently scenes of horror from this period.

In 1874 the abbey and ramparts passed into the care of the State which has restored them considerably for the 375,000 sightseers who flock there annually. (The Mont is, after the principal Paris attractions and Versailles, one of the major tourist sights of France.)

STAGES IN THE ABBEY'S CONSTRUCTION

The Romanesque Abbey (11 and 12C).—Between 1017 and 1144 a church was built on the mount's summit utilising the earlier Carolingian building as a crypt (Our Lady Below Ground —Notre-Dame-sous-Terre) and as support for the platform on which to stand the three final bays of the Romanesque nave.

Additional crypts were built on which to support the transepts and the chancel which extended beyond the rock crest. The conventual buildings were constructed on the mount's west slope and on either side of the nave.

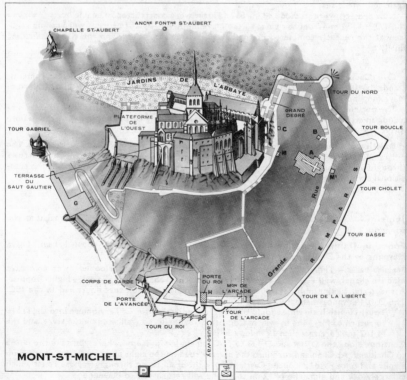

MONT-ST-MICHEL

The Gothic Abbey (13–16C).—In these four centuries there were constructed:
—the magnificent Merveille buildings (1211–1228), to the north, for the monks, pilgrims and the reception of notable guests;
—the abbatical buildings (13–15C), to the south, including administrative offices, the abbot's lodging, and the garrison's quarters;
—the redoubt and the advanced defences to the east defending the entrance (14C);
—the church's Romanesque chancel which had collapsed was rebuilt (1446–1521) even more magnificently in Flamboyant Gothic over a new crypt.

Alterations (18 and 19C).—In 1780 the final three bays of the nave were demolished together with the Romanesque façade. The present belfry, surmounted by a beautiful spire crowned with a statue of St. Michael, dates from 1897.

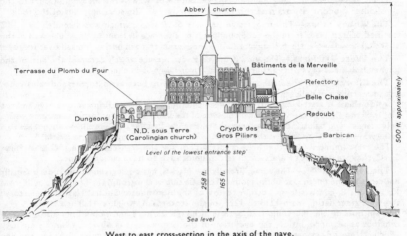

West to east cross-section in the axis of the nave.

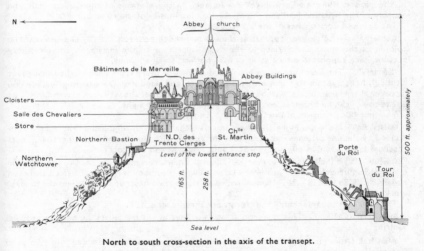

North to south cross-section in the axis of the transept.

PRINCIPAL SIGHTS (tour: 2 hours)

THE ASCENT TO THE ABBEY

Leave the car in one of the official car parks (1 F.).

The Town's Outer Defences.—The outer gate, which is the only breach in the ramparts, opens on to a fortified courtyard. On the left is the 16C burgesses' guardroom, on the right the Michelettes, English mortars captured in a sortie during the Hundred Years War. A second door leads to a second court and a third door dating from the 15C, complete with machicolations and portcullis and known as the King's Gate since above it was lodged the token contingent maintained on the mount by the king in assertion of his rights. You come out finally into the Grande-Rue where the abbots' soldiers lived in the fine arcaded house on the right.

Grande-Rue★.—This narrow uphill main street, lined with 15 and 16C houses and ending in steps, is picturesque and, in the summer, full and bustling with visitors crowding past the souvenir shops even as it was in the Middle Ages.

The Abbey's Outer Defences.—The Grande-Rue leads to the Grand Degré, a stairway to the abbey which formerly could be obstructed by a swing door. To the right is the entrance to the gardens and from there a stairway to the ramparts. Go beneath an old doorway arch to a fortified court overlooked by the redoubt or châtelet. This consists of two high towers, each shaped like a mortar standing on its breech and linked by battlements—even this military fortification shows the constructor's desire for artistry with alternating courses in the wall of rose and grey granite. The Stairs down to the Pit (L'Escalier du Gouffre), a low roofed staircase, ill lit and steep, starts from this point to the fine Guardroom or Porterie.

THE ABBEY***

Open 9 to 11.30 a.m., 1.30 to 4 p.m. (6 p.m., 16 May to 30 September). 3 F., 1.50 F. Sundays and holidays. Cameras: 0.50 F. a day. Visitors wishing to attend the 12.15 p.m. Mass during the season should be at the abbey entrance between noon and 12.15 p.m.

When the mount is crowded—as many as 6,000 are admitted daily—there are sometimes delays on the Pit Stairs. Visitors are directed from the guardroom to the almshouse to get their ticket of admission. Guided tours (official qualified guides), 5 July to 10 September daily at 10 and 11 a.m., 2, 3 and 4 p.m., include the Lacework Staircase; time: 1½ hours; 4.50 F.

The tour takes you floor by floor through a maze of passages and stairways and not by building or period—the effect is confusing, we therefore suggest you read on.

The Guardroom or Porterie.—This hall was the focal point of the abbey: indigent pilgrims were directed there before being passed on by way of the Merveille Court to the almshouse; modern visitors pass through on their way to the starting point of the tour.

The Abbey Steps.—This impressive stairway of 90 steps, which was defended by a 15C fortified bridge, leads from the abbey buildings to a terrace in front of the south wall of the church, known as Gautier's Leap after a prisoner is said to have hurled himself over its edge.

The West Platform.—The view from this vast terrace which occupies the site of the former last three bays of the church extends over Mont-St-Michel Bay.

The Church.—The east end with its buttresses, flying buttresses, turrets and balustrades is a masterpiece of delicacy and grace.

Inside there is a striking contrast between the simplicity of the Romanesque nave and the elegance and light of the Gothic chancel. One of the flying buttresses forms a staircase with a delicately carved balustrade—the **Lacework Staircase**—Escalier de Dentelle—which leads to a gallery 394 ft.—120 m—above the sea from which there is a magnificent **panorama**.

The most impressive of the three crypts supporting the transepts is the 15C **Great Pillars Crypt** (Crypte des Gros Piliers) with ten columns each 16 ft. in circumference.

The Merveille*.**—The name, literally the Marvel, has been given to the superb Gothic buildings on the north side of the mount. The east side of the group, the first to be built from 1211 to 1218, consists from bottom to top of the Almshouse, Guests' Hall and refectory; the west side, dating from 1218 to 1228, of the storeroom, Knights' Hall and cloister.

From outside the Merveille is a fortress although its pure and noble lines also give it a religious appearance. Inside, the evolution of the Gothic style is obvious from a simplicity which is almost Romanesque in the lower halls to the total mastery of grace, lightness and line in the cloister. Intermediary stages can be seen in the elegance of the Guests' Hall, the majesty of the Knights' Hall and the mysterious luminosity of the refectory.

The second floor consists of the cloister and refectory.

Cloister*.**—The cloister appears as though suspended between the sky and the sea. The colours of the stone add variety to the overall harmony of the intricately carved gallery arcades, each supported on a cluster of five, perfect, small columns.

Refectory*.—The first impression is one of disbelief for there is a diffused light throughout although light appears to come only from the two end windows. On entering further you discover that the architect, without lessening the strength of the walls cut narrow windows at the top of the embrasures, so adding an upper, secondary light.

The first floor consists of the Guests' and Knights' Halls.

Guests' Hall* (Salle des Hôtes).—It was in this elegant and graceful hall 115 ft. long—35 m divided by slender columns into two aisles and roofed with Gothic style vaulting, that abbots received kings come in pilgrimage—St. Louis, Louis XI and François I.

Knights' Hall.* (Salle des Chevaliers).—The hall's name certainly goes back to the chivalric order of St. Michael founded in 1469 by Louis XI with the abbey as its seat. This vast and even majestic hall, 85 × 58 ft.—26 × 18 m—divided by three rows of stout columns was the monks' workroom.

The lower chambers include the storeroom and the alms hall.

Storeroom. (Cellier).—This storeroom has two lines of square pillars supporting groined vaulting.

Alms Hall (Aumônerie).—The alms hall—now the waiting room—is divided into two by a line of pillars which still support the early Romanesque groined vaulting.

Abbatical buildings.—Only the guardroom is open.

Old Romanesque Abbey.—The Monks' Walk, the Aquilon Crypt (the original alms centre), the dungeons, and such of the dormitory as remains are visited on the tour.

THE RAMPARTS**

After seeing the abbey, walk round the 13-15C ramparts by bearing left to the steps leading to the Grand Degré Stairway. The watchpath commands good views of the bay, particularly from the North Tower. Take the stairway before the King's Tower (Tour du Roi) to come out just before the King's Gate (Porte du Roi) on the Grande-Rue.

ADDITIONAL SIGHTS

Abbey Gardens*.—0.25 F. The gate is on the left going down the Grand Depré.

Historical Museum (M).—Open 8 a.m. to 7 p.m.; 3 F. also valid for the Historical Museum. Guided tours. Waxwork dioramas of the mount's history and outstanding collection of 25,000 clock balance cocks (the incised pieces supporting old clock mechanisms). Periscope.

Mont St-Michel Historical Museum (M¹) Open 1 March to 30 November, 8 a.m. to 6.30 p.m.; 3 F. also valid for the Historical Museum. Historical dioramas and clock balance cocks.

Parish Church (A).—Much restored 11C church with the apse spanning a narrow street.

Tiphaine's House (B).—1 F. Du Guesclin, who was commander of the Mont, is said to have lodged his wife, Tiphaine, in this house while he went off to the wars in Spain.

The Truie qui File House (C).—Literally, the House of the Spinning Sow, where the ground floor consists only of a series of arcades.

MONT-ST-MICHEL Bay **—Michelin map ⑤⑨ ⑦ ⑧.

If you follow the line of the Cotentin coast you will get wonderful views of Mont-St-Michel across the bay.

"St. Michael in Peril from the Sea".—Until a date which can only be fixed approximately as between the 4 and 8C but which tradition firmly maintains as the early 8C the site of the present Bay of Mont-St-Michel was covered by the vast Scissy Forest. The sea invaded the area transforming Mount Tombe into an island.

The swing of the tides is fantastic, the difference between the levels at high and low tide being as much as 45 ft.—14 m—the greatest in France. As the bottom of the bay is flat, the sandbanks, often quicksands, are uncovered sometimes as far as 9 miles out—15 km. The tide comes in very fast and can be dangerous.

**FROM GRANVILLE TO MONT-ST-MICHEL along the coast

35 miles—56 km—about 1¾ hours—plus ¾ hour sightseeing

The roads proposed are crowded in the tourist season.

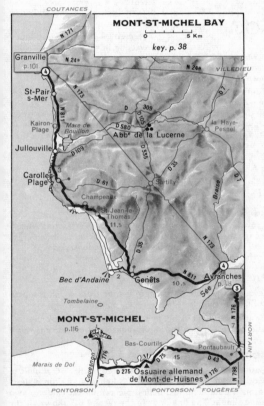

Granville*.—Description p. 100.
There is a wide view of the bay as soon as you begin the drive between Granville and Carolles. The view south is cut by Carolles cliffs, but over to the west, on a clear day, you can see the Brittany coast around Cancale.

St-Pair-sur-Mer.—Description p. 102.

Jullouville.—Place to stay (see p. 36). The houses in this resort are scattered among pine trees.

Carolles.—Description p. 64.
There is a brief glimpse of Mont-St-Michel from the road between Carolles and St-Jean-le-Thomas (place to stay: see p. 36). Beyond the resort the **view**** of the mount becomes quite splendid.

> **Andaine Bill*** (Bec d'Andaine) —Excursion of 1 mile—2 km —from Genêts. Good close **view*** of Mont-St-Michel.

Genêts.—Good walkers can cross the sands from this point to the Mont. *Guide essential; apply to M. Jugan, Place des Halles.* There is an annual pilgrimage made in early July across the sands from Genêts to Mont-St-Michel.
The solid granite 12 to 14C **church** is preceded by an attractive porch with a wooden roof. The transept crossing, inside, leaves an impression of considerable strength.

Avranches*.—Tour: ¾ hour. Description p. 47.

At Bas-Courtils, turn left into the D 75 and a mile further on—2 km—right into the D 107.

Mont-de-Huisnes German Ossuary.—Good view of Mont-St-Michel from the belvedere at the top of the monument.
Continue along the D 275 which is lined on one side by the sea and on the other by the salt marshes on which flocks of sheep can be seen grazing.

Mont-St-Michel***.—Description p. 116.

MORTAGNE-AU-PERCHE *—Michelin map ⑥⓪ ④ local map p. 122—pop. 4,708.

The former capital of the Perche Region stands on a mound overlooking a green and valleyed landscape, the home of the Percheron horse.

The best view of Mortagne, its brown tiled roofs attractively grouped together, is as you approach from the north along the N 830.

Church of Our Lady.—The church was erected from 1494 to 1535 and is an example of Flamboyant Gothic and early Renaissance styles being combined in one building with a resultant loss of unity in the exterior.

Magnificent 18C **woodwork*** surrounds the absidal altar. This, the altarpiece, two panels from the altar surrounds to above the aisles, the choir stalls and pulpit, all come from the Valdieu Carthusian Monastery which was built, and of which a few traces remain, in the nearby Réno Forest.

Hospice.—Ask for permission to visit at the porter's lodge in the Chemin du Cloître.
There remain a delightful 16C cloister and an 18C chapel of the former Convent of St. Clare.

St. Denis Gate.—The gate is the only sizeable piece of the fortifications still standing. The original 15C arch was crowned by a two-storey building in the 16C.

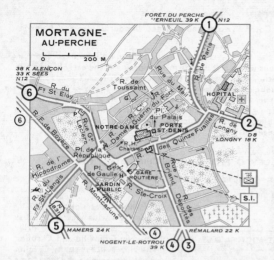

Tour in the Normandy Perche★.—71 miles—115 km—about 3 hours. This drive, described on p. 122, starting from Bellême can be equally well undertaken from Mortagne.

Autheuil; Tourouvre; Perche Forest; the Trappist Monastery.—Tour of 32 miles—51 km—about 1½ hours. Leave Mortagne by ①, N 12; turn right after 7 miles—11 km—into D 290.

Autheuil. — The Romanesque church has a very styled apse. Inside, the arches of the nave and the capitals surmounting the pillars at the transept crossing are remarkable.

Turn back along the D 290 to Tourouvre.

Tourouvre.—Those who enjoy walking in the woods will enjoy this town (see p. 122 the walk described in Réno Forest).

The church still has its 15C stalls and, more importantly, above the altar a 15C **canvas**★, The Adoration of the Magi, which has been incorporated in the 17C altarpiece.

Take the road on the left before Tourouvre church which, at the top of a steep climb, enters the **Perche Forest**. After about 1 mile—2 km—you come on the clearly marked Etoile du Perche crossroads, a relic of the days when the forest was used for hunting and was pierced by rides. Continue straight ahead. At the beginning of the Avre Valley you will notice a series of small lakes in one of which stands reflected the white Château des Etangs surrounded by dark pine trees. Turn left out of the valley and continue through Bresolettes, across the N 830 and into the D 251 to the monastery.

The Trappist Monastery.—Description p. 155.

Return to the N 830 and turn right. Chaumont Lake can be seen through the trees. You get a good view of the town in its setting as you approach Mortagne.

MORTAIN ★—Michelin map ⑤⑨ ⑨—pop. 2,601—Place to stay (see p. 37).

This small pleasantly well kept town is built halfway up a hillside in an attractive **setting**★ where the River Cance, cutting through the last of Lower Normandy's southern hills, emerges on to the vast wooded Sélune Basin, leaving in its wake a rock strewn countryside.

The town has been rebuilt over the ruins of 1944 (see p. 25).

PRINCIPAL SIGHTS (tour: about ½ hour)

Grande Cascade★.—Leave the car in the Abbaye-Blanche Avenue from which the path branches off to the waterfall cascading down 82 ft.—25 m—in a woodland setting.

Petite Chapel★.—Leave the car at the top of the hill in a car park by a pine avenue. Walk down the avenue, past the Petite Chapel, to the belvedere and table from where there is an immense **view**★.

ADDITIONAL SIGHTS

St. Evroult's.—This old collegiate church which was reconstructed in the 13C is built of limestone in a somewhat severe Gothic style. The gabled façade is lightened by three tiers-point windows and, below, by the main door. The 13C belfry, pierced on each side by two single lancets, is attractively plain and simple. The fine door in the second bay shows all the decorative elements known to Norman Romanesque. The single arch relies neither on columns nor capitals but rests directly on wall supports.

Blanche Abbey.—Open July to September, 9 a.m. to noon, 2 to 6.30 p.m.; the rest of the year, Sundays and holidays only, 2 to 6.30 p.m. No visits during services. Apply to the porter's lodge. The park is not open.

This former monastery in a landscape of rock outcrops, was founded in the 12C and is now a seminary. The 13C chapterhouse, one of the galleries of the 12C cloister, the late 12C chapel with its easily recognisable Cistercian plan of a flat east end and transept chapels and a storeroom with groined vaulting are open.

ENVIRONS

Petite Cascade★.—¾ hour on foot. Take the downhill path on the left from the Place du Château. Follow the path along the garden wall and at the corner turn right (signpost). Cross the Cance River and take the narrow footpath which goes past the Aiguille Rock. Cross the Cançon over the stepping-stones and follow the stream to a rock amphitheatre where the waters fall 121 ft.—35 m.

Upper Valley of the Sée★; **St-Michel-de-Montjoie.**—Tour of 35 miles—56 km—about 2 hours. Leave Mortain by the N 177, the Vire road. As you make the winding descent beyond La Tournerie you will see the vast Sourdeval Basin, through which runs the Upper Sée. Turn left in Sourdeval into the N 811 which wanders along the narrow **Sée Valley** following the curves in the river's course and offering a new view at each bend.

Go through Chérencé-le-Roussel and, after the church, turn right into the D 33. As you reach St-Pois notice the views on the left extending to the Sée before entering the village and turning right and right again into the uphill D 39.

At the entrance to **St-Michel-de-Montjoie** turn left to go up to the church. From the burial ground there is a good view, which, on a clear day, extends to Mont-St-Michel (car park).

Return to the D 39 and make for Gathemo where you turn right. There is another view of the Sée Valley before you enter Perriers-en-Beauficel and, as you leave, further extensive views from the winding road to Chérencé-le-Roussel where you turn left into the D 33. Woods and valleys bring you to La Hardière, where you turn left into the D 179 which runs almost level with a rushing stream along the bottom of a narrow wooded valley.

You rejoin the N 177, the road by which you came out, at Bellevue.

NEUBOURG Plain —Michelin maps 54 ⑲ ⑳, 55 ⑤ ⑥ ⑮ ⑯.

The open and monotonous Neubourg Plain, the best cultivated land south of the Seine,

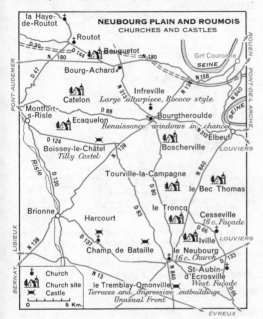

and the Roumois area which adjoins it to the northwest (*map p. 13*) are reminiscent of the Caux Plateau and are not visited by many tourists. Those who enjoy the picturesque, however, will be drawn by small country churches always guarded by a yew tree which, in the Middle Ages, was considered as having power to cleanse the atmosphere and therefore had pride of place among the other trees in the burial ground surrounding a church. There are several noble castles upon the plain.

Boissey-le-Châlet.—On leaving the town take the second avenue on the left, lined with poplars. **Tilly Castle** was constructed by Guillaume le Roux, Lord of Bourgtheroulde, in about 1500. The front is faced with a lozenge design in stone and glazed brick; the perimeter wall, which is still standing, is quartered by pointed turrets.

Bouquetot.—The 11 and 12C church contains good statues in wood and stone and three restored 18C paintings.

The giant hawthorn beside the church is 600 years old. Note the yew trees in the burial ground.

Bourg-Achard..—The church has some beautiful 16C glass in the chancel and north transept and outstanding 15 and 16C woodwork which includes, in addition to the stalls, a celebrant's chair carved with delightful imagination and, in the south transept, four panels illustrating the lives of St. Eustace and St. Placid.

Champ de Bataille Castle.—This huge and beautiful 17C mansion is set in a deer park.

Guided tours 1 July to 14 September, 10.30 a.m. to noon, 2.30 to 6.30 p.m.—closed Tuesdays and Wednesdays; 15 September to 14 March, 2 to 5 p.m. Thursdays and holidays only; 15 March to 30 June, 10.30 a.m. to noon, 2.30 to 6.30 p.m. on Sundays, Mondays, Thursdays and holidays; 3.50 F.; time: ¾ hour.

Twin brick and stone wings, long and low and joined at the far end by porticoes, line the main court making a most impressive whole. Inside, in rooms adorned with fine panelling, and period chimney-pieces, are historical souvenirs, art objects, paintings by Drouais, Van Loo and Fragonard and sculpture by Pigalle, J.-B. Lemoyne, Canova and Carpeaux.

Ecaquelon.—The church, in this pretty village in the heart of a wood, contains a magnificent 15C alabaster **altarfront**★ of the Passion, which was brought over from England.

Harcourt★.—*Open 15 March to 15 October, 10 a.m. to noon and 2 to 6 p.m. (closed Wednesdays) 16 to 30 November and 1 February to 14 March, 2 to 5 p.m., Thursdays, Saturdays and Sundays; 3 F. Follow the numbered panels.*

The Harcourt domain **park**★ has a great variety of trees. Follow the avenue, marked by two enormous cedars at its start, to the mediaeval castle entrance, fortified, flanked by towers and surrounded by a 66 ft. wide moat—20 m.

A path on the left, in line with the castle, leads round the old perimeter wall.

Harcourt **parish church** has a remarkably elegant 15C apse.

La Haye-de-Routot.—The small village is known for the two giant thousand year old **yews**★ in the church burial ground and its St Clair firework display on 16/17 July (p. 27).

Routot.—The church's Romanesque belfry has intersecting arches in its blind arcade.

NEUFCHÂTEL-EN-BRAY —Map 52 ⑮—local map p. 86—pop. 6,133.

Neufchâtel, former capital of the Bray Region, is the home of the *bondon* which first brought fame to this part of Normandy as a cheese region.

Church of Our Lady.—*(Restoration in progress)*. This vast edifice has not yet been entirely restored. Beyond the belfry porch where the late 15C door has been badly mutilated is an early 16C nave with Renaissance capitals. The transept, which went back to the 12C, was reconstructed in the 19C; the chancel is 13C.

Mathon Museum.—*Open Saturdays and Sundays and holidays, 2 to 5 p.m. (4 p.m. on Saturdays)*. Inside are Bray arts and traditions; outside, a typical well, apple mill and press.

The Perche appears, if you have come from a flat area, as an undulating landscape of wooded hills, wide green valleys, rolling pastures grazed by cattle. There are delightful villages that one discovers on leaving the hedge bordered main roads.

GEOGRAPHICAL NOTES

The Perche has a somewhat complicated geological structure, lying as it does between the Paris Basin and the Armorican Massif.

A predominance of non-porous soils and a damp climate produced perfect conditions for a dense vegetation of oak and beech woods on the primary limestone, pastures and fertile arable crops on the secondary marls and clay.

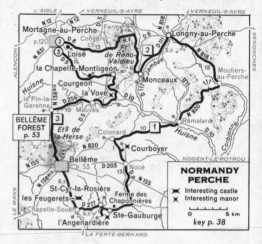

The Normandy Perche has, therefore, evolved with its rich grasslands as a stock breeding area and particularly as the cradle of the Percheron (see p. 14).

THE PERCHE MANOR HOUSES

While Auge manors (see p. 45) appear as welcoming country houses, those in the Normandy Perche emerge as small castles, standing a short distance from the road, built of stone and more or less fortified. Although most of these late 15 or early 16C lordly houses have long since been converted to farmhouses, they have retained such defensive features as towers, turrets and watch towers. But these towers, elegant turrets and the delicate carved ornament decorating many façades have nothing to do with military architecture.

1 *FROM BELLÊME TO LONGNY-AU-PERCHE

34 miles—55 km—about 1½ hours

Bellême.—*Description p. 53.*
The drive begins through an open landscape out of which an occasional tower can be seen on the horizon.

Feugerets Castle.—*Temporarily closed.*
A harmonious group of buildings—two square pavilions with a fine balustrade and moat and an elegant 16C main living quarter—stand out against the green setting.

St-Cyr-la-Rosière.—The church in this small village has a beautiful Romanesque doorway with a triple archivolt. Inside there is a remarkable 17C polychrome terracotta **Entombment***.

Angenardière Manor.—This manorhouse built in the 15 and 16C, although restored, retains a feudal air. Note the massive towers. *Exterior tours allowed.*

Ste-Gauburge.—Behind the now deconsecrated church which is in a very pure Gothic style, there remain the buildings of a former priory (*not open*) which depended, in the 17C, on the royal Abbey of St. Denis. The buildings, which have now been converted into a farmhouse, include a graceful and finely decorated pentagonal tower.
On the left as you leave the village is the **Chaponnières Farm**. A round tower links the living area and a late 16C square pavilion.

Courboyer Manor*.—This delightful manor built of white stone at the end of the 15C, stands out on a hillside, and is one of the finest in the Perche. Four graceful watch towers on machicolations quarter the main wing. The massive round tower, which greets the visitor below the level of the road, is linked by a heavy ridge-pole to the slender octagonal staircase turret which adds considerable elegance to the west front.
The road beyond Rémalard, in a more hilly and green countryside, is very picturesque, crossing the delightful valley in which Moutiers stands and then, bordered with trimly cut hedges and white gates, continues to Longny.

Courboyer Manor.

Longny-au-Perche.—*Description p. 112.*

2 FROM LONGNY-AU-PERCHE TO MORTAGNE

16 miles—25 km—about ½ hour

Longny-au-Perche.—*Description p. 112.*

Monceaux.—This village in the green Jambée Valley stands at the junction of two small valleys.

Réno-Valdieu Forest.—The forest has beautiful clumps of very old trees—oaks and beeches. A farm in a restful setting has replaced the former Abbey of Valdieu which gave its name to the forest which in 1789 was joined with that of Count de Réno.

The undulating D 8 crosses a remarkable landscape of hills, leaving Cohyère Castle on its right as it rises to Mortagne.

Loisé.—The 16C church is flanked by a monumental square tower.

Mortagne-au-Perche.—*Description p. 119.*

③ FROM MORTAGNE TO BELLÊME
22 miles—35 km—about I hour

The drive is through the beautiful and peaceful Percheron countryside.

Mortagne-au-Perche.—*Description p. 119.*

Courgeon.—The late 11C Romanesque church was flanked in the 17C by two aisles and a four-storey tower crowned by a stone shingle dome topped by a lantern. The unity of style will be appreciated by admirers of classical ecclesiastical architecture.

La Chapelle-Montligeon.—*Place to stay (see p. 37).* This apparently modest village, dominated by an immense Neo-Gothic basilica with modern stained glass windows, links in odd association religious and industrial affairs.
The pilgrimage basilica and a printing works with 170 operatives recall by their grouping around a central courtyard their traditional association. *Dates of pilgrimages: Ascension and Assumption Days and first Sunday of November.*
There is a good view of the surrounding countryside from the basilica terrace.

La Vove Manorhouse.—The austere façade, flanked by a massive keep, brooks no denial of the manor's former role as a strongpoint. The façade on the court is more gracious. At the corner of two buildings constructed at right angles, the octagonal staircase tower is embellished by a watchtower supported on corbels. The manor chapel has been converted to a barn.
Beyond Pin-la-Garenne, the road rises towards Bellême Forest where the trees are glorious and the Le Herse Pool is extremely pleasant.

> **Bellême Forest*.**—By turning at La Herse Pool you can go to Bellême through the forest (*described on p. 53*). *Extra distance: 15 miles—24 km.*

As you emerge from the forest there is a good view from the road of Bellême.

Bellême.—*Tour: ½ hour. Description p. 53.*

Ô Castle *—Michelin map ⑥⓪ ③—local map p. 44.

The composite but graceful outline of this castle, reflected in the calm waters of the moat, displays in an original way through its best known parts, the imagination used in Normandy by architects of the first Renaissance.
No entry from 1 July to 10 September. At other times go up to the moat and walk left to get a general view of the façade from the south, or right, beyond the sheet of water, when you will be able to see the main court and buildings lining its three sides. Time: ½ hour. The castle is not open.
The castle consists of three main buildings lining three sides of the courtyard open on its north side to the moat.

East Pavilion.—This, the oldest part of the castle, dates from the end of the 15C. On a Gothic inspired structure the new designs of the French Renaissance can be clearly seen: windows open widely on to the countryside and military features are virtually excluded. The whole, with its variety of sloping roofs, graceful turrets and walls partially faced in a marquetry of brick and stone is altogether charming.

South Wing.—The wing which was added in the 16C consists of one storey with large windows above an arcade in which the arches rest upon slender columns decorated with ermines—the emblem of the house of O.

West Pavilion.—This main living area was entirely rebuilt in the 18C.

OMAHA BEACH —Michelin map ⑤④ ④ ⑭.

The name Omaha Beach, which until 6 June 1944 existed only as an operational code name, has continued jointly for the beaches of St. Laurent, Colleville and Vierville-sur-Mer in memory of the American soldiers of the 1st and 29th Infantry Divisions which landed east and west of Colleville and suffered great casualties in the most costly of the D-Day battles.

A Dramatic Clash.—Here nature in the form of a strong coastal current which swept landing craft off course and shingle which proved at first impossible to heavy armour combined with an extremely well organised defence by the Germans.
Companies at first baulked, later rallied and by evening had taken the Port-en-Bessin–Grand camp road enabling the motorised units to gain the plateau.
A Mulberry harbour (*see details p. 45*) lasted only until a storm, such as had not been seen for forty years, broke it up on 19 June.
The austere and desolate appearance, at least in its eastern part along the narrow beach backing on barren cliffs, make the invasion scene easy to imagine even today.

FROM COLLEVILLE-SUR-MER TO VIERVILLE-SUR-MER by the battlefields
6 miles—9 km—plus ¾ hour on foot Rtn

This drive can be incorporated in the run from Bayeux to Carentan (*described on p. 64*).

Colleville-sur-Mer.—The last Germans did not leave the area around the village church until 10 a.m. on 7 June. The church has been entirely rebuilt.

American Military Cemetery.—*Open 8 a.m. to 6 p.m. (8 p.m. Sundays and holidays).* The 9,385 Carrara marble crosses stand aligned in an impressive site. A memorial with a pool before it in the central alley, is surrounded by young trees. Make for the belvedere overlooking the sea. Monuments have also been erected just outside the cemetery to the 1st Division and the 5th Brigade.

5th Engineer Special Brigade Memorial.—The monument built on the remains of a German blockhouse, and the best local belvedere, commemorates the sacrifices made by the specialists

OMAHA BEACH (concluded)

whose task it was to maintain contact between the ships offshore and the units which had landed and to prepare the beach for further heavy traffic.

Return to the car and the N 814 which you follow to St. Laurent.

St-Laurent-sur-Mer.—The village was captured by the Americans on the evening of D-Day. Turn right into the N 814c which runs down a valley to the sea.

Les Moulins.—Turn left opposite the monument to the D-Day landing (Monument du Débarquement) towards Vierville. The N 814c is transformed for just over a mile—1,800 m—into a superb seafront boulevard marked at its start by a memorial to the American combatants at Omaha. It was at the foot of this promenade—since rebuilt—that the first units sheltered at dawn on 6 June. A stele a little further on, on the left, marks the spot where the first to fall in the Battle of the Beaches were temporarily buried (the first American cemetery on French soil of the Second World War). By 7.50 a.m. on 6 June a company had left the promenade shelter to mount the first assault. The end of this section corresponds with the sector known as Dog Green, the most bloody of Omaha Beach, where within minutes of landing 70%, including all officers and non-commissioned officers, of the 116th Regiment were either dead or wounded.

Vierville-sur-Mer.—*Place to stay (see p. 36).* The road leaves the coast by another "beach exit". A monument has been erected on one of the most redoubtable German blockhouses to the American National Guard who served in France in both World Wars.

The village was invested on 6 June when the church was severely damaged as the belfry fell.

ORBEC—Michelin maps 54 ⑱, 55 ⑭—pop. 3,529.

Orbec, a small and lively town with considerable character, goes back over the centuries as can be seen from the commercial Rue Grande, where there are still some old houses. It stands close to the source of the Orbiquet in one of the pleasantest valleys in the Auge.

Church of Our Lady.—The church is flanked by a massive tower of which the base was built in the 15C and the upper part in the 16C.

The four 16C windows have been twice restored—in the 19C and since the last war. A small 17C carved wood statue of St. Rock stands in the south aisle. In the north aisle are a statue of the Virgin also of carved wood and also 17C and a 14C tombstone engraved with the effigy of Dame Juliane Chardonnel.

ENVIRONS

Source of the Orbiquet.—*3 miles—4·5 km.* Leave Orbec by the Vimoutiers road but continue straight on without crossing the river, along the pleasant La Folletière–Abenon road.

OUISTREHAM-RIVA-BELLA ★—Michelin maps 54 ⑯, 55 ②—p. 62—pop. 5,247—

Place to stay (see p. 36).

Ouistreham is a well known international yachting centre.

Church★.—This ancient 12C fortress church was remodelled inside in the 19C and has been very well restored since the war.

The gabled façade with three superimposed lines of blind arcades above the doorway is particularly remarkable. Step back to get a good view of the late 12C belfry supported by buttresses. Inside, the chancel is a good example of Norman Gothic.

Yacht Harbour.—Leave the car on the Place du Port where the Canal de Caen à la Mer comes out. A 2½ acre—1 ha—basin on the right bank affords mooring for a considerable number of yachts in the season. There are plans to extend this already colourful quarter.

Riva-Bella has arisen as a seaside resort on the ruins produced by German occupation and evacuation at the Allied Invasion. The

4th Anglo-French Commando reduced the enemy strongpoints on the morning of 6 June.

The magnificent fine sand beach bustles with activity, one solitary blockhouse between the Place Alfred-Thomas and the harbour being all that remains of the war.

Le PIN Stud *—Michelin map ⑥⓪ ③—local map p. 44.

The lordly **setting*** of the Le Pin Stud is a perfect reflection of the respect given in France to anything to do with horse breeding.

TOUR (about ½ hour)

Open 9 a.m. to noon, 2 to 6 p.m. Apply to the lodge, left of the gate; free; a groom accompanies. The full complement of stallions is at the stud only between 15 July and 1 March.

The magnificent woodland rides converge on the main courtyard known as Colbert's Court after the statesman who founded the stud. The main building, the château, built from 1716 to 1728 to plans by Mansart, serves as the manager's residence.

In stables in the wings are about 100 stallions grouped by breed, coat colour and size (English thoroughbreds, French trotters, hacks, Anglo-Arabs, Norman cobs, Percherons).

The departure and return from daily exercise nearby is well worth seeing.

The annual steeplechase on the second Sunday in October at the Le Pin Racecourse and the annual meeting including flat races and steeplechasing on the first Sunday in August are popular local events.

ENVIRONS

St-Germain-de-Clairefeuille.—6 miles—9·5 km—by the N 24 bis to Nonant-le-Pin and the D 116.

The **church** (open 2 March to 31 October, 9 a.m. to 7 p.m.; 1 November to 1 March, 9 a.m. to 5 p.m.) is known for its magnificent woodwork including 13 **painted panels***, by the early 16C Flemish school, of the Life of Our Lord.

PONT AUDEMER *—Michelin maps ⑤④ ⑲, ⑤⑤ ④—local map p. 144—pop. 9,248.

Pont-Audemer, a tanners' town standing at the beginning of the embanked Lower Risle, still has quite a character although it was badly damaged in 1944. There are many old houses left and the several arms of the river provide picturesque waterside views.

St-Ouen Church*.—*Time: about ½ hour.* The church was begun in the 11C and although enlarged in the 16C its west face was never completed. The nave, which has a coffered vault, was given a Flamboyant veneer at the end of the 15C.

The triforium has an unusually rich decoration.

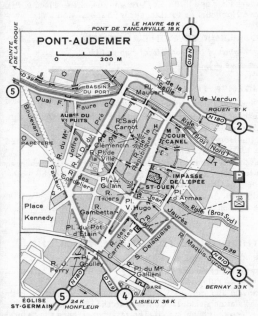

The aisles, in which hanging keystones depend, are lit through the magnificent Renaissance **stained glass windows*** of the side chapels. The first in the north aisle contains a 16C font and, beneath the window, two 15C alabaster low reliefs of St. George and the Holy Trinity.

The modern glass, including reds and greens in a striking Crucifixion, in the chancel, the south aisle, to the right of the main door and above the organ, is all by Max Ingrand.

ADDITIONAL SIGHTS

Cour Canel.—Picturesque old houses.

Vieux Puits Inn.—Old Norman style interior.

St. Germanus' by ⑤ on the map.—This very old building, parts of which date back to the 11C, was considerably remodelled in the 14C and truncated in the 19C. The arches of its squat Romanesque tower have been rebuilt in the Gothic style.

PONT-L'ÉVÊQUE —Michelin maps ⑤④ ⑰ ⑱, ⑤⑤ ③—pop. 3,592.

Pont l'Evêque, famous since the 13C for its cheese, was badly damaged during the war.

Only a few old houses remain mostly in the Rue St-Michel and Rue de Vaucelles. No. 68 in the latter, now the picturesque Aigle d'Or Hotel, was a staging post in the 16C and still has the Norman courtyard of the period.

St. Michael's.—Good Flamboyant building flanked by a square tower.

Former Convent of the Dominican Sisters of the Island.—The building, at the end of the Place du Palais de Justice, has an interesting wooden balcony.

PONTMAIN —Michelin map ⑤⑨ ⑲—4 miles—6 km—southwest of Landivy—pop. 659.

Large pilgrimages to the Virgin make their way to this village on the borders of Normandy and Brittany especially on 17 January.

In 1871, during the Franco-Prussian War, when the Germans had outflanked Paris and were overrunning the west, the Virgin appeared before the village children with a message of prayer and hope. The visitation was on 17 January; eleven days later an Armistice was declared.

The vast Neo-Gothic basilica with its twin spires was erected near the small parish church at the end of the 19C.

PONTORSON —Michelin map ❺❾ ⑦—3,690.

Pontorson, the last Norman village before you enter Brittany, is a favourite stopping place for visitors on their way to Mont-St-Michel.

Church of Our Lady.—The church is said to have been founded by William the Conqueror in gratitude to the Virgin for having saved his army from the Couesnon quicksands. It goes back to the 12C, was given pointed vaulting at a later date and has been remodelled several times. The massive rough granite façade pierced by a wide and just pointed arch has, like the south door with its interesting capitals, kept its original Romanesque appearance.

QUILLEBEUF —Michelin maps ❺❷ ⑫, ❺❹ ⑨, ❺❻ ④—local map p. 152—pop. 1,245.

The onetime Viking port of Quillebeuf retained its importance until the 19C—the *Télémaque* sank offshore in 1790 with, reputedly, the crown jewels on board. Today the port is overshadowed by the petroleum installations of Port Jérôme on the far bank of the river and is scarcely in use, the town, however, has kept its seaport atmosphere.

Quillebeuf Point.—From the lighthouse on the point at the end of the angled promontory separating the disused Vernier Marsh and the Old Port, there is a good view up and down river, across to Port-Jérôme and the Tancarville Bridge.

Grande-Rue.—The street is lined with old houses with sculptured cornices and inscriptions carved on the façades. In the centre stands the 16C house, known as the House of Henri IV—the Vert-Galant or Gay Old Spark showered his favours on the town as it was the first in Normandy to recognise him as King of France.

Our Lady of Safe Homecoming (Notre-Dame-de-Bon-Port).—The church, surmounted by a fine but incomplete Romanesque tower, has a 12C door. The nave is purely Romanesque in style with archaic capitals, the upsweeping chancel, 16C.

The RISLE Valley —Michelin map ❺❺ ④ ⑤ ⑮ ⑯.

The Risle, a river whose waters run cold and swift, rises west of the town of L'Aigle and flows at first through the dark **Ouche Region**, draining the well wooded plateau, the quarry area where the red iron agglomerate used for building in the past was mined and the metal-working area of **Rai, Rugles, Bonneville-sur-Iton, St-Sulpice-sur-Risle** in which factories with thousands of workmen have replaced small local forges.

The river, augmented by the waters of the Charentonne, goes on to divide the Lieuvin Plateau in the west from the Neubourg Plain and Roumois Plateau in the east (*see map p. 13*), before entering into the Seine above Honfleur. Its total lenght is 93 miles—150 km.

① FROM HONFLEUR TO PONT-AUDEMER

16 miles—26 km—about ¾ hour—see local map p. 144

From Honfleur to Pont-Audemer follow drive ④ *, p. 145.*

② FROM PONT-AUDEMER TO LA RIVIÈRE-THIBOUVILLE

21 miles—34 km—about 1 hour—plus ½ hour sightseeing

The road follows the Risle Valley except for a short section in the Bec-Hellouin Valley.

Pont-Audemer*.—*Description p. 125.* Leave Pont-Audemer by ②, N 180.

Corneville-sur-Risle.—The carillon at the Hôtel des Cloches (*played on payment*) was instituted following the runaway success of a 19C operetta *Les Cloches de Corneville*.

Appeville-Annebault.—The large church was rebuilt in the 16C, conserving the 14C chancel, when the governor of Normandy laid plans to make the river navigable up to this point. Inside is a good collection of Brothers of Charity staffs (*see p. 27*).

Monfort-sur-Risle.—The village lies close to the rolling Montfort Forest.

Le Bec-Hellouin**.—*Tour: ½ hour. Description p. 52.*

Brionne.—*Description p. 55.*

③ FROM LA RIVIÈRE-THIBOUVILLE TO CONCHES-EN-OUCHE

22 miles—35 km—about 1 hour

The Nassandres sugar refining factory is a reminder of the valley's manufacturing activities. Leave La Rivière-Thibouville by the D 23 going south.

St. Eligius Chapel (St-Eloi).—*Excursion of 1 mile—1·5 km.* Take the D 46 across the Risle Valley and bear right immediately after a viaduct. Continue to the third turning on the left which leads to grounds in which the chapel stands. The 11C chapel, once the chancel of the conventual church which formed part of a dependent priory of Bec-Hellouin Abbey, has been for centuries, and remains, a popular pilgrimage. The spring which rises beneath the chapel is an object of particular devotion, thus giving rise to the belief that the local cult goes back to pre-Christian times. Recent excavations have uncovered Gallo-Roman constructions beneath the present building.

Beyond two Romanesque blind arcades, facing the chapel, are the remains of a martyrium, inset in a 16C house.

Beaumontel.—The belfry on the well sited church is 16C.

Beaumont-le-Roger.—St. Nicholas' Church, built in the 14 and 16C, has been restored following war damage, modern windows now supplementing its fine old ones. At the top of a slope, on a terrace, stand the ruins of a 13C priory church.

The only section of the French Mint outside Paris is in the town (*not open*).

Gallerand Valley.—*Excursion of 4 miles—7 km—from Beaumont-le-Roger, D 123.* Beautiful farm.

La Ferrière-sur-Risle.—15C church.

Beaumesnil*.—*Excursion of 4 miles—7 km—from La-Ferrière-sur-Risle, D 140.* The 17C **chateau***, a masterpiece of the Louis XIII style, stands with its impressive façade coolly mirrored in its moat, its other sides surrounded by formal gardens. *Tours on application to the keeper (path to the left of the gate) from 10 a.m. to 5 p.m. except on Sundays and in August.*

Conches-en-Ouche*.—*Description p. 72.*

126

ROUEN ***—Michelin maps 52 ⑭, 54 ⑩, 55 ⑥, 97 ① ②—local maps pp. 143 and 145—pop. 124,577.

Rouen, capital of Upper Normandy, numbers 320,000 inhabitants in 22 communes if one includes the surrounding built-up areas. The Museum Town, burnt in 1940, bombed in 1944, has since rebuilt and restored its famous monuments; the port has been reconstructed and more industries than ever attracted to play their essential part in the city's life.

THE SITE

The town has been developing since the Roman Rotomagus was established at the first point on the river at which a bridge could be built. The site is in many ways similar to that of Paris, being at the start of a bend protected by encircling hills and where valleys provide access to the hinterland; it is also above the floodwater mark and where islands in the river course facilitate bridge building. The hills surrounding Rouen, however, are higher and therefore afford better views down on to the city (see p. 133).

HISTORICAL NOTES

Rollo the Forerunner.—After the St-Clair-sur-Epte pact (see p. 88), Rollo was baptised at Rouen, the capital of the new Duchy, and took the name Robert. This administrator proved himself to be a far sighted planner: he narrowed and deepened the river bed, built up unused marshlands, linked the downstream islands to the mainland and reinforced the banks with quays. His constructions lasted until the 19C.

The Goddons.—Rouen was hard hit during the Hundred Years War: in 1418 Henry V besieged the town which capitulated, famine stricken, after six months. Revolts and plots followed against the Goddons—the nickname for the English derived from their swearing "God damned"; terror reigned until hope was reborn in the hearts of the Normans by the exploits of Joan of Arc and the coronation of Charles VII. But Joan was taken prisoner at Compiègne by the Burgundians. The English threatened the Duke of Burgundy with economic sanctions and through the mediation of Cauchon, Bishop of Beauvais, Joan was handed over against a payment of 10,000 gold ducats.

The Trial of Joan of Arc.—Bishop Cauchon promised "a fair trial" and opened the first session on 21 February 1431. An amazing dialogue began between Joan and her judges: bold but "without pride or concern for herself, thinking only of God, her mission and the king", the Maid replied to all the tricks and subtleties of the churchmen and lawyers. The questioning went on for three months. On 24 May, in the cemetery of the Abbey of St. Ouen, tied to a scaffold, Joan was pressed to recant; she gave way, was granted her life but condemned to life imprisonment.

The English were furious and threatened the judges; Cauchon replied "We will get her yet". On Trinity Sunday the guards took away Joan's woman's clothes which she had promised to wear, and gave her men's clothing instead. At noon "for the necessities of the body, she was constrained to go out and indulge in the said habit". She was thus said to have broken her promise and was condemned to the stake. On 30 May she was burned alive in the Place du Vieux Marché. Her heart when not consumed by the fire, was thrown in the Seine. The English, afraid, murmured that they were lost as they had burned a saint.

In 1449 Charles VII entered Rouen; in 1456 Joan was rehabilitated and in 1920 she was canonised and made Patron Saint of France.

The Golden Century.—The period between the French reconquest and the Wars of Religion was a golden century for all Normandy and particularly for Rouen. Cardinal d'Amboise (see under Gaillon, p. 155), archbishop and patron, introduced the Renaissance style to wear. Local dignitaries began to build sumptuous stone mansions and carved woodwork adorned the façades of burgesses' houses. The Law Courts built by Louis XII for the Exchequer were transformed into a parliament by François I.

Rouen businessmen in cooperation with Dieppe navigators (see p. 82) traded all the main maritime routes: the coat of arms of the powerful merchant haberdashers guild showed three ships built and masted of gold and the device "O sun, we will follow you to the ends of the earth". The former linen weaving town now wove silk and cloth of silver and gold. In 1550 the first Colonial Exhibition was mounted in the town.

Industrial Upsurge.—Early in the 18C a rich merchant unable to sell his stock of candle-wick spun and wove the fibre into a cloth that had an immediate success: dyed indigo blue and known as Rouennerie, it outstripped all others. In 1730 came the first velveteen and twill. Dyeing made equal progress, keeping pace with textile production, transformed by mechanisation. Finishing, bleaching and textile printing followed.

In 1969, 28,000 tons of material were handled.

Industrialisation called for changes in the port: in the 19C docks were constructed, the railway brought to the harbour; the old city on the right bank spread to the tributary valleys.

THE MODERN CITY

Industrial expansion accelerated at the beginning of the 20C and Rouen's urban development increased considerably with the creation of industries associated with its port (see p. 141).

The 1939–1945 war destroyed the old quarter between the Seine and the cathedral, razed the bridges and partially destroyed the industrial zone on the left bank. The people of Rouen rebuilt their city, removing damaged factories to industrial zones and converting the centre of the left bank into a residential area with high rise and other buildings which already house nearly as many as live on the right bank, and an administrative centre with a semicircular prefecture (1966) flanked by a 262 ft. tower—80 m—for the local archives.

Lacroix Island, formerly industrial, is gradually becoming residential. The right bank remains the heart of Rouen, having recovered its commercial vitality and tourist attraction.

In addition to the two old bridges, the Pont Boïeldieu and Pont Corneille which were rebuilt, two new bridges have been constructed, the Pont Jeanne d'Arc as a continuation of the street of the same name and the Pont Guillaume le Conquérant further downstream.

The quays have been reconstructed to separate port and other traffic but the plan is being undone by ever growing traffic. Housing is also going up apace in the outlying suburbs.

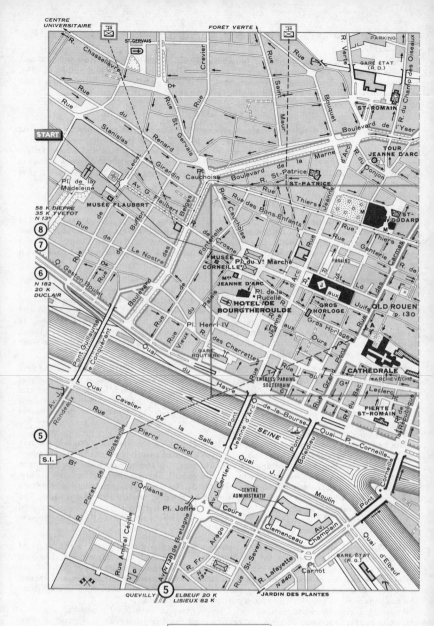

THE TOWN

PRINCIPAL SIGHTS

Although the city has lost part of its old quarter it has kept its intrinsic character; many wooden houses have been cleaned up and now stand clear of disfiguring surroundings; aged façades have been remounted and fit well into the old streets.

Some picturesque old houses are on the route of the walk described below, others are in the Rues Beauvoisine and Beffroi, the Rue des Bons-Enfants and the Rue Etoupée.

WALK THROUGH OLD ROUEN

Time about 4 hours; the Tourist Office hires out for 3 F. ear-pieces enabling visitors to listen to local commentaries in eight areas in Old Rouen.

Place du Vieux Marché.—It was on this square that Joan of Arc was burnt at the stake on 30 May 1431. The square has been enlarged and the covered market built, but it still has character. Beside the statue of Joan in the southwest corner of the market is a plaque describing her ordeal and a plan of the 15C square. A gilt mosaic marks the position of the pyre.

Walk along the right side of the market and at the end, turn right.

Bourgtheroulde Mansion★★.—This famous building (pronounced Boortrood), inspired simultaneously by Gothic and the first precepts of the Renaissance, was built in the first half of the 16C by Guillaume le Roux, Counsellor to the Exchequer and Lord of Bourgtheroulde.

Get a little away to look at the façade then enter the justifiably well known inner court (*open during banking hours; Saturdays, Sundays and holidays, ring for the caretaker*).

The end building is pure Flamboyant Gothic, with gables, pinnacles and an octagonal staircase tower. The left gallery is entirely Renaissance with six wide basket handle arches. It is surrounded by friezes: the upper one, disfigured, shows the Triumphs of Petrarch, the lower, the Field of the Cloth of Gold (1520) at which besides Henry VIII and François I, Abbot Aumale, son of Guillaume le Roux, was also present. It was he who later erected the mansion.

Return to the Place du Vieux Marché and turn right into the Rue du Gros-Horloge.

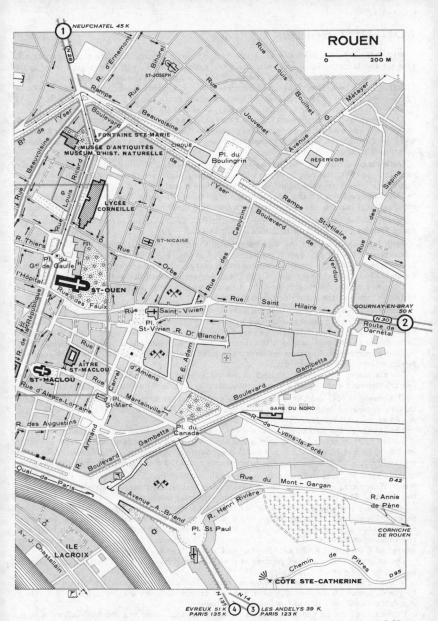

Belfry.—*Open Palm Sunday to Second Sunday in September, 10 a.m. to noon and 2.30 to 5.30 p.m.; closed Tuesdays. Enter through the small clock keeper's door; 3 F.—valid also for the Le Secq and Fine Arts Museums.*

This plain building of 1389 replaced an earlier tower destroyed by Charles VI in 1382 following a popular revolt. The bells which sounded the start of the uprising still ring the curfew at 9 p.m. The old iron clock's mechanism can be seen beneath the dome at the top of the tower from which there is a good view of the cathedral.

The fountain abutting on the belfry is 18C, the loggia—where the Great Clock keeper used to stand—Renaissance.

The Great Clock★ or **Gros Horloge.**—The most popular monument in Rouen.

The clock was originally on the belfry but the people of Rouen wanted to make it more conspicuous and so, in 1525, built the arch in which it is now incorporated (twice restored: 1892 and 1969). The hour signs marked by the single hand are complemented by signs of the weeks on the lower half of the face. The upper bull's eye showed the phases of the moon.

Go through the arch and up the crowded street.

Cathedral★★★.—Of the first 11 and 12C building, there remain the St. John and St. Stephen doors and the first three tiers of the St. Romanus Tower. The present cathedral is a reconstruction made after a devastating fire in 1200. The major part was completed by the end of the 13C. In the 15C the church took on its final appearance when the master builder, Guillaume Pontifs, built the Library, the staircase to the library and the clerestory to the Booksellers' Court (1482). He had just completed the Butter Tower when he died in 1497. In the 16C Rouland le Roux, architect of the Law Courts and the Treasury, gave the cathedral its main door and the upper tier of the lantern, which in the 19C was crowned with its present spire.

The considerable war damage has been repaired.

Exterior.—The attraction of Rouen Cathedral lies in its infinite variety including an immense façade bristling with openwork pinnacles and framed by two totally different towers: the St. Romanus on the left and the Butter Tower on the right.

ROUEN*** (continued)

West Face.—The St. John and St. Stephen doorways on either side are richly decorated, that on the left, the St. John, being a superb example of 13C art. Above each door are a profusion of niches and delightful statues which are late 14C. The central door is early 16C. Flanking it are two massive pyramid buttresses which support the façade and above, on the tympanum, a Tree of Jesse; higher still is an elegant gable cut by a latticework gallery.

The St. Romanus Tower (Tour St. Romain), a relic of the 12C church, is early Gothic.

The sumptuous Butter Tower (Tour de Beurre), thus named in the 17C when it was believed that it had been paid for by dispensations granted to those who wished to eat and drink butter and milk during Lent, was never completed, being crowned not by a spire but by an octagon.

Inside is a carillon of 55 bells.

South Face.—Go round the Butter Tower to the south side which has had to be largely rebuilt since 1944. Standing back you will see the central lantern tower and a 492 ft.—151 m—openwork iron spire—the tallest in France and Rouen's glory.

The Calende Door off the right transept is a 14C masterpiece. The lower embrasures, the most original feature, are decorated with four leaf medallions inspired by French ivories.

Return to the cathedral square where on the Rue du Petit-Salut corner stands the Renaissance **Treasury** (now the Tourist Office), built in 1510.

North Face.—Walk along the Rue St-Romain. On the right, separated from the street by a Flamboyant Gothic stonework trellis, restored in the 19C, is the Booksellers' Court (Cour des Libraires) and the door to the north transept, the Booksellers' Door. As with the Calende Door, the chief interest lies in the lower medallions filled with extravagant figures.

Continue along the Rue St-Romain, past the **passage to the Accounts Court** (A on the plan) to the square and the main door into the cathedral.

Interior.—The **nave** of eleven bays with three tiers of arches, lesser bays and large windows beneath which runs a gallery, is flanked by tall aisles intended to include galleries which were never, in fact, installed although the supporting clusters of columns were placed in position. Dominating the **transept crossing** is the lantern, rising with incredible boldness, 164 ft.—50 m—from pavement to keystone on enormous piles, which in groups of 27 or more columns sweep upward in a single thrust.

The attractive carvings on the back of the transept gables are 14C. In the north arm is the Library **stairway*** opening off a door surmounted by a gable. The first two flights are 15C.

The **chancel** is 13C and the most noble part of the cathedral: sweeping pillars end at round capitals decorated with charming formal plant motifs. The upper part is pierced with great windows, of which three, depicting Calvary, are 15C.

The Joan of Arc chapel opens off the south transept. The windows are by Max Ingrand.

Guided tours of the crypt, the church and the tombs during the Easter and summer holidays: weekdays, 10 and 11 a.m., 2.15, 3, 4 and 5 p.m.; Sundays and holidays, afternoons only; at other times of year, Saturdays, Sundays and holidays only at 2.15, 3 and 4 p.m.; 1 F., apply in the nave.

The **crypt** is 11C and still possesses its single altar and 16 ft.—5 m—curbstone well of sweet water. Fragments of columns discovered during excavations are displayed. A casket with the heart of Charles V can be seen inlaid into the east end wall.

Interesting monumental **tombs** in the ambulatory and Lady Chapel, include those of Richard Lionheart, Dukes of Normandy and Bedford, **Louis de Brézé** (1535-1544), Seneschal of Normandy and husband of Diane de Poitiers who can be seen weeping at his head and the **Cardinals of Amboise***. This last, a family tomb by Rouland le Roux, shows the kneeling figures of Georges of Amboise, Minister to Louis XII and his nephew.

The chapel's 14C windows portray the bishops of Rouen; the 1643 altarpiece frames a picture by Philippe de Champaigne.

In the ambulatory are five 13C **windows**: one of St. Julian the Hospitaler, others of Joseph by the Chartres glassmaker, Clément, and still others with remarkable colours, illustrating the Passion and the story of the Good Samaritan.

Come out of the cathedral through the north transept door and the Booksellers' Court. Walk past the **Archbishopric** (*closed*) with its 15C façade, on the right, and a half-timbered house on the left. Cross the Rue de la République to the Church of St. Maclou.

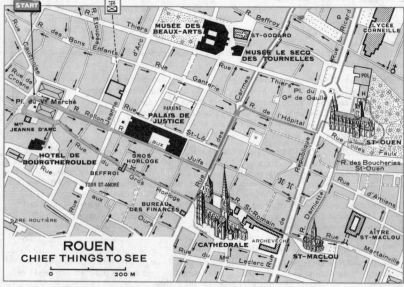

ROUEN
CHIEF THINGS TO SEE

0   200 M

St-Maclou★★.—This delightful Flamboyant church dedicated to St. Maclovius was built between 1437 and 1517 and although erected in the Renaissance period is pure Gothic in style. The only modern part, apart from restored areas, is the belfry steeple.

The most beautiful section, the west face, is preceded by a large five sided fan-shaped porch (note the picturesque Norman houses opposite). The central and left of the three doors have Renaissance **panels★★** divided into two. The lower area is adorned with small bronze heads of lions and fauns and pagan inspired reliefs, the upper with medallions showing the Circumcision and Baptism of Christ and God the Father before and after the Creation.

On the left door the medallion shows the Good Shepherd; the statuettes are of Samson, David, Moses and Solomon; the rear figures of men and women symbolise Error.

Inside, the 1521 **organ loft** has outstanding Renaissance panelling, marble supporting columns and a beautifully carved **spiral staircase★** of 1517 leading to a contemporary organ.

Go along the Rue Martainville, past the north door of St-Maclou where the panels depict the Virgin, to the cloister.

St-Maclou Cloister★ (Aître St-Maclou), 184–186 Rue Martainville.—*Open free until midnight in summer.*

This 16C group (from the Latin *atrium*) is one of the last examples of a mediaeval plague cemetery. The south gallery dates from 1640, the lower gallery at one time being open like a cloister. The upper gallery is 18C. The frieze is somewhat macabre.

Return to the front of St-Maclou and take the old Rue Damiette on the right. Note the picturesque blind Hauts-Mariages street on the right, and on the left, the Rue d'Amiens with the 17C Etancourt Mansion adorned with large statues. Continue straight ahead down the Rue des Boucheries-St-Ouen beside the south wall of the church.

St-Ouen★★.—The beautiful chancel, the proportions of the nave and the pure lines of the building generally make this former abbey church, dedicated to St. Andoenus, one of the jewels of French 14C architecture. Work began in 1318 (chancel, ambulatory, transept and first bay of the nave), was interrupted by the Hundred Years War and completed (nave) in the 15C. The west face was replaced between 1845 and 1851 by the cold uninspired façade evident today. The church is 440 ft.—134 m—long.

Interior★★★.—The outstanding feature of the nave is its superb proportioning. The organ is one of the major ones of France.

The chancel is perhaps even more harmonious. Above the great arches, as in the nave, there runs a rich but delicate clerestory triforium. Higher still are great windows filled with 14C glass except for the central one which is modern. The grilles closing the chancel are 18C, as are those at the north end of the ambulatory.

The attractive south door is known as the Candlemakers' Door—Porte des Ciriers—from the name of the merchants who sat round it.

Exterior.—Coming out walk along the north wall, where a gallery of the old cloister remains, and through the town hall to the former abbey garden.

The church is flanked on its north side by the Clerks' Tower, a Romanesque relic of the earlier building; at its east end by individually roofed radiating chapels and flying buttresses. Above the transept the square central tower rises two tiers before ending decoratively in a ducal coronet.

Above the great rose window in the Flamboyant south transept gable are statues of kings and queens of Juda; below is the strange Urchin or Marmouset Door in which the arching, on one side, rests disconcertingly on false keystones.

Walk along the Rue de l'Hôpital, turn left into the Rue des Carmes and right into the Rue des Juifs which brings you to the Law Courts.

(After Archives photographiques)

Façade of St. Maclou

Law Courts★★ (Palais de Justice).—This building, erected as the Normandy Exchequer, is attributed to Rouland le Roux. It was badly damaged in 1944 but has since been restored.

The decoration of the façade, which is the most beautiful part of the building, is typical of the Renaissance, infinite care being taken to enrich the ornament at each level—the base is therefore quite plain, the crest line a forest of chiselled stone, pinnacles, turrets, gables and flying buttresses above a rich balustrade. (Inside is a monumental 16C grand staircase.)

Continue along the Rue des Juifs, then the Rue Rollon to the Place du Vieux Marché.

ADDITIONAL SIGHTS

Fine Arts Museum★★.—*Open 10 a.m. to noon, 2 to 6 p.m. (4.30 p.m. 1 November to 31 March); closed Tuesdays, Wednesday mornings, 1 January, 1 May, Ascension Day, 14 July, All Saints and Christmas Days; 3 F., also valid for the Le Secq Museum and the Belfry.*

Rouen Ceramics★★★.—The first floor presents a collection of the world famous Rouen pottery in chronological order showing also foreign influences and fashion in its decoration.

Art Gallery**.—In addition to international masterpieces, the collection represents a panorama of painting beginning with the altarpiece of the *Virgin and the Saints* by Gerhaerd David, one of the greatest Flemish primitive paintings, followed by Veronese, Caravaggio, Velasquez, French 17 and 18 and 19C masters (particularly those with Norman associations: Poussin, *Venus Arming Aeneas*, Géricault, Ingres and Delacroix), the Impressionists (Monet, Sisley) and the 20C (Dufy, Villon).

Le Secq des Tournelles Museum**.—*Same conditions as for the Fine Arts Museum; ticket valid for the Fine Arts and Belfry.*

The museum, in the former St. Lawrence Church, a Flamboyant building, is of ironwork. In the nave are large items such as balconies, grilles and signs, locks, door knockers and keys —their development is traced from the 3 to 19C. Domestic utensils and tools are on the first floor. There are also jewels, clasps, combs, medals, tools and 17 and 18C objects.

15 and 16C glass and statues from the bombed-out Church of St. Vincent are also displayed.

Antiques' Museum*.—*Open 10 a.m. to noon, 2 to 5 p.m.; 2 F.; closed Wednesdays.*

The museum in the old Visitandines Convent contains mediaeval and Renaissance stained glass, gold and silver work, ivories, enamels, sculptures, tapestries (*The Winged Stag*) and an interesting collection of carved panelling from old houses in Rouen.

There are, in addition, Egyptian, Oriental, Greek, Merovingian and Gallo-Roman departments and also the Lillebonne mosaic, *Daphne pursued by Apollo*.

Natural History, Ethnography and Prehistory Museum.—Entrance to the right of the Antiques' Museum. *Open 10 a.m. to noon, 2 to 6 p.m.; closed Mondays and Tuesdays; 2 F.*

Lycée Corneille.—The school is in the former 17 and 18C Jesuit college and was attended not only by Corneille but later by Flaubert, Maupassant and Maurois.

St. Godard's.—This late 15C church contains wonderful **stained glass windows***, in particular a 16C one at the end of the south aisle showing the Tree of Jesse. The three aisles are covered by a wooden roof pierced by sky-lights.

St. Patrick's.—This early 16C Gothic church is again remarkable for its **stained glass*** made between 1538 and 1625. In the south chancel is Christ Triumphant, in the adjoining chapel, Sts. Fiacre, Eustace and Louis and an Annunciation in Italian Renaissance style; in the south aisle are the stories of Job, St. Patrick and St. Barbara. The gilt baldachin is 18C.

Joan of Arc's Tower.—*Open 9 a.m. to noon, 1.30 to 7 p.m. (summer); 10 a.m. to noon and 2 to 6 p.m. (winter). Admission: 3 F.* This is the former keep in Philippe Auguste's castle where Joan was threatened with torture on 9 May 1431.

Joan of Arc Museum.—In the Place du Vieux Marché.—*Open 9 a.m. to noon, 1.30 to 7 p.m. (summer); 10 a.m. to noon, 2 to 6 p.m. (winter); 2 F.*

Corneille Museum, 4 Rue de la Pie.—*Open 10 a.m. to noon, 2 to 6 p.m.; closed Tuesdays, Wednesday mornings, 1 January, 1 May, 1 and 11 November, 25 December, the last three Fridays in January and November and the first two Fridays in December; 0.50 F.* Corneille's birthplace.

Flaubert and History of Medicine Museum.—In the old hospital, 52 Rue de Lecat. *Guided tours 10 a.m. to noon, 2 to 6 p.m.; closed Tuesdays, Wednesday mornings and holidays.* The 17 and 18C hospital was where Flaubert's father worked as a surgeon and the author was born.

Fierte St-Romain.—An original Renaissance building. The stone canopy used to contain, on Ascension day, the relics of St. Romanus.

The building adjoins the Linen Hall, a modern construction with exhibition, conference and banqueting rooms.

THE PORT

The Joffet company runs motorboat trips round the port and as far as La Bouille in summer. Apply at the bus station. ℡ 71 20 01.

Rouen is France's fourth port, after Marseilles, Le Havre and Dunkirk, with traffic amounting to 12,000,000 tons in 1966. One of its great advantages is its proximity to Paris—137 miles upstream—220 km—or 75 miles by motorway—137 km.

Many works and factories, profiting from the readily accessible mineral and primary products, have been steadily crowding the river banks since the beginning of the century, producing typical harbour surroundings (see p. 141—*The Economy of the Lower Seine*).

By 1949 the port, which had been devastated by the war, had equalled its pre-war traffic.

As imports of coal and petroleum products have decreased (because of the Le Havre–Paris pipeline) new items have taken their place particularly cereals (major French port), early vegetables and citrus fruit. Improved access, new quays and equipment now allow ocean going vessels and 20,000-ton tankers to dock in all weathers. Further expansion is planned.

TOUR

The Guillaume-le-Conquérant Bridge marks the upstream limit for larger shipping apart from ships with dismantling superstructures which can go up to Gennevilliers.

Right Bank Quays.—Below the bridge you can see the usual ships' bustle. From the end of the landing stage's second pontoon you get a good view of the port and the forest of cranes.

Walk along the Boulevard Ferdinand-de-Lesseps which serves a vast jetty for the North African trade. To the right is the Port Authority wine store (220 million gallons); the Antilles Quay on the far side of the dock handles bananas, its continuation, the Africa Quay, the products of the west coast of Africa.

You can walk on to a peninsula from where you will see the downstream river bend. On the right is the Skalli granary and on the left the 40,000-ton capacity port silo.

Left Bank Quays.—A walk along the raised quays of the left bank between the Corneille Bridge and the Avenue J.-Rondeaux, affords interesting views of the historic buildings on the far bank. Factories and quays succeed one another as far as Moulineaux on the left bank.

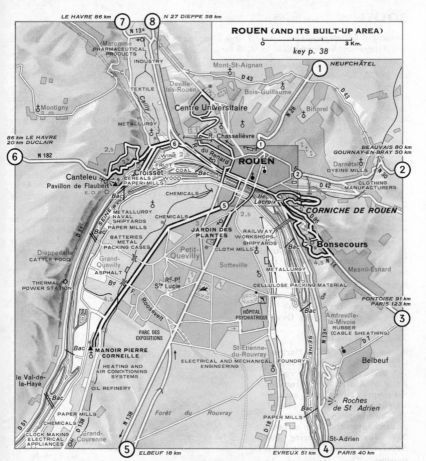

ENVIRONS

Within the Rouen built-up area

Rouen Corniche*.—*6 miles—10 km—plus ¼ hour sightseeing. Preferably at sunset.* Starting from the Place St-Paul, drive along the Rue Henri-Rivière and its continuation the Rue du Mont-Gargan. Branch right into the Rue Annie-de-Pène. The road climbs by a hairpin bend to the top of the Ste-Catherine Hill, a chalk spur separating the Robec and Seine Valleys.

Ste-Catherine Hill*** (Côte Ste-Catherine).—Leave the car on a terrace in a sharp bend to the left. There is a strikingly beautiful **panorama***** (*viewing table*) over the river bend and the town with all its belfries.

Continue along the D 95 which meets the N 14 *bis* by a school. Turn left and 200 yds later turn right in front of the Café de la Mairie.

Bonsecours**.—The Neo-Gothic Basilica of Bonsecours (1840) which crowns the Mount Thuringe spur is a popular pilgrimage and also an excellent **belvedere**** from which to see shipping and industrial Rouen. The bell, the Great Lion, at the cemetery entrance was offered to the basilica but proved too heavy to be installed in the belfry. It is rung on solemn occasions. From the foot of the Calvary (*viewing table*) there is a **panorama**** straight down to the river bend with the left bank with its industry, the port and the bridges going away downstream and on the right bank, the cathedral.

The 19C Joan of Arc monument approached by a horseshoe staircase stands on a platform from which there is an upstream **view*** of the Seine.

Continue along the N 14B going towards Paris but turn off right into the N 14 which brings you back to Rouen along a fine *corniche* stretch of road.

University Centre.—*3 miles—5 km*—Leave Rouen by the Rue Chasselièvre, northwest on the map. From the road which ends on the Mont-aux-Malades Plateau on which the University Centre has been built, there is a good **panorama**** of the city, the port and the curve in the river. *Return by the Rue du Renard.*

Croisset; Canteleu*.—*6 miles—9 km—plus ¼ hour sightseeing.* Leave Rouen by ⑥ on the map, going towards Duclair. Take the D 51 on the left towards Croisset.

Croisset.—*Guided tours of a wing of Flaubert's house, 10 a.m. to noon, 2 to 6 p.m.; closed Tuesdays and Wednesday mornings, 1 January, 1 May, 1 and 11 November, 25 December, three last Fridays in January and November and two first Fridays in December; 0.50 F.* This wing, now a museum, is all that remains of the house in which Flaubert wrote *Madame Bovary* and *Salambô*. (His library is in the Canteleu-Croisset town hall.)

Turn back towards Rouen along the same road and the N 182 on the left which climbs picturesquely to Canteleu.

Canteleu*.—There is an interesting but limited **view*** of the port and part of the town from the church terrace. To return to Rouen, go along the street facing the church, lined by utility and residential buildings. At the end of the built-up area turn left and immediately right by a school. As you go down a steep wide road, you get a good **panorama**** of the Cailly Valley, Rouen and the port. At the bottom of the hill turn left into the N 182 for Rouen.

133

ROUEN*** (concluded)

Botanical Gardens.—1½ miles—2.5 km—along the N 840. Open 8 a.m. to 8 p.m. (5 p.m. in winter); tropical hot houses 8.30 to 11.30 a.m., 1.30 to 5 p.m.

Petit-Couronne.—5 miles—8 km—plus ½ hour's sightseeing. Leave Rouen by ⑤ on the map, the D 138. Turn right by the first houses of Petit-Couronne into the Rue Pierre-Corneille. Leave the car before No. 502.

Pierre-Corneille Manor.—Guided tours 9.30 a.m. (10 a.m. in winter) to noon, 2 to 6 p.m. (4 p.m. in winter); closed Wednesdays. The "house in the fields" was bought in 1608 by the poet's father so that his child, who was delicate, could enjoy country air. The Norman house has now been transformed into a museum. At the bottom of the garden is a thatched bakery reconstructed to look exactly as it did in the 17C.

Beyond the Rouen built-up area

Tour of Roumare Forest; St-Martin-de-Boscherville*; Canteleu*.—Tour of 29 miles —46 km—about 1½ hours—plus ¼ hour sightseeing. Leave Rouen by the Croisset road. After looking at the wing of Flaubert's house, continue along the D 51 which runs between the river and the cliff face crowned by Roumare Forest.

Le Val-de-la-Haye.—The column on the right, facing the Grand Couronne ferry as you leave the village, commemorates the return of Napoleon's body to France—brought from St. Helena to Cherbourg in the frigate La Belle Poule, transhipped to the Normandie, and on 9 December 1840 transferred at this spot to the Dorade No. 3, which sailed up to Paris.

The road continues beside the Seine.

Sahurs Church.—A shaded road, on the left, leads to the church overlooked from the far bank by the ruins of Robert the Devil's castle.

Turn left off the D 51.

Sahurs. — The 16C Marbœuf Chapel, which stands in a manor, was made famous by the vow of Anne of Austria who promised the chapel a silver statue equal in weight to the child she desired. The twelve-pound silver statue dispatched on the birth of Louis XIV disappeared during the Revolution. Return to the D 51.

Quevillon.—The castle of La Rivière-Bourdet, on the left, a sumptuous 17C building, has been abandoned but the monumental dovecote remains well preserved.

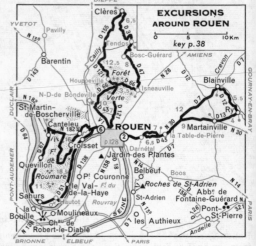

EXCURSIONS AROUND ROUEN

St-Martin-de-Boscherville*.—Description p. 136.

Turn right into the N 182; at the oak crossroads in Leu, take the first on the right and after 500 yds. turn left. The road winds between the oaks, beeches and hornbeams of Roumare Forest to come out at the Treize Chênes crossroads where you turn left.

Canteleu*.—View and return to Rouen described p. 133.

Verte Forest; Clères*.—Tour of 30 miles—48 km—about 1½ miles—plus 1 hour sightseeing. Leave Rouen by the Rue Bouquet, north on the map. Continue by the Rue de la Corderie, the Avenue Gallieni and the D 121 which crosses the Verte Forest. Take the D 155 to Clères (description p. 72). Come out of Clères by the D 3 and at Bosc-Guérard bear left into the D 47 and, after the church at Isneauville, right along the D 66 which goes along a beautiful wooded valley in the Verte Forest.

Before a lower road, turn left to return to Rouen by the D 43 and the V 1, the Rue Pasteur.

Martainville; Ry; Blainville.—Tour of 27 miles—44 km—about 1½ hours—plus ¼ hour sightseeing. Leave Rouen by ②, the N 30 which climbs to the plateau.

Martainville.—Guided tours 9 a.m. to noon, 2 to 6 p.m. (4.30 p.m., 1 October to 31 March). Closed on Tuesdays.

Martainville Castle is an elegant residence of brick and stone, erected at the end of the 15C by some rich Rouen merchants. From outside the great brick chimneys have a remarkable Gothic decoration. The interior is much as it was originally and is gradually being refurbished and arranged as the Upper Normandy Folklore Museum.

Take the D 13 on the left as you leave the village.

Ry.—This village in the Crevon Valley is said to be the setting for Flaubert's Madame Bovary. The **church** (access by a slope behind the town hall), which goes back, in part, to the 12C, is preceded by a beautiful carved wood Renaissance **porch***. Inside note the 16C medallion in the south aisle, of the Eternal Father, and in the chancel a Renaissance altarfront.

Former French Resistance (maquis) leaders founded, on their return from deportation, the **Maquiparc**: open 9 a.m. to 7 p.m. (8 p.m. on Sundays). Admission: 3 F (4 F on Sundays and public holidays) amusement park in the grounds in which they had been hiding when discovered by Germans occupying the Louis XIII house.

Continue along the D 12 up the Crevon Valley.

Blainville.—Inside the Flamboyant church stands a monumental 16C statue of St. Michael and, in the south transept chapel, a 15C group of St. Anne and the Virgin as well as the tombstone of Lord Mouton of Blainville. The stalls are 15C.

By the D 7 make for the N 30; at La Table de Pierre continue straight ahead into the D 43. At the start of the descent you will see Rouen Cathedral straight before you.

Excursions can also be made along the Seine Valley (pp. 142 to 146) and to Lyons Forest (p. 113).

ST-ANDRÉ-D'HÉBERTOT *—Michelin maps 54 ⑱, 55 ④—4 miles—7 km— southwest of Beuzeville.

St. Andrew's Castle (St. André) stands in a particularly attractive valley setting.

Castle★.—*Not open to the public.*
The castle surrounded by a moat stands in a park with centuries old lime trees. A fine 17C corbelled tower abuts on the graceful 18C façade.

Behind the castle through the trees, can be seen the small parish church (12C Romanesque chancel) dominated by a handsome belfry.

ST-LÔ —Michelin map 54 ⑬—pop. 19,613.

St-Lô, the prefecture of the Manche Department, has the sad privilege of having earned the title of Capital of the Ruins. By 19 July 1944, the day the town was liberated, there remained standing only the battered towers of the Collegiate Church of Our Lady and a few outlying houses. The town is therefore a modern one.

HISTORICAL NOTES

St-Lô, the ancient Gaul Briovère, which in the 6C took the name of its local lord, Bishop of Coutances, and in 1944 became a war casualty, has a history worthy of respect.

The Key Town.—St-Lô was a vital communications centre in the Battle of Normandy; it was bombed regularly from 6 June onwards. Early in July began the battle for St-Lô proper, prior to the capture of the Lessay – St-Lô road, the base for operation Cobra (see p. 25).

The town, principal pivot of German resistance, fell on 19th. A monument (A on the map) raised in memory of Major Howie of the American Army recalls a moving episode during the advance. The major had been killed on the 18th but so great had been his anxiety to be among the first to enter the town, the first column to invest the town brought his coffin and deposited it on the ruins of the belfry of the Holy Cross Church.

A week later, after an unprecedented air raid in which 5,000 tons of bombs were dropped over an area of 4 sq. miles – 11 km² – the enemy front to the west broke, and the Avranches breakthrough could be launched.

Reconstruction.—From the ruins, a new town has arisen, planned so that one can now see clearly outlined the rocky spur, ringed by ramparts and towers, which gives the town its individual character. The oldest quarter, the Enclos, in the upper part of the town includes the prefecture and administrative buildings, which make an interesting postwar architectural group. The extremely modern tower on the Place de l'Hôtel-de-Ville is an amazing contrast to the nearby old prison porch.

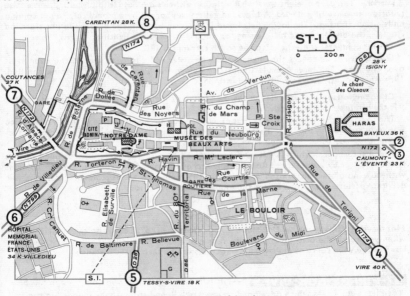

TOUR (about 1 hour)

Church of Our Lady (14 and 15C).—The church's façade with the two towers, strengthened but otherwise left exactly as they were, indicate the violence of the 1944 attacks. The building has a remarkable plan with two pillars in the centre of the nave supporting an 18C glory beam. There is an outside pulpit against the north wall.

If you continue straight ahead you will come to the edge of the spur on which the old town stands.

Fine Arts Museum.—*Open 2.30 to 5 p.m.; closed Mondays and Fridays.*
The three galleries display the late 16C series of tapestries, *The Loves of Gombaut and Macée*, 19C French painting (Corot, Boudin, Millet) and portraits of the Matignon-Grimaldi princes.

Stud★.—*Open 10 to 11.30 a.m., 2.30 to 5 p.m. A groom accompanies. The full complement of stallions is present only on Saturdays at 10 a.m., 29 July to 9 September.*
The full complement of stallions, which numbers 230, are mostly English and Norman thoroughbreds selected for the breeding of race horses, French trotters, Norman cobs and Percherons.

French-American Memorial Hospital, Villedieu road by ⑥ on the map.—The hospital was built jointly by the two nations and has a Fernand Legér mosaic on one of its façades. *The chapel is open.*

ST-LÔ (concluded)

ENVIRONS

Vire Valley.—*25 miles—40 km. Leave St-Lô by ④, the N 174.*

Torigni-sur-Vire.—The old Matignon Castle, destroyed in 1944, has been rebuilt (*open 1 April to 30 September, 10 a.m. to noon, 2 to 5 p.m.*). The east wing contains Louis XIII and XIV furniture and tapestries. Pleasantly shady park with two pools.
Turn round and take the D 286 on the left.

Ham Rocks★★ (Roches de Ham).—*2 miles—3 km—south of Condè-sur-Vire; on the right; signpost.*

From the first platform on this magnificent escarpment you can look down 260 ft—80 m—on a deep bend carved by the slowly moving river through the ancient shale rock below, while from the second, 150 yds further on, there is a wide **view**★★ along the Vire Valley.

Troisgots-la-Chapelle-sur-Vire.—This small village has been a pilgrimage centre since the 12C. A 15C statue of Our Lady of Vire stands on the left inside the church which also contains an unusual low-relief in alabaster of St. Anne, the Virgin and Holy Child and 15C low reliefs. Return to St-Lô along the D 551, D 286 and the N 174.

ST-MARTIN-DE-BOSCHERVILLE ★—Michelin maps 52 ⑭, 54 ⑩, 55 ⑥, 97 ①—local map p. 145—pop. 970.

The Abbey of St. George of Boscherville was founded in 1050 by Raoul of Tancarville, Grand Chamberlain to William the Conqueror, for the canons regular of St. Augustine who were later succeeded by the Benedictines of St-Evroult (see p. 69).

The abbey church, which became the St. Martin parish church at the time of the Revolution and so was saved from destruction, is now one of the Seine Valley's finest small monuments.

FORMER ABBEY CHURCH OF ST. GEORGE★ (*tour: ¼ hour*)

Church.—*Guided tours; apply to the caretaker.*

The building, which was constructed from 1080 to 1125, apart from the vaulting in the nave and transept which is 13C, has a striking unity of style and harmony of proportion.

The façade is plain: the ornament on the main door archivolts geometric, in typical Norman Romanesque fashion (*see p. 17*); the capitals which are remarkably delicately carved are by craftsmen from the Ile-de-France or the Chartres region.

Interior.—The nave of eight bays with aisles on either side, has Gothic vaulting and a false triforium in place of galleries. A big open gallery supported by a monolithic round column ends either transept. The low reliefs inlaid in the wall beneath the balustrade illustrate, on the left, the bishop giving his blessing, on the right, warriors fighting.

The monumental confessional in the south transept is 18C.

Groined vaulting covers the chancel and side aisles and a heavier version the oven vault over the apse. The black marble tombstone before the high altar is to Antoine the Red, 19th Abbot of St. George's, who died in 1535.

Chapterhouse.—*To visit, ring at the door to the right of the church and wait a few minutes; 1 F; the caretaker accompanies you.*

The tour affords the opportunity first of letting you see the north face of the church which was reconstructed in the 14C—the cornice modillons are outstanding—and, even more interesting, the massive lantern built over the transept.

The chapterhouse, which is 12C and surmounted by a 17C building used to open on the former cloister by way of three Romanesque arches supported on groups of slender columns with now mutilated historiated capitals. On the right are statue columns. Inside, a fine decorative frieze runs above where the monks' stalls once stood.

ENVIRONS

Hénouville Viewpoint★.—*One mile—2 km—along the D 67. Leave the car in a right bend when you reach the plateau. A path down on the left leads to a wall from which there is a* **view**★ *of the wide curve of the river; St. George's can be seen in the distance.*

ST-PIERRE-SUR-DIVES ★—Michelin maps 54 ⑦, 55 west of ⑬—pop. 3868.

St-Pierre-sur-Dives which developed round a rich Benedictine Abbey founded in the 11C, still possesses a remarkable old church.

Church★.—*Tour: ½ hour.* The original church was burnt down during the wars between William the Conqueror's sons. An examination of the west face reveals several periods of reconstruction: the Romanesque south tower dates back to the 12C; the west face itself and the north tower are 14C reconstructions; the window above the main doorway is late 15C.

Inside, the nave is light and harmonious, the upper parts, including the triforium bays surmounting each wide arch, dating back only to the 15C. The fine lantern above the transept is 13C as is the chancel encircled by wide pointed arches. The bases of the columns dividing the chancel from the ambulatory and south tower once formed part of the old 12C church.

The history of St-Pierre-sur-Dives can be seen illustrated in the three modern stained glass windows of the chancel.

Chapterhouse.—*Apply at the town hall to visit.* The early 13C chamber has a 13C glazed brick pavement (*see Norman Ceramic Art p. 20*).

Covered Market (11–12C).—The market, which was burnt down in 1944, has been rebuilt faithfully in the original style even to the use of 290,000 chestnut pegs. *To enter ask for the key at the Café du Marché on the square.*

ST-SAUVEUR-LE-VICOMTE—Michelin map ➏ ②—pop. 2329.

St-Sauveur-le-Vicomte in the heart of the Cotentin, suffered, together with its castle, very considerably in June 1944. Pilgrims visit the abbey in memory of St. Marie-Madeleine Postel, 19C foundress of the Order of Sisters of Mercy.

Church.—The church, which has a 13C transept, contains interesting works of art, including a 16C *Ecce Homo* (*at the opening of the chancel on the left*) and a 15C statue of St. James of Compostella.

Barbey-d'Aurevilly Museum.—*Guided tours 9 a.m. to noon, 2 to 7 p.m.* (*in winter apply to the keeper of the old people's home*). *Admission: 2 F.*

Go through the castle walls (now a house of retreat) and up the stairs on the left beyond the covered way. The museum contains mementoes of the great writer, Barbey d'Aurevilly (*see p. 21*) who was born in the town.

ST-SEVER-CALVADOS—Michelin map ➎ ⑨—pop. 1478.

This large market town in the Normandy Bocage Region developed from an abbey founded in the 6C of which there still exist the church and a conventual building, now occupied by the town hall and local schools. The nearby St-Sever Forest provides an attractive setting.

The Church.—The old abbey church, a severe 13 and 14C granite building, is preceded by the free standing 17C belfry of the former parish church. A graceful lantern on pendentives rises above the transept; tall lancet windows, two with 13C glass, light the chancel and in the south aisle a 15C window portrays the monastery's early abbots.

ENVIRONS

St-Sever Forest—*2 miles—4 km.* Leave St-Sever by the St-Pois road. Bear left ½ mile—1 km —after passing the D 299 on the left. 300 yds further on continue straight along a tarred road to the Hermitage Avenue on the left. The forest massif includes oaks, beeches and pines as well as fir and larch plantations.

The Hermitage (L'Ermitage).—A small colony of Camaldulian hermits established a retreat in this spot in the first half of the 17C.

ST-VALERY-EN-CAUX—Michelin map ➋ ③—local map p. 67—pop. 3174—*Place to stay (see p. 36).*

St. Valéry, a former fishing and coastal trading port, has become a seaside resort thanks to its own remarkable efforts to re-establish and re-equip itself.

The centre of the town was razed in June 1940 during the desperate rearguard action fought by units of the British 10th Army driven back to the sea after the collapse of the Somme front. Two monuments and a military cemetery recall the sacrifice of the 51st Highland Division and the French 2nd Cavalry Division.

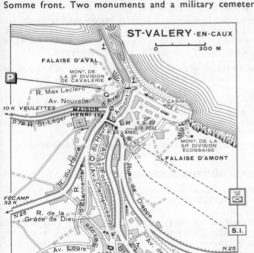

ST-VALERY-EN-CAUX

WALK TO THE AVAL CLIFF★ (Falaise d'Aval)
¼ *hour on foot Rtn*

Leave the car at the end of the Avenue Nouvelle, at a roundabout encircled by seats.

Take the cliff path to the 1940 Memorial from which there is a **view**★ east extending to the Ailly Lighthouse and, in clear weather, to Le Tréport.

ADDITIONAL SIGHTS

Amont Cliff (Falaise d'Amont).— A stairway leads to the 51st Highland Division Monument which overlooks the town, harbour and beach of St-Valéry.

Henri IV House, Quai du Havre.—Beautiful Renaissance house.

St-Valéry Stadium (Stade Valériquais).—Tennis courts in a pleasantly green setting, a stadium and the Etennemare Woods stand invitingly close together.

ST-WANDRILLE ★★—Maps ➋ ⑬, ➏ ⑨, ➎ ⑤—local map. p. 145—pop. 1061.

St. Wandrille Abbey and the renascent Abbey of Bec Hellouin are a moving testimony to the continuity of the Benedictine Order in Normandy since the earliest times.

HISTORICAL NOTES

God's Athlete (7C).—All at King Dagobert's court were celebrating the marriage of the wise and handsome Count Wandrille who seemed brilliantly destined when, by common accord, the young newly-weds decided to consecrate their lives to God. The bride entered a convent and Wandrille joined a group of hermits. The king ordered Wandrille to return to court, but the new hermit placed his cause in the hands of God and, in time, Dagobert enlightened by a miracle, resigned himself to the loss of his subject. Wandrille, after staying in far off monasteries, returned to St-Ouen in Rouen where he was ordained. His saintliness and his magnificent physique earned him the nickname of God's True Athlete.

The Valley of the Saints (7 to 9C).—In 649 Wandrille founded a monastery in the Fontenelle Valley. The monks cleared the forest and planted the first vines. **Fontenelle** library and schools became famous (the abbey had not yet taken the name of its founder). A succession of learned men were appointed as abbots: Einhard, Charlemagne's historian and Ansegise who organised the first collection of the emperor's capitulary ordinances. In 831 the *Epic of the Abbots of Fontenelle* appeared—the first history of a western monastery. But even more important, Fontenelle, "where saints flourish as rose trees in a greenhouse" became for the people living locally the Valley of the Saints and St. Wandrille remains to this day the only monastery in Christendom to celebrate its own feast of All the Saints of the Monastery.

Benedictine Continuity.—In the 10C some monks began to rebuild the ruined abbey, destroyed by the fury of the Northmen. The new abbey, which took the name of its original founder, became one of the most flourishing centres of the Benedictine Order which spread widely throughout Normandy in the 11C (*details p. 140*). The Wars of Religion brought only a temporary decline; the Maurian Reform sustained its influence but the Revolution led to the dispersal of the monks and the buildings fell into ruin. In the 19C the abbey passed successively into the hands of a textile mill owner and the English peer, the Marquis of Stacpoole. In 1894 the Benedictines returned, but seven years later were again dispersed. For several years the author Maurice Maeterlinck lived in the abbey. In 1931 however the Gregorian chant began once more to be heard in the church.

THE ABBEY** (tour: ½ hour)

Guided tour of some of the abbey buildings, Sundays and Benedictine feast days, 11.30 a.m. to 12.15 p.m., 3 to 7 p.m. (except during vespers); other days, 10.15 to 11.45 a.m., 3 to 7 p.m. (except during vespers). Tickets at the porter's lodge; men only are allowed in the cloister.

The monumental gateway was erected in the 19C by the Marquis of Stacpoole. The entrance to the abbey is through a 15C door surmounted by a symbolical pelican. The porter's lodge and its twin are 18C; the gate between the two is known as the Jarente Gate.

The Abbey Church Ruins.—The bases of the columns which supported the main arches of the 14C nave can be seen rising out of the grass. The only parts still standing are the tall columns in two groups of massive and slender pillars which stood at the opening of the north transept. The 13C chancel, with six bays, was circled by an ambulatory and fifteen chapels.

Cloister*.—All four galleries of the cloister remain. The 14C south gallery, parallel with the nave, was linked to it by a fine door surmounted by a now mutilated tympanum illustrating the Coronation of the Virgin. A niche, in a wall at right angles, contains the deeply venerated and graceful 14C statue of Our Lady of Fontenelle.

The remaining three galleries are 15C; in the north gallery, beside the highly ornate refectory door, is a half Gothic, half Renaissance **lavabo**. Above is a gable decorated with a fretwork of leaves and a blind arcade with six sections each containing a tap. Scenes from the New Testament are illustrated in an exquisitely delicate Flamboyant decoration.

Church.—*The monastery church is open to all. Mass with the Gregorian chant is at 9.15 a.m. on weekdays, 10 a.m. Sundays and feast days; Vespers at 5.30 p.m. on weekdays (6.45 p.m. Thursdays), 5 p.m. Sundays and feast days.*

The church is an old 15C tithe barn, the Canteloup Barn, which was transported piece by piece in 1969 from La Neuville-du-Bosc in the Eure and re-erected at St. Wandrille. The Chapel of the Holy Sacrament, which is characterised by its wood beams, is the barn's one-time porch.

To the right of the chapel's opening is a 1970 shrine containing the head of St. Wandrille.

WALK TO ST. SATURNINIUS' CHAPEL (¾ hour Rtn)

As you come out of the abbey take the path downhill on the right which passes by a 16C Entombment beneath a sort of porch. Skirt the wall for 150 yds, go round a field and take the path along the abbey wall to the chapel.

St. Saturninius' Chapel built at the edge of the abbey porch is a small trefoil plan oratory, rebuilt in the 10C on what were probably Merovingian foundations. The façade was remodelled in the 16C but the building has preserved its thickset appearance with three apsidal chapels dominated by a heavy square tower.

The building has been restored inside (*entry permitted*). The tops of three pillars embedded in the base of the tower and decorated with roses, palms and fantastic animals come, no doubt, from an earlier construction probably of the Carolingian period.

STE-MÈRE-ÉGLISE—Michelin map 54 ② ③—pop. 1389.

This large town at the centre of the traditional Normandy livestock breeding area (*see p. 14*) entered the news headlines brutally on the night of 5/6 June 1944 when troops from the American 82nd Airborne Division landed to assist the 101st Division clear the Utah Beach exits (*see p. 76*). The action is commemorated by a monument in the square and an **airborne troops' museum** (*open 1 April to 31 October, 9 a.m. to noon, 2 to 7 p.m.; 1 November to 31 March, Sundays and holidays only, 10 a.m. to noon, 2 to 5 p.m.; 1.50 F*).

Ste-Mère-Eglise was liberated on 6 June but fighting continued all around until tanks advanced into the town from Utah Beach the following day.

Church.—The solid 13C church was damaged particularly during the dislodging of German snipers from the belfry. The American parachute drop can be seen recorded in the modern glass in the main door.

Milestone O on Liberty Road.—This is the first symbolic milestone planted along the road followed by the American forces to Metz and Bastogne. From Avranches onwards they recall especially the rapid advances of the 20th Corps of the US 3rd Army (General Patton).

STE-SUZANNE —Michelin map 60 ⑪—pop. 888.

This peaceful city occupies a picturesque **setting*** on the summit of a rock promontory commanding the right bank of the Erve and chosen in the 11C by the viscounts of Beaumont as the site on which to build one of the most important Maine strongpoints.

A tour round the town enables one to see the remains of the fortress which William the Conqueror was unable to take even after a three-year siege.

TOUR (about ½ hour)

Leave the car on the Place Ambroise-de-Loré from which one can see standing in now private grounds the massive south tower, one of the walls' most impressive fortifications.

Go up the Rue de la Cité and along the Rue du Grenier à Sel, on the right.

North Tower (viewing tower).—*To visit apply at the café on the corner of the Rue de la Cité and Rue du Grenier à Sel.* From the top, where there is a viewing table, you look down on the small town grouped round its stalwart 11C **keep** and the ramparts. The **view** extends north to the Coëvrons chain, east to the Grande Charnie Forest and along the Erve Valley.

Continue along the Rue du Grenier à Sel to the postern where you turn left.

Postern or Rampart Walk.—The path circles the fortifications, skirting first the 16C castle. (*Tours of the castle, 11C keep, 11 and 13C ramparts, Easter to 30 September at 11 a.m., 3, 4, 5 and 6 p.m.; 1 October to Easter, Sundays and holidays. Apply to Mme. Boiteau, Rue des Coëvrons or at the Tourist Office.*)

The walk continues in front of the old Iron Gate, the Wicket Gate, with attractive **views** across the countryside. Go through the Wicket Gate to the Grand'Rue (left) and the church.

Son et Lumière performance at weekends from 2 July to 3 September.

Church.—The church contains behind the altar a graceful 14C Virgin and Child, and, on the north side of the chancel, a very old polychrome wood statue of St. Suzanne.

The Rue de la Cité brings you back to the Ambroise-de-Loré Square.

ENVIRONS

Viviers Signal.—*Tour of 16 miles—25 km.* Leave Ste-Suzanne by the D 9 going northeast towards Viviers. On leaving the village which now adjoins Torcé-en-Charnie, turn right into uphill road which ends at the edge of a steep wooded drop from which you can see the dense Grande Charnie Forest. A path on the left leads to a rock crowned with a statue of the Sacred Heart, from which you will get a good view of the Coëvrons Range.

Return to Viviers and bear left into the D 210 for 3½ miles—5.5 km—when you turn first into the D 156 on the right, then the D 7 from which there is a remarkable view of Ste-Suzanne just before you cross the Erve.

Excursions described starting from Evron (see p. 93) can also be made from Ste-Suzanne. Extra distance: about 4 miles—7 km.

SÉES *—Michelin map 60 ③—local maps pp. 44 and 87—pop. 4,904.

Sées is a calm and quiet old cathedral town. Numerous monasteries, institutions and seminaries grouped round the magnificent cathedral combine to create a hushed atmosphere.

THE CATHEDRAL* (tour: ¼ hour)

The edifice, which has known many vicissitudes, remains nevertheless one of the finest examples of 13 and 14C Norman Gothic.

Exterior.—The main façade is pierced by a huge porch. When this west face was seen to be inclining dangerously due to subsidence in the 16C, massive buttresses were set against the porch, disfiguring it considerably.

Interior.—Above the great arches of the nave which are separated by cornerstones adorned with fretted roses, is a triforium and above that a delicate frieze. The triforium is pierced over the **chancel**** and the **transept****. All this part of the church, an interesting example of Norman Gothic, forms an immense clerestory, lit, in the transept, by 13C **stained glass*** and rose windows. The double Louis XVI high altar has a gilt bronze low relief, facing the nave, illustrating the Entombment and, on the chancel side, a marble low relief of the Discovery of the Bodies of St. Gervase and St. Protase.

In the south transept the marble figure of Christ is 18C and the Virgin, Our Lady of Sées, facing the altar, 14C.

ADDITIONAL SIGHTS

Church of Our Lady on the Square (Notre-Dame-de-la-Place).—The organ loft is Renaissance and the twelve **low reliefs***, in groups of three illustrating scenes from the New Testament, 16C.

Former Abbey of St. Martin.—Now a children's home. *Tours on application in advance to the director.*

Through the great main door with its Classical entablature you can see the gracious 18C abbot's lodging.

Old Bishop's Palace.—This majestic group of buildings was constructed for Mgr. Argentré in 1778. The court opens through a beautiful wrought iron gate complete with escutcheon and foliated scrolls.

Great Seminary. — The major buildings which stand at the eastern exit to Sées consist of a cloister and a good "modern" chapel completed in 1938 and decorated with several stained glass windows and fine panelling.

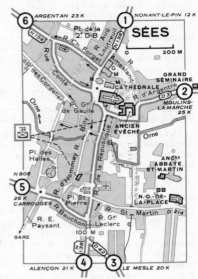

SÉES

The River Seine, which rises in Burgundy, flows successively through Champagne, the Ile de France and finally Normandy on its 485 miles course—776 km—to the sea. The valley's history, natural beauty, the castles and other monuments built upon its banks and its ever increasing economic importance make it Normandy's greatest inland tourist feature.

GEOGRAPHICAL NOTES

The winding river.—The name Seine is said to derive from the Latin *sequana* from the Celtic *squan*, meaning to curve or bend—the river perhaps being likened to a coiled snake.

The Seine has almost no fall being only 52 ft.—16 m—above sea-level at Vernon although still more than 50 miles—100 km—as the crow flies, from the Channel. It is almost certain that originally it flowed over the countryside, following the lie of the land and progressing capriciously, possibly by wide curves. The volume gradually hollowed out the valley we know today with its enclosed bends which, in their turn, have greatly influenced Norman topography.

Concave banks and convex promontories.—The concave river banks have an almost uniform appearance. At point (a) the river flows with all its force into a bank topped by steep slopes

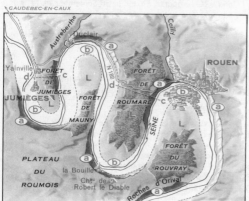

or even by cliffs extraordinarily similar to those along the coast. These relative heights with sheer drops to the river make good defensive positions and several were crowned with such fortresses as Gaillard and Robert the Devil's Castles. These concave areas were also, by the river's flow, the deepest parts and where a tributary entered the mainstream, good sites for river ports. Andelys, Duclair, Caudebec and Lillebonne, once a great port, and finally Rouen which is particularly well placed (see p. 127) were all established and developed apace.

In contrast, at (b) the current flows more slowly along the convex stretch of bank, depositing part of the debris collected upstream. The land behind the bank slopes only gently upward. The convex promontories (L) are often stony and have, therefore, been left over the centuries as forest areas.

The spread of the valley.—If one takes the line c d one notices that at c the river is flowing swiftly, driving against the promontory and undercutting the bank ever more steeply whereas at d the current is slack and much of the alluvium caught upstream can be deposited, making the riverbed ever more shallow.

Over the centuries the stream's cutting away of the banks and depositing of silt have thus moved the river's course downstream a considerable way at the bends and produced an alluvial arc that even now continues to expand (*the white area on the map above*).

Finally, near the estuary (see *map p. 144*), the promontories have been reduced to triangular headlands as at Quillebeuf and La Roque and further on to hillocks such as Cape Le Hode and Tancarville Point.

In the Vernier Marshland one can see the semicircle of hills which once formed the outer bank of a bend in the river.

At Duclair there is an unusual example of "river capture". The tributary Ste-Austreberthe originally entered the Seine at Yainville, but owing to the westward movement of the Duclair bend suddenly found itself flowing into the mainstream at Duclair, leaving a dead valley between Duclair and Yainville. This disused course is now used by the N 182.

The Bore.—When the great tides are running, the seas entering the estuary are trapped between the river banks and, as they rush forward, meet the normal river flow. The sea current prevails, reversing the stream and causing a bore or, as it is called in Normandy, *le mascaret*. The phenomenon, which used to be seen at its most impressive at Caudebec during the equinoxial tides, and which caused the death by drowning, when they were suddenly caught in the rushing waters, of Victor Hugo's daughter and her husband at Villequier in 1843 (see *p. 154*), is now seldom seen and then much diminished, having been "tamed" by engineering work on the river banks.

HISTORICAL NOTES

Highway to the sea, highway to Paris—such has been the dual role of the Valley of the Seine, together with that of cradle of the Duchy of Normandy, throughout its history.

The Tin Road.—In the Bronze Age—c. 2500 B.C.—rivers provided the only possible thoroughfares through densely wooded country. Boats sailed upstream to river sources; where the bed was too shallow, boats and goods were carried overland to the next deep water. Gradually all those sending ships across the Channel to Cornwall for tin to alloy with copper and make bronze, congregated on the banks of the Seine.

With the Roman occupation, the paths of Gaul became the glorious roads of Caesar—the road beside the Seine from Troyes was extended to the great base at Juliobona (Lillebonne) and on to Caracotinum (Harfleur).

The Castles of God.—Christianity penetrated in the 3C to the Second Lyonnaise, a province with Rouen as its capital. From the 6C, monasteries developed into centres of learning and intellectual life as well as religion, and also of economic development. Merovingians and Carolingians supported the monastic surge with concessions of land, bringing about the foundation of abbeys such as Fontenelle (now St-Wandrille) and Jumièges. Monastery discipline was inspired equally by the rule of St. Benedict and that of St. Columban.

Churches were built in honour of the saints and to contain their relics; every abbey established a school where children learnt "reading the psalter, counting, singing and how to write".

The Vikings.—From the 9 to the 11C the Northmen, intrepid navigators and warriors from Scandinavia, voyaged to wherever there were riches, pillaging and ravaging (see p. 23).

These pirates or **Vikings** were a race apart. Setting sail in their *drakkars* they harassed western Europe, landed on the coast of Africa and even entered the Mediterranean. For a hundred years they dominated the Atlantic, colonising Iceland and Greenland and landing in America four centuries before Columbus.

The Valley of the Seine with its prosperous towns, rich churches, abbeys and monasteries, offered an open invitation to the plunderers: at the beginning of the 9C the *drakkars* advanced up river under sail and oar. Each ship was 79 ft. long by 16 ft. broad with a draught of 7 ft.— 24×5×2 m; they lacked superstructures but had graceful lines, boldly carved prows and each carried some sixty warriors. On land these Normans, as they came to be called, proved to be good horsemen and redoubtable fighters, masters at guerrilla warfare, ambush and surprise attack. They massacred, pillaged and burnt. Caught in a tight corner, they negotiated a truce, had themselves baptised—some would boast of as many as twenty baptisms!—and promptly joined another band of marauders.

Terror reigned: the monks fled with their precious relics; the peasants abandoned their houses amidst the fields to group together in villages around local seignorial castles where the chapel became the parish church.

No king could stop these devastating raids which recurred with sinister regularity, threatening the countryside as far as Paris and Chartres. Eventually, however, the Normans lost their passion for plunder as the booty became more rare. King Charles the Simple, who was in fact far from simple, decided to neutralise the pirates he could not overcome by getting them to settle down. In 911, the king met the Viking, Rollo, at St-Clair-sur-Epte (see p. 88) and conceded to the "Normans on the Seine" the lands they were occupying: the Duchy of Normandy had been born; Rollo was the first Duke.

Normandy's Great Century.—The country, within a century, became a well ordered state—the first to emerge in the Middle Ages—so adept did the former pirates prove as administrators. A wonderful civilisation began to flourish.

Rollo and his descendants made it a point of honour to repair the damage caused by the Vikings and outrivalled each other in their generosity towards the Church. It was through this contact with the Church that the Scandinavians first mixed with and began to be absorbed by the native Gallo-Franks.

The 11C was the century of epic deeds of war: of the adventures of the sons of Tancrede of Hauteville in southern Italy and Sicily (see p. 75) and of the undertaking of William the Bastard Conqueror who gathered his knights at Lillebonne to set out on the "great Norman adventure", the conquest of England (see p. 73).

In the spiritual compass, it was the time of Benedictine flowering, quickened by the Cluniac reform introduced at Fécamp by Guglielmo da Volpiano (see p. 95) and encouraged by the dukes.

St. George's Abbey was constructed at Boscherville and Jumièges was gloriously rebuilt.

Finally the Norman style was to develop and dominate religious architecture for more than a century and influence architecture abroad from Sicily to England.

THE MARITIME SEINE

A difficult street to cross.—Napoleon declared "Le Havre, Rouen and Paris are but a single town of which the Seine is the main street". The phrase depicts exactly the Seine Valley, the vital artery which links Paris to the sea but also the barrier which, throughout history, has separated the Caux from the Roumois. Today, however, the great suspension bridge at Tancarville (see p. 149) joins the north to the south and Caux has ceased to be an isolated "peninsula".

The Embankment of the Seine.—Work has been going on for over a hundred years to enable large merchant ships to steam up river. For a thousand years, from the time of Duke Rollo, nothing was done to the navigation channel. In 1848 embanking was begun and has continued ever since. At that time sailing boats took 4 days to reach Rouen—but many did not get that far: from 1830 to 1852, 105 vessels sank in the stretch alone between Quillebeuf and Villequier. With the advent of large steamships the situation became urgent.

The undertakings of the last century have included the extension of the alluvial plain between Rouen and the sea by 59 sq. miles—15,000 ha; the construction in 1887 of the 15½ mile long Tancarville Canal—25 km—to enable river barges to reach Le Havre without entering the estuary; and the construction, in 1948, of a dyke along a new course from the mouth of the Risle to the Butin lighthouse and between Honfleur—now linked to the estuary by a channel—and Vasouy to control the silting up of the estuary. An interesting overall view of the undertaking and its attendant dredging and filling-in operations can be gained from the Plateau de Grâce (see p. 108).

The Economy of the Lower Seine.—The Seine Valley has been developing apace industrially since 1900 with the two ports of Rouen and Le Havre, which handle 30% of France's merchant trade, playing a capital role in the general scheme.

The textile industry, the oldest in the region, retains pride of place. Elbeuf alone remains faithful to the wool trade; cotton has gone to the area around Rouen, the Andelle, Cailly and Austreberthe Valleys and Bolbec Valley. The Norman mills with 387,500 spindles and 4,450 looms represent more than 10% of the national cotton industry. The cotton market remains, as always, at Le Havre.

Metallurgy includes four great shipyards—two at Le Havre and one each at Quevilly and Le Trait—the Renault works at Sandouville and Cléon, electrical and electronic factories, besides the foundries and wireworks and metal construction shops established around Le Havre and Rouen.

The SEINE Valley*** (continued)

The chemical industry, born of a need for finishing and dyeing products for textiles, has diversified and now includes chemical fertilisers; around Rouen there are large papermills producing paper for domestic consumption and 55% of France's newsprint, factories making acid and pharmaceutical products, bleach, etc; the first synthetic rubber factory outside the U.S.A. was built at Port-Jérôme; two plastics factories and a sulphur recovery works have also been built.

To satisfy the ever increasing demand for electric power, stations are under construction at Dieppedalle and Yainville and the vast station at Le Havre is being enlarged (see p. 103).

The most spectacular activities now, however, derive from the oil refining industry and its by-products in petro-chemistry including large hydrocarbon factories.

The river of petrol.—The capacity of the Seine-Maritime's four great refineries at Gonfreville, Port-Jérôme, Notre-Dame-de-Gravenchon and Petit-Couronne now amounts to 33 million tons a year or nearly 32% of the total French refining capacity.

Production includes car petrol, high octane fuels and the gamut of products from liquid gas to bitumens and primary products for the petro-chemical industry which, in turn, produces detergents and solvents, manmade fibres and synthetic rubber and plastics. The refineries and factories can be seen from afar, their aluminium painted storage tanks and superstructures clearly visible by daylight and floodlit at night.

The Le Havre–Paris pipeline.—The transport to Paris of petroleum products refined or stored in Le Havre or further refined or manufactured in the Seine-Maritime works, was undertaken by ship or rail until 1953. The increase in demand then necessitated the construction of a pipeline—and for the first time in Europe liquid carburants were transported by permanent pipeline.

The first line consisted of a steel pipe conduit 10 inches—25 cm—in diameter and 149 miles—240 km—long. A second, 12 inches—30 cm—in diameter was laid parallel to the first in 1961, and finally a third was constructed in 1964 with a diameter of 20 inches—50 cm. The capacity of the three combined amounts to 1,600,000 tons a month.

The pipeline's contents flow at between 3¾ and 5 m.p.h.—6 to 8 km.p.h.; 45 different types of petroleum and other light products are carried without interruption and without undue contamination and any consignment can be located within the pipeline at any time within seconds. Individual deliveries are made direct from any refinery to any depot in the Paris area.

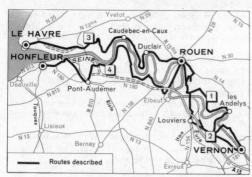

TOURS

1. ****From Vernon to Rouen** along the right bank. — *Description below.*

2. ***From Rouen to Vernon** by the direct tourist road.— *Description p. 143.*

3. *****From Rouen to Le Havre** along the right bank. —*Description p. 144.*

4. ****From Honfleur to Rouen** by the Lower Risle Valley and the left bank.— *Description p. 145.*

1 ****FROM VERNON TO ROUEN along the right bank**
52 miles—83 km—about 3 hours—plus 1 hour walking and sightseeing

The road in the main runs parallel to the right bank of the Seine, sometimes at a distance through the farmlands of the alluvial plain, sometimes close at hand between the bank's edge and the bare escarpment to be found at each hollow bend.

Vernon*.—*Description p. 153.*

Between Pressagny-l'Orgueilleux and Port-Mort, the N 313 crosses a plain ringed by a semicircle of hills. As you approach the junction with the D 10 look out on the right for a dolmen, known as Gargantua's Pebble, standing in a field.

Gaillon.—*Description p. 155.*

There is a view of a bend in the river from the D 65 between Aubevoye and Villers-sur-le-Roule and an even pleasanter **view*** from the curve on the D 176 between Villers-sur-le-Roule and Tosny. The road enters Les Andelys over the suspension birdge, bringing you face to face with the ruins of Gaillard Castle perched high on the cliff-top.

Les Andelys**.—¾ hour on foot Rtn. Description p. 42.

From Les Andelys to Muids, the N 313 runs at the foot of strangely jagged chalk escarpments bordering the river. The La Roque Rock has an almost human profile. From the D 65 one can see how the escarpment has changed banks, or rather the river altered course, so that the cliff now dominates the concave left bank. There are fine private properties between the Herqueville crossroads and Amfreville-sous-les-Monts.

Deux Amants Hill**.—Excursion of 3 miles—4·5 km—from Amfreville-sous-les-Monts—plus ¼ hour on foot Rtn. Leave by the D 20 which climbs rapidly to the top of the hill where there is a magnificent **view**** for miles over the Valley of the Seine. (Car park 50 yds. beyond the TCF viewing table.)

Continuing on to Le Plessis, take a narrow road on the left at a Calvary and after 300 yds. bear left again to a signpost: Panorama des Deux Amants, then left for a further mile —2 km. Park the car; follow the path to the edge of the plateau to see a **panorama**** which includes the Amfreville Locks and another bend in the Seine.

The legend of the two lovers, Caliste and Raoul, was first told by Marie de France in the 12C, the first woman writer in France. The King of the Pitrois would only let his daughter Caliste marry a suitor strong enough to carry her at a run to the top of the hill; Raoul succeeded but dropped dead from exhaustion at the top and Caliste immediately died too. The lovers were buried where they fell and the hill was named after them.

The SEINE Valley*** (continued)

Amfreville Lock*.—*Tour: ¼ hour. Description p. 42.*

    Le Manoir.—*Excursion of 1 mile—1·5 km—from the N 321.* The new church preceded by a detached belfry is a plain, modern building. A vast composition in glass by Barillet makes up the pierced façade also giving a warm light to the interior.

The N 13 *bis* cuts away from the river at Igoville and across the base of the Elbeuf promontory by two valleys which almost meet, to come out at Port-St-Ouen.

    Les Authieux.—*Excursion of ½ mile—1 km—by the D 13 from the N 13 bis.* The church has a fine series of Renaissance stained glass windows.

Industrial plants on the outskirts of Rouen appear on the left bank facing Port-St-Ouen.

The D 7 beyond St-Adrien climbs rapidly to the plateau at Belbeuf.

    St. Adrien Rocks*.—*1 hour on foot Rtn or 1 mile—1·5 km—by car along a poor road.* The road to the rocks branches sharply off to the right from the D 7 shortly before Belbeuf (signpost: Rue de Verdun). Bear left, then right, cross a forest crossroads and take the first path on the right. Leave the car on the edge of the wood. A path leads to the bare rock spur from which there is a most attractive view of the river.

Belbeuf.—The small church guarded by its old yew tree is pleasantly situated. The castle is 18C. A stupendous **panorama**** opens out as the N 14, below the Bonsecours church, descends, *corniche* fashion, to the river, scattered at this point with overgrown islands. Rouen lies ahead in its unique setting, the cathedral spire tall and slender against the sky.

    Bonsecours**.—*Excursion of ½ mile—1 km—from Mesnil-Esnard. Description p. 133.*

    Rouen***.—*Description p. 127.*

② *FROM ROUEN TO VERNON by the direct tourist road
39 miles—63 km—about 2 hours—plus ½ hour sightseeing

This more rapid road passes through several small towns with interesting buildings.

Rouen***.—*Description p. 127.*

Rouen's industrial area now extends to Amfreville-la-Mi-Voie and on the left bank even further. The road cuts away from the river at Port-St-Ouen to cross the base of the Elbeuf promontory by two valleys which almost meet and come out at Igoville.

    Les Authieux.—*Excursion of ½ mile—1 km—by the D 13 from the N 13 bis.* The church has a fine series of Renaissance stained glass windows.

Pont-de-l'Arche.—This small town gets its name from its bridge which was the first, preceding even those at Rouen, to span the Lower Seine.

The **church, Our Lady of the Arts,** has a highly ornate Flamboyant south face and door. Inside, among the 16 and 17C stained glass windows (restored) is one (2nd window, south aisle) showing the town boat-hauliers pulling a boat through an arch in the bridge; also a Louis XIII altarpiece at the high altar setting off a Resurrection, an organ and a 16C font.

Two popular 16C paintings illustrate the *Birth of the Virgin* and the *Adoration of the Magi.*

Shortly beyond the town the N 13 *bis* enters the Bord Forest where the pines, which surround Pont-de-l'Arche and give it a somewhat southern appearance, are replaced by beeches. The road leaves the woods for the Eure Valley at Louviers.

    Louviers*.—*Tour: ½ hour. Description p. 112.*

The N 182A climbs up out of Louviers affording a good view of the Eure Valley as it levels off.

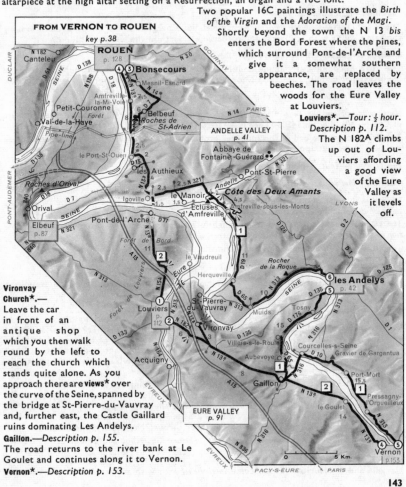

Vironvay Church*.—Leave the car in front of an antique shop which you then walk round by the left to reach the church which stands quite alone. As you approach there are **views*** over the curve of the Seine, spanned by the bridge at St-Pierre-du-Vauvray and, further east, the Castle Gaillard ruins dominating Les Andelys.

Gaillon.—*Description p. 155.*

The road returns to the river bank at Le Goulet and continues along it to Vernon.

Vernon*.—*Description p. 153.*

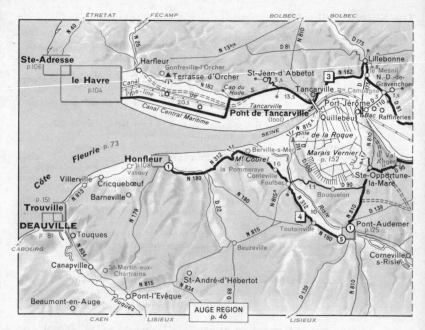

③ ***FROM ROUEN TO LE HAVRE along the right bank

68 miles—109 km—about 3½ hours—plus 1½ hours sightseeing

This road is the sightseeing one—it is the **abbey road**. Another of its attractions is the variety of views one gets from it of the meanderings of the Lower Seine. After Caudebec the countryside, up till then covered with trees, alters to the reclaimed alluvial plain.

Rouen***.—*Description p. 127.*

A **view*** of Rouen looking back eastwards can be glimpsed as far as Canteleu through a small valley.

Canteleu*.—*Description p. 133.*

The N 182 crosses Roumare Forest from which you emerge to a view once more overlooking the Seine Valley with St-Martin-de-Boscherville Church in the foreground.

St-Martin-de-Boscherville*.—*Tour: ¼ hour. Description p. 136.*

The road between La Fontaine and Mesnil-sous-Jumièges follows the outer side of the bend (*see map p. 140*), constructed, for several miles, to skirt the river bank and the cliff.

Duclair.—*Description p. 85.*

Mesnil-sous-Jumièges.—It was in the 13C manorhouse at Mesnil that Agnès Sorel, the favourite of Charles VII, died in 1450. There is an attractive covered well in the courtyard.

The drive across the end of the Jumièges promontory is through typically Norman scenery and is at its best at apple blossom time.

Jumièges***.—*Tour: ½ hour. Description p. 109.*

Yainville.—The square church tower and nave are 11C.

Le Trait.—Ships of all classes, including the first French methane gas tanker, the *Jules Verne*, have been launched from the La Ciotat shipyards at Le Trait.

The 16C parish church includes some delightful alabasters (*Adoration of the Magi* and *Coronation of the Virgin*) on the pedestals beneath the statues surrounding the altar.

Turn off from Caudebecquet for St. Wandrille.

St. Wandrille**.—*Tour: ½ hour. Description p. 137.*

Monument "To the Latham 47 Company".—The monument is a memorial to the fatal expedition made by Amundsen, with Guilbaud and others, to the Arctic in 1928.

Caudebec-en-Caux*.—*Tour: ¼ hour. Description p. 65.*

> **The Brotonne Forest.**—*Excursion of 19 miles—30 km—from Caudebec.* Take the D 40 on the far side of the river. The road passes picturesque half-timbered houses and colourful gardens on its way to St-Nicolas de Bliquetuit after which it enters the forest. At Rond Victor take the D 131 and continue towards the Rond-de-Nagu, a vast six-point-star-shaped clearing half a mile off the main D 131.
>
> Go from Rond-de-Nagu by the straight forest road going north to Le Quesnay. Then bear left into the D 65 which runs southwards beside the Seine. Shortly before La Vaquerie, turn left into the D 116 which rises, affording a view over the valley, and crosses the D 131. One and a half miles—2·5 km—beyond the crossroads turn left into the D 40 which brings you back to Caudebec through the heart of the forest.

There are some delightful views of the river between Caudebec and Villequier.

Villequier*.—*Description p. 154.*

Norville and St-Maurice-d'Etelan come into view, each with an attractive stone belfry.

144

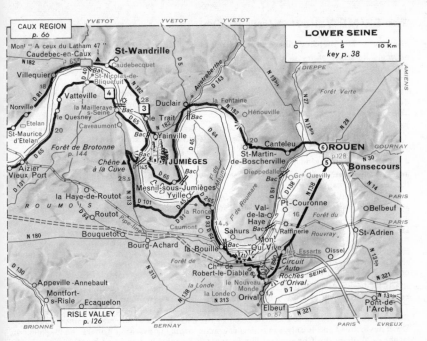

Tall pylons—the one on the left bank is 371 ft. high—113 m—carrying the high-tension cable across the river appear, followed by the refineries of Notre-Dame-de-Gravenchon and Port-Jérôme.

Notre-Dame-de-Gravenchon.—*Excursion of 1 mile—1·5 km—from the D 81. Interesting modern church with a lead and copper composition on the façade of St. George slaying the dragon.*

Alternative road by Port-Jérôme.—*See p. 142, the River of Petrol.*
Return to the D 81 at Le Mesnil.

Lillebonne.—*Description p. 110.*
The whitish cliffs around Tancarville emerge in the distance; the road bridge suddenly comes clearly into view; the alluvial plain extends even further.

Tancarville★.—*Tour: ½ hour. Description p. 149.*
Below Tancarville, the N 182, which passes at the foot of the northern pylon of the suspension bridge, continues to hug the cliff until it reaches Le Hode. There are views of the southern shore of the estuary and then of the industrial zone lying south of the Tancarville Canal.

St-Jean-d'Abbetot.—*Excursion of 2 miles—3·5 km—from the N 182. To see the church apply at the first house on the left in the road which runs parallel to the church front. The church, which dates from the first half of the 11C, contains 12, 13 and 16C frescoes★, the most remarkable being in the crypt.*

Cross the bridge at Le Hode to enter Le Havre through its somewhat spectacular industrial zone where you will see between the Tancarville Canal and the Central Maritime Canal refineries, the Lambert-Lafarge cement works (left), the Renault-Sandouville car assembly plant (painted blue, on the right) and the petroleum plant of the Compagnie Française de Raffinage.

Le Havre★★.—*Description p. 102.*

4 **★★FROM HONFLEUR TO ROUEN by the Lower Risle Valley and the left bank**
70 miles—113 km—about 3½ hours—plus ½ hour sightseeing

There are fewer buildings to look at on this bank, but the road goes through several woodland areas and there are many bird's-eye views of the river which are most attractive.
The route proposed has to be taken slowly.

Honfleur★★.—*Description p. 107.*
The best **view★** of the estuary between Honfleur and Berville occurs after you have passed La Pommeraye Castle on your right, as you round Mount Courel.
The road goes on to follow the course of the Lower Risle Valley. The landscape is particularly attractive in the spring when the apple orchards are in blossom, especially around Toutainville.

Alternative road by Bouquelon.—*Reduction of drive: 4 miles—7 km. Views over the Vernier Marsh.*
Between Foulbec and Ste-Opportune-la-Mare follow the itinerary described in the opposite direction on p. 153.

Pont-Audemer★.—*Tour: ½ hour. Description p. 125.*
The road climbs to the Le Roumois Plateau.

Ste-Opportune-la-Mare.—*Description p. 153.*
From the fine *corniche* section between Le Val-Anger and Vieux Port you can see right along the valley from Quillebeuf to Caudebec.

The SEINE Valley*** (concluded)

Vieux-Port.—The thatched village cottages stand half-hidden by their orchards.

Aizier.—The stone belfry of the 12C Romanesque church looks very old.

The D 65 crosses the Brotonne Forest (see p. 144), all the while remaining near the banks of the Seine, to get from Aizier to Le Quesney.

Vateville-la-Rue.—An emblazoned mourning band can be seen where it was painted on the death of a local lord in black on the walls of the church nave which dates from the Renaissance. The chancel is Flamboyant, the windows 16C.

After La Mailleraye, the D 65 returns to the river bank, following it closely between the Yainville and Jumièges ferries. Continue along the road, now the D 143.

The La Cuve Oak.—100 yds. from the N 313, opposite the 11 km post. Four oak trunks growing from a single bole form a kind of natural cup, 23 ft.—7 m—in circumference.

Jumièges Viewpoint*.—The abbey can be seen towering up on the far bank over to the right. It is particularly spectacular at sunset.

By the time you reach the downhill D 45 you will get a new series of views of the river and also be able to see Jumièges Forest and, immediately below, the beautiful 18C Château of Yville. The road again follows the river course from La Ronce to La Bouille.

La Bouille.—La Bouille has a most attractive setting at the foot of the wooded slopes of the Roumois Plateau on the first concave bend of the Seine below Rouen. The village was a favourite of Monet and has remained so with the citizens of Rouen. Between La Bouille and the Qui Vive Monument the D 64 climbs the hillside so that one gets a view of the river bend commanded by Robert the Devil's Castle and of the Rouen industrial suburbs.

Robert-the-Devil's Castle*. (Château Robert le Diable).—The feudal ruins have recently been reconstituted inside as a waxworks. There are also a tea room and amusements.

The castle, which commands a splendid view of the river, which by tradition was built by Robert the Devil was, in fact, constructed by the early Dukes of Normandy, since Robert the Devil never lived and is only a mythical character probably based on Robert the Magnificent, father of William the Conqueror. The fortress was probably destroyed by the French in the 15C to prevent its falling into the hands of the English.

The subsequent drive through the La Londe Forest and along a corniche road above a deep wooded valley is briefly reminiscent of mountain country.

Qui Vive Monument.—At the D 64 and D 67A crossroads. There is a remarkable view* from the monument (viewing table) of the Seine as it curves round to encircle the Roumare Forest.

Moulineaux.—The delightful church with its slender spire dates from the 13C. Inside there is an attractive woodwork group formed by the pulpit and rood screen, of which one side is Gothic decorated, the other Renaissance.

Orival Rocks* (Rochers d'Orival).—Excursion of 1 mile—1·5 km—from Le Nouveau Monde by the N 138 and the D 18 on the left—plus 1 hour on foot Rtn. Park the car at the signpost: Sentier des Roches and walk up the steep and difficult path on the left (slippery if wet). The path passes in front of some caves hollowed out of the rock, improves, runs at the foot of a cliff on the right and about 300 yds from a grass-covered crest, affords an open view** of the Seine and the rock escarpment along which the path continues as a grass corniche.

The church at Orival is a curious mid 15C half troglodyte structure.

The Rouvray Forest on the outskirts of Rouen with its groves of pine trees and extensive bare acres resembles a heath rather than a forest in places.

Rouen-les-Essarts Car Circuit.—4 miles 100 yds. long—6·542 km. The permanent track climbs and falls as it runs through the forest. Free access except when trials are being held.

Rouen***.—Description p. 127.

The SÉLUNE Dams—Michelin map ⑤⑨ ⑧.

The enclosure of the Sélune by the great granite cliffs of the Armorican Massif enabled dams to be built to control the river flow. These barrages have created two picturesque sheets of water much enjoyed by anglers and water sports enthusiasts.

FROM DUCEY TO ST-HILAIRE-DU-HARCOUËT

15 miles—24 km—about 1 hour

No road runs along the shores of the Vézins and Roche qui Boit reservoirs—one gets good views of these artificial lakes, however, from the route suggested below.

The Vézins shores are crowded on Sundays during the season. Take care when driving along the narrow private (but open) road linking the D 582 and the Auberge du Lac.

Ducey.—The old bridge over the Sélune stands upstream from the more modern one used by the national highway. Take the D 78 which goes down the Sélune Valley.

The Roche qui Boit Dam.—700 yds. from the D 78. Not open.
This small dam, built between 1915 and 1919, is the French prototype of the multi-arch straight dam.

Take the D 582 on the left at a road fork, which will bring you back in view of the valley. After the river bridge, a narrow road leads off on the right uphill to the crest of the Vézins Dam.

Vézins Dam.—This curved multi-arched dam which is 115 ft. high—35 m—and 273 yds. long and was completed in 1931, controls an artificial lake which runs back for a distance of 10 miles— 16 km. The surroundings* are extremely pleasant.

A road on the right goes from the Auberge du Lac to the D 85 which crosses the reservoir over the bridges at Les Biards. At St-Martin-de-Landelles, take the D 30 on the left to St-Hilaire-du-Harcouët.

St-Hilaire-du-Harcouët.—The town has been rebuilt since 1944 and is interesting on that account. Wednesday is market day and very lively.

The small town of Sillé-le-Guillaume, built in a semicircle on the southern slope of the Coëvrons, had a rich and eventful past since it was one of the strongpoints, like Ste-Suzanne and Mayenne which protected northern Maine from Norman invasion.

Castle.—At the end of the Hundred Years War, the English sacked the fortress which had been built in the 11C at Sillé. In the 15C Antoine de Beauvau constructed on the ancient ruins the castle which today houses a college. Although considerably restored, the keep built into the living rock and the round towers linked by 16 and 17C buildings, give the old castle a proud air.

Church of Our Lady.—The church stands upon the site of a former Romanesque church of which the crypt and the south transept gable remain. A beautiful 13C door restored in the 15C has withstood the many other rebuildings that have occurred since.

ENVIRONS

Sillé Forest.—*Tour of 17 miles—28 km—about 1 hour.* Leave Sillé-le-Guillaume by the N 805 which rises before entering the forest.

Sillé Forest covers the eastern crest of the Coëvrons chain of hills, extending like a skein for 10 miles—nearly 17 km. There are few outstanding trees as the forest was badly exploited at the turn of the century but the reafforestation promises well.

Take the first forest road on the left and after 900 yds. bear left again into a road which comes out at the Defais Pool which it skirts along the north shore.

Defais Pool.—This stretch of water, also known as Lake Sillé, with its attractive green surroundings, is a favourite with the local townspeople. A beach has been arranged at one point.

Make for the D 16 and turn right. As you reach the edge of the forest there is a good view north of wooded farmland.

Turn left at La Boissière to reach St-Pierre-sur-Orthe and the N 823 which you follow left. It is a picturesque road which goes over the wooded Coëvrons crest and from which as you descend towards Sillé you will get an attractive view of the La Mare Cross, the highest point at 952 ft.—290 m—of the west area of the forest.

This extraordinary name denotes an area in Normandy which has neither mountains nor lakes in the Swiss sense, and does not even include Normandy's highest rises (*see map p. 11*), but is nevertheless an attractive tourist area particularly enjoyed by walkers, canoeists and anglers.

The River Orne as it cuts its way through the ancient rocks of the Armorican Massif produces a kind of hollow relief of which the most typical elements are a pleasantly winding river course bordered by steep banks surmounted by rock cliffs. An occasional isolated "peak" rises up from which one can view the rolling, wooded countryside.

1 ****FROM THURY-HARCOURT TO PONT-D'OUILLY**
by the Orne Valley

17 miles—27 km—about 1 hour

Roads around Clécy must be taken slowly.

Thury-Harcourt.—*Description p. 150.*

The N 162, on leaving Thury-Harcourt, drops down into the valley. On the way you will see the small Bonne Nouvelle Chapel perched on a hillock, followed by an abandoned limestone quarry, on the left and immediately afterwards, Caumont, then St-Rémy and its mining installations covered in red powder.

St-Rémy.—The St-Rémy iron mines, where the richest ore in Normandy was mined, were worked from 1875 to 1967.

From the burial ground surrounding the small restored church flanked by its old yew tree on top of the hill some 750 yds. from the N 162, there is a good view of the Orne Valley.

The D 133 crosses the Orne over the Le Vey bridge as it drops sharply down to Clécy.

Clécy*.—Clécy, the tourist centre of the Suisse Normande, is within reach of the most picturesque parts of the Orne Valley and is an excellent starting point for walkers. It lies at the centre of a majestic river curve in a countryside of woods and rock escarpments.

The 16C **Placy Manor** is now a small folklore museum (*open: 15 June to 1 October, 9 a.m. to noon, 2 to 7 p.m.; 2 October to 14 June, Sundays only: 2 F.*).

> **The Pain de Sucre*** or **Sugar Loaf.**—*Excursion from Clécy of 1 mile—1·5 km—plus ½ hour on foot Rtn.* from the old Clécy-Bourg station. Bear right after 100 yds. into the La Serverie path and continue to the plaque indicating the start of the Pain de Sucre path. From the top there is a **panorama*** with the wide curve of the Orne as the focal point. Return to Clécy.

> **The Eminence.**—*Excursion from Clécy of 1¼ miles—2 km—plus ½ hour on foot Rtn.* Leave Clécy by the D 133, the St-Pierre-la-Vieille road; after Grand Camp, bear left in front of a garage, into the Hauts-Vents road. The path up the northern flank of the Eminence begins in the village. Before reaching the top—860 ft.—262 m—which is anyway covered in thorny scrub, you get a panorama of the Normandy Bocage and the Orne Valley.

> **Le Vey Bridge.**—*Excursion from Clécy of ½ mile—1 km—east along the D133A.* The bridge spans the Orne at a delightful spot.

Leave Clécy by the Croix Faverie road which begins between the church and the post office. Bear left at the fork and continue on foot left to the **Faverie Cross*** from which there is a typical Suisse Normande **view*** including the Parcs Rocks on the far side of the river spanned by the Lande Viaduct.

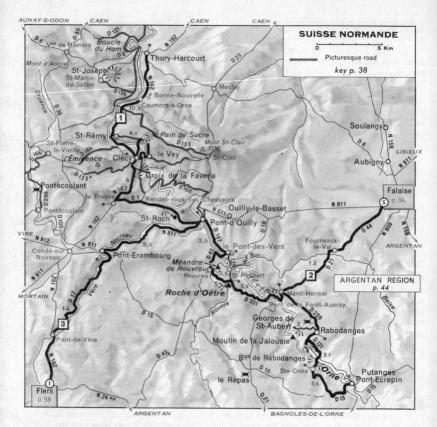

Return to the car and the N 162. Towards the top of a climb after a right bend there is a bird's-eye view of the valley and Clécy and, on the horizon, the Eminence and slightly to its right, Mount Ancre, at 1086 ft.—331 m—one of the tallest summits of the Bocage. Leave the N 162 at Le Fresne for the D I which follows the crestline of the ridge separating the Orne and Noireau Valleys. It is later joined by the Béron crest. 550 yds. after the Rendez-Vous-des-Chasseurs you will get a brief view to the north of the Orne Valley and, above, of the Parcs Rocks.

As you drop down, before you reach the St. Rock Chapel, ahead and to the right, in the distance, you can see the cliff like promontory of the Oëtre Rock.

St. Rock Chapel.—This 16C pilgrimage chapel with modern frescoes, is the goal of a "pardon" held on the Sunday after 15 August in full local Norman costume.

Pont-d'Ouilly.—The village at the meeting of the Orne and Noireau Rivers is also the major junction of the tourist crossroads of the Suisse Normande.

② **FROM PONT-D'OUILLY TO FALAISE by the Oëtre Rock

17 miles—27 km—about I hour—plus ½ hour sightseeing and walking

Pont-d'Ouilly.—*Description above.*

The D 167, as it leaves Pont-d'Ouilly, passes at the foot of the rock which in its upper part resembles a lion's head. The road runs beside the Orne to Pont-des-Vers where you branch off into the D 43 which climbs, enabling you to get a look at the Rouvre with its almost geometrically enclosed curves—the most outstanding being the Rouvrou Bend.

Rouvrou Bend.—*Excursion of ¼ hour on foot Rtn.* To see this stretch of the river at its best, leave the car by the war memorial which stands at the end of the bend where it is only a few feet wide and where it is most confined by the rock crest above it. The surroundings are pleasantly shaded by pine trees.

Oëtre Rock★★.—The rock, in its grandiose **setting★**, dominating the wild and winding Rouvre gorges with its steep escarpment, is the most mountanous feature to be found in the Suisse Normande. The belvedere is part of a café (*purchase of a drink or souvenirs obligatory*).

Go from the café to a viewing table and then along the cliff edge on the left to descend to a second natural balcony. On the return turn left at the viewing table to see, below it, a ridge of rock with an almost human profile.

From the Oëtre Rock to the Pont-des-Vers by way of St-Philbert (*described as a descent, the only way recommended*).—*Alternative road of 2 miles—3.5 km. Narrow road from St-Philbert to Le Pont-des-Vers with a short uphill section of I in 8—+12%—going through St-Philbert.* From the road you get renewed views of the Orne as it winds on its way and on the final descent you come into view of the Cul du Rouvre, a curious curved rock spine overlooking the meeting of the Rouvre and the Orne.

Beyond the Oëtre Rock, the road runs along the hillside affording views once more of the Orne Valley, where the north slope is particularly wild. At the La Forêt-Auvray bridge you get your last glimpse of the Orne Valley. The countryside begins to level out after Ménil-Hermei and beyond La Baise you get more open views of the Bocage. As at Fourneaux-le-Val you cross one of the limestone ridges to be found in the Falaise area you will get a good view south of the Bocage and north of the Falaise countryside.

Falaise★.—*Description p. 94.*

148

3 *FROM FLERS TO PONT-D'OUILLY by the Vère and Noireau Valleys

15 miles—24 km—about ¾ hour

There are several blind turns on the roads described.

Flers.—*Description p. 98.*

After Pont-de-Vère, the D 17 enters the cut made by the Vère, which grows ever narrower and more austere as the river, sometimes more a rushing torrent, flows on beside it. You pass several factories—formerly textile mills and now manufacturing electronic equipment and asbestos sheeting and a large flint quarry.

Pont-Erambourg.—The village lies pleasantly at the meeting of the Vère and Noireau rivers which further downstream curve in a wide bend.

> **Pontécoulant Castle.**—*Excursion of 7 miles—12 km.* Leave Pont-Erambourg by the N 811 and D 105 to Pontécoulant where you take the D 298 going north out of the village to the castle. The castle now owned by the Calvados Department has been transformed into a museum (*guided commentaries 9 a.m. to noon, 2 to 6 p.m. in summer—5 p.m. in winter; closed Tuesdays and in October; 1 F*). The ground and first floors are open with displays of fine old furniture, also the library. The castle is surrounded by a landscaped park.

The Noireau River passes at the foot of tall escarpments all the way from Pont-Erambourg to Berjou station after which the slopes diminish until you come to Pont-d'Ouilly.

Pont-d'Ouilly.—*Description p. 148.*

4 *FROM PUTANGES TO THE OËTRE ROCK
by the St-Aubert Gorges

12 miles—20 km—about ¾ hour—plus 1 hour on foot Rtn

The roads suggested afford views of the Orne Valley.

Putanges-Pont-Ecrepin.—*Place to stay (see p. 37).* This little old town makes a good starting point for a tour of the St-Aubert Gorges.

You get a good view of the reservoir lake behind the Rabodanges Dam as you cross the Ste-Croix Bridge on your way to the D 121 which continues for some way along the shore.

Rabodanges Dam.—The dam is of the multi-arch type; a belvedere has been arranged on the right bank.

Rabodanges.—The 17C castle is set in a park overlooking the Orne Valley.

> **La Jalousie Mill.**—*Excursion of 1 mile—2 km—from Rabodanges by a narrow road, plus ½ hour on foot Rtn by a descending sunken path on the left and a second path again first on the left.* The mill ruins stand isolated facing the remains of an ancient Devil's Bridge.

The gorge's northern slope is particularly rugged between Ménil-Hermei and the Oëtre Rock.

Oëtre Rock**.—*Description p. 148.*

TANCARVILLE *—Michelin maps (52) ⑫, (55) ④—local map p. 144.

Tancarville Castle, built upon the last promontory of the chalk cliffs constricting the Seine before its estuary finally splays out into the Channel, commands the finest panoramic view of the right bank of the river.

The great suspension bridge springs from the same cliff to cross the river.

THE ROAD BRIDGE**

Toll bridge: for rates see the current Michelin Guide France.

Until 1959 no bridge spanned the Seine between Rouen and Le Havre—a distance of 80 miles—127 km. Boats sailed upstream to Rouen, the capital of Normandy and communication was maintained between the two banks of the river by numerous ferries.

By 1955 it was evident a bridge had to be built and the present bridge—one of the largest in Europe—was undertaken. It was opened in July 1959.

The vital statistics of the bridge, from which there is a good **view*** of the Seine Estuary are: length: 4,953 ft.—1,400 m; height above water at high tide 156 ft.—48 m; height of the pylons: 410 ft.—125 m; central span: 1,995 ft.—608 m.

At the left bank end: telescope 1 F; recorded commentary on the bridge's construction in English: 1 F.

The effect of the bridge on the local economy has been outstanding linking as it does various parts of Normandy and also the port of Le Havre with western France.

THE CASTLE *(not open to the public)*

The approach road branches off the D 39.

Terrace**.—From the terrace in front of the modern 18C castle there is a wide **view**** of the final section of the Seine Valley as it flows towards the sea with the bridge in the foreground. On the far bank are Port-Jérôme and the Vernier Marsh.

Feudal Castle.—The Eagle Tower is the only part intact of the feudal castle, some of whose buildings date back to the 10C. The tower with a base in the shape of a spur, stands to the left of the terrace. The guide will take you round other towers, halls and the dungeons.

—Michelin maps **54** ⑮, **55** ⑪—local map p. 148—pop. 1,238 —*Place to stay (see p. 37).*

Thury-Harcourt where the 15C poet, Pierre Gringoire, was born has been pleasantly rebuilt on the banks of the Orne and is now a tourist centre on the edge of the Suisse Normande.

A fine park, open to visitors, surrounds the ruins of the castle of the dukes of Harcourt which was burnt down in 1944. The church's 13C façade is original, the rest reconstructed.

ENVIRONS

The Hom River Loop*.—*Tour of 3 miles—5 km.* Leave Thury-Harcourt by the D 6 but remain close to the left bank of the Orne by taking the D 212. This skirts the loop's steep bank (*read the paragraph on river bank formation, p. 140*). Turn right at Le Hom where the road, leaving the Orne, enters a deep cutting through the rock at the end of the curve's promontory. Return to Thury-Harcourt.

St. Joseph's Chapel.—*Tour of 11 miles—17 km.* Leave Thury-Harcourt by the D 166 which goes up the Orne Valley. Turn right at Mesnil-Roger into the picturesque road to St-Martin-de-Sallen where you turn right again into a narrow uphill road from which a minor road leads off to the right to St. Joseph's.

As you approach the chapel there is a beautiful **panorama***** of the Orne Valley and the Suisse Normande heights.

Return to St-Martin-de-Sallen where you turn right into the D 6 for Thury-Harcourt.

Mount Pinçon*.—*Tour of 22 miles—36 km.* Leave Thury-Harcourt by the D 6 going west. Turn left at the Hamars Valley into the D 36 and, after a crossroads, right into the D 108. Turn sharp right at the entrance to Plessis-Grimoult into the D 54.

Mount Pinçon*.—At the top of the climb of 1,201 ft.—365 m—near a television transmitter, turn left and continue for 650 yds. On leaving the car to walk over the surrounding heathland you will get a vast **panorama***** of the Bocage.

Return to Thury-Harcourt by way of **Aunay-sur-Odon** (*description p. 155*) and the D 6.

*—Michelin map **52** ⑤—local maps pp. 150, 151—pop. 6,328—*Place to stay (see p. 36).*

Le Tréport, a small fishing port at the mouth of the Bresle, is a seaside resort which owes much of its popularity to its being so near Paris. During the summer gay crowds around the harbour turn the town into a fair. The long shingle beach, backed by tall cliffs, is crammed with visitors at weekends, but is wide enough to take them all.

Mers-les-Bains, on the right bank of the Bresle, is less commercial than Le Tréport and has many devotees, as has Ault, a beach further north.

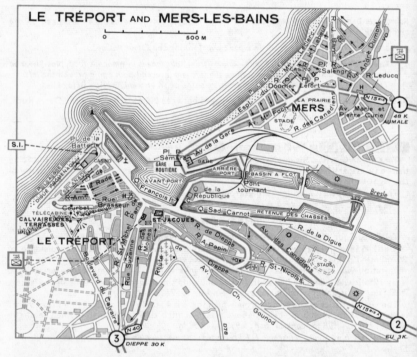

Ascent to the Terrace Calvary*.—*About ½ hour Rtn.* The Calvary on the top of the cliff is linked to the town hall by a 378 step stairway and to the beach by a tele-cabin (*ascent: 2 F*). Take the Rue St-Michel and the Boulevard du Calvaire to go up by car.

There is a **view*** from the terrace on which the Cross stands, which extends north beyond the last of the Caux cliffs to the Hourdel Point and the Somme Estuary and inland, over the lower town's slate roofs and along the Lower Bresle Valley to Eu. *Telescope.*

St. James's (Eglise St-Jacques).—The building, which dates from the second half of the 16C, although much restored, stands halfway up a hill in a good situation. The modern porch shelters a Renaissance doorway.

Inside are several interesting 16C features including remarkable hanging keystones, a *pièta* in the Chapel of Our Lady of Mercy (north aisle) and a low relief above the altar showing the Virgin encircled by Biblical emblems. At the far end of the church, in which the chancel is on a lower level than the nave, is the fine statue of Our Lady of Tréport.

TROUVILLE ** —Michelin maps 54 ⑰, 55 ③—pop. 6,577—*Place to stay (see p. 36).*

Trouville, situated where the cliff of the Normandy Corniche ends at the mouth of the River Touques, to be replaced on the far bank by a wonderful beach of fine gold sand, has all the latest amenities and so maintains its reputation as the seaside resort which, as long ago as the start of the Second Empire (1852), launched Côte Fleurie.

THE RESORT

As at Deauville (see p. 81), the *Planches*, the wooden plank promenade lining the beach for its entire length, is the main gathering place for all holidaymakers.

The quays along the Touques are also extremely popular and bustle with humanity.

Trouville has sufficient citizens not concerned with tourism —fishermen, office workers and others—to remain truly alive outside the season as well as during the height of summer.

The Corniche★.—Make for the Corniche road by way of the Boulevard Aristide-Briand. Come down it into the town to get a magnificent **view★** of the Trouville and Deauville beaches and the Côte Fleurie.

Stop at the Bon Secours Calvary (*viewing balcony*).

ENVIRONS

All the excursions, walks and air trips starting from Deauville described on p. 81 can be made equally well from Trouville.

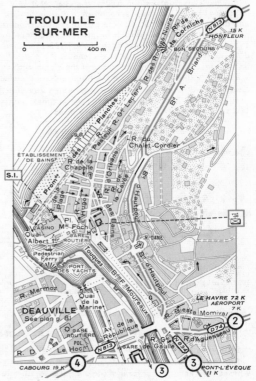

VALOGNES —Michelin map 54 ②—pop. 6,106.

Valognes is a Cotentin market town which specialises in the production and sale of butter.

A modern city has replaced the town destroyed in June 1944. A few large old houses do however remain recalling the descriptions of Barbey d'Aurevilly (see p. 21) and the 18C, when local high society made Valognes the Versailles of Normandy.

Beaumont House.—*Open 1 July to 15 September, Tuesdays, Thursdays, Sundays, 2 to 6 p.m.; 2 F.* The façade of this noble mansion overlooking a terraced garden is 164 ft. long—50 m.

VERNEUIL-SUR-AVRE ★—Michelin maps 60 ⑥, 97 ㉓—pop. 6,463.

Verneuil is the descendant town of a fortified city created in the 12C by Henry I, Duke of Normandy. Together with Tillières and Nonancourt it formed the Avre defence line on the Franco-Norman frontier, and before it was finally won by the French in 1449, therefore, saw many bloody battles including that of 1424 when Charles VII was defeated.

Verneuil is divided into three quarters with, respectively, the Madeleine, Gambetta and Notre-Dame Streets as their main arteries, and formerly a fortification surrounding each ending, like the city wall which encircled them all, in a moat filled from the Iton River.

MAIN SIGHTS

(tour: about 1 hour)

The Magdalene Church★. —*Stand at the corner of Nouveau-Monde and Poissonerie Streets.*

The **tower★** is reminiscent of the famous Butter Tower of the Cathedral at Rouen. It stands apart from the church and consists of three tiers surmounted by an octagonal lantern. The twenty-four statues which decorate it are superior to those at Rouen.

All the different materials used at each reconstruction, particularly during the Gothic

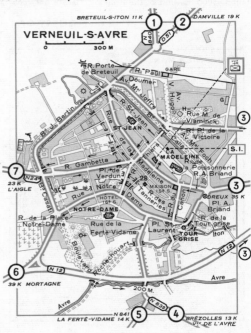

VERNEUIL-SUR-AVRE* (concluded)

period, can be clearly seen as you walk round the church. The 16C porch is flanked to right and left by mutilated but still beautiful 16C statues of the Virgin and of St. Anne.

The nave has Romanesque arches; the chancel is in a desiccated Flamboyant Gothic style.

Some 15 to 19C works of art are worth noting: St. Giles and his deer, against a pillar at the end of the north aisle; St. Crispin patron saint of shoemakers, in the south aisle; St. Theresa of the Infant Jesus with a surprising, grave countenance, in the transept; a 16C Holy Sepulchre, the tomb of Count de Frotté (one of the last leaders of the Chouans in Normandy) by David d'Angers (1783–1856); finally at the end of the south aisle and left of the altar to the Holy Sacrament, a 15C polychrome statue of the Virgin with an Apple.

The softly tinted windows on the north side of the chancel are 16C.

Church of Our Lady*.—The church, which was built of red coloured agglomerate stone in the 12C, and has been remodelled several times, possesses an outstanding number of early 16C statues, mostly carved by local sculptors.

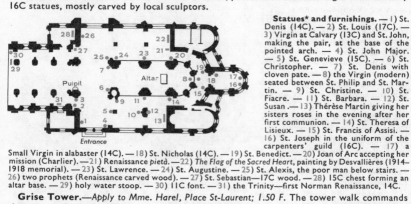

Statues* and furnishings. — 1) St. Denis (14C). — 2) St. Louis (17C). — 3) Virgin at Calvary (13C) and St. John, making the pair, at the base of the pointed arch. — 4) St. John Major. — 5) St. Genevieve (15C). — 6) St. Christopher. — 7) St. Denis with cloven pate. — 8) the Virgin (modern) seated between St. Philip and St. Martin. — 9) St. Christine. — 10) St. Fiacre. — 11) St. Barbara. — 12) St. Susan. — 13) Thérèse Martin giving her sisters roses in the evening after her first communion. — 14) St. Theresa of Lisieux. — 15) St. Francis of Assisi. — 16) St. Joseph in the uniform of the carpenters' guild (17C). — 17) a Small Virgin in alabaster (14C). — 18) St. Nicholas (14C). — 19) St. Benedict. — 20) Joan of Arc accepting her mission (Charlier). — 21) Renaissance pietà. — 22) The Flag of the Sacred Heart, painting by Desvallières (1914–1918 memorial). — 23) St. Lawrence. — 24) St. Augustine. — 25) St. Alexis, the poor man below stairs. — 26) two prophets (Renaissance carved wood). — 27) St. Sebastian—17C wood. — 28) 15C chest forming an altar base. — 29) holy water stoop. — 30) 11C font. — 31) the Trinity—first Norman Renaissance, 14C.

Grise Tower.—Apply to Mme. Harel, Place St-Laurent; 1.50 F. The tower walk commands the town and surrounding countryside. Like the church, it is built of red agglomerate.

ADDITIONAL SIGHTS

Old St. John's.—The partly ruined building has a 15C tower and a Gothic doorway.

Rampart Walk.—If you walk along the Boulevard Casati and the continuing streets you will see the remains of several of the old outer fortifications.

Old Houses.—**Corner of the Rue de la Madeleine and the Rue du Canon:** 15C and on the right 18C balconied houses; **corner of Rue Notre-Dame and Rue du Pont-aux-Chèvres:** 16C mansion; **No. 28 Rue des Tanneries:** Renaissance house; also old wooden houses in the Rue de la Madeleine, Rue de la Poissonnerie and Place de Verdun.

ENVIRONS

Avre Valley.—Tour of 16 miles—25 km—about ¾ hour. Leave Verneuil by ④, the N 839. Turn left into the D 316 which continues as the D 102 along the pleasantly shady right bank of the Avre. On your way you will see the water catchment works which supply the aqueduct built in 1892 and still conveys 8 million gallons of drinking water daily—110,600 m³—to Paris 63 miles away—102 km. Return by way of Montigny-le-Bérou, Tillières (p. 155) and the N 12.

The VERNIER Marsh (MARAIS VERNIER)—Michelin maps 54 ⑧ ⑨, 55 ④.

The Vernier Marsh, once a bend in the River Seine, cuts a vast bay of just under 20 sq. miles—5000 ha—out of the Roumois Plateau between Quillebeuf and Roque Point.

THE CONQUEST OF THE SEA

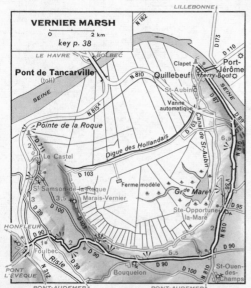

In 1847, 350 landowners formed themselves into a syndicate to complete the drainage project first outlined in the reign of Henri IV. It was he who had summoned a group of Dutchmen to build the so-called Dutchmen's Dyke (Digue des Hollandais) which forms the northern limit of the marshlands. The drainage undertakings were abandoned until 1950 since when 22 miles—35 km—of canals have been dug to drain excess water into the Great Marsh (Grande Mare) from where it travels by way of the St-Aubin Canal to the Seine. The canal is controlled by a sluice gate to prevent water flowing back at high tide.

Land reclamation has followed so that nearly 8 sq. miles—2000 ha—have been cleared of fossilised tree trunks (the marsh was a coalmine in the making) and generally restored. The area is kept drained by ditches 50 yds. apart and is now given over to cultivation.

FROM QUILLEBEUF TO FOULBEC by way of Bouquelon

11 miles—18 km—about ¾ hour

The drive will take you from the Seine Valley to that of the Risle.

Quillebeuf.—*Description, p. 126.*

Between Quillebeuf and Ste-Opportune-la-Mare, the road overlooks the wide Valley of the Seine on the far side of which can be seen the refineries of Port-St-Jérôme.

Ste-Opportune-la-Mare viewpoint.—*Excursion of ½ mile from Ste-Opportune.* Leave the car just before a left turn on the V 36. The view extends over the Great Marsh and beyond to the reclaimed marshland.

After Bouquelon, from a hairpin bend to the left on the D 103 (*viewing table*), you get a good view over the marsh to the Tancarville Bridge. Between the fork where the D 100 and the Foulbec roads meet, the D 90 continues as a *corniche* road with a view down onto the Risle Valley.

Alternative by the Roque Lighthouse.—*Extra distance 5 miles—8 km—by the D 100 and D 711.*

The **panorama**★ extends across the Seine Estuary, straight ahead to Cape La Hève and the Côte de Grâce. Tancarville cliffs and bridge can be seen in the foreground.

VERNON ★—Michelin maps ⑤⑤ ⑰ ⑱, ⑨⑥ ①, ⑨⑦ ⑭—pop. 19,724.

Vernon, which lies on the banks of the Seine, close to the forest of the same name, was created by Rollo, first Duke of Normandy, in the 9C. It became French during the reign of Philippe Auguste early in the 13C and is now an extremely pleasant residential town with a number of fine avenues.

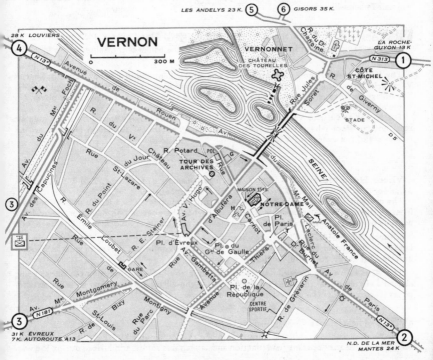

SIGHTS

Church of Our Lady★.—This 12C collegiate church was remodelled several times before the Renaissance. The 15C west front has a beautiful rose window flanked, on either side, by galleries.

The nave, also 15C, is higher than the transept and chancel, its triforium and tall windows having considerable beauty of line.

The great Romanesque arches in the chancel were superimposed by an upper tier in the 16C, which is the period also of the organ loft and the windows in the second chapel off the south aisle. The Louis XIII tapestries illustrate the Virtues.

Wooden Houses.—An attractive 15C house stands to the left of the church. There are others in the Rue Carnot (police station) and Rue Potard.

Archives Tower.—The tower was the keep of the 12C castle.

Bridge Viewpoint.—From the bridge you get a view of Vernon, the wooded islands in the Seine and the ruined piles on which the 12C bridge stood.

On the right bank amidst the greenery can be seen the towers of Tourelles Castle which formed part of the defences of the old bridge.

ENVIRONS

St-Michel Hill★.—*½ hour on foot Rtn.* View of Vernon and the Seine Valley.

Notre-Dame-de-la-Mer★; **Coutumes Beacon**★.—*5 miles—8 km—by a road which narrows beyond Coutumes village.* Leave Vernon by ② but bear right into the D 89; turn left at a tobacconist's in Notre-Dame-de-la-Mer.

*VERNON (concluded)

Notre-Dame-de-la-Mer*.—There is a most entertaining **aerial view*** of the right bank of the Seine from Bonnères to Villez from the belvedere on the chapel forecourt.
Continue along the D 89. Turn sharp left at the Jeufosse town hall (leaving a surfaced road on your right). Turn right by the last houses in Coutumes and left at the next fork.

Coutumes Beacon*.—From the hill's lower slopes there is a wide and pleasant **view*** of the Bonnières bend in the river.

VILLEDIEU-LES-POÊLES —Michelin map 59 ⑧—pop. 4,445.

The procession which has been held in the town every four years since 1655 and is known as the *Grand Sacre* or Great Coronation (*see p. 27*) recalls the town's early history. It was at Villedieu that the first commandry of the Knights of St. John of Jerusalem was established in the 12C. In the 17C the skill of its craftsmen and coppersmiths brought the town its present name—*poêles* means frying pan or pot. For a long time the great round bellied copper milk flagons or *cannes* to be found on every Norman farm came from Villedieu; today the craftsmen make kitchen utensils in copper—and aluminium—and also souvenirs.

Church.—The 15C Flamboyant church has a highly ornate square tower over the transept.

Bell Foundry, Rue du Pont-Chignon.—*Open 8.30 a.m. to noon, 1.30 to 5 p.m.; Sundays, Mondays, holidays, by appointment; 2 F.* An insight into this highly specialised craft is extremely interesting.

ENVIRONS

Champrepus Zoo.—*5 miles—7.5 km—by the N 24 bis. Open 8 a.m. to noon, 2 to 8 p.m.; 3 F.* Animals in semi-liberty.

VILLEQUIER * —Michelin maps 52 ⑬, 54 ⑨, 55 ⑤—local map p. 145—pop. 773.

Villequier stretches out in a beautiful **setting*** along the banks of the Seine, at the foot of a wooded hill crowned by the local castle.

The Villequier Tragedy.—Victor Hugo's daughter, Léopoldine, and her husband, Charles Vacquerie were drowned in the Seine at Villequier six months after their marriage in 1843. The village was brought literary fame when the poet expressed his sorrow in his poem, *Les Contemplations*.

The tombs of Charles Vacquerie and Léopoldine, Victor Hugo's statue on the Caudebec road not far from where the drowning took place and the Victor Hugo Museum are all reminders of the century-old tragedy.

SIGHTS

Victor Hugo Museum*.—*Quai Victor Hugo. Open 10 a.m. to noon, 2 to 7 p.m. (6 p.m. 1 October to 31 March). Closed Wednesdays and in November; 1 F.*
The museum is in the house once owned by the Vacqueries, a rich family of boat builders from Le Havre. On display are family letters between the poet and his daughter, portraits, a painting of Villequier as it was in 1832 and views of contemporary Normandy, furniture, etc.

Church (12, 14, 16C).—The church has a fine coffered roof and a 16C stained glass window known as the "naval battle". By the south wall are the tombs of Charles Vacquerie, Léopoldine and Victor Hugo's wife, Adèle.

The Quays on the Seine.—As you walk along the quayside you may see pilots going aboard and coming off the ships on the Seine, for the village is the station at which estuary pilots take over from the upstream pilots and vice versa.

VIRE —Michelin map 59 ⑨ ⑩—pop. 12,107.

Vire, well placed on a hillock from which one can look out over the rolling Normandy Bocage, was also an important road junction and as such was almost annihilated during the war.

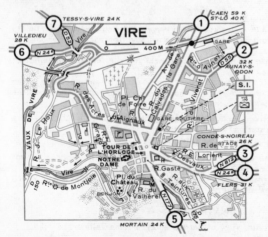

SIGHTS

Clock Tower.—The 15C belfry crowning a 13C gate was spared and now forms the centre-piece of the new main square.

Church of Our Lady.—The 13–15C church has been rebuilt in warm toned granite.

Place du Château.—Standing on the square on a spur overlooking, on the right, the Vaux de Vire, are the remains of the early 12C castle's square keep.

The Vaux de Vire.—The Vaux de Vire is the name by which the steeply enclosed Vire and Virenne Valleys are known close to where they meet. *Vaux de Vire* is also the name of the collection of songs of a textile worker, Olivier Basselin, who lived in these parts in the 15C and from which the word 'vaudeville' was later derived.

ANET*—⑤⑤ ⑰, ⑨⑥ ⑪, ⑨⑦ ⑬ ⑭—map p. 91. Diane de Poitiers, favourite of Henri II, began building **Anet Castle*** in 1548 and died there in 1566. A triumphal entrance, court of honour, 17C wing, chapels and 13C church are open. Many representations of Diana the goddess. *Open Easter to All Saints Day, Sundays and holidays, 10 to 11.30 a.m., 2.30 to 6.30 p.m., Thursday afternoons 2.30 to 6.30 p.m.; winter 2 to 5 p.m., Thursdays, Sundays, holidays; 3.50 F.*

AUMALE—⑤② ⑯—Milk marketing town with Flamboyant and Renaissance **church** with historiated keystones and 16C stained glass.

AUNAY-SUR-ODON*—⑤④ ⑮. Totally reconstructed in record time—November 1947–August 1950. Good example of town planning, rehousing; large modern church.

BARENTIN—⑤② ⑭, ⑤④ ⑩, ⑤⑤ ⑥, ⑨⑦ ①. Brick viaduct of 552 yds. carrying Paris–Le Havre railway at approach to industrial town; ornamented with profusion of Rodin and other 19/20C statues.

BOSC-BORDEL—⑤② ⑮, ⑤⑤ ⑦, ⑨⑦ ②. 16C wooden church porch.

BRECY—⑤④ ⑮ east of Bayeux. Sumptuous monumental 17C **entrance*** to the castle and terraced **garden***. 2 F.; *closed Tuesdays.*

BRESLE Valley—⑤② ⑤ ⑥. Wide valley, former border between Normandy and Picardy, now a glass-making area (perfume bottles). At **Rambures**, 15C brick fortress (*closed*); at **Gamaches** 12 to 15C church surmounted by Flamboyant belfry and interesting interior.

BRETEUIL-SUR-ITON—⑤⑤ ⑯, ⑥⑥ ⑥, ⑨⑦ ⑫ ㉓. The town, close to the forest area of the Ouche Region, is circled by the Iton River. The **church** dates back in part—transept pillars—to William the Conqueror.

CARENTAN—⑤④ ⑬—map p. 76. Carentan, in the Cotentin, is a large cattle market and milk product town. The vast 12 to 15C **church** is elegantly Flamboyant with a belfry surmounted by a spire visible for miles.

CONDEAU—⑥⑥ ⑮—The Perche village church has a robust exterior—belfry porch and buttresses—and delicate rounded Gothic vaulting inside.

CREULLY—⑤④ ⑮. This town and its 15C castle (remodelled—*open*) flanked by a 16C round turret and abutting a square keep, overlooks the Seulles Valley. Nearby is Creullet Castle where General Montgomery set up his caravan H.Q. in June 1944.

DREUX*—⑥⑥ ⑦, ⑨⑥ ㉑, ⑨⑦ ㉔. Dreux, in the Blaise Valley close to the Ile-de-France, is a bustling regional market town. Formerly a border town, it was repeatedly under siege, the cruellest being by the Burgundians in 1412 and the English in 1421 when King Henry V occupied it. It suffered also in the Wars of Religion. The town passed to the royal family in the 16C and became the necropolis of the Orleans.
The ground and first floors of the **belfry*** (1512–1531) are Flamboyant, the 2nd floor and dormer windows Renaissance, the campanile 17C (*limited access*). The **St. Louis Royal Chapel** (*guided tours summer 8 a.m.—winter 9 a.m.—to noon, 1.30 to 7 p.m.—winter 6 p.m.; 2.50 F.*). Rich interior; royal tombs; **painted glass***. The 13C Church of St. Paul (reconstructed 15 and 17C) has good 15 and 16C glass.

ERNÉE—⑤⑨ ⑲. A Romanesque tower, Gothic chancel and nave complete **Charné Church** (on the N 12).

La FEUILLIE—⑤② ⑯, ⑤⑤ ⑧, ⑨⑦ ③. The slender 167 ft. church **spire*** is a bold piece of carpentry.

FOULLETORTE Castle—⑥⑥ ⑫. Late 16C moated granite castle (*closed*) with well ordered spectacular façade.

GAILLON—⑤⑤ ⑰, ⑨⑦ ⑬—map p. 143. Cardinal Georges of Amboise, on returning with Louis XII from Italy, transformed the castle to the Italian style (1497–1510), thus launching Renaissance design in Normandy. The castle entrance is in best repair.

GRANDE-TRAPPE Abbey—⑥⑥ ④ ⑤. The abbey founded in 1140 in the forest was the site of the 17C Cistercian reform which gave rise to the Trappist Order.

MONTIVILLIERS—⑤② ⑪, ⑤④ ⑧, ⑤⑤ ③—map p. 68. Founded on a monastery and now an industrial suburb of Le Havre, the town possesses a church, **St. Saviour***, with a Romanesque belfry and 11C lantern, and adjoining naves inside—one Romanesque, the other 16C Gothic —added when the church passed to the parish. Note two beautiful English alabaster reliefs at the end of the north ambulatory. The **Brisegaut Cemetery** was a charnel house—one 16C gallery remains with a timber roof.

NONANCOURT—⑥⑥ ⑦, ⑨⑦ ㉔. A mediaeval Norman fortress town against the French. **St. Martin's**, built in 1511, has a belfry of 1204. 16C glass; Renaissance organ; 14 and 15C statues. At St. Lubin-des-Joncherets the church which has been reconstructed in Flamboyant Gothic has a Renaissance façade. The nave is coffered, the aisles groined with hanging keystones and Renaissance medallions. 16C font.

RANES—⑥⑥ ②. Castle rebuilt in 18C conserving the 15C keep.

ST-CHRISTOPHE-LE-JAJOLET—⑥⑥ ② ③. The village church—the north transept chapel contains a remarkable Flemish Primitive, the *Burial of the Virgin*—has become a pilgrimage centre to St. Christopher (25 July and following Sunday). Processions past monumental statue.

TILLIÈRES-SUR-AVRE—⑥⑥ ⑥, ⑨⑦ ㉓. The first Norman strongpoint to be constructed, in 1013, to guard the Avre line against the French (see p. 151).

VAUSSIEUX Château—⑤④ ⑮. (*not open*).—Franco-American friendship was sealed in this fine 18C country house when the owner, an American, invited the French, including Marshal de Rochambeau who had led French forces in the U.S. against the English, to use it as a headquarters from which to conduct manoeuvres further to harass the British in 1778.

VILLERS-BOCAGE—⑤④ ⑮. Village largely rebuilt since 1944; interesting modern buildings including St. Martin's Church and a covered market.

INDEX